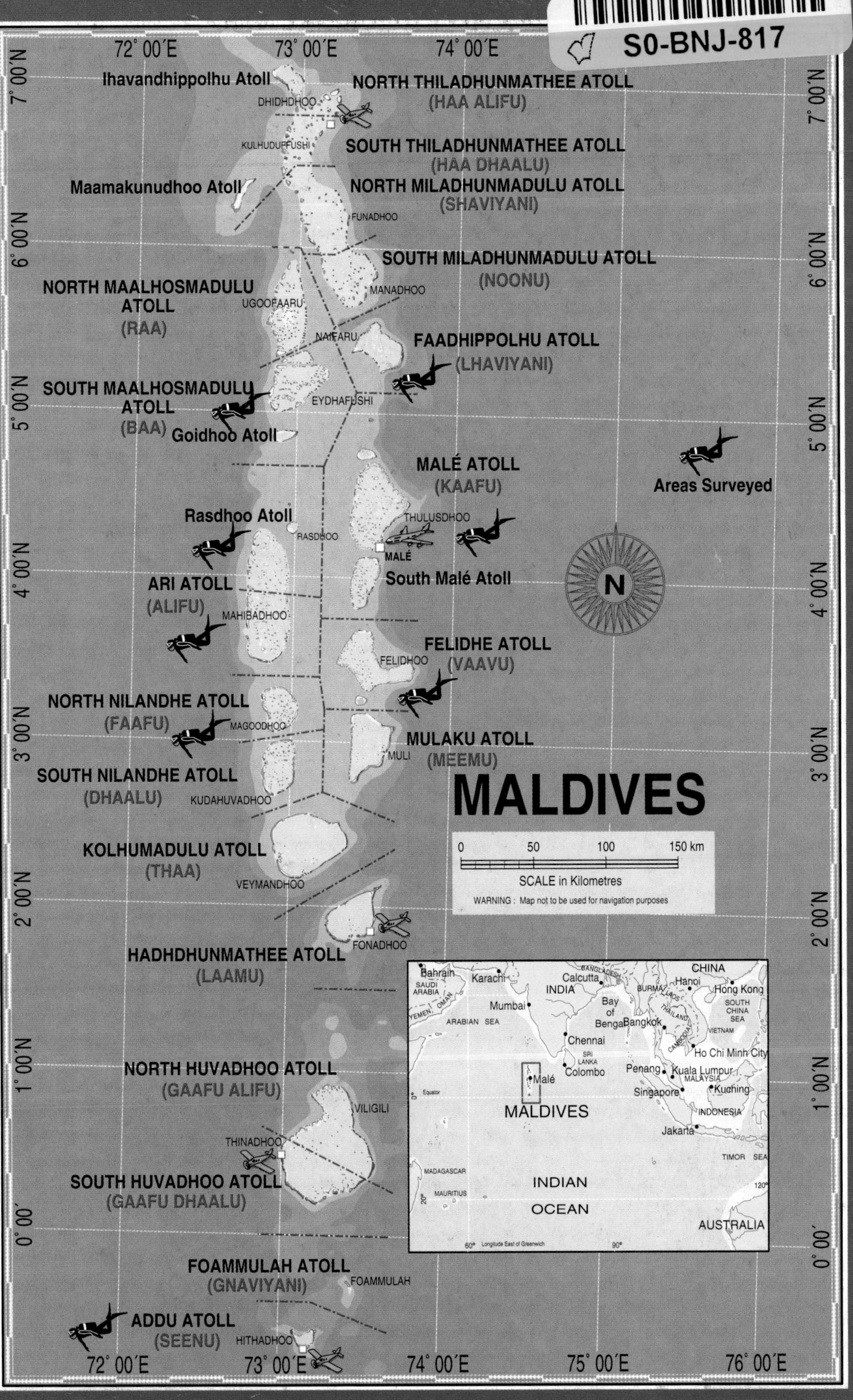
MALDIVES
72° 00´E
73° 00´E
74° 00´E
75° 00´E
76° 00´E
7° 00´N
6° 00´N
5° 00´N
4° 00´N
3° 00´N
2° 00´N
1° 00´N
0° 00´
Ihavandhippolhu Atoll
NORTH THILADHUNMATHEE ATOLL
(HAA ALIFU)
DHIDHDHOO
KULHUDUFFUSHI
SOUTH THILADHUNMATHEE ATOLL
(HAA DHAALU)
Maamakunudhoo Atoll
NORTH MILADHUNMADULU ATOLL
(SHAVIYANI)
FUNADHOO
SOUTH MILADHUNMADULU ATOLL
(NOONU)
MANADHOO
NORTH MAALHOSMADULU
ATOLL
(RAA)
UGOOFAARU
NAIFARU
FAADHIPPOLHU ATOLL
(LHAVIYANI)
SOUTH MAALHOSMADULU
ATOLL
(BAA)
EYDHAFUSHI
Goidhoo Atoll
MALÉ ATOLL
(KAAFU)
Areas Surveyed
Rasdhoo Atoll
THULUSDHOO
RASDHOO
MALÉ
South Malé Atoll
N
ARI ATOLL
(ALIFU)
MAHIBADHOO
FELIDHE ATOLL
(VAAVU)
FELIDHOO
NORTH NILANDHE ATOLL
(FAAFU)
MAGOODHOO
MULAKU ATOLL
(MEEMU)
MULI
SOUTH NILANDHE ATOLL
(DHAALU)
KUDAHUVADHOO
KOLHUMADULU ATOLL
(THAA)
VEYMANDHOO
0
50
100
150 km
SCALE in Kilometres
WARNING : Map not to be used for navigation purposes
FONADHOO
HADHDHUNMATHEE ATOLL
(LAAMU)
NORTH HUVADHOO ATOLL
(GAAFU ALIFU)
VILIGILI
THINADHOO
SOUTH HUVADHOO ATOLL
(GAAFU DHAALU)
FOAMMULAH ATOLL
(GNAVIYANI)
FOAMMULAH
ADDU ATOLL
(SEENU)
HITHADHOO
Bahrain
SAUDI ARABIA
OMAN
YEMEN
Karachi
Calcutta
BANGLADESH
CHINA
Hanoi
Hong Kong
INDIA
Mumbai
BURMA
LAOS
THAILAND
SOUTH CHINA SEA
ARABIAN SEA
Bay of Bengal
Bangkok
VIETNAM
CAMBODIA
Chennai
Ho Chi Minh City
SRI LANKA
Colombo
Penang
Kuala Lumpur
MALAYSIA
Malé
Equator
Singapore
Kuching
MALDIVES
INDONESIA
Jakarta
TIMOR SEA
MADAGASCAR
MAURITIUS
INDIAN
OCEAN
AUSTRALIA
120°
20°
0°
60°
Longitude East of Greenwich
90°

MARINE LIFE OF THE MALDIVES

NEVILLE COLEMAN

First published in 2000 by Atoll Editions.
PO Box 113
Apollo Bay
Victoria 3233
Australia
www.atolleditions.com.au
Fax: (+61) 3 52376332
Email: info@atolleditions.com.au

To contact the author, visit www.nevillecoleman.com.au or
Fax: (+61) 7 33418148
Email: worldofwater@nevillecoleman.com.au

Designed by Publishing Solutions Pty Ltd
Cover design by David Constable Design
Typeset by Scott Howard

National Library of Australia
Cataloguing-in-Publication entry

Coleman, Neville
Marine Life of the Maldives.

ISBN 1 876410 36 1

1. Natural History – Maldives. I. Title.

Printed in Singapore by Tien Wah Press Pte Ltd

Contents

Acknowledgments

The photographs in this book are from the files of the Australasian Marine Photographic Index, a private collection of photographs offered by Neville Coleman's Underwater Geographic Pty Ltd.

Thanks to Toshikazu Kozawa, the creator of Nexus camera housings, and Sea Suits Australia for the use of their excellent products.

Besides the reference photographs housed in the Australasian Marine Photographic Index many of the identifications for this book were supplied by specialist taxonomists and marine scientists with their own reference materials of specimens and pictures. Without their knowledge, experience and expertise this book would have assumed a lot lesser perspective. I would like to thank the following people for all their valuable assistance.

Dr Phil Alderslade (Alcyonarians); Dr Richard C Willan (Molluscs) of the Northern Territory Museum of Arts and Sciences; Dr Carden Wallace and assistant Paul Muir (Stony corals, Acroporidae); Dr John Hooper (Sponges); Dr Patricia Kott (Ascidians); Peter Davie (Crustaceans) of the Queensland Museum; Dr Sandy Bruce, honorary research associate Queensland Museum (Crustaceans); Ian Loch (Molluscs) of the Australia Museum; Loisette Marsh (Echinoderms) honorary research associate of the Western Australian Museum; Dr Charlie Veron (Corals) of the Australia Institute of Marine Science; Dr Allan Miller (Algae) of the Royal Botanic Gardens (Sydney).

To Drs Lori and Pat Colin of the Coral Reef Research Foundation (Palau) whose comparative work on Maldivian sponges was critical to our presentation of this important group, our sincerest gratitude. (Original identifications made from specimens by Dr Michelle Kelly).

Many thanks to compatriot underwater photographers Rudie H. Kuiter, Toshikazu Kozawa, Jorg Aebi, Musthag Hussain, Wally Rowlands for the use of their photographs (see individual credits beneath pictures) and their companionship, assistance, goodwill and hospitality in the field.

Moosa Shafeeu, Mariyam R Saleem, Ali Rasheed, Sea Explorers, Musthag Hussain and Jorg Aebi all assisted in various ways, from dive mastering and finding subjects to providing equipment and locating dive sites. Musthag Hussain shared his excellent knowledge on local dive areas and was an enthusiastic participant on the project supplying equipment and his new dive boat to visit out of the way sites.

I also thank William Allison, Anne Thomson, Mohammed Ibraheem Loutfi and Miriam Iselin for their help in the research and production of the manuscript.

Preface

About the Maldives

by Tim Godfrey

Geography

The Republic of the Maldives lies south-west of the southern tip of India, and spans a vast area of the west Indian Ocean from 7° 6' 30"N to just south of the equator, 0° 42' 30"S, and between longitudes 72° 32' 30"E and 73° 46' 15"E. It forms the central part of an underwater mountain range stretching for over 2000 kilometres from the Laccadives (islands of Lakshadsweep) in the north, to the Chagos Archipelago in the south. The area of the Maldives is about 90,000 square kilometres, yet less than an estimated 0.5% is dry land. There are 1190 islands with some kind of vegetation on them, whether grass, bushes or trees, 990 of which are uninhabited and 200 inhabited. An estimated 200,000 people make up the local population but many are concentrated in or near Malé, the capital. The islands are divided into 26 geographic atolls but for convenience, these are divided into 19 administrative groups. The atolls vary in size from the tiny atoll of Thoddoo with a diameter of 2.5 kilometres and only one island, to the great Huvadhoo Atoll with a length of 82 kilometres, a width of 67 kilometres and comprising 244 islands. Most of the north and central part of the Maldives is made up of two separate chains of atolls separated by a plateau with depth ranging between 300 metres and 500 metres. In the south, the atolls form a single chain and are separated by wider and deeper channels. The widest channel, Huvadhoo Kandu, otherwise known as the One and Half Degree Channel is 96 kilometres across with depths reaching 900 metres. On both the east and west sides of the archipelago depths of 2000 metres can occur within 5.5 kilometres of the outer reefs. The inside of the atolls are usually at depths between 30 and 50 metres, but depths up to 90 metres occur in Huvadhoo Atoll.

An aerial overview of islands and submerged reefs, part of the many thousands which make up the Maldivian Archipelago. (Photo: Adrian Neville)

Geology

Charles Darwin proposed that the atolls of the Maldives developed as the mountain range gradually subsided into the sea or sea levels rose. The fringing reefs surrounding these mountains built up and became more distant from the centre of the range until there was nothing left but a circle of reefs enclosing a lagoon, called an atoll.

Coral reefs are created by a tiny animal, called a polyp, that secretes a hard limestone skeleton and provides the reef's framework. Fragile branching coral may grow between 20 and 30 centimetres per year, while massive boulder-shaped coral may grow only a few millimetres per year. Coralline algae, which thrives in areas exposed to wave action and places too deep and dark for the coral, cement the framework of dead and broken coral together forming a solid limestone base. During ice ages, rise and falls in sea levels forced migration of reef building corals to colonise new areas. At some stage during these times, reefs were left high out of the water.

The limestone reefs were readily eroded by fresh water and this led to the formation of caves and canyons of all shapes and sizes. After they were again flooded by the sea, marine life re-established itself and layers of coral and coralline algae continued to grow upon the eroded gutters and valleys. These eroded substrata largely govern the shapes of modern reefs and today, many of these features remain submerged providing divers with spectacular natural attractions.

Greater depths and increased clarity of water generally distinguish the outer reef slopes of the atolls. In some cases the visibility may exceed 50 metres. Looking down the reef slope, the coral communities change rapidly with increasing depth. At depths greater than 20 metres, wave surge is non-existent and extensive coral growth may occur to depths of 50 metres and more. Light availability is the main factor limiting the range of the coral here. The upper parts of the outer reef slope may be affected by wave action, restricting the growth of more delicate plate coral. Coral growth can be wiped out in a single freak storm in this zone. In areas less exposed to wave action, extensive stands of staghorn corals can dominate and a great variety of fish life occurs.

The reef front is the part of the reef which takes the full force of the ocean swells and the coral here tends to be gnarled and stunted as a result of the pounding by waves. The reef flats can range in width from a few metres to a few kilometres. Rainwater can damage or completely destroy the coral in this zone if heavy or cyclonic rainfall coincides with very low tides.

Lagoons with good circulation of water may have large stands of branching corals growing and they can trap many fish varieties as the tide recedes.

On the inner reef slope, coral growth may be rich if the slope is not too steep. Steep or vertical slopes may be bare. Many interesting caves, overhangs and gullies can occur in this zone. Rising from the floor are separate coral reefs or coral patches, known as *giris* and *thilas*. The *giris* nearly reach the surface, whereas the *thilas* lie below at depths between five and 15 metres.

Nilandhoo Island, Faafu Atoll, scene showing lush vegetation and small sandy beach with excellent formations of beach rock that underlies the sand and protects the shoreline from erosion. (Photo: Tim Godfrey)

There are many words in *Dhivehi*, the local language, used to describe islands and reefs. A *fushi* is a big island usually on the outside reef of the atoll and a *finolhu* is an island with few or no coconut trees. *Dhoo* and *Huraa* are other words for an island. Reefs are usually called *farus* or *falhus*. A *faru*, is a reef partially exposed at low tide and *falhu* is often a reef encircling a lagoon, sometimes with one or more islands inside. *Gaa* and *haa* are other words used to describe coral reefs.

Water temperatures
Ocean water temperatures rarely vary beyond 27–30° although thermoclines can sometimes be experienced at depths below 20 metres. During hot periods, water temperatures inside the lagoons increases measurably, influencing water temperatures inside the atolls. During these periods most divers are comfortable diving without a wetsuit, although those of slight build may shiver a little. Lycra and 3 mm wetsuits are popular in tropical waters but some divers prefer a 5 mm suit if doing more than one dive a day during the south-west monsoon. During overcast periods with wind and rain squalls, it is wise to carry extra clothing on the boat after a dive.

Global warming – *coral reef meltdown* (Neville Coleman)
There is no doubt that the Earth's climate is changing, devastating many of the world's coral reefs, reducing populations of many species and threatening a large number with extinction.

The staghorn corals are the fastest growing corals and as such are the first ones to show signs of stress. (Acropora clathrata*)*

The single most significant factor in the world today is that abnormally high sea surface water temperatures have resulted in mass mortality of worldwide corals. Global warming has been increasing since the beginning of the Industrial Revolution. In short, the industrial nations of the world produce billions of tonnes of air pollution (especially from fossil fuels, refineries and chemical production) per decade, which, over the past century, has built up 'greenhouse' gases that has had an overall warming effect on the Earth's atmosphere. (Depletion of the ozone layer by CFC gases allowing elevated levels of ultra violet radiation may also prove damaging in many ways. However, significant studies have shown this modification is not the main cause of coral bleaching.)

Animals in the oceans of the world have evolved to certain life-sustaining temperatures necessary for their survival. Most corals can only stand a 1 to 3°C increase before they begin to stress. (25°C to 29°C appear optimum for most tropical species). Fish also are only able to maintain life without stressing in waters which have a maximum 5°C rise or fall in temperature. We know what effects increases in water temperature have on adult population of sedentary and mobile animals, but the wholesale mortality on eggs, larvae, plankton etc, due to rises in temperature must be immense.

The facts

Since the early 1980s, the consequences of sustained increases in the sea surface temperatures (down to at least 40 metres) have been unprecedented. In 1983, 90% of corals bleached and died on many reefs in the Galapagos Islands. In 1990 the Caribbean waters warmed up and huge areas of coral reef bleached and died, leading experts to announce it as an ecological disaster. By 1991, nearly every coral reef system in the world was affected by coral bleaching, which in most cases, was due to higher than normal sea surface temperatures.

Coral reefs off Australia, China, Japan, Panama, the Philippines, India, Indonesia, Malaysia, Thailand, Kenya, Red Sea states, Puerto Rico, Jamaica and the Bahamas were all showing signs of major distress with widespread bleaching.

In 1994, 1995, 1996 significant warming caused massive devastation to many of the coral reefs in the northern Milne Bay area of Papua New Guinea and throughout the Bismarck and Solomon Seas. Severe bleaching was also reported by Greenpeace to have occurred in French Polynesia with over 70% of live corals bleached down to 25 metres. American and Western Samoa and the Cook Islands also reported massive die off. In 1997 the corals in the Seychelles and the Maldives showed the first signs of stress (personal observation). By April 1998 widespread bleaching occurred with up to 80–90% of shallow water corals being affected due to the huge area of abnormally hot water which remained stationery across the Indian Ocean.

Coral bleaching

Most hermatypic corals (reef building stony corals) have a symbiotic relationship with microscopic unicellular algae called zooxanthellae which inhabit the living tissues of the corals and in most cases are responsible for the corals colour.

Zooxanthellae are plants and as such produce carbon enriched organic compounds from sunlight and carbon dioxide which is passed on to reef building corals providing up to 98% of their required nutrients. The zooxanthellae are the key to the growth rates of reef building corals and their presence governs the ability of the reef building corals to build calcium carbonate skeletons at speeds far in excess of corals without zooxanthellae present in their tissues. When the water gets too hot the zooxanthellae become heat stressed and leave the tissue of the corals. With their colour coating gone the white coral skeletons can be seen through the coral animal's transparent tissue, giving a bleaching appearance. If in a short while the water temperature goes down the zooxanthellae may return. Should the water temperature remain high the corals will die, remaining white and bleached until settled by other algal forms. Skeletons may be light green the first year, dark green the second year and black by the third year after death.

The dead coral is a rocky limestone reef that represents shelter to some fish and provides surfaces for alga, ascidians and corals as well as a substrate for the burrowers. However most of the coral dependant animals can no longer survive, for example, some butterflyfishes which live on a diet of coral polyps and mucous will disappear. Commensal associate species such as some shrimps, crabs and worms will also die and species diversity will be reduced.

As recently as 1999, small colonies of shallow water corals were still being affected by higher than normal sea surface temperatures. (Acropora humilis)

Global warming – a reality

Whether the increased sea surface temperatures of the world's oceans is induced by global warming due to greenhouse gas emissions (and therefore human induced), whether it is El Niño cycles, or some natural climatic change, is still open to discussion and debate by world climatologists. Whatever the reasons, it appears that global warming is on the increase and that sea surface temperatures are rising consistently across the world.

The overall mortality of coral reefs and their dependant fauna will have an enormous impact on future species diversity and composition in many areas. As most species of tropical marine life have planktonic larval dispersal there is every chance that the limestone reefs will be recolonised by corals over time. However, if the sea surface temperatures stay up and continue to rise then the entire species composition will change.

After a cyclone has destroyed a reef, records show that the newly settled corals grow at almost twice the speed as normal. Even so it takes a cyclone destroyed reef 20 years or more to grow and recover and, of course, nothing is ever the same. Growth cannot be correlated between cyclone damage recovery and bleaching recovery for it all depends on the conditions and the water quality and temperature.

In time, coral reefs will spread further south where the water is of optimum temperature. Only those species which can endure warmer water will remain and become dominant. There are encouraging signs of new coral settlement in many of the hardest hit areas with new colonies beginning to be seen. However, here and there some new colonies have succumbed and even small colonies are bleaching due to the continued presence of warmer water.

Maldivian outlook

There are still enough limestone reefs and enough resorts and live-aboards to keep even the most avid diver enthralled for a long time. Local guides, dive masters and instructors know where all the good diving is and use their knowledge to show visitors the best. Even reefs which are almost totally devoid of corals in some places still support myriads of fish because there is so much more plankton to go around; at some reefs planktivores have increased immeasurably.

The deeper water gorgonian sea fans, corals and soft corals show little effect, (though some shallow water soft corals have died), sponges and ascidians have increased at some localities and the cave faunas are still as healthy as ever. Animals such as pincushion sea stars which are incidental coral feeders are still common and going strong on a diet of detritus and algae; like many other life forms they are adaptive.

For most underwater people a lot of the changes will only be aesthetic, some places won't be as pretty in the shallows and snorkellers may be a bit disappointed swimming around the inshore areas. Some species of invertebrates will be easier to find; others more difficult. Whatever the eventual outcome, diving will still be the greatest adventure activity and underwater the nicest place to be.

Facing the facts (Tim Godfrey with William 'Bill' Allison)

Legend

There is an old Maldivian legend recorded by Captain Robert Moresby during his survey of the Maldives in 1834–36 that prophesises the future of this group of islands. It reads: "When the white men come in large numbers to these islands, the seas will flood the islands and people will sail over the top saying, 'Once there were people living here on islands...'"

The white man has come in the form of tourists and the sea level is rising. If there were any truth in legends, then we'd be wise to take note of this one. If the islands of Maldives are to persist they need continual production of calcium carbonate and protection from the physical energy of waves and currents. The calcium carbonate producing corals and similar organisms provide both protection from erosion and raw materials for continued island growth. If the growth of these reefs is arrested or does not keep pace with sea level rise the islands will be washed away. Unfortunately, there are indications that reef growth is being inhibited.

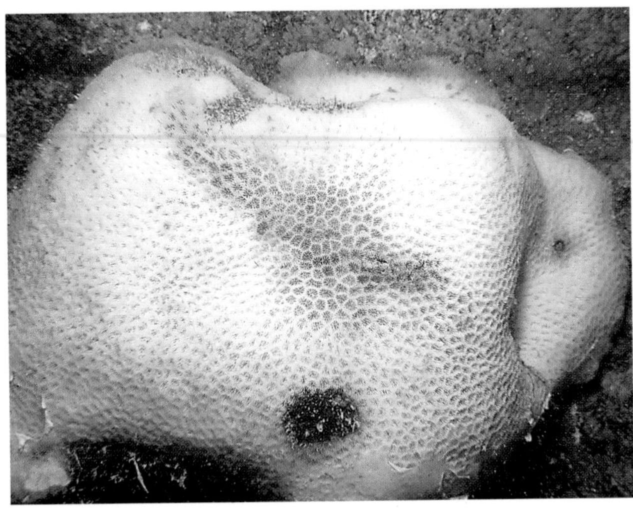

Mound corals are more tolerant of warmer water and only reject their zooxanthellae over extended periods of adverse conditions.

In April 1998 a severe reef bleaching event, triggered by abnormally high water temperatures, struck the Indian Ocean. Corals live close to their upper thermal tolerance level and temperatures several degrees above the usual seasonal high produced rapid bleaching and subsequent mortality. Most of the shallow water branching and table corals were killed. Boulder corals and corals in deeper water were less affected but still sustained appreciable damage. Estimates of recovery time are largely guesses but the reeftop branching and table corals did recover from a serious 1987 bleaching event in about a decade (Allison, 1995) so recovery from this apparently more serious event could take 10 to 20 years. On the positive side the process may be likened to a brush fire ecology which sweeps away weed species and reinvents the community. New coral colonies are already appearing in some locations on Maldivian reefs. However, if there are more rises in water temperature before the corals recover and coral bleaching occurs like it did in April and May of 1998, then corals will probably again die. This will restrict the upward growth of coral reefs and should this coincide with rising sea levels, the Maldives will be in serious trouble.

Climate

The Maldives experiences a tropical, monsoonal climate with warm temperatures year round and a great deal of sunshine. There are two seasons, the north-east monsoon, known locally as the *Iruvai*, and the south-west monsoon, the *Hulhangu*. Whatever the season, there is considerable variation in climate between the northern and southern atolls. In the south the rainfall is greater but showers are not as heavy as in the north. There are greater extremes of temperature in the north also, as the seasons are more evident further away from the equator.

The north-east monsoon

This season is between December and mid-April. It is the driest period, when hot days, cooler nights and slight seas are more common. There is generally little cloud except in the south. Frequent light winds from the north-east and variable sea breezes with an average of 9 knots are experienced. The transitional period between monsoons begins in April when calm, windless days are more likely to be experienced than at any other time of the year. A fortnight of strong winds and rain from the SW usually ushers in the change of the new season and occasionally the tail end of cyclones from the Bay of Bengal can be felt. By the end of May the winds are predominantly W–SW.

The south-west monsoon

This season is from May to November. It is the wettest period when moderate to rough seas and cloudy days are more common. Frequent strong, gale force winds from the south-west with an average speed of 11–15 knots per hour occur and wind gusts of 35–45 knots and above are occasionally recorded. September and October can be more calm and November is again a transitional period with variable winds swinging towards the north-east. The effects of cyclones from the Arabian Sea can be experienced during the south-west monsoon. The north-east monsoon gradually travels down the Maldives from the north and is ushered in by a fortnight of very strong winds from the north-east with heavy rain squalls.

Currents and tides

The exposure of the Maldives to the vast Indian Ocean ensures that an immense body of water is constantly flowing across the plateau on which these atolls are built. The currents can be extremely strong and in the channels near Malé they have been recorded at four knots or more. Oceanic currents are largely influenced by the direction of the trade winds and can be of great strength. Tidal currents which flow according to the height of the tide and the direction of the prevailing winds, are said to be much weaker than oceanic currents, though they cause velocity variations in the flow. The Tidal Range over Malé and nearby islands varies from a Mean Spring Range of about 0.7 metres to a Mean Neap Range of about 0.3

metres. On the eastern side of Malé Atoll, currents predominantly flow into the atoll when the north-east monsoon is firmly set and flow outside during the south-west monsoon. The opposite applies to the western side of the atoll. This is by no means the rule, as changes in wind direction and tides can offset the influence of the oceanic currents. If the winds ease off for a few days, then currents are more likely to flow both in and out of the channels. Inside the atoll, current speeds are more settled and leisurely dives in the lee of reefs can always be found.

Protected marine areas

In 1995, the Government of the Maldives announced the establishment of 15 Protected Marine Areas within the major tourist atolls to protect popular dive sites from the detrimental effects of over-fishing, coral mining, anchor damage and rubbish. A further 10 sites were declared in October 1999 but the financial and practical measures needed to enforce the protection of these sites is yet to be established. However, a new project to develop wide-ranging parks is currently being implemented in a joint project between AusAid of Australia and the Government of the Maldives. The initial phase of the marine parks project will start with developing three model areas to establish the mechanisms and processes by which the tourism industry and the local communities can co-exist, and to further establish the financial structure to pay for the ongoing management of the Protected Marine Areas.

North Maalhosmadulu Atoll (Raa): Vilingili Thila.
South Maalhosmadulu Atoll (Baa): Dhigalihaa (Horubadhoo Thila).
Faadhippolhu Atoll (Lhaviyani): Fushifaru Thila, Kuredhdhoo Kanduolhi.
North Malé Atoll (Kaafu): Makunudhoo Kandu, Rasfari Faru, Thaburudhoo Thila (H.P Reef), Gaathu Giri (Banana Reef), Giraavaru Kuda Haa, Miyaruvani (Lions Head), Kollavaani (Hans Hass Place), Lankan Thila (Nassimo Thila).
South Malé Atoll (Kaafu): Embudhoo Kandu, Guraidhoo Kandu.
North Ari Atoll (Alifu): Maaya Thila, Orimas Thila, Mushimasmigili Thila (Fish Head), Karibeyru Thila.
South Ari Atoll (Alifu): Kudarah Thila, Faruhuruvalhi Beyru (Madivaru).
Felidhoo Atoll (Vaavu): Miyaru Kandu, Vattaru Kandu.
Mulaku Atoll (Meemu): Lhazikuraadi.
North Nilandhe Atoll (Faafu): Filitheyo Kandu.
South Nilandhe Atoll (Dhaalu): Fushi Kandu.

The world of water means many things to many people. For us, it's exciting, adventurous and enjoyable. The more we explore and understand, the more mindful we all become of the need to protect it as a valuable asset for future generations.

Introduction

Over the edge of the reef every nook and cranny is 'painted' with living colour. Each flash of the torch beam reveals a kaleidoscopic macro-world portrayed by encrusting invertebrates.

Well known as a major tourist attraction for many years, the Maldives attracts vast numbers of scuba divers to its clear waters and wondrous reefs bustling with over 1000 species of fishes and an immense but as yet unknown number of invertebrates.

Although there have been many books published which show a large perspective of the reef's beauty and some of the more well known marine life, little has been managed to display the myriad life forms which exist within the reefs themselves. Yet, it is the very existence of these obscure life forms that has allowed such a rich diverse fauna to develop in the Maldivian Archipelago.

With the popular pastime of fish watching encouraged by easy to use fish identification books ("Photo Guide to the Fishes of the Maldives" Rudie H Kuiter, Atoll Editions) divers are becoming much more aware of the creatures they see and can now recognise underwater.

Apart from corals, shells and some of the larger brightly-coloured sea creatures such as sea stars or sponges, few visitors to the Maldives have had the opportunity to know what it was they were actually looking at. To most, much of the invertebrate fauna remained a mystery or was delegated to the "pretty stuff" category. Because photographic evidence to the multitude of beings is not available, there has been little to establish a reference value this vast unknown resource could be to the tourism industry and to the national heritage of the Maldives.

The author and publisher hope that this book will establish a greater understanding towards the so-called lower forms of life (the invertebrates) and that it will advance knowledge in a degree of visual identification that will allow recognition, reference and value to be shared by all who turn its pages.

New records and species

In the course of preparation for this book a great deal of information and many thousands of pictures were accumulated. Many of the animals and plants pictured are new records established here for the first time and as such are now published in the literature as part of the Maldivian flora and fauna. Those species which remain unidentified or that are new (undescribed) have their visuals recorded as examples of their existence which may aid or encourage a new generation of explorers to carry on discovering.

About the book

This book has been developed as a general visual identification guide for divers and students and is not presumed to be more than its intention. The aim is to provide the average person (who is unlikely to ever try and decipher a scientific key or dissect sea creatures) a means by which a basic level of information can be referred to and systematically absorbed.

Although there are over 1000 photographic examples shown, these are only representative examples of the existing fauna and flora and are by no means complete. However, they do portray the existence of most major phyla of known sea creatures that are liable to be seen by divers.

Those phyla which do not lend themselves to straightforward visual identification (for instance, those which are too small) are not included here as the concept is illustrative, rather than textbook biology. This book covers life from sea shores down to deep ocean sea floor, and there are illustrations showing representative external features of each phylum included.

Although visual identification is possible for the majority of the larger groups of marine animals, our knowledge is far from complete. Scientific assistance and preserved specimens must still be studied before accurate identification can be made; for some species this research is likely to extend well into the 21st century. Any system of identification must depend on a reference and the preserved specimen, the first of its kind to be described, is essential. This is the *type specimen*.

Chapters are based on phyla and each has an introduction giving a general overview of each phylum, and a basic introduction of its natural history and biology. In addition, each *class* has its own basic introduction, natural history and biology which is illustrated with photographic examples.

Arrangement of species

Due to the very real fact that not all taxonomic details are agreed to by individual scientists or in some cases may not be available for every species, they have been arranged in the following ways. Where a taxonomic hierarchical system was available it was followed.

In all other groups positioning follows an alphabetical order by family, genus and species similar to an encyclopedia.

To make it easy for the viewer these introductions are organised along similar headings: Title – Features – Lifestyle – Reproduction – Associations – Identification. Next to, above or below the photograph of each species is a list of information with a range of details. The information has been arranged under the following categories:

FAMILY NAME:
COMMON NAME:
SCIENTIFIC NAMES:
HABITAT:
DEPTH:
SIZE:
GENERAL REMARKS:

How to use the book (Understanding science)

The basic classification method used to organise this book is a scientific one based on a hierarchical system, whereas the principles are arranged by descent from the highest (largest principle **KINGDOM**) to the lowest (smallest principle – **SPECIES**)

Accepted classification sample

LEVEL	SCIENTIFIC TERM	COMMON TERM
Kingdom	Animalia	Animals
Phylum	Echinodermata	Echinoderms
Class	Asteroidea	Sea stars
Order	Spinulosida	Spinulosids*
Family	Asterinidae	Asterinids*
Genus	*Pateriella*	Pateriellids*
Species	*nuda*	Naked sea star*

* Note: Anglicised Latin terms may be used as common terms where no other word is in usage.

Although this structure will apply to the arrangement of species within each phylum the book begins in the traditional scientific way by presenting the lower life forms by the present status of scientific knowledge.

(1) **Kingdom of plants** – algae

(2) **Kingdom of animals** – sponges to marine mammals

Rather than provide a strict and sometimes over-scientific view of every example the arrangement in most cases refers only to the phylum, the class, the family, genus and species. Explanations have been kept as simple as possible so as not to confuse beginners with what may often appear to very complex issues.

Phylum: A primary taxonomic division of animals and plants
Class: A comprehensive group of animals or plants ranking below a phylum
Order: A comprehensive group of animals or plants ranking below a class
Family: A comprehensive group of animals or plants related to each other ranking below order

Common names

Common names are those which are in general use, have already been published, or are directly based on the original scientific name interpretations. Where no such common name is available (for example, for undescribed species), terminology has sometimes been constructed from outstanding features of the species' external anatomy, colour, pattern, design or failing this, the locality where it was discovered.

Scientific names

It's important to distinguish one thing from another, to recognise, identify, talk about, teach or learn, animals and plants must have a reference point – a name. Common names, while providing a beginning are of little use in multiple languages or if several species on a worldwide basis have the same common name. In order to overcome this confusion in the middle of the 18th century the Swedish botanist, Carolus Linnaeus, published *Systema Natura* and provided the basis of scientific nomenclature which is accepted throughout the world today.

The concept was exceptionally well thought out. The names given to organisms when they are described and published scientifically are written in Latin. In this way it does not matter which language a book is written in, the organism's scientific name will be the same and recognisable throughout the world.

Each scientific name consists of two Latin words and is known as "binominal nomenclature'. the First name always begins with a capital letter (for example, *Cassis*) and is known as the genus (which might be considered the organism's surname). The second name, which always begins with a lower case letter, (and which might be thought of as the organism's Christian name) is the species name (for example, *pelagicus*).

Generic names are unique within the animal kingdom but species names can be re-used to describe the animal in question. Thus the edible sea-urchin in the United Kingdom is *Echinus esculentus* and in the Caribbean is *Tripneustes esculentus*. It is customary to write the name of the author after the scientific name, for example, *Echinus esculentus* Linnaeus, and to add the date that this name was first published. If the species is transferred to another genus, the author's name is placed in brackets to show it has been re-assigned, eg, *Echinus esculentus* (Linnaeus, 1785).

Linnaeus' system was good because it indicated natural relationships. He also grouped similar genera together into families and similar families into orders. Likewise orders are grouped into classes and classes into phyla. Thus we end up with an hierarchical system which tells us about the supposed relationships and links between the animals we are dealing with. At the top is the phylum, containing all the animals supposed to have a common evolutionary origin. At the bottom is the species, a unique example of that phylum.

If an animal new to science has not had its name published, or if we are examining an animal for which we know the genus but not the species, it is referred by its accepted generic name followed by sp. which is short for species, for example, *Cassis* sp.

If we want to refer to a group of species within a genus we can use spp, for example, *Cassis* spp. (*Cassis* is a genus of large marine predatory snails known as helmet shells).

All the names in the hierarchy above the species name are there for the convenience of seeing how the species relate to each other. Family names have been used in this book as well as genera and species because they help to provide an understanding between the relationships of closely allied genera.

Explanations of terms

Distribution

The distribution of benthic marine animals and plants within the Maldivian Archipelago is not established, yet with minimal understanding and experience it is apparent that many atolls and reefs have a restricted fauna which often contains species that have not been observed at other reefs and atolls.

The northern atolls and reefs may not always support the same species of flora and fauna found on the southern ones. It appears that the influences of currents and the opposing monsoonal winds bring pelagic larvae from a number of places across the Indian Ocean and there is also the pattern of local currents which keep species unique to the Maldives within the Archipelago confines.

All these influences may change at any time and depending on their route provide fauna and flora which becomes established in only one atoll or island group. No attempt is made within the book to give individual species status to one area or reef as next season there may be a different species make-up. However, where known, information is provided on the known range of particular species, for example, Indo-Pacific.

Habitat

Only general information on major habitats is given. Where space allows micro-habitats and obligate associations and relationships are given in the captions.

General water depth
Lines on maps and depth indicators mean very little to marine animals. These things can only serve as a point of reference, not as a fixture. Animals go where they please and can survive. Depths have been given in metres and feet; fractions have been taken to the nearest whole figure.

Food habit
Little is known about the specific food habits of marine animals in general, especially in the Southern Hemisphere. Much of the material in this book is from my own observations and discoveries. Other information has been referenced from the few publications available. With regard to the planktonic food references, the information has been separated into two categories. *Carnivorous: plankton* = animals that have selective devices (such as Nematocysts) which enable them to capture specific prey. *Omnivorous: plankton* – animals which are less selective feeder, for example, suspension feeders, filter feeders, detrital feeders.

Many marine animals are opportunistic carnivorous scavengers; others can actively hunt and catch prey, yet have the ability to survive on plankton if their hunting ability is no longer functional. Some marine animals change their food habits with the seasons, depending on whatever is in good supply.

Size
Within the framework of this book, sizes of animals most often refer to the adult size, or individual size which has been recorded in the past. Sizes which refer to colonies are general indications only, as colonial animals such as corals, sponges or investing ascidians may cover quite large areas. Sizes in these cases are those which have generally been observed in regard to the average width or height or the size of the photograph. Where metric or imperial figures have been converted, these are only estimates to the nearest millimetre or inch.

Description
Only visual features have been listed, with as few scientific terms as possible being used where the author considered it necessary. In most cases, references are made to living colours and forms. In this way, people can become familiar with, and more aware of, the ocean as a place of wonderment and consideration.

Identifications
Given the inadequate state of our knowledge identifications in some cases are only tentative. Although a great number of the identifications have been checked by experts in each field we all acknowledge that without actual specimens definite determination is not always possible and educated opinions must suffice. As the first step in the staircase of knowledge there are bound to be updates. As science advances, so too will the processes of marine identification.

One could assume that over 1000 pictures and 70,000 words might be an adequate representation of the marine life of the Maldives yet in relation to the extraordinary wealth of life that exists, it is barely an introduction. Yet it references the largest number of invertebrate species shown together for the first time.

Simple in construction and terms of reference this book is an invitation into an adventure of discovery that can be shared by one and all; a visual experience that will help develop a greater awareness of the Maldivian reefs and their inhabitants and encourage worldwide interest in their preservation.

Symbols used (colour coded)

ALGAE 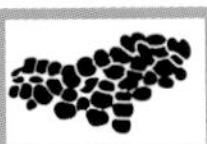

SPONGES 

HYDROIDS 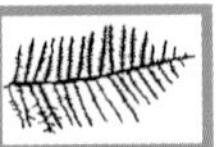

BLACK CORALS 

SOFT CORALS 

GORGONIAN SEA FANS 

SEA ANEMONES 

ZOANTHIDS 

CORALLIMORPHS 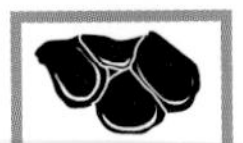

STONY CORALS 

FLATWORMS 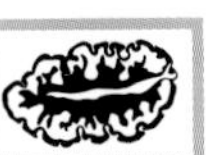

SEGMENTED WORMS 

CHITONS 

UNIVALVES 

OPISTHOBRANCHS 

BIVALVES 

CEPHALOPODS 

MANTIS SHRIMPS 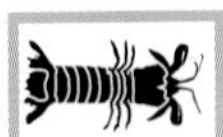

SHRIMPS 

ROCK LOBSTERS 

HERMIT CRABS 

SQUAT LOBSTERS 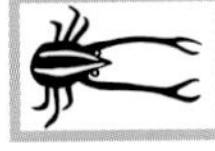

CRABS 

FEATHER STARS 

SEA STARS 

BRITTLE STARS 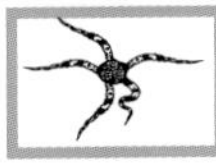

SEA URCHINS 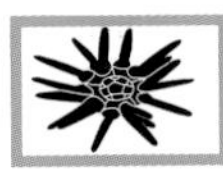

SEA CUCUMBERS 

ASCIDIANS 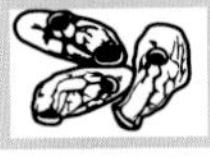

REPTILES 

BIRDS 

MAMMALS 

Glossary of terms

Asexual: reproduction by means other than sexual action, for example, by budding or splitting from the parent body
Atoll: a group of reefs and islands that surround a central lagoon
Autotomy: the spontaneous casting off of part of an animal's body, often to facilitate escape; for example, breaking off a captured limb
Branchial: respiratory function of an organ (gill) or region of body
Buccal: relating to the oral cavity (mouth)
Budding: the process of polyp duplication in the forming of a colony
Byssus: a tuft of strong filaments or thread-like strands with which some bivalves attach themselves to objects, such as rocks
Calcareous: composed of or containing calcium carbonate
Calice: the opening of the corallite, bounded by the wall
Carapace: chitinous and/or calcareous skin fold enclosing part or whole of the dorsal part of crustaceans and turtles
Carnivorous: flesh-eating
Cerata: tentacular processes on the backs of some nudibranch molluscs
Chela: the prehensile nipper or claw of some arthropods such as crabs; plural chelae
Chemoreception: sensitivity to water or airborne chemicals, especially developed in marine animals
Chitin: a horny organic compound forming part of the skin or shell of some marine animals
Ciliary motion: movement caused by the microscopic threads borne on the outer membranes of cells (cilia) of some marine animals which beat back and forth
Cirrus: a slender appendage; plural cirri
Cloaca: common opening for respiratory, reproductive and anal systems in a number of animals
Colonial: pertaining to communal animals of the same species living together, sometimes with organic attachments to each other, as in corals, or sometimes social links, as bees or wasps
Colonial organisms: organisms that live together in social or structural colonies
Commensal: a term applied to two species living in close association with one another, neither one at the expense of the other
Conspecific: of the same species
Corallite: skeleton of an individual coral polyp
Detritus: accumulation of dead animal and plant tissue and fine sediment, usually found on the sea floor
Dioecious: having separate sexes
Dorsum: the back or top (dorsal) surface
Endemic: native to and restricted to a particular locality
Endoecism: an habitual relationship between two animals where one takes shelter in the tube or burrow of another
Eversible: capable of being turned inside out
Fission: reproduction by splitting of a body into two or more parts

Flabello-meandroid: the type of coral colony formation where the valleys are elongate and have separate walls
Flange: a lip
Foot: muscular extension of a mollusc's body used for locomotion
Gastropod: a class of molluscs including snails, having a shell of a singular valve and a muscular foot
Genus: rank in taxonomic hierarchy: group of animals or plants with common characteristics and origins, usually containing more than one species
Gregarious: found together in groups
Herbivorous: plant-eating
Hermaphroditic: having both male and female reproductive organs in one animal
Intertidal: between the extremes of high and low tides
Invertebrate: animal without a backbone
Magilid: a mollusc belonging to the family Magilidae (coral shells)
Mantle: an outgrowth of the body well which lines the shell in molluscs
Nematocyst: a coiled thread that can be projected as a sting from the cnidoblast cells that contain it (cnidarians)
Notochord: rudimentary spinal cord found in protochordates (ascidians)
Nudibranch: a marine gastropod without a shell and true gills, but often with branching external gills on the back or sides of the body
Obligate: dependent
Operculum: lid or stopper; for example, a plate on the foot of a gastropod that closes the aperture of the shell when the animal is retracted
Ovulid: a mollusc belonging to the family Ovulidae (allied to cowries)
Papilla: a small projection extending from the body tissue; plural papillae
Pelagic: inhabiting open waters of oceans or lakes or the water column by swimming or drifting: not living on the sea bottom
Phylum: a primary taxonomic division of animals and plants
Pinnate: having branches on either side of an axis
Plankton: animals or plants, especially minute or microscopic forms, that drift suspended in seas, rivers, lakes and ponds
Polyp: a sac-like individual within a group of animals such as coral It can be of solitary or colonial existence
Proboscis: prehensile snout of a mollusc
Radiole: respiratory and/or feeding tentacles of some tube worms
Radula: a ribbon-like tongue bearing rows of teeth with which a mollusc reduces food to digestible particles or drills through other shells
Rhinophore: sensory tentacle on the head or anterior section of the mantle of opisthobranchs (order Mollusca)
Rhizoids: slender hairlike structures that function as roots in mosses, ferns, fungi and related plants
Sedentary: immobile; refers to animals that remain attached to a substrate or that are unattached but do not move
Sessile: attached by the base (generally to a substrate)
Seta: bristle; plural setae
Siliceous: composed of or resembling silica, a glass-like material

Species: a group of individuals closely related in structure, capable of breeding within the group, but not normally outside it

Spicule: a minute, hard, needle-like body found in some invertebrates, such as sponges, soft corals, sea fans, and sea cucumbers

Subspecies: a geographical or other subdivision of a species that is sufficiently different to be recognised as such; a race

Substrate: the sea bed on which animals and plants live or are attached; rock, coral, mud or sand

Subtidal: below low tide level

Swimmeret: an abdominal limb or appendage adapted for swimming (of a crustacean)

Synonymy: collective names that designate the same species

Test: the hard covering of some invertebrates such as crustaceans, sea urchins

Type specimen: the original specimen from which a species was described

Valleys: the opening of the corallite in meandroid and flabello-meandroid coral colonies (brain corals)

Veliger: the free-swimming larva of many molluscs

Vertebrate: an animal with a backbone

Viscera: the intestines

Water-column: area of water between the sea floor and the surface

Zooid: an individual forming part of a colony and produced asexually by fission; this term is often used in place of 'polyp'

Algae

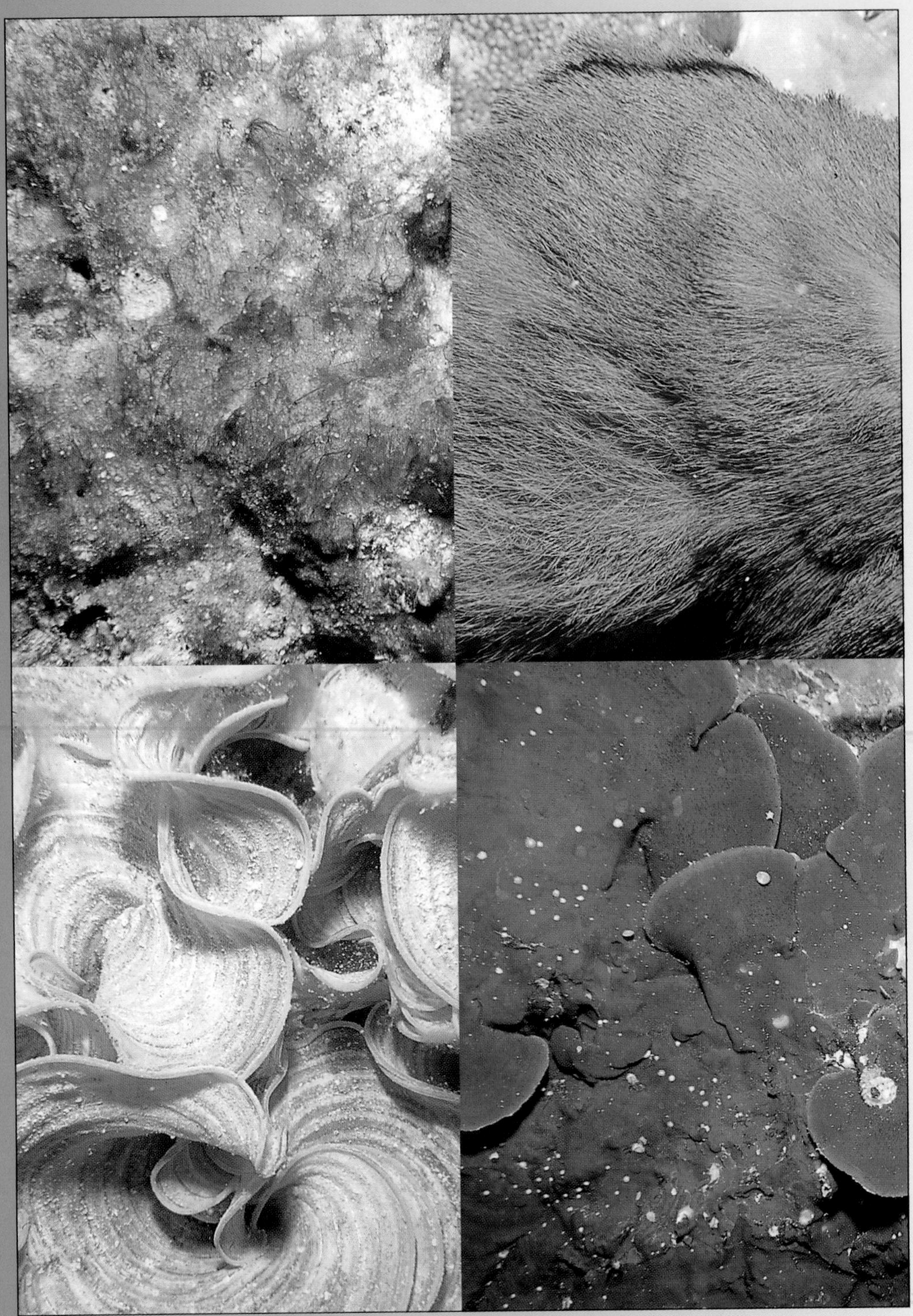

Kingdom of plants

Chapter 1
Algae (Marine plants)

Features: There are more than 9000 species of algae in the world's oceans. Of these, the largest and most dominant occur in temperate waters ranging in size from filamentous turfs only millimetres in height to giant kelps, which can be 30 metres long and may grow at the rate of half a metre a day. Other forms are seen merely as a slippery scum on the rocks.

Tropical reefs may support around 1000 species yet many remain undescribed. Although 63 intertidal species have been recorded from the Maldives very little work has been done in establishing a subtidal resource listing. There is every reason to suspect that there will be a number of new discoveries when more work is done in the future.

Compared to the higher land plant communities algae are more primitive in structure and although they have less distinctive features there are an amazing number of shapes, designs, patterns and textures.

Lifestyle: Algae grow wherever there is enough light and life-supporting conditions exist. They live on coral reefs, rocky reefs, rubble, sand and mud from above the intertidal zone down to hundreds of metres. Whereas land plants have leaves that extract carbon dioxide from air and roots that absorb moisture and minerals from soil, algae have no true roots; their 'holdfasts' simply anchor them to the bottom.

Like all plants they live by using their photosynthetic pigments (chlorophyll) to convert sunlight, water, carbon dioxide and dissolved nutrients into organic compounds such as starches and sugars which are rich in energy. The by-product of this conversion is oxygen.

Reproduction: Algae have no flowers but reproduce by way of spores in an often complex fashion which includes both sexual and asexual plants.

Associations: Food to a massive number of herbivores, algae in one form or another support the existence of every other group of marine life.

Identification: In the past, the identification of algae was entirely based on microscopes and a degree in marine botany. However, although a degree in botany and a specimen is still the most accurate way to go, diving botanist/photographers have made enormous inroads into visual identification over the past 20 years.

In general terms, the subdivision of algae is based on colour: (1) blue-green algae (the most primitive), (2) green algae, (3) brown algae, (4) red algae. However, although this would appear an easy method it's amazing just how many green-looking species are browns and brown-looking species are reds. The colours are broadly based in photic zones according to light penetration at depth; blue-green and green algae are found towards the top of the scale (maximum light), browns at the intermediate level (medium light) and reds at the bottom (reduced light). However, this may not always appear to be the case, especially in tropical waters. As light decreases due to depth or to increasing turbidity, algae give way to dominant animal communities.

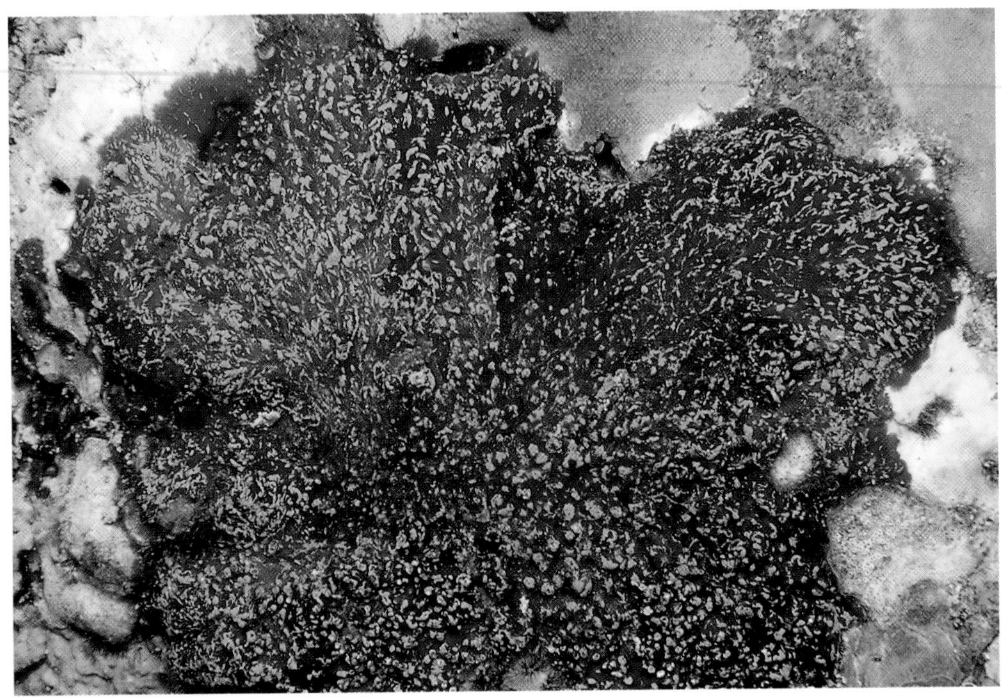

Maldivian red algae, unknown.

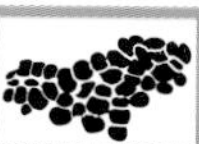

Blue-green algae

PHYLUM: CYANOPHYTA

Features: Far more easily seen on rocky shoreline substrates than underwater, blue-green algae appear as black or dark-coloured scum at the water's edge. Blue-green algae are extremely slippery to touch and even more so to walk on sending many an intertidal reef walker or shore entry diver skidding. Most blue-green algae occur in fresh water with only 75 per cent of the 200 known species living in the sea.

These single-celled microscopic plants form clusters of filamentous cells within a gelatinous mass; their colour generates from their main photosynthetic pigments of chlorophyll and phycocyanin. Although they look insignificant the blue-green algae are related to the oldest recognised life forms on earth. By consolidating sediments into permanent growing rocky structures called stromatolites they are able to convert atmospheric nitrogen into compounds (such as sugars) suitable for plant nutrition.

Living fossils by today's standards, stromatolites are over three billion years old and have been credited with having created the necessary levels of oxygen that led to the evolvement of higher forms of life as we see it today.

Reproduction: By way of spores.

Associations: None known.

Identification: Most blue-green algae are very difficult to identify unless they occupy a known micro-habitat or are subjected to microscopic study by a trained botanist.

Stromatolites are the oldest living life forms known. Shark Bay, Western Australia.

OSCILLATORIACEAE
Rusty scum algae
Schizothrix calcicola

Lagoons, reefs

1 to 20 metres (3.3 to 66 ft)

180 mm (7 in) across

Commonly visible over wide areas of many shallow water lagoons this very prevalent blue-green algae appears as a rusty, brown scum on the sand and surfaces of dead corals. Although it doesn't seem to be more than an eyesore this algae is capable of producing large amounts of oxygen (often seen as bubbles beneath its mat-like surface. Similar to many other algae it responds to high nutrient level sites.

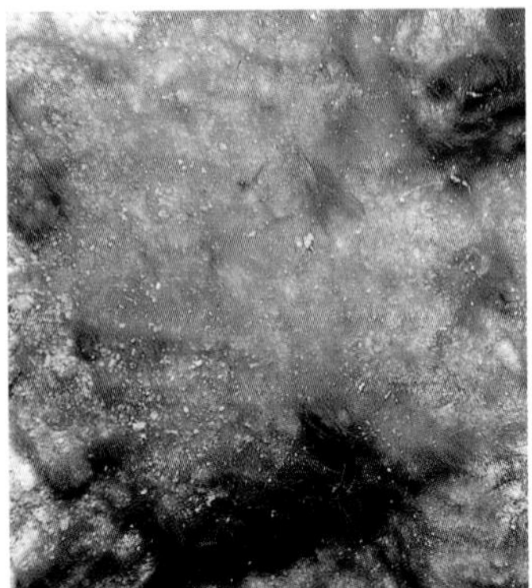

Close up of higher density example, Maldives.

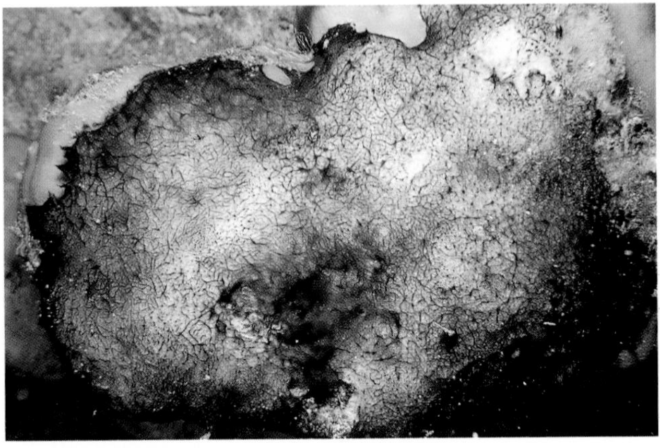

OSCILLATORIACEA
Hair-mat algae
Microcoleus sp.

Coral reefs, rocky reefs

Lt to 20 metres (0 to 66 ft)

170 mm (6.8 in) across photo

This blue-green algae is generally seen covering areas of dead coral on reef slopes and terraces. It will also grow across live coral as a smothering mat, eventually killing the coral.

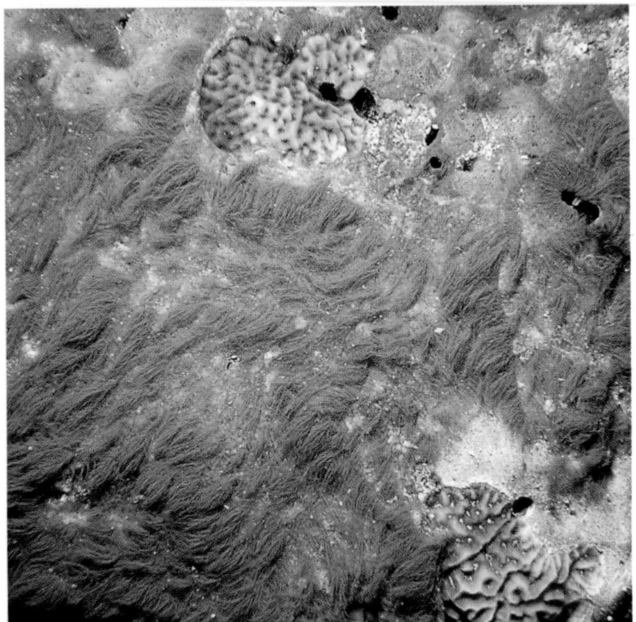

 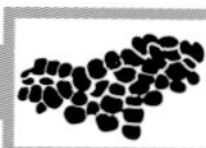

Green algae

PHYLUM: CHLOROPHYTA

Features: For most people the link between land plants (which are mostly green) and green algae can be easily seen. The phyla name chlorophyta is from the Greek words *chloros* for green and *phyton* for plant and although green is green, green algae may vary in colour from light green to yellow and dark green to black. Quite a few green algae, for example, *Ulva* and *Enteromorpha* are cosmopolitan and occur throughout most tropical areas. Both these species flourish where there are high nutrients or welling fresh water. Tropical green algae have an amazing range of forms from huge single cells to encrusting turfs and those with strange calcified plate-like leaves. The *Halimeda* alga are extremely important in the production of sand and marine sediments and also play a big part in the construction of beach rock holding the atolls and reefs together.

Lifestyles: Green algae is found mostly in shallow water though in some areas where the water is very clear it may be commonly seen in depths below 30 metres (98 ft). Vast areas across the Maldivian reefs are now covered with various forms of algae, many of them greens and these are eaten by parrotfish, surgeonfish and many molluscs.

Reproduction: **Sea lettuce**

The green alga *Ulva* undergoes a cyclic alternation and can be a spore-producing plant or a sexual-producing plant. Though each of these plants may look identical, they can only be identified by a specialist with a microscope. The spore-producing plant produces free swimming zoospores which swim to the bottom and attach, each growing into a complete sexual plant (male or female). When mature, these sexual plants release either sperm or eggs into the water. The fertilised eggs hatch into zygotes which settle to the bottom and grow into spore-producing plants to complete the cycle.

Associations: Many smaller molluscs and opisthobranchs are only found on various species of algae. There is no doubt that as interest in the prey and predator associations are studied more many new records of associations will be discovered.

Identification: Due to the difficulty in visually identifying many algae to species, to date only those species showing significant features have been used as examples.

CAULERPACEAE
Grape weed
Caulerpa racemosa
Coral reefs, rocky reefs, sand, rubble
Lt to 20 metres (0 to 66 ft)
70 mm (2.8 in) across

Extremely common across the entire Indo-Pacific this species can be easily recognised by sight due to its bead or grape-like branch tips. There are many forms and variations throughout its wide distribution and it often favours areas of high energy water movement.

CAULERPACEAE
Saw-bladed Caulerpa
Caulerpa serrulata
Coral reefs, rocky reefs, sandy reefs
2 to 10 metres (6.6 to 33 ft)
170 mm (6.8 in) across

A shallow water dweller, this common easily recognised Indo-Pacific species is comprised of short (often twisted) flattened Y-shaped serrated blades growing from a thin runner.

CLADOPHORACEAE
Stout green algae
Chaetomorpha crassa
Rocky reefs, rock walls
Lt to 5 metres (0 to 16 ft)
180 mm (7 in) across

Found on areas of high energy coast this algae grows in small dense clumps of unbranched filaments. The species is common throughout the Indo-Pacific and is prolific in some areas of the Maldives.

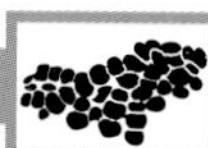

CHLOROPHYCEAE

Turtle weed

Chlorodesmis hildebrandtii

Reef tops, reef rims and slopes

3 to 10 metres (10 to 33 ft)

200 m (8 in) across

Bright green in appearance this easily identified genus occurs over a wide area of the Indo-Pacific. Many clumps in the Maldives are small and raggedy with white around the outside edge. This white area is dead which may indicate that the plants are in poor health, or they have been subjected to long periods of rough conditions thereby wearing along the edges. The tufts are constructed of filaments which continuously divide into equal branches.

ULVACEAE

Green guts weed

Enteromorpha clathrata

Coral reefs, rocky reefs

Lt to 2 metres (0 to 6.6 ft)

170 mm (6.8 in) across photo

Usually seen as a sheet of green slimy weed covering the rocks in the intertidal zone this genus is common throughout most tropical world oceans. It may live in rough or sheltered conditions and has hair-like branched tubes issuing from the base.

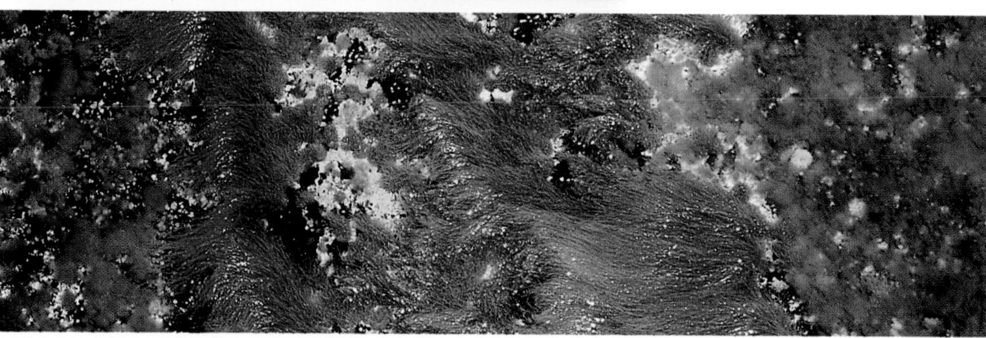

Close up of more developed growth, Lord Howe Island, South Pacific.

HALIMEDACEAE

Cactus algae

Halimeda opuntia

Sandy coral reefs, rocky reefs

5 to 25 metres (16 to 82 ft)

170 mm (6.8 in) across

A widespread form colonising the Indo-Pacific area this common Maldivian species is comprised of hard calcium carbonate tri-radiating segments connected by flexible joints. It grows in randomly branching clumps generally on sand covered pot holes in the reef.

HALIMEDACEAE

Micronesian coralline algae

Halimeda micronesica

Reef edges, slopes and terraces

3 to 10 metres (10 to 33 ft)

170 mm (6.8 in) across

Mostly seen in deeper low-light areas this species has calcified flat, disc-shaped segments that may be dark green or light green and grow in chains up to 150 mm. It does not appear to be particularly common at any of the reef sites visited. Clumps often seem to be ragged.

CHLOROPHYCEAE

Pom Pom algae

Tydemania expeditionis

Reef tops, edges, slopes and terraces

3 to 30 m (10 to 98 ft)

120 mm (4.8 in) across

Extremely common across the Maldives the general structure of this algae allows it to hold large quantities of sand, silt and/or decaying coral within its close-knit fronds. At a distance it gives the appearance of being sponge-like, but closer examination reveals no pores.

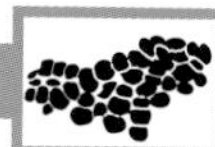

ULVACEAE
Sea lettuce
Ulva sp.
Coral reefs, rocky reefs
Lt to 10 metres (0 to 33 ft)
170 mm (6.8 in) across pic

Intensely grazed by fish and invertebrates this genus is very common across the entire Indo-Pacific and in the Maldives appears to be common as small tufts in areas of high water movement. Larger colonies exist where there are areas of high nutrient dispersal.

Close up of plants showing bubbles of oxygen trapped beneath the fronds.

VALONIACEAE
Sailor's eyeball algae
Ventricaria ventricosa
Coral reefs, rocky reefs
Lt to 20 metres (0 to 66 ft)
50 mm (2 in) across

Growing on hard bottom this very well known common algae is comprised of a single giant cell attached by hair-like threads to the substrate. It is found across the Indo-Pacific and is easily recognised.

Brown algae

PHYLUM: PHAEOPHYTA

Features: While there may be over 1500 species of brown algae most of these occur in sub-temperate and temperate waters with relatively few species living in the tropics. However, what they lack in diversity, browns often make up for in abundance and sometimes entire areas can be covered with filamentous brown algae as well as the larger *Turbinarias*, *Sargassums*, and *Padinas*, while *Dicyotas* dominate the deeper reef slopes.

The phylum name comes from the Greek world *phaios* meaning "brown" and the actual colour is due to the brown pigment fucoxanthin which presumes many shades, from yellow to dark brown verging on black.

Lifestyles: Brown algae can be found throughout the intertidal zone, the inshore subtidal zone and down to several hundred metres. Most brown algae lives on hard bottom or on pieces of rock, shells or dead coral on sand or rubble. Funnel weed (*Padina*) is a very common brown algae growing on dead coral heads and patch reefs in lagoonal situations.

Reproduction: Plants can be sexual or asexual and follow the basic method of reproduction described for green algae.

Associations: There are not as many animals which feed on or are associated with brown algae as there are with greens and reds.

Identification: Some browns are easy to identify visually while others still require a specimen and a trained botanist.

DICTYOTACEAE
Y-shaped algae
Dictyota sp.
Coral reefs, rocky reefs
5 to 10 metres (16 to 33 ft)
170 mm (6.8 in) across photo

Seen as creeping mats of low profile Y-shaped branches on reef tops and slopes, this species has crenulated fronds. The colour is often green or blue (with or without iridescence) with dark brown specks on the upper surface.

DICTYOTACEAE
Funnel weed
Padina commersonii
Coral reefs, rocky reefs, lagoons
5 to 15 metres (16 to 49 ft)
170 mm (6.8 in) across photo

Very common in some lagoonal situations covering areas up to three square metres. The regular growth pattern recurved fronds and chalky appearance make it fairly easy to identify even though it is generally covered with a fine coating of silt. The chalky appearance is due to the presence of calcium carbonate on the upper surface of the flat circular blade.

SARGASSACEAE

Sargassum weed

Sargassum sp.

Coral reefs, rocky reefs, open sea

Lt to 10 metres (0 to 33 ft)

400 mm (16 in)

There are a number of species within this widespread Indo-Pacific genus. This Indian Ocean species is a golden brown with long ragged edged bladed leaves and round floats. Some Sargassums live out their entire lives on the surface of the ocean. Others grow attached to reefs by a holdfast.

CYSTOSEIRACEAE

Ornate Turbinaria

Turbinaria ornata

Coral reefs, rocky reefs

Lt to 10 metres (0 to 30 ft)

200 mm (8 in) height

Very common on reef tops throughout the Indo-Pacific this Indian Ocean form is well known and easily identified. It is very firm and quite spiky to touch.

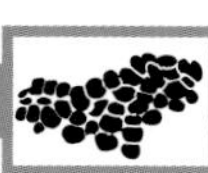

Red algae

PHYLUM: RHODOPHYTA

Features: With more than 4000 species known from tropical reefs the red algae are the most diverse in shape, pattern and design and are found from the intertidal area down to at least 100 metres. They may appear in almost any colour though their phylum name *Rhodophyta* comes from the Greek *rhodon* meaning 'red' rose. The red colour itself comes from having large quantities of the pigment phycoerythrin in the cells which absorbs the green and blue components of the sun's rays.

Some red algae are so calcified that they grow upright in clumps and appear as brittle pink skeletons with articulating joints.

Lifestyle: Coral reefs or tropical biotic reefs are constructed by lime-secreting animals and plants, corals and red coralline algae that live in vast communities under optimum conditions of moderately stable temperatures, good aeration, maximum sunlight, limited nutrients and carbonates. A coral reef is just a large mound of solidified skeletal debris covered by a thin veneer of living coral.

The corals contribute the major bulk of building materials to the reef and may be likened to providing the foundations, or the bricks. Holding the bricks together are various types of red coralline algae which bind and solidify, anchoring the larger formations against the forces of nature. Red coralline algae may not get much attention due to their insignificant appearance, yet they are as important to the function of a true coral reef as are the corals themselves. In fact, red algae dominate and at times exceed corals in importance as reef-building organisms.

Often referred to as lithothamnians, these red coralline algae extract calcium carbonate from sea water and are found all over the reef. Their hard encrusting layers cover the reef rock rim, cementing the living and dead corals together to form protective ramparts against the ever-erosive ocean and making it possible for other life forms to exist.

Reproduction: By spores similar to others previously described.

Associations: Many types of fish and invertebrates feed on red algae and there are some species of crabs and molluscs that mimic it.

Identification: With so many species and variations red algae present a challenge to visual identificationists. However, many have very characteristic forms, patterns and shapes and will prove easy in the future. The coralline encrusting forms may always require a specialised botanist to separate species on specimen based material.

CORALLINACEAE
Pink mat algae
Jania sp.
Coral reefs, rocky reefs
Lt to 3 metres (0 to 10 ft)
170 mm (6.8 in) across photo

Found in places of high energy wave action this algae has hard calcified, jointed branches which are generally forked at the ends. The branches grow quite close together forming dense clumps of mat-like turf over large areas. This genus is widespread throughout the tropical Indo-Pacific.

CORALLINACEAE
Crustose coralline algae
Mesophyllum sp.
Coral reefs, rocky reefs
Lt to 30 metres (0 to 98 ft)
180 mm (7 in) across

Growing flat on the substrate this species has small circular growing edges and can be seen in high energy wave areas or places of moderate wave action. In deeper sheltered water the crustose edges may grow higher and overlap.

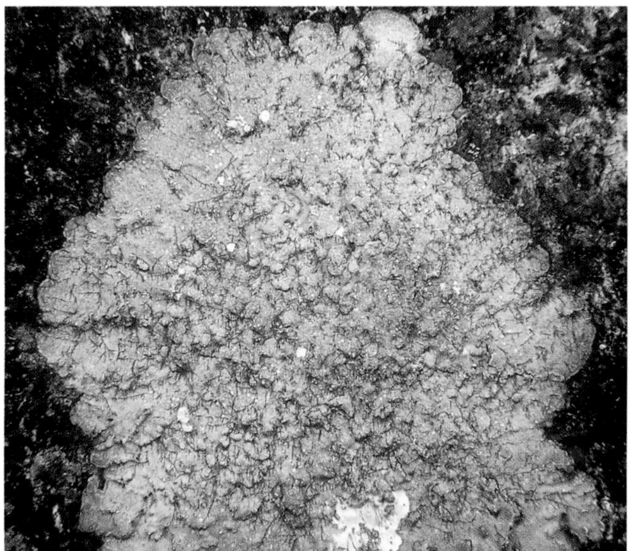

 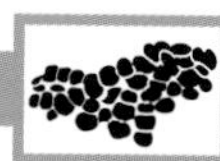

A widespread Indo-Pacific genus this interesting red algae generally lives on shady drop offs, reef walls, slopes and terraces where it grows under ledge edges and on vertical surfaces. The purple, pink, green or yellow fronds have radial striations.

SQUAMARIACEAE

Fungi-form red algae

Peyssonelia capensis

Coral reefs, rocky reefs

5 to 25 metres (16 to 82 ft)

60 mm (2.4 in) across

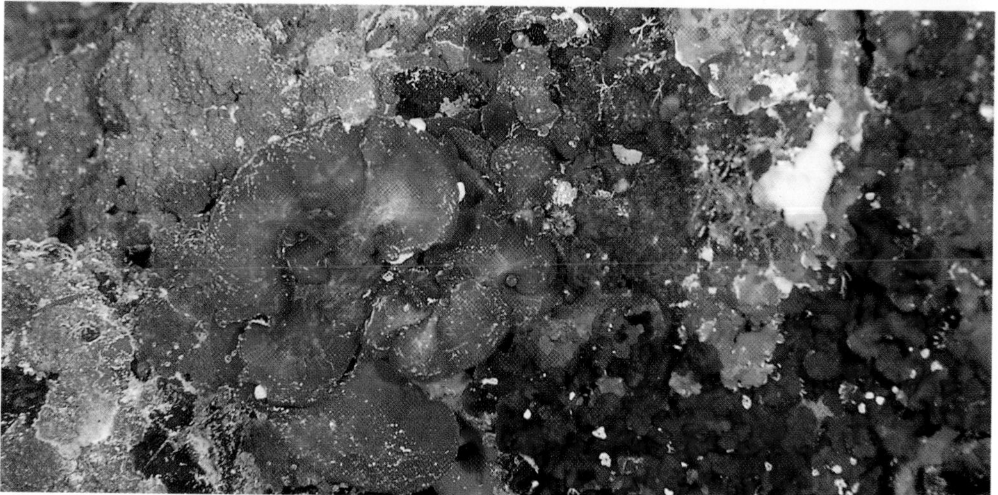

Colour variation, Maldives.

Sponges

Kingdom of Animals

Chapter 2
Sponges (Pore-bearers)

PHYLUM: PORIFERA

CLASSES: *Demospongiae* (Siliceous sponges)
Calcarea (Calcareous sponges)

Features: Sponges are considered by some to be the first multicellular animals; their fossil remains have been traced back to the Precambrian era, some 650 million years ago. These simple, primitive life forms are widespread throughout temperate and tropical seas, with around 15,000 species recognised worldwide.

Sponges are individual animals (not colonies) covered by a thin "skin" which houses multitudes of roving cells. They have no specific body plan, can be any shape, and may be soft or hard in texture. The body is perforated by pores and canals; with or without a fibrous skeleton and the body mass is supported internally by characteristically-shaped non-attached spicules. They are without intestines and have no nervous system.

Sponges usually have a fibrous skeleton that is made up of a keratin-like material called spongin, which is only found in sponges. Spongin is very resistant to decomposition, which accounts for the number of sponge skeletons found washed up on beaches, where they often remain for many years before breaking down.

Lifestyle: Sponges can be found on coral reefs, rocky reefs, on rubble, sand or mud and every microhabitat between. Depending on its environment, a single species may develop an encrusting form in areas open to rough seas, or may grow upright and branched in sheltered areas, or deeper water. Colour is also variable; sponges that grow in shade may be a different colour from those that grow in the sunlight. All sponges are attached to the substrate. Most prefer hard surfaces, though some live on the soft bottom embedded in the sand or mud. There are commensal sponges that live on the valves of live scallops, others bore holes in shells and rocks, and still others that dissolve living corals. Sponges range from minute encrusting species under rocks, to massive structures, one and a half metres (five feet) high, in deep water.

The anatomy of a sponge is complex. The body is perforated by many small inhalant pores called *ostia* and one, or a few large exhalant pores called *oscula* (singular osculum). The ostia lead to the oscula by converging channels passing through the sponge tissue. These channels are wholly or partially lined by special cells called collar cells, thus named because of their shape when seen under the microscope. Each collar cell bears a single filament or flagellum which beats. The combined effect of the beating flagella of the collar cells drives a stream of water through the sponge body from ostia to oscula. Fine protoplasmic extensions on the collar of the collar cells trap suspended fragments of food which are then ingested by the cells. The water stream supplies the sponge with oxygen and removes waste carbon dioxide. One small sponge no bigger than a clenched fist can filter its own body volume of water every four to 20 seconds, which amounts to around 5000 litres (1100 gallons) in one day.

Reproduction: Sponges can reproduce either sexually or asexually, and most are hermaphrodites having both male and female sex cells. Sperm are shed into the water through the exhalant oscula. When sperm are taken in by sponges of the same species through their inhalant ostia, fertilisation occurs inside the parent sponge, where fertilised eggs later develop into small flagellated larvae. The larvae then leave through an exhalant pore to swim in the sea for a time before settling on the bottom and developing into a new sponge. Small pieces of broken-off, or budded-off sponge (gemules) can also grow into an adult animal (asexual reproduction).

Association: Due to the needlesharp spicules, tough bodies and highly toxic chemical deterrents sponges have very few predators. However, they are eaten by nudibranchs, umbrella shells, sea stars and sea urchins. Some nudibranchs actually retain the toxic chemicals in the tissues of their own bodies and in this way are inedible to fish and some other predators. Sponges have a large number of commensal associations including shrimps, crabs, molluscs and brittle stars. Some even have zooxanthellae living in their tissues.

Identification: More than half the known species of marine sponges were described last century. Scientists now have difficulty identifying many species because the original nomenclature is confused and entire families need to be revised. Even today, taxonomists rely on spicule, or skeleton examination under a microscope to identify sponges. The spicules are small skeletal elements embedded either sporadically or in a definite pattern throughout the body of a sponge, helping to support the structure. These spicules can be either calcareous or siliceous and in most cases are minute. The two major classes of sponges are differentiated by their spicules: those of Calcarea are made of lime, while the spicules of Demospongiae are made of silica. Calcarea species have no spongin fibres.

Over the past few years sponges of the Maldives have become important due to the possibility of their having disease-curing characteristics in their pharmacology. In pursuit of these lifesaving properties scientific expeditions have now recorded several hundred species.

Due to the work carried out by modern day underwater taxonomists over the past 15 years it is now possible to visually identify a number of tropical genera and species. It is due to the courtesy, ability and experience of marine scientists (see acknowledgments) that such an outstanding selection of Maldivian sponges can be published for the first time.

Chagos calcite sponge, Maldives.

PLAKINIDAE
Ceylon sponge
Plakinastrealla ceylonica
Coral reefs, rocky reefs
15 to 25 metres (49 to 82 ft)
170 mm (6.8 in) across photo

A simple lumpy growth form and greyish yellow colour provide little individuality for visual identification on this species. It can be encrusting or massive and lives on reef faces, slopes and ledges.

TETILLIDAE
Berry sponge
Paratetilla bacca
Coral reefs, rocky reefs
10 to 25 metres (33 to 82 ft)
60 mm (2.4 in) width

Mostly seen on back reef slopes in areas of sandy rubble and sometimes under ledges on slopes. Specimens observed were all spherical and brown; most had a layer of silt on top in which minute algae grow. Sponges in this family are often referred to as "golf ball" sponges.

TETILLIDAE
Magician's sponge
Craniella abracadabra
Coral reefs, rocky reefs
15 to 25 metres (49 to 82 ft)
60 mm (2.4 in) width

Easily identified by its unique long-spined "pincushion" shape this species did not appear common in any one area and was found on slopes and drop offs.

This small sponge is only tentatively identified to genus although it appears to have very characteristic funnel-shaped inhalant tubes. It lives on walls in deeper water.

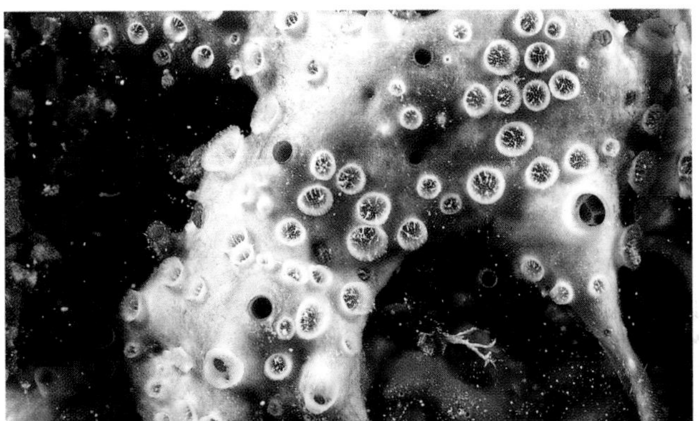

ANCORINIDAE

Funnel tube sponge

Stelleta sp.

Coral reefs, rocky reefs

15 to 25 metres (49 to 82 ft)

35 mm (1.4 in) width

Although this sponge looks like a group it is only one animal that is excavating its way through the substrate by burrowing into the subsurface limestone. It lives on reef tops and appears stable in colour.

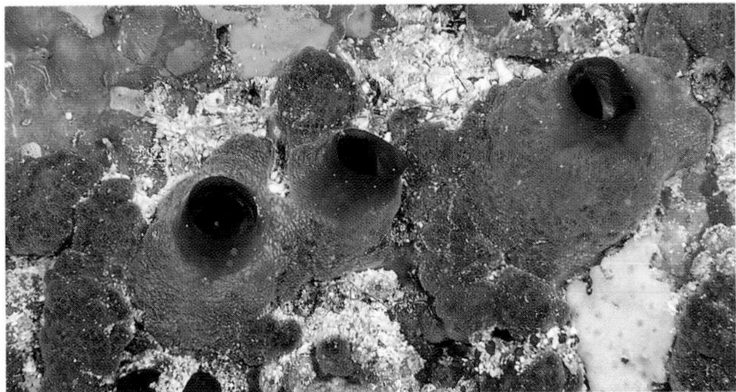

CLIONIDAE

Vagabond sponge

Spheciospongia cf. vagabunda

Coral reefs, rocky reefs

8 to 20 metres (26 to 66 ft)

200 mm (8 in) width

Only found beneath dead coral slabs this interesting little species has a unique pore pattern on its outside surface and was only seen in one colour.

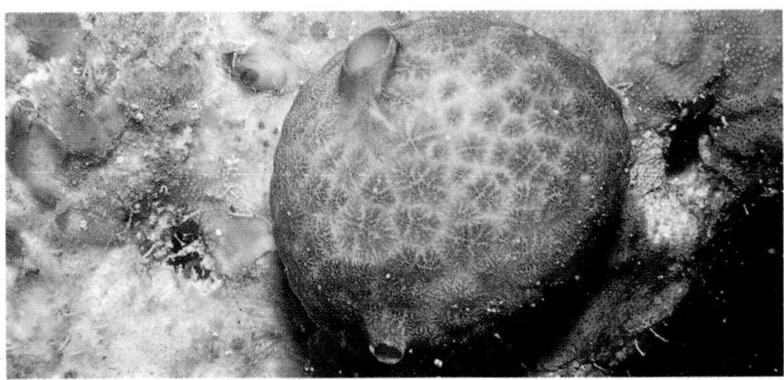

CHONDRILLIDAE

Mosaic sponge

Chrondrosia sp.

Coral reefs, rocky reefs

20 to 30 metres (66 to 98 ft)

50 mm (2 in) width

IOPHONIDAE

Orange-crumble sponge

Acarnus sp.

Coral reefs, rocky reefs

10 to 25 metres (33 to 82 ft)

250 mm (10 in) height

Bright orange to red in colour this sponge had two growth variations. On deeper water slopes it grew larger and at the tops of the slopes individuals were more stunted and spread out.

Dorsal aspect of shallow water form, Maldives.

Lateral aspect of shallow water form, Maldives.

MICROCIONIDAE

Brick-red sponge

Clathria (Microciona) plinthina

Coral reefs, rocky reefs

15 to 25 metres (49 to 82 ft)

170 mm (6.8 in) width

Found on a reef wall ledge this low profile encrusting species is very soft to touch and has numerous exhalant pores evenly distributed across the surface with prominent canals.

Close up of radial canals, exhalant oscula and surface texture, Maldives.

Possible colour variation growing on uneven reef, Maldives.

MICROCIONIDAE

Mauve-lobed sponge

Clathria (Microciona) sp.

Coral reefs, rocky reefs

10 to 20 metres (33 to 66 ft)

200 mm (8 in) width

With thick lobe-like encrusting form this species appears to have an irregular growth pattern. It grows on terraces in areas of moderate current.

COELOSPHAERIDAE

Sandy sponge

Ectyodoryx sp.

Coral reefs, rocky reefs

5 to 10 metres (16 to 33 ft)

35 mm (1.2 in) across photo

Fairly small in size these unlikely looking cushion-shaped sponges are usually found on dead rubble or coral rock in sandy areas. The body of the sponge is always covered in sand.

COELOSPHARIDAE

Yellow sponge

Lissodendoryx sp.

Coral reefs, rocky reefs

20 to 30 metres (66 to 98 ft)

100 mm (4.2 in) width

Attached to the top of a sea whip this tentatively identified species has an excellent feeding platform way out in the current. It is globular in shape and has large translucent oscula.

CRAMBIIDAE

Ungiculate sponge

Monanchora ungiculata

Coral reefs, rocky reefs

8 to 20 metres (26 to 66 ft)

170 mm (6.8 in) across photo

Varying in colour from bright red to pink with bright red oscula this species exhibits a number of growth forms, from flat and encrusting to large lobed or massive.

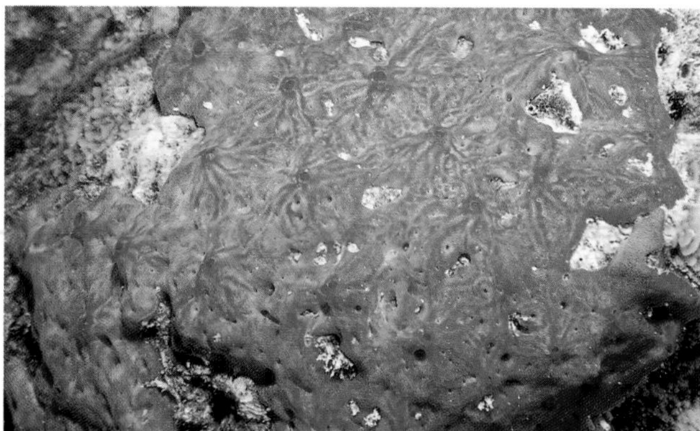

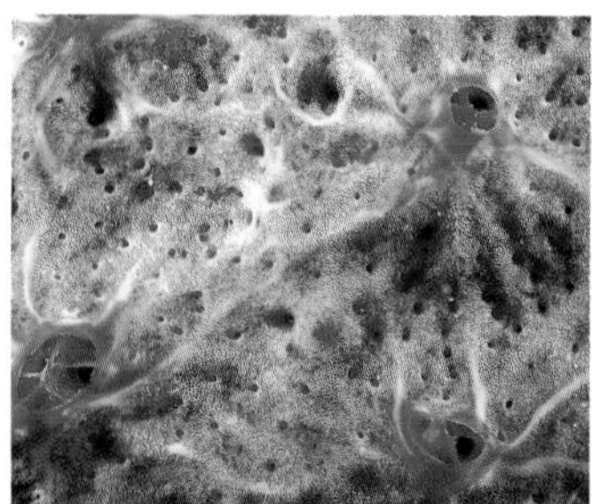

Dorsal close up colour variation, Maldives.

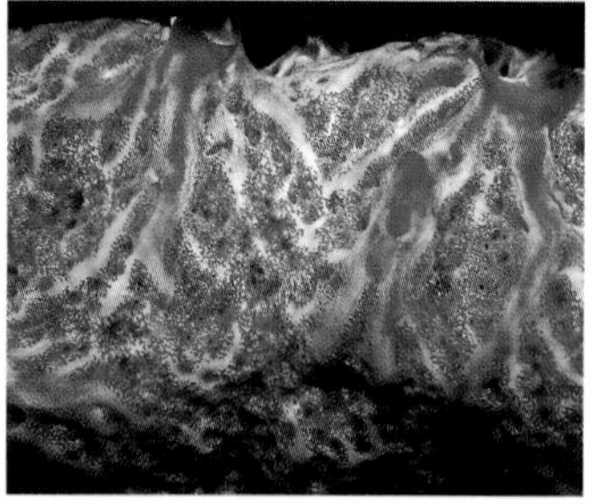

Lateral close up of colour variation, Maldives.

Another colour form of this genus, Maldives.

AXINELLIDAE
Carter's sponge
Phakellia carteri
Coral reefs, rocky reefs
10 to 20 metres (33 to 66 ft)
300 mm (12 in) width

Compressed and flabellate in form this species is quite common and generally grows along back reefs. Although the colour seems stable there is quite a bit of variation in the flabellate shapes growing from the body. Spicules often protrude through the skin.

AXINELLIDAE
Cavern sponge
Acanthella cavernosa
Coral reefs, rocky reefs
15 to 30 metres (49 to 98 ft)
35 mm (1.4 in) across photo

Bright orange in colour this sponge grows in caves and under ledges along walls. It is firm but fleshy with a lot of simple exhalant pores in the centre of the body.

AXINELLIDAE
Nippled sponge
Auletta cf. lyrata
Coral reefs, rocky reefs
5 to 15 metres (16 to 49 ft)
35 mm (1.4 in) width

Only observed in small clumps on dead coral silty sand surfaces. The surface around the oscula is swollen and rounded. All individuals seen were orange.

AXINELLIDAE

Labyrinth sponge

Axinella labyrinthina

Coral reefs, rocky reefs

20 to 30 metres (66 to 98 ft)

200 mm (8 in) width

Growing at the bottom of a dead coral slope this sponge had quite a bit of sediment on the dorsal surface. The body was firm and rough with spicules poking through the skin.

Small labyrinth sponges at 30 metres on a wall, Maldives.

AXINELLIDAE

Sculptured sponge

Pseudaxinella cf. australis

Coral reefs, rocky reefs

10 to 25 metres (33 to 82 ft)

170 mm (6.8 in) width

Found as a low profile encrusting form or as small semi-spherical lumps this species has extremely characteristic texture pattern somewhat similar to brain corals. Colour varies from orange to dark red and it is commonly seen along walls.

Colony growing over live coral, Maldives.

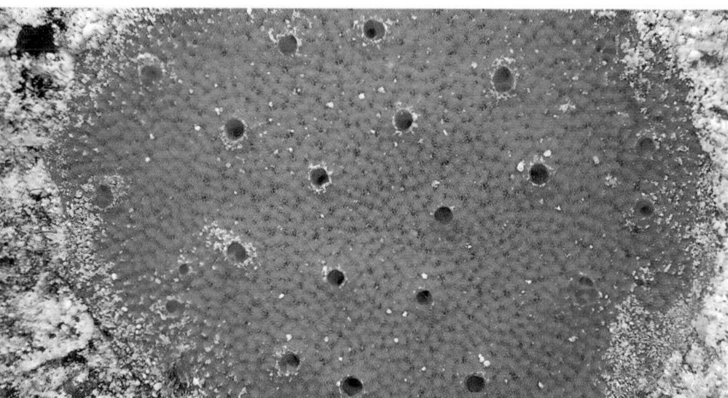

Close up of distinctively patterned surface corrugations, Maldives.

AXINELLIDAE

Red berry sponge

Pseudaxinella coccinea

Coral reefs, rocky reefs

20 to 30 metres (66 to 98 ft)

200 mm (8 in) width

Thick and lobe-like encrustations with little apparent growth pattern this sponge lives along walls where there is good current flow and clean conditions.

AXINELLIDAE

Flabelliform sponge

Stylissa flabelliformis

Coral reefs, rocky reefs

15 to 30 metres (49 to 98 ft)

300 mm (12 in) height

This sponge grows on a stalk attached to the reef. In sheltered deeper water the stalk is long and the sponge may be fan or goblet shaped or it may grow as a number of busy lobes. It lives along drop offs and on slopes.

Dorsal growth form variation, Maldives.

AXINELLIDAE
Imposter sponge
Stylotella sp.
Coral reefs, rocky reefs
10 to 20 metres (33 to 66 ft)
200 mm (8 in) width

An orange thick-bodied encrusting form this species does not appear to have any distinctive oscula on the surface. It grows on ledges along walls.

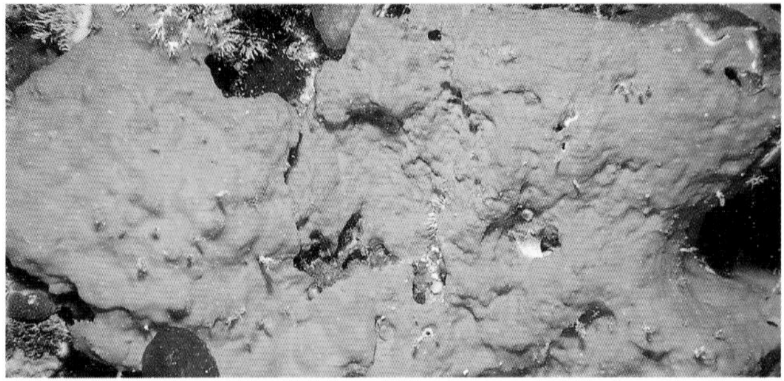

DICTYONELLIDAE
Paradox sponge
Liosina paradoxa
Coral reefs, rocky reefs
10 to 25 metres (33 to 82 ft)
200 mm (8 in) width

Looking more like a bunch of fleshy brown algae than any resemblance to a sponge this extraordinary species lives under ledges where it hangs down into the current. So dissimilar is it to other sponges recognition is easy.

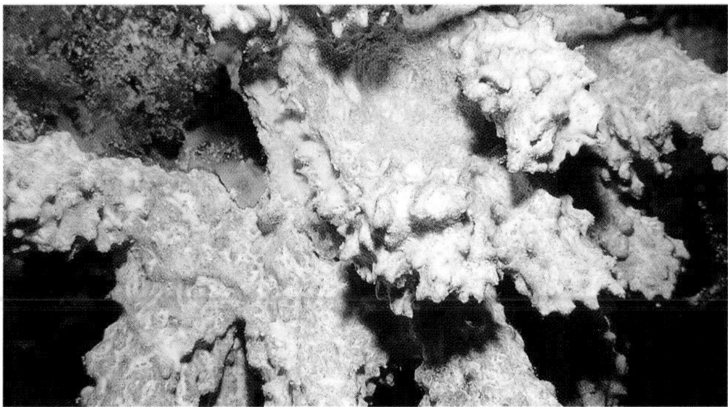

CHALINIDAE
Sickly sponge
Haliclona ostros
Coral reefs, rocky reefs
20 to 30 metres (66 to 98 ft)
170 mm (6.8 in) width

Living beneath ledges and overhangs along drop offs, this very characteristic soft, fleshy sponge first appears to be rotting or half dead but this is not the case.

(left) Close up of surface texture and pattern, Maldives.

CHALINIDAE

Coral-eating sponge

Haliclona nematifera

Coral reefs, rocky reefs

5 to 30 metres (16 to 98 ft)

300 mm (12 in) across photo

This outstanding species of investing sponge is very common throughout the Indo-Pacific. It is fairly stable in its colour and pattern and although fragile to touch the sponge envelopes living corals, dissolving the tissue and taking over the corals living space.

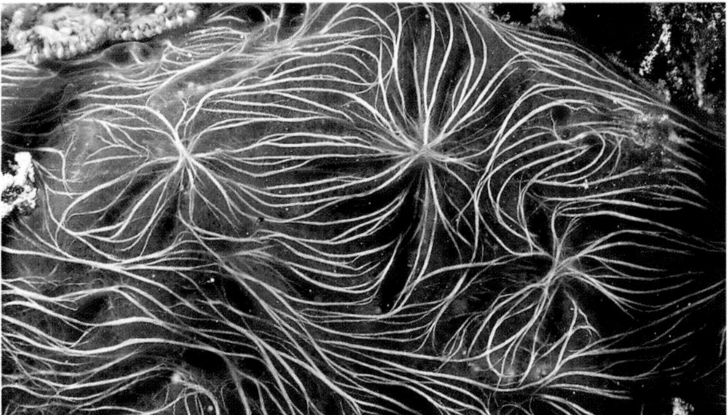

Example of territory invasion on midnight coral, Maldives.

Close up of surface texture, Maldives.

NIPHATIDAE

Brown-boring sponge

Aka mucosum

Coral reefs, rocky reefs

5 to 20 metres (16 to 66 ft)

170 mm (6.8 in) across photo

The black siphons of this species signify that this subterranean sponge has bored its way through the coral head and surrounding reef and will eventually break down the substrate.

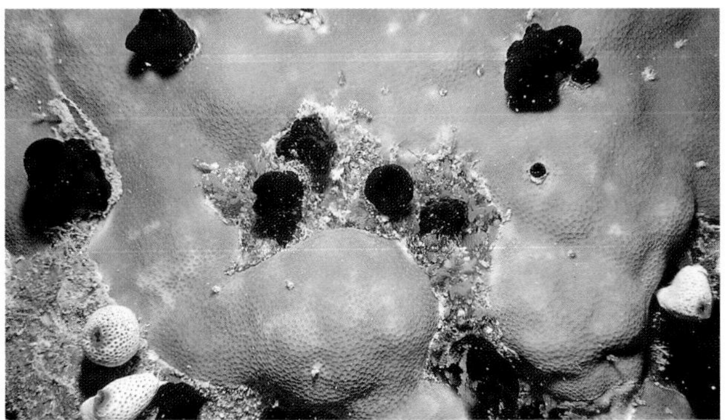

NIPHATIDAE

White-boring sponge

Aka sp.

Coral reefs, rocky reefs

5 to 20 metres (16 to 66 ft)

70 mm (2.8 in) across photo

Boring sponges are common to all tropical coral (limestone) reefs and have major impact in destroying localised areas. This example shows many meshed inlets (ostia) and a larger outlet siphon (oscula).

NIPHATIDAE

White-knobbed finger sponge

Microxina sp.

Coral reefs, rocky reefs

15 to 25 metres (49 to 82 ft)

300 mm (12 in) height

A stalked branching form with long finger-like projections, this species has a light coloured swollen tip on the ends of the branches and very distinctive sieve-like oscules.

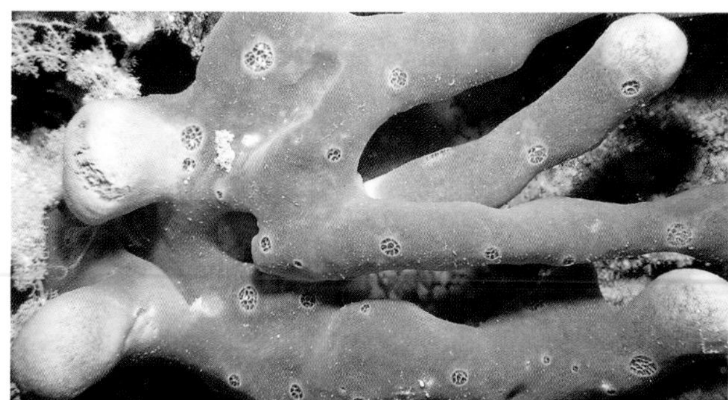

NIPHATIDAE

Blue-finger sponge

Amphimedon sp.

Coral reefs, rocky reefs

10 to 40 metres (33 to 131 ft)

450 mm (18 in) height

Extremely common on some deeper water slopes, gullies and terraces this distinctive species is generally blue or grey and may grow as long finger-like stalks in sheltered deeper water, or as a lobed encrusting form on shallow reefs.

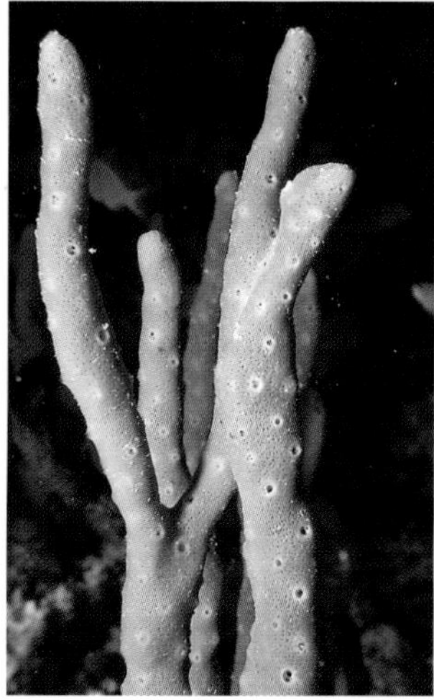

Some clumps may have up to 15 branches, Maldives.

Lobed encrusting form on shallow reef, Maldives.

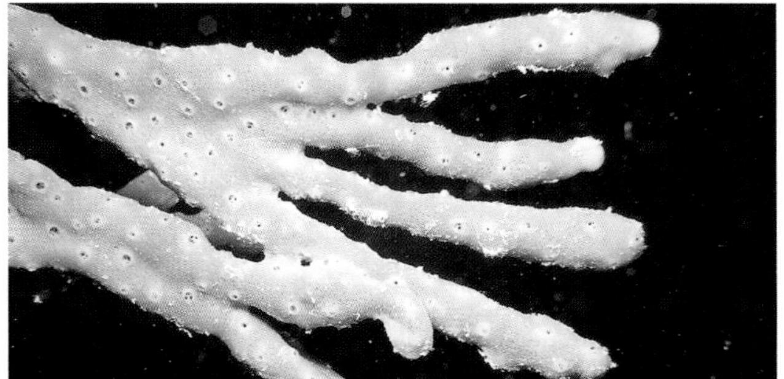

Colour variation, Maldives.

NIPHATIDAE

Sieve sponge

Cribrochalina cribricutis

Coral reefs, rocky reefs

10 to 20 metres (33 to 66 ft)

170 mm (6.8 in) across photo

A globular encrusting sponge with a sieve-like surface this species lives on walls and drop offs. It has a "spongy" surface and is sticky to touch.

PHLOEODICTYIDAE

Digit sponge

Oceanapia sp.

Coral reefs, rocky reefs

20 to 30 metres (66 to 98 ft)

120 mm (4.8 in) width

Seen along the edges of ledges this little sponge has very distinctive projections growing from the surface and is generally white in colour.

PHLOEODICTYIDAE

Puffball sponge

Oceanapia sagittaria

Sandy rubble

8 to 20 metres (26 to 66 ft)

80 mm (3.2 in) height

Locally common from the Maldives to the Great Barrier Reef this unusual very fragile topped long-stalked sponge gives little clue as to its ancestry. It lives in sheltered silty soft bottom areas and is rarely noticed.

PETROSIIDAE

Swollen finger sponge

Strongylophora sp.

Coral reefs, rocky reefs

10 to 20 metres (33 to 66 ft)

200 mm (8 in) length

Although the main body of this sponge is hidden beneath a ledge it grows a number of finger-like projections out over the substrate.

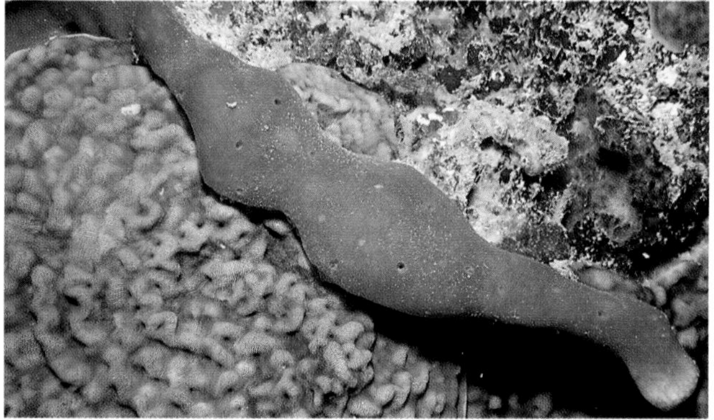

Common on some slopes and terraces this sponge and its relatives are found throughout the Indo-Pacific. As yet the species identity remains uncertain and this form may be undescribed.

SPONGIIDAE

Foliate sponge

Carteriospongia cf. foliascens

Coral reefs, rocky reefs

10 to 25 metres (33 to 82 ft)

180 mm (7.2 in) width

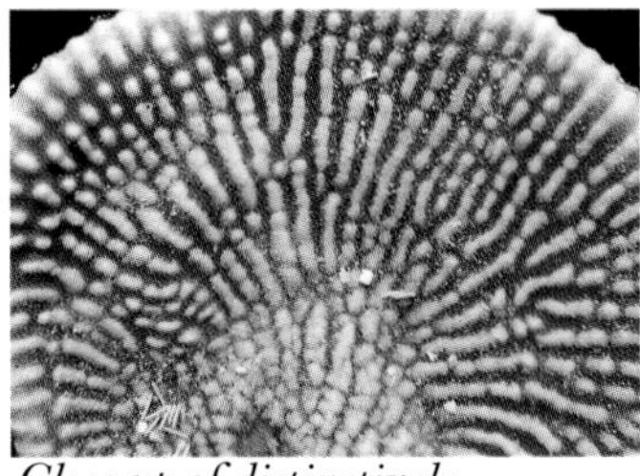

Close up of distinctively patterned surface.

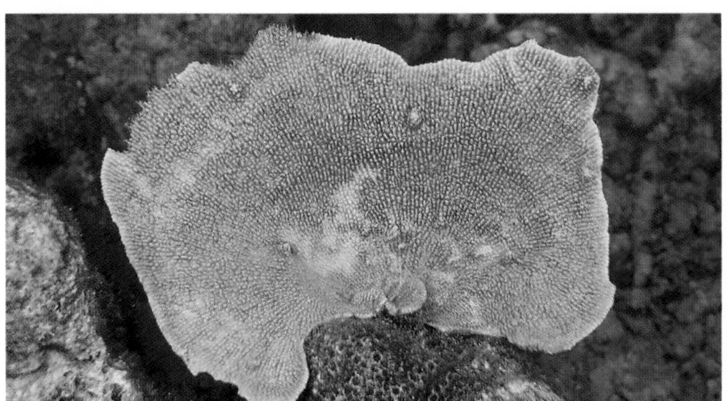

A larger specimen 250 mm (10 in) width has signs of predation.

Although in the Maldives this species is almost always bright yellow in colour, larger forms across the Indo-Pacific appear dirty yellow or greenish depending on associations and locality.

SPONGIIDAE

Yellow-dimpled sponge

Hippospongia metachromia

Coral reefs, rocky reefs

10 to 20 metres (33 to 66 ft)

170 mm (6.8 in) width

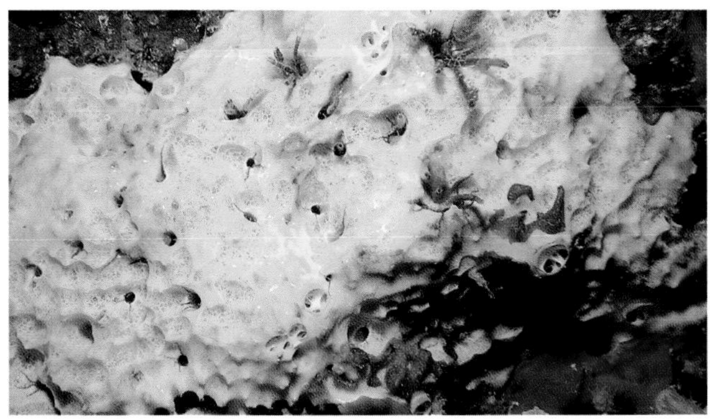

THORECTIDAE

Erect sponge

Hyritos erecta

Coral reefs, rocky reefs

15 to 25 metres (49 to 82 ft)

200 mm (8 in) height

A common species sometimes found on silty areas of reef and rubble slopes this species is generally black or dark brown coated in liberal amounts of silt or sediment. It is food for some nudibranchs and squat lobsters also inhabit it at night.

DYSIDEIDAE

Greenish sponge

Dysidea chlorea

Coral reefs, rocky reefs

5 to 10 metres (16 to 33 ft)

170 mm (6.8 in) across photo

Covering quite a bit of dead coral substrate across the Maldives this thin investing species is often ornamented with numbers of short projections which may or may not have holes (oscula).

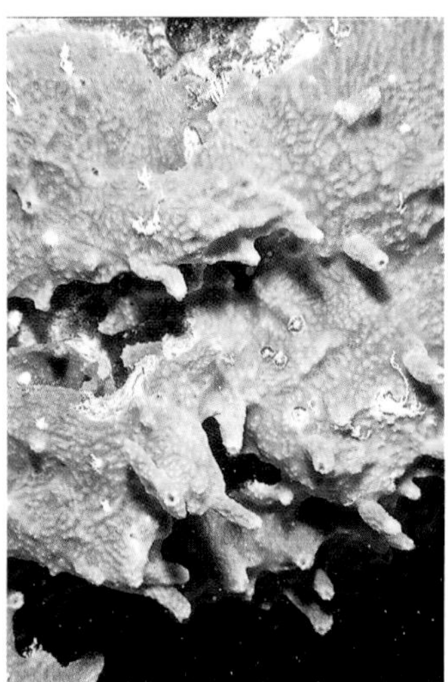

Colour and form variation, Maldives.

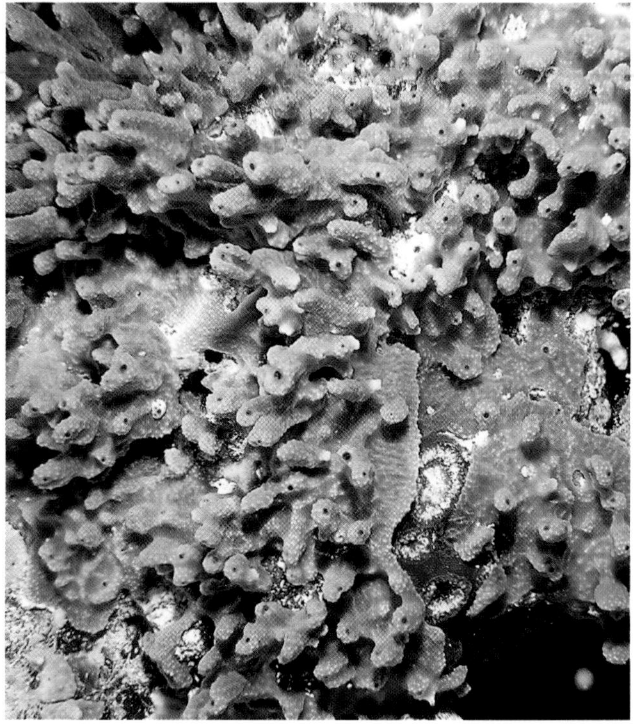

Found in many areas of the Indo-Pacific this sponge does not appear to have any growth pattern; it spreads across the substrate in finger-like projections that seem indiscriminate.

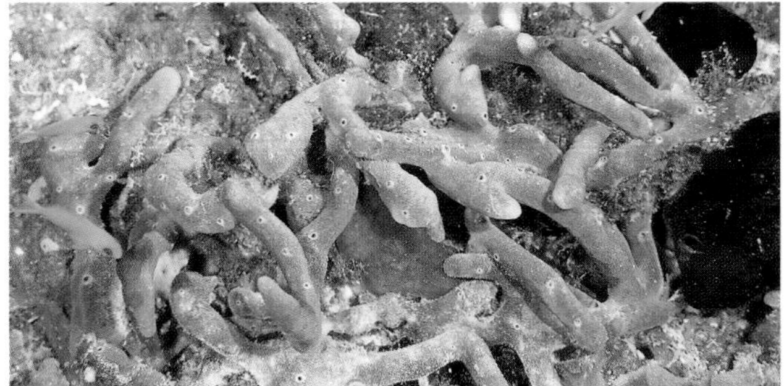

DYSIDEIDAE

Granulose sponge

Dysidea granulosa

Coral reefs, rocky reefs

15 to 25 metres (49 to 82 ft)

170 mm (6.8 in) across photo

Flattened wide-spreading surface with a distinctive pattern this sponge lives in sunlit shallow areas on the tops of reefs and slopes. The greenish tinge is due to symbiotic algae living in the tissues.

DYSIDEIDAE

Algae sponge

Dysidea herbacea

Coral reefs, rocky reefs

5 to 10 metres (16 to 33 ft)

300 mm (12 in) width

Generally mauve or pink in colour this sponge lives on ledges over drop offs and smells strongly of garlic. This species has figured in effective biochemistry by producing an anti-AIDS molecule.

DYSIDEIDAE

Come-again sponge

Dysidea cf. avara

Coral reefs, rocky reefs

20 to 30 metres (66 to 98 ft)

150 mm (6 in) width

CLATHRINIDAE

Yellow calcite sponge

Clathrina sp.

Coral reefs, rocky reefs

20 to 30 metres (66 to 98 ft)

90 mm (3.6 in) length

A very fragile and delicate form this calcareous species has long membranous tubes growing from the surface. It has been observed in other areas of the Indo-Pacific but does not appear to be common across the Maldives.

Another unidentified calcite sponge, Maldives.

Mostly found in deeper water in caves or shady drop offs, this very characteristic bright yellow sponge is firm to touch, has well-developed oscula and grows as lumps or lobes, sometimes growing downwards.

LEUCETTIDAE

Chagos calcite sponge

Leucetta chagosensis

Coral reefs, rocky reefs

20 to 30 metres (66 to 98 ft)

170 mm (6.8 in)

Short-lobed variation, Maldives.

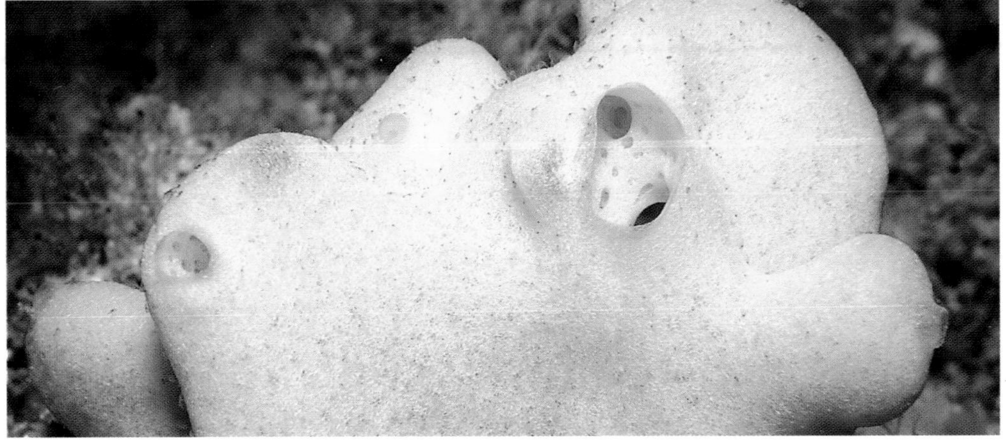

Close up of surface area, Maldives.

Cnidarians

Chapter 3

Cnidarians (Stingers)

PHYLUM: CNIDARIA

CLASS: *Hydrozoa* (Hydroids, Hydrocorals, Fire Corals, Portuguese Man-of-War)
Ceriantipatharia (Black corals)
Alcyonaria (Soft corals, Gorgonian sea fans, Sea whips)
Zoantharia (Sea Anemones, Zoanthids, Corallimorphs, Hard Corals)

Features: At one time all animals with radial symmetry and simple sac-like bodies were placed in the phylum Coelenterata. Instead, scientists today recognise two separate phyla at this level: Cnidaria and Ctenophora. All the animals illustrated in this section belong to the larger phylum, the Cnidaria. The term 'Cnidaria' refers to the power to sting, a feature of those animals which have special stinging cells in their bodies.

There are about 9000 species of cnidarians living in the world's oceans. (This number is only an estimate due to continuing changes in taxonomy and new discoveries.)

Although all cnidarians possess nematocysts, only a few have the capacity to harm humans. Some hydroids, fire corals, sea jellies and sea anemones can injure humans and a few, including the tropical box jellies, have caused the deaths of many people.

The life histories of cnidarians are often varied and complex. The following is only a general account.

Lifestyle: Cnidarians are widely distributed throughout the Indo-Pacific, both in shallow and deep water. However, they are most obvious in the tropics where they form coral reefs. The basic structural unit of a typical cnidarian is a flower-like polyp. This polyp has no breathing mechanism, no blood and no excretory system. In short, it is a sac-like organism with an opening at one end surrounded by one or more circlets of tentacles. The vital functions of respiration, excretion and food distribution are achieved by simple diffusion.

Other types of cells are present including nerve cells, muscle cells, gland cells and reproductive cells. These are all arranged in two layers around the gut, and the inner layer is separated from the outer one by a layer of jelly-like substance called mesogloea.

The tentacles are hollow containing a space which connects to the gut and are armed with cells called cnidoblasts which house multiple numbers of stinging nematocysts. There are a number of different types of nematocysts; some are barbed, some are sticky, some act as a spring to wrap around and ensnare prey. Basically they are coiled up inside the cnidoblast cell and when given the appropriate stimulus, touch or chemical, they discharge by turning inside out. Once the prey is subdued, the tentacles manoeuvre it to the mouth. It then passes to the stomach where it is digested and the useful products are absorbed. The refuse is regurgitated and ejected via the mouth.

Within the phylum cnidaria, there are two main body forms – free swimming medusae (sea jellies) and stationary polyps (hydroids, corals and sea-anemones). Both body forms are radially symmetrical, with the mouth located at the centre. The basic differences between the free-swimming medusa and the stationary polyp are their orientation and their mode of life. Most medusa swims with the mouth and tentacles facing downwards, while the stationary polyp is attached to a substrate with the mouth and tentacles facing upwards, outwards, or downwards. One important feature of many cnidarians is their ability to form colonies.

Reproduction: In the Hydrozoa we find both solitary and colonial forms and within the colonies there may be several types of individual polyps, for example, defensive polyps, reproductive polyps and feeding polyps. Colonies do occur in the Anthozoa but in that instance all individual polyps are equivalent.

Most hydroids and scyphozoa have complex life cycles. These involve a fixed polyp phase and a mobile medusa phase. The Medusae reproduce sexually, each organism being male or female and releasing eggs and sperm into the sea. The fertilised eggs develop into larvae which settle to the bottom and turn into polyp forms, which upon growth and maturation, reproduce asexually to give another mobile medusa phase. In the hydrozoa it is the sedentary polyp phase which is dominant and due to the visually apparent growth forms can be recognised by divers.

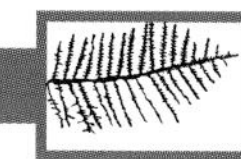

Associations: Even with their outstanding armaments and deadly properties cnidarian defences have been penetrated by a myriad organisms which live in them, on them and around them. These include worms, molluscs, crustaceans, echinoderms and fish.

Identification: Although some cnidarian groups still defy visual identification most are recognisable to class, many to family and a large number to genus and species. With an upsurge in interest and quality publications, knowledge will progress and before too much longer further advancements will be made.

CLASS: *Hydrozoa* (Hydroids, Hydrocorals, Fire Corals, Portuguese Man-of-War)

Features: The order Hydroida (sea ferns) are one of the few cnidarian groups that is more diverse in temperate waters than in tropical seas. Although they flourish across the Indo-Pacific, hydroids are certainly not familiar to most divers until they get stung. The majority are low-profile clusters of fine, fern-like structures that tend to blend in rather than stand out. Many species are very small, and many live on other organisms, such as seaweeds, sponges and shells.

The external tubular supporting structure of a hydroid's sedentary colonial state (skeleton) is composed of flexible chitin. In some cases this merely protects the tubular connections between polyps in the colony, while in other cases it is extended to form tunnel-like hydranths into which the polyps can withdraw for protection. By contrast, the colonial hydrocorals and fire corals have massive, hard, calcified structures.

Lifestyle: Hydroids and hydrozoans live on coral reefs and rocky reefs generally in areas of good water movement, tops of coral heads, channel sides, tops of drop offs, under caves and ledges.

Whereas the chitinous flexible forms are rarely noticed, the brightly-coloured hydrocorals (which includes the stony fire corals) generally stand out. The fire corals and other hydrocorals are able to build calcium carbonate skeletons in a similar fashion to stony corals. However, it is only the genus *Millepora* (fire corals) that have very powerful nematocysts and are able to sting humans. The smaller brightly-coloured species of hydrocorals do not sting humans. Most hydroids feed on plankton. Even though their nematocysts are very powerful only the Portuguese man-of-war (bluebottle) is capable of stinging, killing and eating larger prey such as fish.

Reproduction: Reproduction includes a process of body form alternation of an asexual colonial sedentary stage and a sexual medusa stage. The typical sedentary colonial form is what most divers see as it is attached to the bottom. At a certain time of the year the hydroid colony buds off small medusae which appear as tiny sea jellies. These medusae (sea jellies) are either male or female and when released from the parent colony become part of the plankton where they grow up, mature and release sperm and eggs. The larvae from fertilised eggs eventually settle to the bottom, find a suitable situation, attach to the substrate and begin the process of forming a hydroid colony by asexually budding.

In the case of the Portuguese man-of-war the entire colony is comprised of float, fishing tentacles, feeding polyps and reproductive zooids. The reproductive zooids do not separate from the colony but produce eggs and sperm which are then released into the water.

Associations: Hydroids are eaten by angelfish, nudibranchs and other molluscs, some of which are species specific. Gobies live on the surface of some fire corals and barnacles and worms bury into their skeletons.

Identification: Even though a number of the more prominent tropical sedentary colonies can be identified by the amateur observer (after some practice), the majority need to be identified by a specialist taxonomist from properly collected and preserved specimens. It will be some time before the full details of life histories of all hydroids are known. Many medusae have different names from the hydroid which constitutes the sessile generation and this complicates matters considerably. Careful breeding work may be necessary to establish which hydroid develops which medusa type. Scientists have recorded many species of hydroids in the world's oceans, but relatively fewer hydrocorals.

Pink hydrocoral, Maldives.

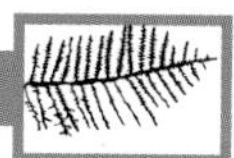

HALICHORDYLIDAE
Alternate Hydroid
Pennaria disticha

Coral reefs, rocky reefs
10 to 20 metres (33 to 66 ft)
25 mm (1 in) across photo

A common Indo-Pacific genus this smaller hydroid grows in clumps around 130 mm (5 in) high and is generally on a reef ledge or edge out in the current. The polyps show well-developed numbers of male and female medusa almost ready to be released to begin their life stage as free swimming sea jellies.

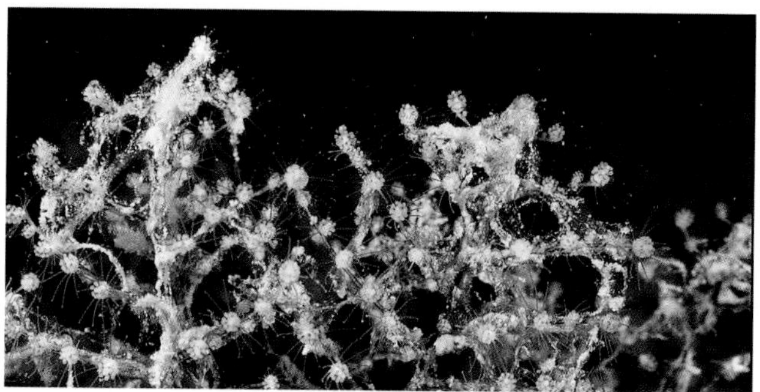

PHYSALIIDAE
Portuguese man-of-war
Physalis physalis

Coastal waters; oceanic waters
Surface waters
229 mm (9 in)

A Portuguese man-of-war is composed of a float, long fishing tentacles, feeding polyps, and reproductive zooids. Although it appears to be a single animal, it is a colony, living on the high seas. The fishing tentacles may be as long as 10 m (33 ft) and are studded with batteries of powerful stinging cells called nematocysts.

PLUMULARIDAE
White-stinging sea fern
Macrorhynchia philippina

Coral reefs, rocky reefs
1 to 25 metres (3 to 82 ft)
450 mm (18 in) colony height

Close up of stinging fronds, Maldives.

(continued)
These white fern-like colonies with dark brown stems occur in clumps and generally grow in areas of surge, or current, throughout the Indo-Pacific area.

PLUMALARIDAE
Delicate Hydroid
Plumularia sp.
Coral reefs, rocky reefs
10 to 20 metres (33 to 66 ft)
170 mm (6.8 in) across photo

A short-stalked spreading form this species is common to the Maldives and the genus is widespread across the Indo-Pacific. It lives on drop offs and reef ledges and prefers sites where there is a steady current flow.

PLUMULARIDAE
Curve-branched Hydroid
Zygophylax sp.
Coral reefs, rocky reefs
5 to 10 metres (16 to 33 ft)
170 mm (6.8 in) colony

Growing site, Maldives.

Difficult to identify without specimen taxonomy, this genus is widespread across the Indo-Pacific generally living on the edges around coral heads or ledges. The short side branches are generally curved and have a row of polyps on each side.

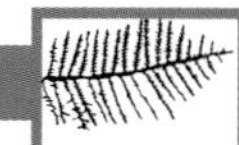

This genus resembles a gorgonian sea fan. However, the polyps are much different than the octocorals and although the branches are all on one plane the growth pattern and pliability are also dissimilar. This species is known from East Africa across to Western Australia.

SOLANDERIIDAE

Small dusky sea fern

Solanderia minima

Coral reefs, rocky reefs

10 to 30 metres (33 to 98 ft)

160 mm (6.4 in) across

Found across the Indo-Pacific this fire coral is generally observed on shallow reefs where there is high energy wave action. The plates are exceptionally strong and often fused together at different angles. This species stings badly.

MILLEPORIDAE

Flat-sided fire coral

Millepora platyphylla

Coral reefs, rocky reefs

2 to 10 metres (6.6 to 33 ft)

1 metre (3.3 ft) colony

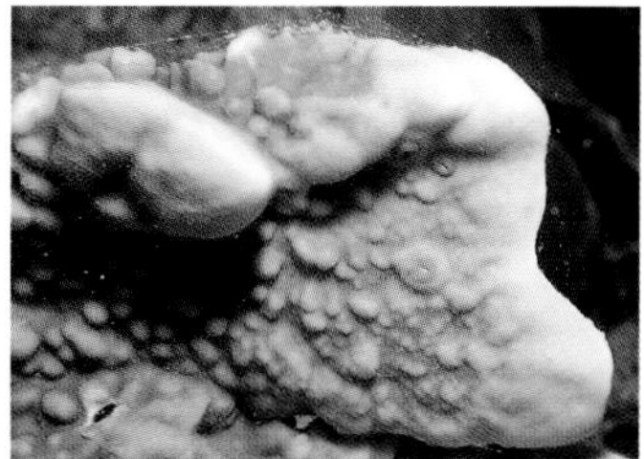

Close up of fused plates showing expanded polyps and barnacles, Maldives.

The delicate fire coral grows on the sides and tops of reefs where maximum water movement prevails. The sting is moderately painful and causes a continuous itch.

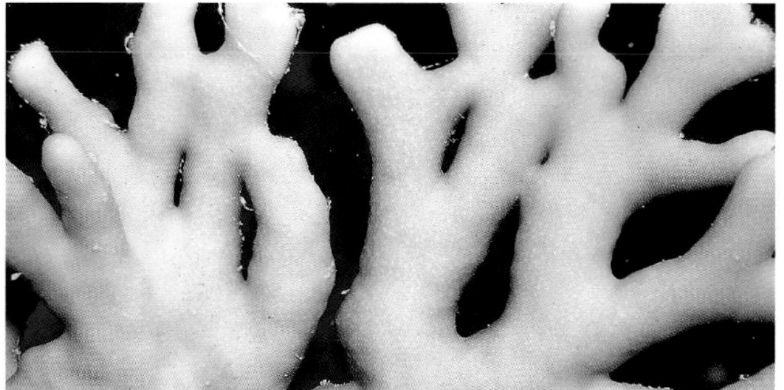

MILLEPORIDAE

Delicate fire coral

Millepora tenera

Coral reefs, rocky reefs

3 to 20 metres (10 to 66 ft)

3 metres (10 ft) colony width

STYLASTERIDAE
Blue hydrocoral
Distichophora violacea
Coral reefs, rocky reefs
1 to 30 metres (3 to 98 ft)
80 mm (3 in) colony

The blue hydrocoral is generally situated under ledges, along cliff faces, swim-throughs and in caves. This stony hydroid colony has its polyps growing along the peripheral edges of the branches, rather than over the entire surface as its fire coral (*Millepora*) relatives.

Close up of stunted colony, Maldives.

STYLASTERIDAE
Pink Hydrocoral
Distichophora sp.
Coral reefs, rocky reefs
20 to 30 metres (66 to 98 ft)
170 mm (6.8 in) across

Well known from the northern atolls this species is very erratic in its distribution and does not appear widespread, occurring at specific locations on some reefs and absent from others. It grows on walls, drop offs and underhangs generally in areas of moderate current.

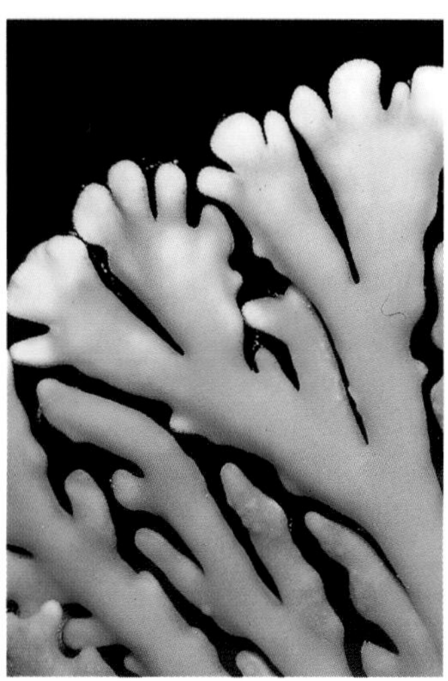

Close up of structure, Maldives.

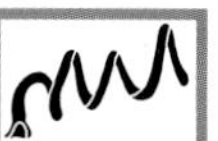

CLASS: *Cerianthipatharia* (Black corals)

Features: Living black corals are covered by a fleshy skin which may be white, pink, yellow, brown, orange, or green. The polyps have six tentacles that cannot retract into the skeleton, though they may shrink when disturbed.

The inner skeleton is black and comprised of an extremely tough, horny, tremendously pliable proteinous material secreted by the polyps. This material gets its strength from being deposited in concentric layers over a long period of time, resembling the growth rings in a tree. Different species may resemble a tree, a bush, a hydroid, a sea fan colony, or be straight like a whip, or corkscrew in shape. Black corals may be seen in tropical and temperate waters. Many black coral forests have been decimated due to their ancient tradition as 'precious' coral which is still sold throughout the world on the semi-precious jewellery markets.

Lifestyle: In the Indo-Pacific area, black corals can occur from low tide level down to and beyond 600 metres (2000 ft). They can live in a number of habitats as long as the larvae have something hard to settle on, but most are seen on coral reefs or rocky reefs on drop offs, slopes, wall, in caves, along walls and terraces where there is moderate current. They are plankton feeders and are long lived. Many large deep water colonies may be up to 300 years old.

Reproduction: Black coral polyps may be male or female and the colony as a whole hermaphroditic with reproductive products being released into the sea. Asexual growth is produced by budding.

Associations: Black corals have an amazing array of small resident predators and symbionts including crabs, shrimps, serpent stars, spindle cowries, barnacles, anemones, worms and fish.

Identification: Without doubt, there are a remarkable number of black coral species in the Maldives and due to the present lack of expertise in the field of black coral taxonomy few can be named even if the specimens were available. However, most can be placed in a genus on the level of understanding available. There is no doubt that when interest and availability of knowledge is updated there will be a number of new species. Until then illustrations are presented as examples of the diverse fauna existing in the Maldives.

ANTIPATHIDAE
Fir-tree black coral
Antipathes abies
Coral reefs, rocky reefs
10 to 30 metres (33 to 98 ft)
250 mm (10 in) height

Found from East Africa to Papua New Guinea this colony has fine elongate branches arranged around a central stem. The polyps are generally white and it can be seen in caves and under ledges on slopes.

Juvenile colony, Maldives.

ANTIPATHIDAE
Delicate black coral
Antipathes sp.
Caves, ledges
20 to 40 metres (66 to 131 ft)
180 mm (7.2 in) across

Occurring from the Maldives to Japan this species grows from the roofs and sides of caves. Compared to many other species of black corals, colonies of delicate black coral were small and obscure. An unidentified spindle cowry *Phenacovolva* sp. (a new record for the Maldives) was observed to live on this black coral.

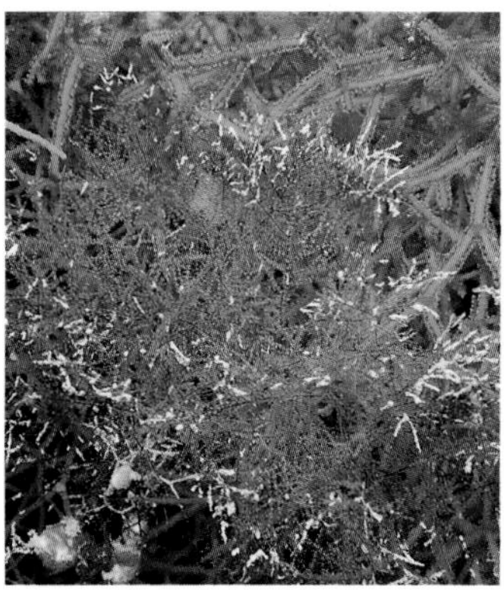

Juvenile colony, Maldives.

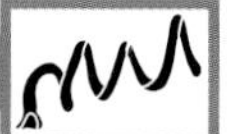

This species is common in caves along drop-offs. The skin is white with pink polyps and the minor branches grow alternatively from the edges of the main stems leaving the underside of the branches bare.

ANTIPATHIDAE

Ferny black coral

Antipathes sp.

Coral reefs, rocky reefs

15 to 40 metres (49 to 131 ft)

1 metre (3.3 ft) height

Frondy black coral has fine branches with white skin and small polyps. Growth is tree-like with branches forming large bushy colonies. A number of other animals such as the giant winged pearl oyster *Pteria penguin*, the cock's comb oyster *Lopha cristagalli* and black coral shrimp *Periclimenes* sp. live amongst the branches.

ANTIPATHIDAE

Frondy black coral

Antipathes sp.

Coral reefs, rocky reefs

20 to 30 metres (66 to 98 ft)

1.5 metres (4.5 ft) height

Close up of branch arrangement.

Spiky black coral is extremely strong with robust trunk-like main stems and thick branches with sharp-pointed straight tips. Its colours range from dark brown to orange or pink and it can be a dense thicket or be sparsely branched. It is host to the black coral spider crab *Xenocarcinus conicus* and ranges across the entire Indo-Pacific.

ANTIPATHIDAE

Spiky black coral

Antipathes sp.

Coral reefs, rocky reefs

20 to 40 metres (66 to 131 ft)

300 mm (12 in)

Spiky black coral variation, Port Moresby, Papua New Guinea.

ANTIPATHIDAE

Pipe-cleaner black coral

Antipathes sp.

Coral reefs, rocky reefs

10 to 40 metres (33 to 131 ft)

300 mm (12 in) height

This species begins its growth as a single bushy frond growing out and expanding in width into a shape resembling a giant pipe cleaner. It is fairly common across the Indo-Pacific area; in the Maldives it is host to the granulose black coral crab *Quadrella granulosa*.

ANTIPATHIDAE

Wiry black coral

Antipathes sp.

Coral reefs, rocky reefs

20 to 40 metres (66 to 131 ft)

200 mm (8 in) height

A small colony shaped somewhat like a pot scourer, this species is very finely branched and tightly formed. It does not appear to be common but is known to be another host for the granulose black coral crab *Quadrella granulosa*. In the Maldivian area it lives beneath ledges, on the ceilings of caves and along walls.

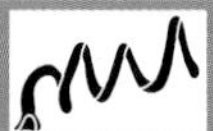

ANTIPATHIDAE

Giant black coral whip

Cirrhipathes sp.

Coral reefs, rocky reefs

25 to 40 metres (82 to 131 ft)

3 metres (10 ft) height

There are at least four or five species of black coral sea whips common to the Maldives. This giant species has polyps encircling the entire circumference of the whip leaving no bare area. It occurs throughout the Indo-Pacific and is found on reef slopes and terraces.

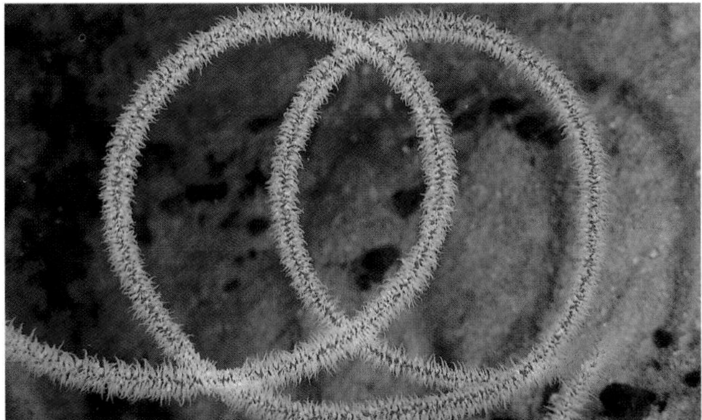

Close up of expanded polyps.

Small colony, Bali, Indonesia.

ANTIPATHIDAE

Tortured black coral whip

Stichopathes sp.

Coral reefs, rocky reefs

15 to 40 metres (49 to 131 ft)

600 mm (2 ft) height

Quite common in the Maldives and across the Indo-Pacific this species is very sinuous and generally seen on slopes, terraces and drop offs. The skin is brown and the finger-like pointed tentacles white or yellow. This genus has polyps on front and sides leaving one side of the whip bare.

Close up of expanded tentacles, Maldives.

CLASS: *Alcyonaria* (Soft Corals, Blue Corals, Gorgonian Sea Fans, Sea whips)

Features: All of the types of sedentary colonial organisms belonging to the class Alcyonaria can be distinguished from other members of the cnidarian phylum by the fact that their polyps have eight tentacles (Octocorals) and the tentacles are always fringed, or pinnate.

Lifestyle: Unlike the stony corals, most soft corals have no true skeleton as such. Their soft tissue-like bodies are flexible and various species may be soft and squelchy (*Xenia*) or firm and leathery (*Sarcophyton*) while others (*Dendronephthya*) hold themselves erect by pumping water into their interconnecting body cavities. All species however, no matter how soft or pliable contain minute spicules of silica or calcium which in many cases help to strengthen the body walls. It is these spicules which scientists use to describe different species of alcyonarians, and in the genus *Dendronephthya* some types of these spicules can be seen in the body walls.

Being cnidarians, soft corals have nematocysts in their polyps which sting and catch planktonic prey but these do not affect humans. However, some of the spiky soft corals (*Dendronephthya*) have protective spikes arranged around their polyp clumps (which act in a similar fashion to the thorns on rose bushes) that may help to protect the soft coral from some predators.

Soft corals also have extremely potent chemical defences and some even have chemicals which attack and kill other organisms whose territory they wish to invade. Many of these substances are being investigated by bio-chemists to see if they have properties which will inhibit cancer cells, or cure other diseases in humans.

Some shallow water dwelling soft corals (those in the light) have symbiotic zooxanthellae living in their tissues.

Reproduction: Similar to stony corals, soft corals may be separately sexed or hermaphrodites and release their reproductive products into the sea after the full moon on a particular month. On the Great Barrier Reef, for example, in some areas the spawning takes place in October and November. At Lord Howe Island it takes place in December or January, at Exmouth Gulf in Western Australia it occurs in April/May. A few days before spawning eggs can actually be seen through the body walls. The colonies grow by asexual reproduction and the process of budding.

Associations: Soft corals are food and/or shelter to many different groups of marine animals including worms, ovulid cowries, coral shells, nudibranchs, shrimps, squat lobsters, crabs, barnacles, brittle stars and fish.

Identification: As yet, many soft corals can only be identified to genus (even with a good picture available). Others still require the specimen and an experienced taxonomist. Some are unable to be named due to taxonomic problems.

HELIOPORIDAE

"Blue coral"

Heliopora coerulea

Coral reefs, rocky reefs, lagoons

Lt to 20 metres (0 to 66 ft)

1 metre (3.3 ft) across

Found from the Red Sea to the Great Barrier Reef "blue coral" is unique, its polyps constructing a deep blue calcium carbonate skeleton. This blue is due to the high presence of iron salts. Colonies may be small blade-like projections in deeper water to massive wavy folds covering an area of two metres (6.6 ft) in shallow water.

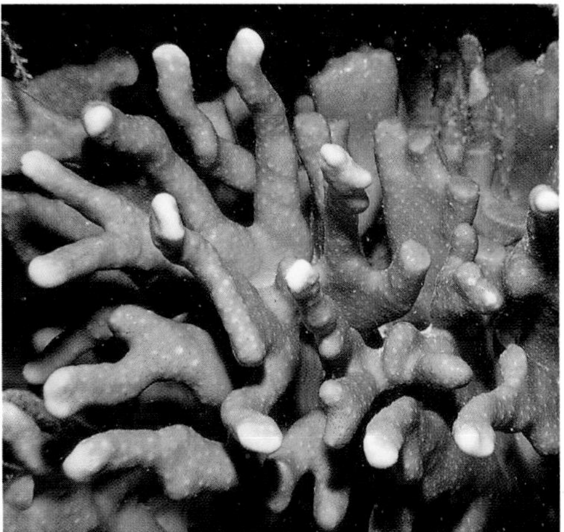

Stumpy form from deeper water, Maldives.

CLAVULIRIIDAE

Orange Carijoa

Carijoa sp.

Coral reefs, rocky reefs

20 to 30 metres (66 to 98 ft)

180 mm (7.2 in) colony width

Only observed in small isolated colonies this soft coral lives on reef slopes and terraces. Unlike other species it does not appear to be covered in the epizoic sponge growth that this genus is well known for. The genus *Carijoa* is found throughout the Indo-Pacific.

Close up of polyps, Maldives.

TUBIPORIDAE
Organ-pipe "coral"
Tubipora "musica"
Coral reefs, rocky reefs
Lt to 20 metres (0 to 66 ft)
200 mm (8 in) colony

Close up of variation from Kimbe Bay, Papua New Guinea.

Although this complex was once thought to contain only one species it's now known that a number of different species occur throughout the Indo-Pacific. The common name "organ-pipe" was taken from the distinctive red skeleton which when viewed up close resembled the pipes of an organ.

Close up of eggs being released during coral spawning season.

ALCYONIIDAE
Indian carrot coral
Paraminabea indica
Coral reefs, rocky reefs
20 to 80 metres (66 to 262 ft)
50 mm (2 in) retracted colony

Recorded from the Seychelles to the Maldives and Sri Lanka this easy to identify carrot-like soft coral was first named from a dredged Seychelles specimen in 1905. The species is very common on the sides of caves, under ledges and on walls and shaded sides of coral heads throughout the Maldives. The colonies are retracted during the day and only expand their long polyps for feeding at night.

Colour variation showing expanded polyps. Maldives (night time).

Colour variation showing extremely well developed polyps. Maldives (night time).

Although not common in all areas in the Maldives this rather distinctive leather coral is easy to recognise and appeared to have a stable growth form. The colonies were all circular with various sized finger-like lobes.

ALCYONIIDAE

Finger-lobed leather coral

Lobophytum sp.

Coral reefs, rocky reefs

5 to 10 metres (16 to 33 ft)

250 mm (10 in) colony

A high profile flat-bladed leather coral this species lives on reef tops and slopes and has a fairly distinctive appearance. Small short-stalked polyps were expanded both day and night.

ALCYONIIDAE

Bladed leather coral

Lobophytum sp.

Coral reefs, rocky reefs

8 to 20 metres (26 to 66 ft)

250 mm (10 in) colony

With over 40 species of this genus spread across the Indo-Pacific accurate identification requires a preserved specimen and a taxonomist to check out the spicules. This form is relatively common in the Maldives and even small colonies show very well developed ridging.

ALCYONIIDAE

Ridged leather coral

Lobophytum sp.

Coral reefs, rocky reefs

Lt to 20 metres (0 to 66 ft)

170 mm (6.8 in) colony

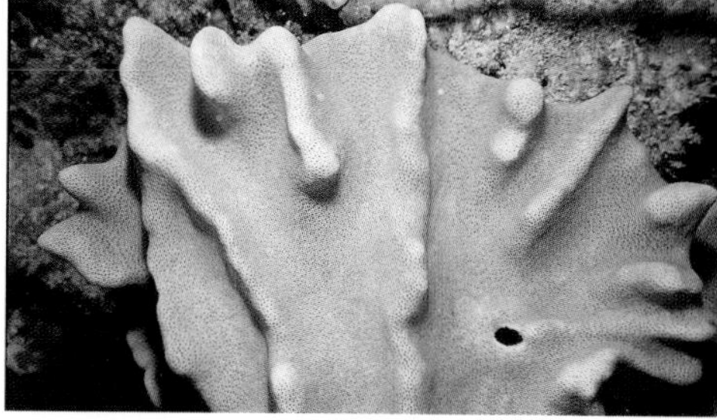

Colour variation, Maldives.

ALCYONIIDAE
Mushroom leather coral
Sarcophyton sp.
Coral reefs, rocky reefs
5 to 10 metres (16 to 33 ft)
300 mm (12 in) colony

Mushroom leather corals are common across the entire Indo-Pacific; there are, at present, around 36 different species recorded. This form is grey on top and elongate in shape with deeply folded, strongly convoluted margins. It grows on reef tops and slopes.

ALCYONIIDAE
Long polyp leather coral
Sarcophyton sp.
Coral reefs, rocky reefs
10 to 30 metres (33 to 98 ft)
170 mm (6.8 in) colony

Small and circular in shape this form is flat on top (like a mushroom) without folded margins. It's extremely long feeding tentacles may be extended during the day and night especially when there is a flooding tide. Mushroom leather corals are able to produce toxic compounds which when exuded kill or prevent other colonies of sedentary animals colonising their territory.

Close up of polyps, Maldives.

ALCYONIIDAE
Brassy leather coral
Sinularia brassica

Coral reefs, rocky reefs

10 to 30 metres (33 to 98 ft)

170 mm (6.8 in) colony

Growing in a number of different forms this species is relatively thin and leafy compared to others in the genus. However, the characteristic flat-bladed lobes and the distinctive prominent yellow or orange subsurface spicules are always present.

Variation, Maldives.

ALCYONIIDAE
Rugose leather coral
Sinularia sp.

Coral reefs, rocky reefs

8 to 20 metres (26 to 66 ft)

170 mm (6.8 in) colony

Uncommon in the Maldives area the rugose leather coral lives on reef tops and slopes. It has a very characteristic shape and was easy to recognise in the field. Colours were stable on those observed.

ALCYONIIDAE
Finger-tip Cladiella
Cladiella sp.

Coral reefs, rocky reefs

8 to 20 metres (26 to 66 ft)

250 mm (10 in) colony

When the polyps are out its general shape is like a rock. However, when the polyps are retracted the shape is revealed. This species lives on reef slopes. The finger-tip lobes are dense and the colony is firm but slimy.

ALCYONIIDAE

Long-lobed Cladiella

Cladiella sp.

Coral reefs, rocky reefs

10 to 20 metres (33 to 66 ft)

250 mm (10 in) colony

There are over 40 species of *Cladiella* throughout the Indo-Pacific. This long-lobed form from the Maldives is easy to recognise and colonies are generally seen in small groups.

NEPHTHEIDAE

Orange spiky soft coral

Dendronephthya sp.

Coral reefs, rocky reefs

5 to 50 metres (16 to 164 ft)

200 mm (8 in) colony

Extremely colourful and common throughout the Maldives this genus is widespread across the entire Indo-Pacific area. However, due to there being total confusion as to which species is which, the 250 or more described species names are unavailable until a complete revision and new study of the genus is undertaken.

Colony with retracted polyps, Maldives.

Close up of body wall spicules.

NEPHTHEIDAE
Magenta spiky soft coral
Dendronephthya sp.
Coral reefs, rocky reefs
10 to 40 metres (33 to 131 ft)
170 mm (6.8 in) colony

One of the most spectacular and prolific forms of spiky soft coral in the Maldives it is host to the spiky soft coral crab *Holophrys oatesii*. This species lives along drop offs and slopes and grows in a tightly bunched manner. Although soft corals do not sting the sharp spines are capable of penetrating soft skin and drawing blood.

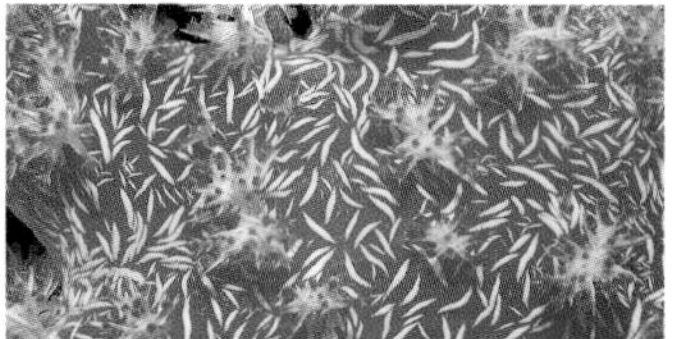

Close up of body wall spicules, Maldives.

NEPHTHEIDAE
Mauve spiky soft coral
Dendronephthya sp.
Coral reefs, rocky reefs
25 to 40 metres (82 to 131 ft)
170 mm (6.8 in) colony

One of the most spectacular spiky soft coral forms, this one appears to be restricted to deeper water where it lives along walls and drop offs. Soft corals are described on the basis of spicules in their body walls.

NEPHTHEIDAE
Branching spiky soft coral
Dendronephthya sp.
Coral reefs, rocky reefs
20 to 40 metres (66 to 131 ft)
170 mm (6.8 in) colony

Sometimes this form is found growing down from the underside of ledges and may only be a morphological variant of some other species caused by the fact that it doesn't have to support itself growing up from the bottom.

NEPHTHEIDAE
Bushy lemnalia
Lemnalia sp.
Coral reefs, rocky reefs, rubble
5 to 20 metres (16 to 66 ft)
170 mm (6.8 in) colony

Common on rubble and dead coral reef flats and slopes, the colony grows as a dense confusion of branches and has polyps which close on disturbance but do not completely withdraw. This genus is well represented across the Indo-Pacific from East Africa to Australia.

NEPHTHEIDAE
Cauliflower soft coral
Scleronephthya sp.
Coral reefs, rocky reefs
20 to 40 metres (66 to 131 ft)
170 mm (6.8 in) colony

Common on the ceilings and sides of caves and ledges in deeper water throughout the Maldives this brightly coloured short-stalked knobbly species is (for a soft coral) fairly easy to recognise visually.

Colour variation, Maldives.

NEPHTHEIDAE
Dappled soft coral
Scleronephthya sp.
Coral reefs, rocky reefs
20 to 30 metres (66 to 98 ft)
250 mm (10 in) colony

Growing down from overhangs and cave ceilings this long-branched, small-spiculed form has a unique dappled appearance. It seems to be unique to the Maldives area.

NEPHTHEIDAE
Orange-mouthed soft coral
Scleronephthya sp.
Coral reefs, rocky reefs
20 to 30 metres (66 to 98 ft)
100 mm (4 in) height

Recorded from the Maldives across the Indo-Pacific to Lord Howe Island, this small but easily recognised species is quite common in caves and along shaded vertical walls where there is abundant current. It has a short thick, heavily spiculed body and the polyps have bright orange centres.

Inactive colonies hang down from a cave ceiling.

Close up of polyps, Maldives.

NEPHTHEIDAE
Raspy soft coral
Scleronephthya sp.
Coral reefs, rocky reefs
20 to 40 metres (66 to 131 ft)
200 mm (8 in) colony

Protruding, well-developed spicules (sclerites) form diamond shapes on the body and short branchlets. Spicules are present even around the polyps capsule; the polyps close, but do not completely withdraw.

NEPHTHEIDAE
Thorny soft coral
Stereonephthya sp.
Coral reefs, rocky reefs
8 to 20 metres (26 to 66 ft)
170 mm (6.8 in) colony

Uncommon in the Maldives this species has tightly bunched thorn-like projections housing the polyps. It lives on reef flats and slopes and almost always has several spiny brittle stars amongst its lobes.

NIDALIIDAE

Brittle soft coral

Siphonogorgia sp.

Coral reefs, rocky reefs

10 to 30 metres (33 to 98 ft)

170 mm (6.8 in) colony

Found on drop offs along walls and around caves, this genus is recorded from the Maldives to Australia. There are a number of species known across the Indo-Pacific. This one has a brown trunk and branches with yellow polyps and is very brittle.

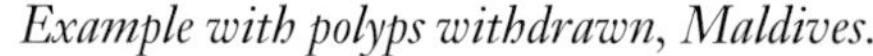

Example with polyps withdrawn, Maldives.

NIDALIIDAE

Flat-sided soft coral

Siphonogorgia sp.

Coral reefs, rocky reefs

25 to 40 metres (82 to 131 ft)

150 mm (6.2 in) colony

Although growth appears similar to other species the trunk and some branches have lines of spicules along them with the polyps growing on the sides, giving the colony a flattish look.

NIDALIIDAE

Sea fan soft coral

Siphonogorgia sp.

Coral reefs, rocky reefs

20 to 30 metres (66 to 98 ft)

250 mm (10 in) colony

This form was the most commonly observed in the Maldives and grew along walls and drop offs. The spicules are dark in colour and are situated lengthwise along the growing line.

Close up of polyps and spicules.

NIDALIIDAE

Naked soft coral

Chironephthya sp.

Coral reefs, rocky reefs

20 to 30 metres (66 to 98 ft)

130 mm (5.2 in) colony

Recorded from the Maldives across the Indo-Pacific to the Great Barrier Reef this deeper water denizen lives along walls, drop offs and on cave walls. The bright purple branch tips and polyps stand out against the stark white of the trunks making it an easily recognised form.

NIDALIIDAE

Yellow naked soft coral

Chironephthya sp.

Coral reefs, rocky reefs

20 to 30 metres (66 to 98 ft)

150 mm (6 in) colony

More common in the Maldives than the previous form this soft coral has bright yellow stems and short branches with red polyps. There are no polyps on the actual stems and the spicules are also bright yellow. It lives along walls and drop offs and on ledges in caves.

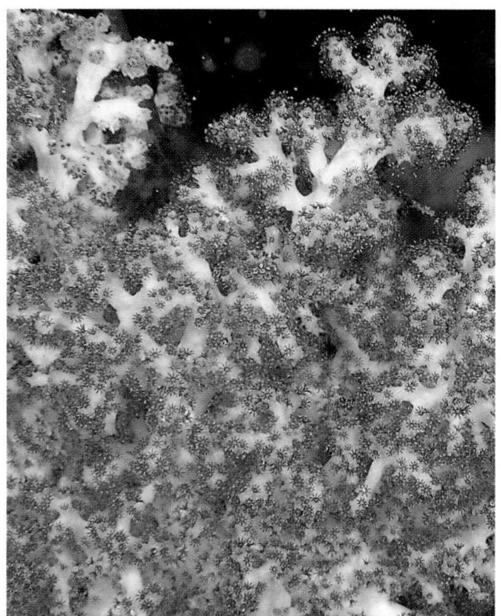

Colony with retracted polyps. Notice spiky-armed brittle star in residence, Maldives.

SUBERGORGIIDAE
Smooth sea fan
Annella mollis
Coral reefs, rocky reefs
20 to 40 metres (66 to 131 ft)
Up to 2 metres (6.6 ft) colony

Easily determined by visual features this species has characteristic wide fans which grow on a single flat plane either upright or on walls and cave ceilings. The branches are smooth and they form patterns with many variously sized oblongs and squares. Colour varies from pink to yellow or brown.

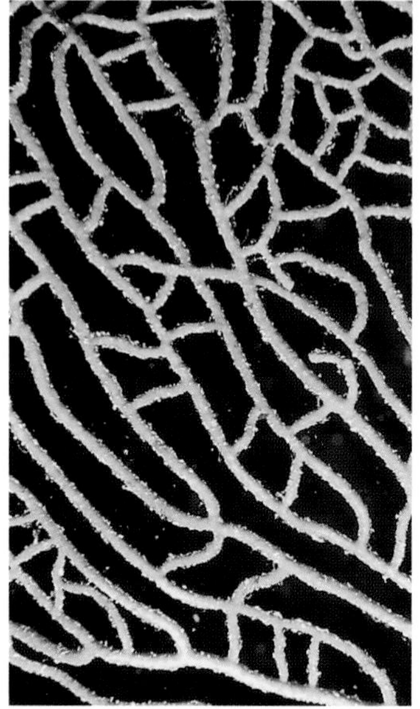

Colour variation close up of growth pattern.

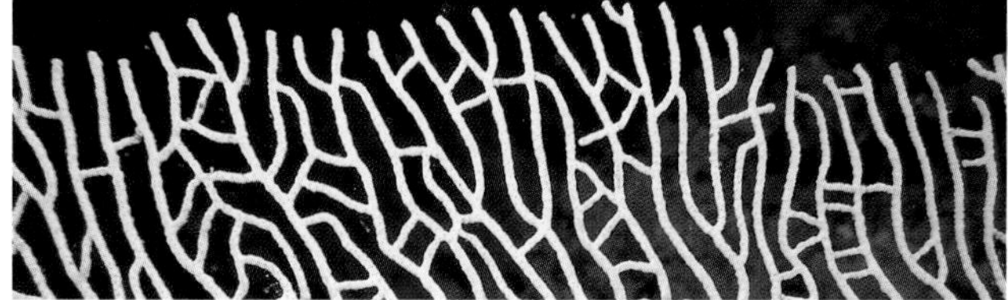

Close up of the bicoloured growing edge, Maldives.

SUBERGORGIIDAE
Corky gorgonian
Subergorgia suberosa
Coral reefs, rocky reefs
10 to 30 metres (33 to 98 ft)
400 mm (16 in) height

With a distribution spanning the entire Indo-Pacific this gorgonian is free branching with a very distinct medial groove running along the underside of every branch and polyps on each side. It lives along walls and drop offs, in caves on slopes and channel sides and is very common.

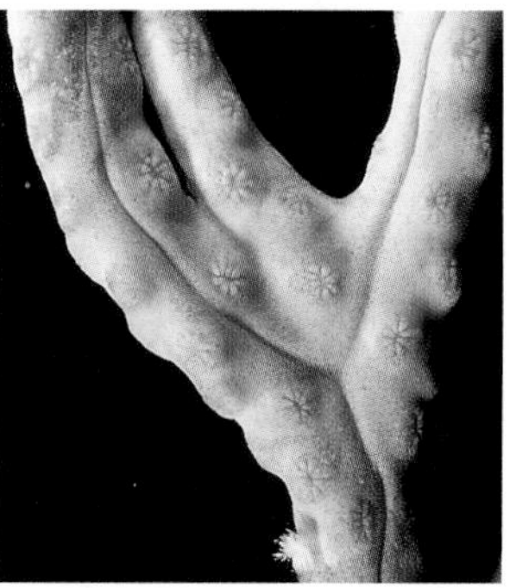

Medial line bordered by a row of polyps.

Polyps expanded, Maldives.

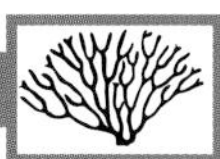

Seen here with its two colour forms this gorgonian is only found beneath flat slabs of dead coral which are situated on broken bottom allowing water to flow underneath. Only three individual colonies were located and they all grew along under the rocks in the same general direction.

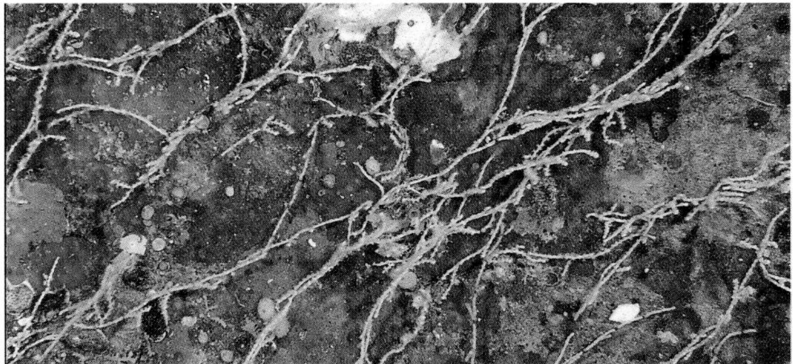

MELITHAEIDAE
Creeping Acabaria
Acabaria sp.
Coral reefs, rocky reefs
10 to 20 metres (33 to 66 ft)
170 mm (6.8 in) colony

A flat-bladed low profile rambling gorgonian this species was only seen in one colour; pink with white polyps. It lives on slopes and was only observed in small clumps.

MELITHAEIDAE
Pink Acabaria
Acabaria sp.
Coral reefs, rocky reefs
10 to 20 metres (33 to 66 ft)
170 mm (6.8 in) colony

Growing a bit like a bramble bush this species has short, flat-bladed branches with white polyps along each side. The branches are unique in the way there are three, four or five growing out of each pink axis. This gorgonian lives under ledges and is easily recognised.

MELITHAEIDAE
White Acabaria
Acabaria sp.
Coral reefs, rocky reefs
10 to 20 metres (33 to 66 ft)
170 mm (6.8 in) colony

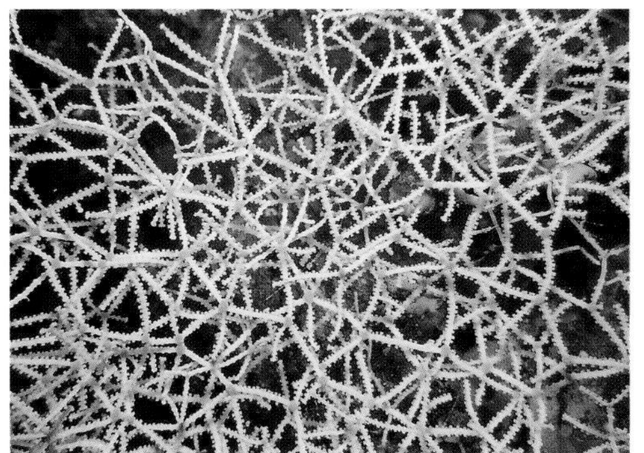

Example showing polyps expanded, Maldives.

MELITHAEIDAE

Red and yellow Clathria

Clathria sp.

Coral reefs, rocky reefs

10 to 30 metres (33 to 98 ft)

170 mm (6.8 in) colony

Visually there appears very little difference between this genus and *Acabaria*, as some forms appear to grow exactly the same. This species is the classic Maldivian gorgonian. It is very common and generally lives on the edges of underhangs, in crevices on slopes, terraces and drop offs. Small colonies are usually in shallow water and the bigger colonies in deeper water.

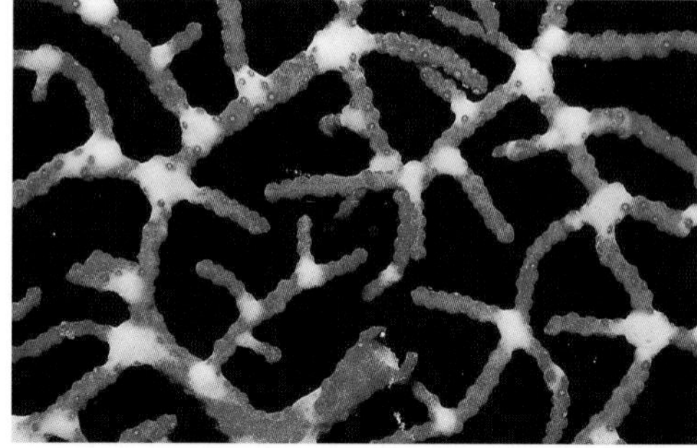

Colony example with retracted polyps, Maldives.

Close up of colour variation, Maldives.

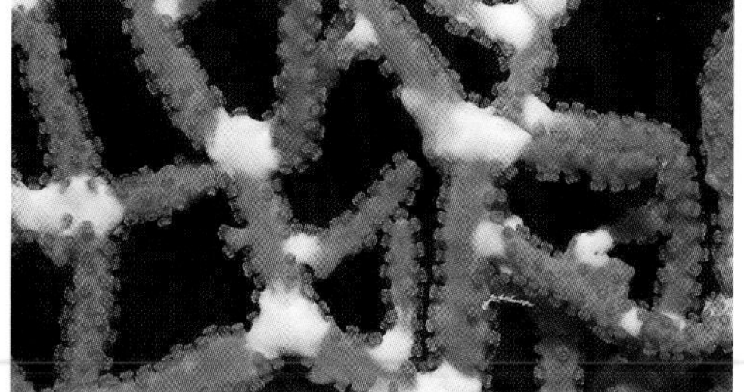

Single plane growth form, Maldives.

MELITHAEIDAE

Yellow and white Clathria

Clathria sp.

Coral reefs, rocky reefs

10 to metres (33 to ft)

60 mm (2.4 in) colony

This gorgonian has a totally different growth structure than the previous species. The branches grow as a disorganised bunch on numerous planes and from all directions.

Another Clathria, *Maldives.*

In Clathria *the distance between the branches and the axis is shorter than* Acabaria.

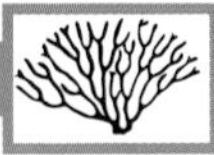

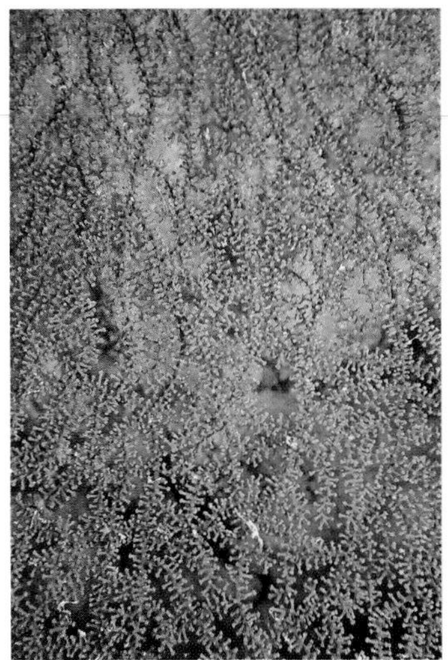

Most sea fans of this genus have very thin wiry branches with a black horny skeleton. The polyps are not able to retract into the branches and fans may be on a single plane or with several planes of branches growing out of various parts of the main fan.

ACANTHOGORGIIDAE
Orange wire sea fan
Acanthogorgia sp.
Coral reefs, rocky reefs
20 to 30 metres (66 to 98 ft)
170 mm (6.8 in) colony

Multiple plane growth pattern.

This species generally grows as a single plane fan with multiplane branches, a fine meshed pattern and non-retractable polyps as seen in most of this complex. It is often seen growing down beneath ledges.

ACANTHOGORGIIDAE
Yellow wire sea fan
Acanthogorgia sp.
Coral reefs, rocky reefs
10 to 25 metres (33 to 82 ft)
200 mm (8 in) colony

The gorgonians of this genus can have a knobbly branch, smooth branch or flat branch appearance depending on where the polyps are growing. The different forms have polyps with an opaque white or yellow stripe on the back of each tentacle. This species lives on slopes and drop offs.

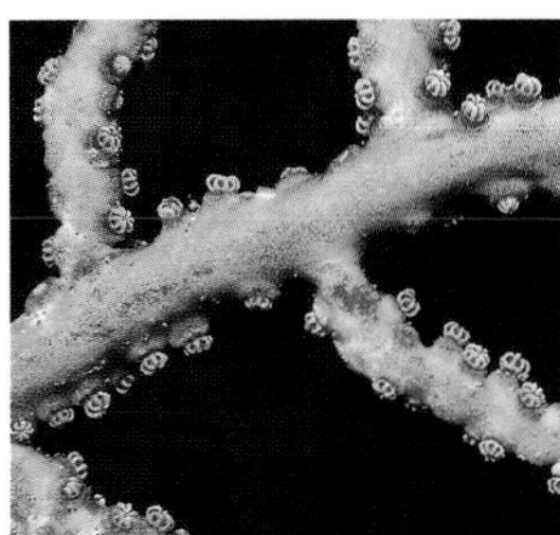

Green colour is due to zooxanthellae growing in the tissues.

Close up of polyps.

PLEXAURIDAE
Striped polyp sea fan
Astrogorgia sp.
Coral reefs, rocky reefs
5 to 25 metres (49 to 82 ft)
250 mm (10 in) colony

PLEXAURIDAE

Fine meshed sea fan

Echinogorgia sp.

Coral reefs, rocky reefs

10 to 30 metres (33 to 98 ft)

250 mm (10 in) colony

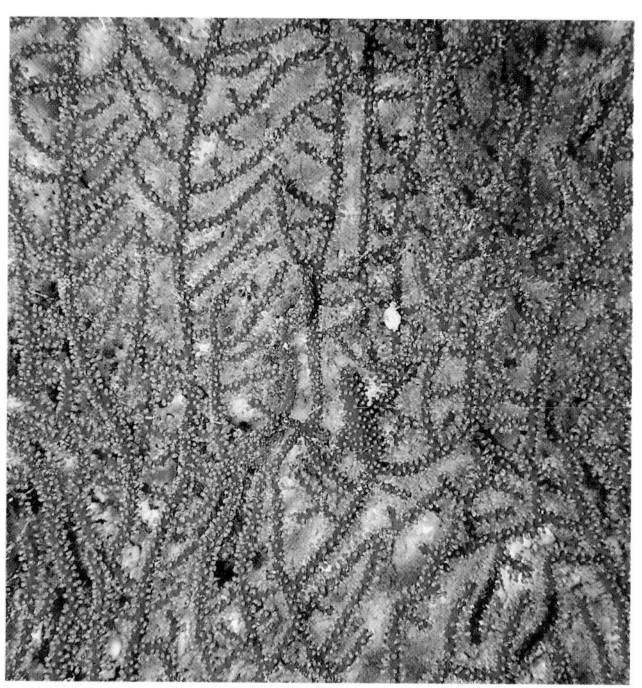

This species has a very thin branching bright red fan with yellow polyps and is generally seen growing from dead coral clumps or heads on slopes. The mesh pattern is easily distinguished and it has commensal barnacles living in it.

PLEXAURIDAE

Magenta Menella

Menella sp.

Coral reefs, rocky reefs

30 to 50 metres (98 to 164 ft)

600 mm (24 in) height

Close up of polyps, Maldives.

Mostly seen on deeper water terraces or at the bottom of drop offs or cave floors this very distinctive bright red species grows as a bunch of long whip-like fronds with few side branches and red polyps. Deep water colonies may be up to a metre (3.3 ft) in height.

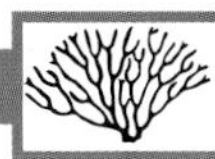

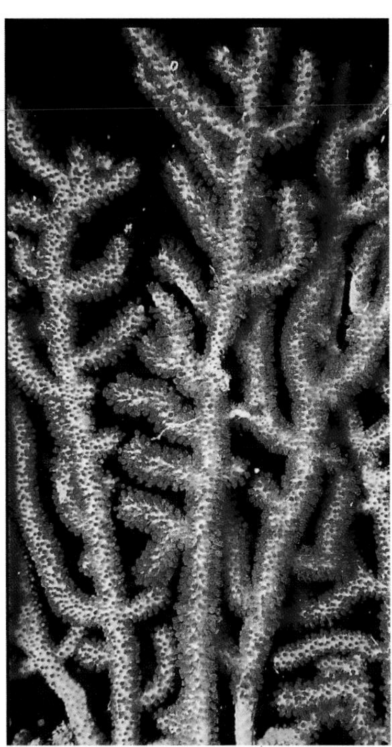

A common Indo-Pacific genus this species is well distributed on drop offs and terraces throughout the Maldives. Easily recognisable with its thick yellow or white elongate branches, short knobbly side branches and bright wine red polyps it generally grows in an upright stance.

PLEXAURIDAE

Yellow and red Menella

Menella sp.

Coral reefs, rocky reefs

20 to 40 metres (66 to 131 ft)

250 mm (10 in) height

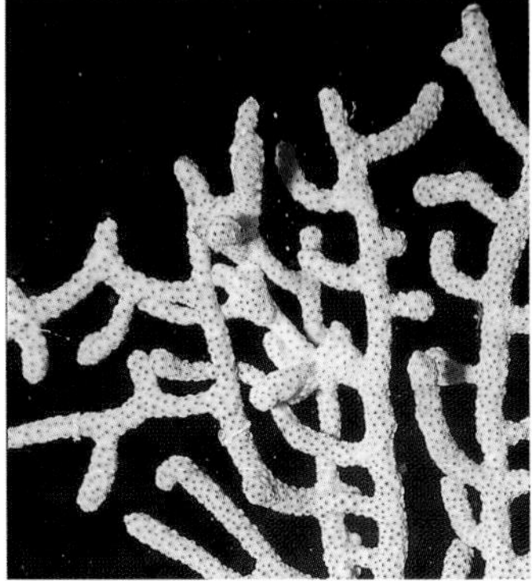

Colony with retracted polyps, Maldives.

Occurring on deeper reefs, cave floors and terraces, these spectacular whips occur throughout the Indo-Pacific where they may often be seen in groups. The colour varies from light orange to dark orange and the myriad well-developed polyps are packed in around the entire surface area.

Close up of polyps, Kimbe Bay, Papua New Guinea.

ELISELLIDAE

Orange sea whip

Junceella (Junceella) sp.

Coral reefs, rocky reefs

25 to 40 metres (82 to 131 ft)

1 metre (3.3 ft) height

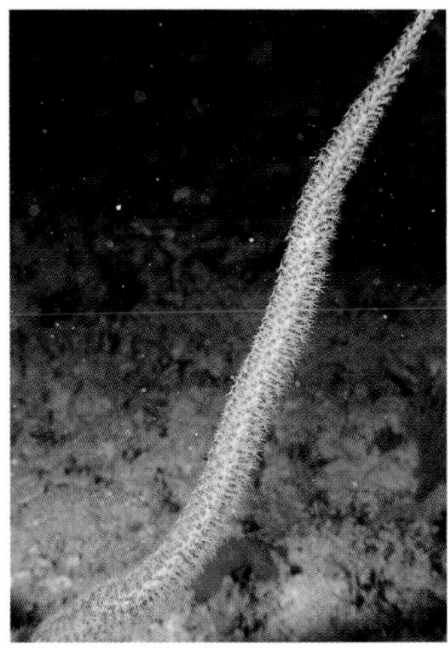

Colour variation, Maldives.

CLASS: *Zoantharia* (Sea Anemones, Zoanthids, Corallimorphs, Stony Corals)

Sea anemones

Features: Basically, a sea anemone is a large solitary polyp which has no skeleton with a basal or pedal disc which is capable of movement either by crawling, digging or both. This disc can be extremely adhesive and when attached to a hard substrate, nothing short of partial destruction can move it.

The highly muscular body, called a column, is capable of enormous expansion and contraction and may be smooth, lumpy or rough. At the top of the body (column) is the oral disc which is fringed with numbers of tentacles amounting to six or multiples of six arranged in various ways according to the species.

At the centre of the oral disc is the mouth leading to the stomach. The stomach has powerful enzymes and can digest most prey but as the animal has no rectum any indigestible matter and waste is ejected through the mouth. The body and tentacles have thousands of microscopic stinging cells called nematocysts embedded in the skin; those in the tentacles are more powerful and act in defence and prey-catching roles. Most feed on plankton, but are able to kill and eat anything that blunders into them including medium-sized fish.

Lifestyle: Tropical sea anemones can be found in many habitats and micro-habitats. Some are huge in size (*Heteractis*), (*Stichodactyla*) and may grow to one metre across and be in a prominent situation on top of a reef and inhabited by anemonefish. Others are so well camouflaged that few divers or snorkellers ever see them (*Phyllodiscus*) until they brush them and get stung. Sea anemones can live in crevices in the reef where they can expand or withdraw (*Cryptodendrum*). Some live completely inside the reef during the day and crawl out at night to feed (*Alicia*). There are small anemones that only grow 12 mm across and live on the underside of rocks and dead coral slabs and some that are commensal (*Nemanthus*) and live only on sea whips, gorgonians and black corals.

Most sea anemones live on reefs but some are specialised to live in the sand (*Actinodendron*) where they can be seen in lagoon channels and sea grass meadows. Sea anemones live in captivity for extended periods up to 30 years and it is thought that the large clown or anemone fish anemones may live beyond a hundred years.

Reproduction: Sea anemones can reproduce sexually and asexually. Each animal is either male or female and during the spawning season eggs and sperm are released (generally at night). A fertilised egg grows into a free-swimming larva called a planula (same as corals) which is then carried around by the currents until it settles to the bottom.

Asexual reproduction is by way of splitting whereby one polyp splits down the middle and forms two polyps. However, this is not common in larger tropical anemones and seems to be restricted to smaller anemones which live as groups, or it may happen during juvenile stages.

Associations: **Colour**

Much of the greens and brown colours seen in the tentacles of day time reef dwelling sea anemones is due to the presence of millions of microscopic single-celled algae called zooxanthellae which inhabit the anemone's body.

Specific colours and body patterns other than those produced by the zooxanthellae are the result of individual pigmentation produced by the sea anemone itself. Some of the colours, patterns and designs are very indicative of a species and allow simple visual identification to be established.

There are around 10 different species of sea anemones recorded as being hosts to anemone fish. These anemone fish have a very special relationship with their host anemone which is developed from when the fish first settle out of their larvae form and live beneath the "skirt" of the sea anemone's tentacle-fringed oral disc. Many crabs, shrimps and brittle stars live commensally in sea anemones.

Identification: As there is no skeleton to determine species identification (as with corals) the task of field recognition is sometimes difficult. Even with a properly preserved specimen there just aren't very many sea anemone taxonomists around. The original literature is very old and often in European languages and original descriptions are without suitable photographic examples of living species.

As yet, the Maldivian sea anemone fauna is still being discovered. There are however, enough species to give a credible series of examples and these can all be identified by their shape, the shape of the tentacles, their habitat, patterns and colours. Where some are unable to be identified due to the present stage of our knowledge, examples are shown.

Magnificent Sea anemone, Maldives.

ACTINIIDAE
Bulb-tentacle anemone
Entacmea quadricolor
Coral reefs, rocky reefs
5 to 25 metres (16 to 82 ft)
400 mm (16 in) across

Occurring throughout the entire tropical Indo-Pacific this species is easy to identify in the field due to the presence of a swelling which appears a short distance from the tip. Sometimes the tips are pink or red. This species has been recorded as the host to 13 different kinds of anemonefish.

Close up of extreme bulb swellings, Port Moresby, Papua New Guinea.

ACTINODENDRIIDAE
Hell's fire anemone
Actinodendron arboreum
Sand
1 to 20 metres (3.3 to 66 ft)
300 mm (12 in)

Living mostly in sheltered lagoons, in channels or around seagrass meadows this sand-dwelling retractive species is recorded across the Indo-Pacific and is relatively common in the Maldives. It has an extremely painful sting and is inhabited by commensal shrimps (*Periclimenes*).

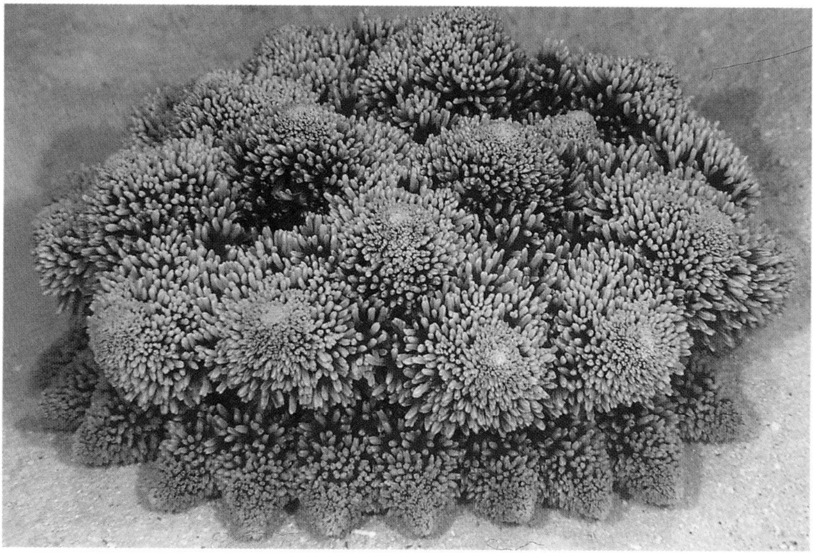

ACTINODENDRIIDAE

Hemprich's anemone

Megalactis hemprichii

Sand, rubble

8 to 20 metres (26 to 66 ft)

250 mm (10 in) across

Known across the Indo-Pacific this species is a virulent stinger causing skin damage and aggravated pain. It has small beads along the tentacles and can vary from green to yellow or grey in colour. Commensal shrimps (*Periclimenes*) live on some specimens.

ALICIIDAE

Semon's anemone

Phyllodiscus semoni

Coral reefs, rocky reefs

8 to 20 metres (26 to 66 ft)

250 mm (10 in) across

Looking like a clump of very dead algae covered coral this unbelievably cryptic anemone appears anything but alive. It lives on slopes amongst broken and dead reef and without previous knowledge a diver can be badly stung by touching it. At night a "second storey" tentacled-fringed mouth rises out of the centre of the column.

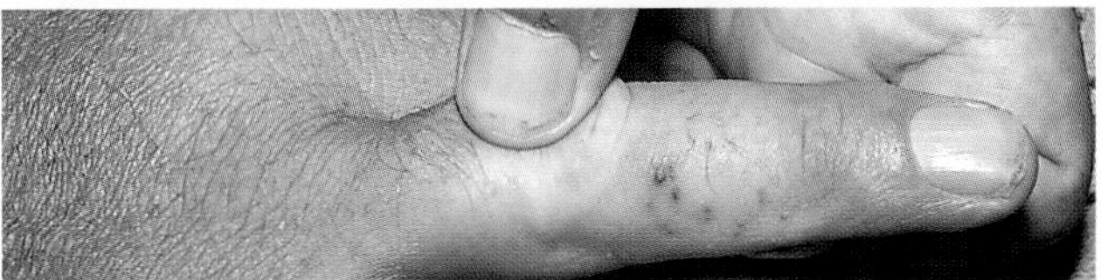

Injury to diver's finger 24 hours after contact with Semon's anemone.

The "second storey" section which is only seen at night. Bali, Indonesia.

EDWARDSIIDAE

Star anemone

Edwardsia sp.

Sand

5 to 20 metres (16 to 66 ft)

25 mm (1 in)

Known from the Seychelles to the Great Barrier Reef these small sand-dwelling anemones can be seen out during the day or night. They generally have around 15 larger tentacles and these are often arranged in threes.

HORMATHIIDAE

Hermit crab anemone

Calliactis miriam

Coral reefs, rocky reefs, sand

2 to 15 metres (6 to 49 ft)

20 mm (0.8 in)

The hermit crab anemone has a symbiotic relationship with hermit crabs and their shells. When disturbed, the anemone ejects large amounts of pink nematocyst-laden stinging threads called acontia .

STICHODACTYLIDAE

Beaded anemone

Heteractis aurora

Rubble, sand, mud

8 to 20 metres (26 to 66 ft)

250 mm (10 in) across

A very distinctive species living in sediment, the foot of the disc is attached to a buried rock. If disturbed it can completely retract beneath the sand. The beaded tentacles are unique and allow easy recognition across its Indo-Pacific range.

STICHODACTYLIDAE
Leathery anemone
Heteractis crispa
Rubble, sand on reef, coral reefs
8 to 20 metres (26 to 66 ft)
350 mm (14 in) across

The long-tapering tentacles often tinged with purple or characteristically striped (Maldivian form) are easily recognised visually significant features of this anemone. It is known to host up to 15 different species of anemonefish across its Indo-Pacific range.

Colour variation, Maldives.

STICHODACTYLIDAE
Magnificent sea anemone
Heteractis magnifica
Coral reefs, rocky reefs
5 to 15 metres (16 to 49 ft)
1 metre (3 ft) (width)

The magnificent sea anemone is one of the largest single structured tropical anemones. It is generally seen in areas of relatively strong water movement along the fringes and slopes of coral reefs. The column is mostly a dark orange-brown to purple and the tentacles range from bright green to greenish black.

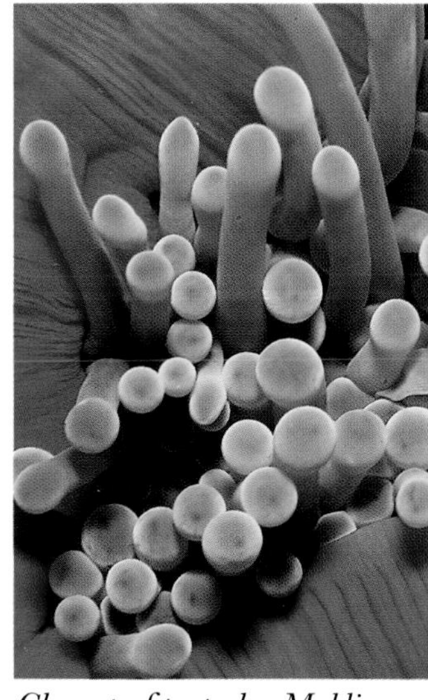

Close up of tentacles, Maldives.

STICHODACTYLIDAE
Haddon's anemone
Stichodactyla haddoni
Coral reefs, seagrass meadows, sand
Lt to 20 metres (0 to 66 ft)
500 mm (20 in) across

Haddon's anemone occurs from East Africa across to the Fiji islands. The specimen illustrated is typical of the Maldivian forms with short sticky tentacles..

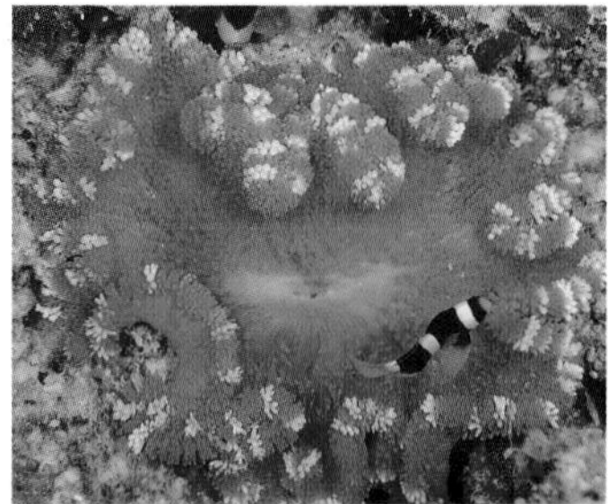

Variation, Queensland.

STICHODACTYLIDAE
Merten's anemone
Stichodactyla mertensii
Coral reefs, rocky reefs
5 to 10 metres (16 to 33 ft)
1 metre (3.3 ft)

This species is only found on reef and prefers areas of moderate current on slopes. Merten's anemone is distributed from East Africa to the Fiji islands and the tentacles are finger-like and non-adhesive.

THALASSIANTHIDAE
Adhesive anemone
Cryptodendrum adhaesium
Coral reefs, rocky reefs
5 to 20 metres (16 to 66 ft)
300 mm (12 in) across

Highly variable in colour, this species grows on reefs across the Indo-Pacific. When touched it will retract into its crevice and although the tentacles are "sticky" they will not dislodge from the animal.

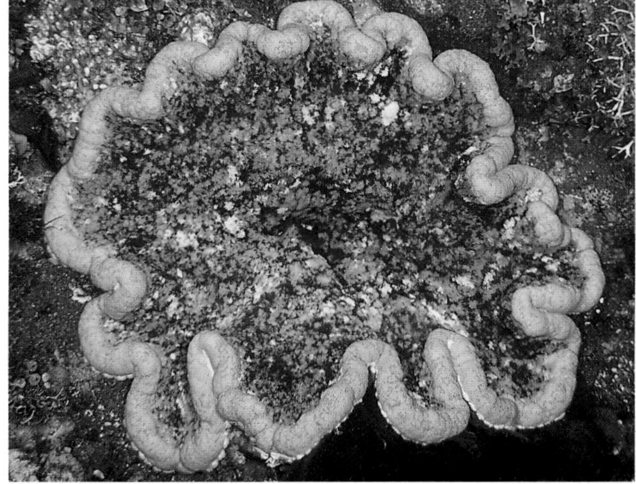

ZOANTHIDS

Features: Mostly colonial by nature zoanthids look for all the world like groups of small sea anemones. They have no skeletons or individual basal disc and are either attached to their related clone by a communal base, or the polyps may be embedded in a common creeping stolon which infests the surfaces of rocks and dead coral. The investing types (*Palythoa*) are able to absorb sand and shell grit into their stolon giving the colony test a more rigid composition. This is especially necessary for this particular group as they often inhabit very rough habitats such as reef edges and high energy coasts.

Lifestyle: Zoanthids live from the intertidal zone down to hundreds of metres (1000 ft) and can be found on coral reef, rocky reef, rubble, sand or mud. Whereas the commensal zoanthid polyps are sensitive to touch and may close on contact many of the colonial investing species don't seem to react in the same fashion.

It appears that some species attract zooxanthellae while others living in the darkness of caves have natural pigmentation. While their nematocysts do not cause harm to humans at touch they are, as a group, very poisonous and it's known that the Hawaiian warriors of old dipped their spearheads into the juices of zoanthids to render them deadly.

It's interesting to note that although these animals are plankton feeders the encrusting forms rarely close an individual polyp during the day. Perhaps the cilia on the surface of the oral disc move food to the mouth or the colony may close together at a given signal.

Reproduction: Zoanthids reproduce sexually in a similar fashion to stony corals, but the colonies increase their size by budding which is converse to the sea anemone's habit of splitting in order to reproduce asexually.

Associations: Some zoanthids (*Parazoanthus*) live in an epizoic, semi-parasitic fashion on gorgonian sea fans and black corals eventually growing over and smothering the host animals. Others live commensally, embedded in sponges which grow on other sessile animals.

Identification: Although these animals are being studied by a world authority, as yet, there is no comprehensive text book relating to visual identification of the many species. The few samples shown represent the more commonly known fauna of the Indo-Pacific that are present in the Maldives. Most of these can be identified to genus from a good photograph.

ZOANTHIDAE
Encrusting Zoanthid
Palythoa caesia
Coral reefs, rocky reefs
Lt to 5 metres (0 to 15 ft)
1 m (3.3 ft) colony width

The encrusting zoanthid is one of the few species which frequent intertidal areas; as a species it is easy to identify as its shape and colour don't seem to vary greatly over its entire range. The texture of the encrusting zoanthid is quite tough in relation to its soft-bodied relatives and is not unlike sandy leather.

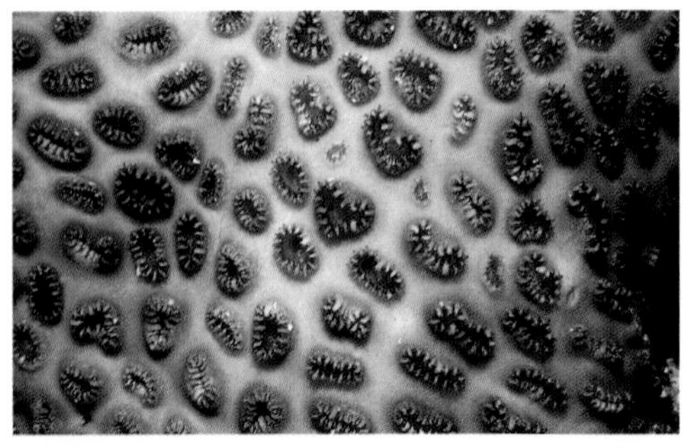

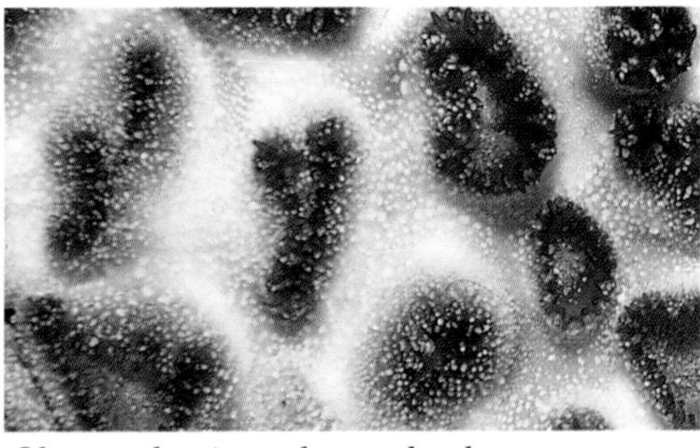

Close up showing polyps and stolon texture.

ZOANTHIDAE
Sea whip Zoanthid
Parazoanthus sp.
Coral reefs, rocky reefs
20 to 40 metres (66 to 134 ft)
35 mm (1.4 in) photo area

A deeper water dweller this zoanthid was only found on black coral sea whips along drop offs and in caves in areas of moderate current. The external stolon was rough in texture and appeared red in colour, while the polyps were yellow to orange.

ZOANTHIDAE
Camouflage Zoanthid
Protopalythoa sp.
Coral reefs, sand
covered rocky reefs
5 to 20 metres (16 to 66 ft)
170 mm (6.8 in) colony width

Uncommon to many places in the Maldives, this species was only seen where the reef had a covering of sand. The nodules are very well-developed around the edges of the disc and occur alternatively with the tentacles.

Common along drop offs and reef slopes throughout the Maldives the polyps are expanded both day and night; the radiating white lines and yellow or white nodules at the edge of the disc appear at the terminus of every alternate white line. The intermediate lines end with a tentacle. Colour can vary between green, grey and brown.

ZOANTHIDAE

Stripe-disc Zoanthid

Protopalythoa sp.

Coral reefs, rocky reefs

8 to 20 metres (26 to 66 ft)

170 mm (6.8 in) colony

Close up of zoanthid colony with its polyps retracted showing the underlying tissue connecting the colony.

Close up showing pattern arrangement of lines, nodules and tentacles.

Extremely common in some lagoons in the northern Maldivian atolls but was rarely seen during southern atoll surveys, the intense green colour and red centre make it easy to identify in this form. Polyps are extended both day and night and in some dead reef areas in sheltered waters it is the most visually dominant species.

ZOANTHIDAE

Manton's Zoanthid

Zoanthus mantoni

Lagoons, on dead coral

5 to 15 metres (16 to 49 ft)

1 metre (3.3 ft) colony width

Close up colour variation, Maldives.

Corallimorphs

Features: Similar to sea anemones in structure, life style and mode of habit, corallimorphs are taxonomically between sea anemones and corals, but unlike corals they have no skeletons. They resemble flat anemones and most have short club-tipped tentacles or multiple branched fringing tentacles arranged in rings around the mouth which is at the centre of the circular disc. They can be solitary or colonial living deep in the reef, in shaded cracks and crevices or beneath rocks in shallow or deeper water. Some species are brightly-coloured while others are drab brown, or grey and carpet large areas of dead coral reef.

Lifestyle: Corallimorphs live on coral reef, rocky reef and rubble and appear very adept at taking over huge areas where stony corals have difficulty getting established. Once they have a suitable substrate they reproduce very quickly and dominate entire habitats. Although they have nematocysts in their surface tissue these are not powerful enough to sting humans. However, when disturbed they can shoot out stinging threads called acontia which are able to sting very badly and have been known to sting divers through a lycra suit. Large species (*Amplexidiscus*) may grow to 300 mm while the smallest secretive species may only be 20 mm in diameter. Most species feed on plankton and while some are daylight dwellers and live in the open, other species are nocturnal and are only seen at night.

Reproduction: Corallimorphs reproduce sexually and asexually with the aggregational species splitting at regular intervals increasing the size of their communal living area and aggressively destroying all other sedentary life forms in their expansive progress.

Associations: This group has few recorded associations though some shrimps (*Pliopontonia furtiva*) inhabit the larger species.

Identification: With little work available on living species there are only a few genera known and although there may be over twenty or more different species, visual recognition in the field is still in its infancy. Species have been included to give representation to the Maldivian fauna.

Found from the Maldives to the Great Barrier Reef the balloon corallimorph is the largest species known. It is generally seen in groups and may be fully expanded in a dish shape with a myriad short tentacles, or contracted when it has a bowl-like shape, emphasising the smooth underside. The corallimorph shrimp *Pliopontonia furtiva* is a resident commensal on some colonies in some areas.

ACTINODISCIDAE

Balloon Corallimorph

Amplexidiscus fenestrafer

Coral reefs, rocky reefs, rubble

3 to 25 metres (10 to 82 ft)

300 mm (12 in)

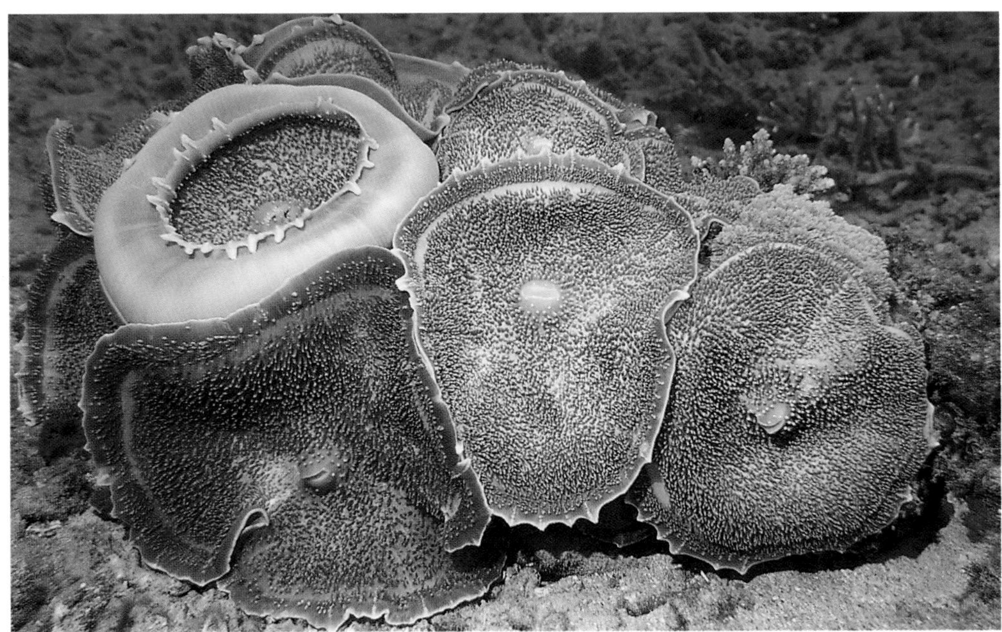

Close up of the balloon corallimorphs white contraction/expansion ring.

Expanded balloon-like form.

Close up of tentacles, mouth and extruded stinging acontia threads.

ACTINODISCIDAE

Dish-disced Corallimorph

Metarhodactis sp.

Coral reefs, rocky reefs

5 to 20 metres (16 to 66 ft)

150 mm (6 in) across

Similar in general shape and appearance to the balloon corallimorph this species does not grow as large, is much firmer to touch, has fewer and shorter tentacles, does not "balloon" and has no expansion/contraction joint around the outer disc rim. The dish-disced corallimorph is fairly common in the Maldives and is also found across the Indo-Pacific to the Great Barrier Reef.

Close up of disc and tentacles.

ACTINODISCIDAE

Carpet Corallimorph

Discosoma sp.

Coral reefs, rocky reefs, rubble

5 to 20 metres (16 to 66 ft)

40 mm (1.6 in) across disc

Extremely common on dead coral reef in some protected lagoons and back reefs this species is a very vigorous expansionist covering large areas of substrate throughout the Maldives. It is recorded throughout the Indo-Pacific area and is an extremely potent stinger.

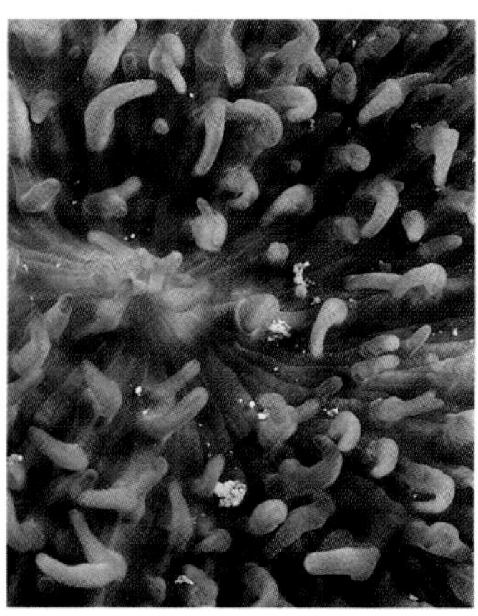

Close up of tentacles, Maldives.

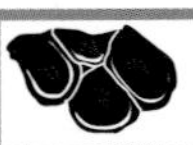

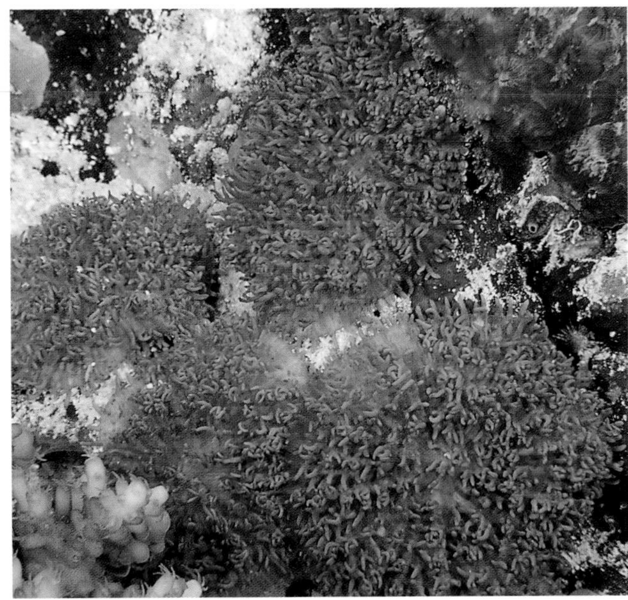

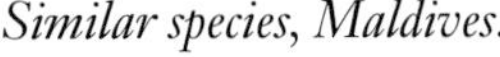

Similar species, Maldives.

Close up of acontia stinging threads being extruded from all over the body disc.

Known from the Seychelles across to Micronesia this attractive little corallimorph has a very distinctive pattern which is characteristic and doesn't appear to vary much across its range. Generally found in small colonies on walls, or shaded rock slopes.

ACTINODISCIDAE

Fringe-mouthed Corallimorph

Discosoma sp.

Coral reefs, rocky reefs

5 to 10 metres (16 to 33 ft)

20 mm (0.8 in) across disc

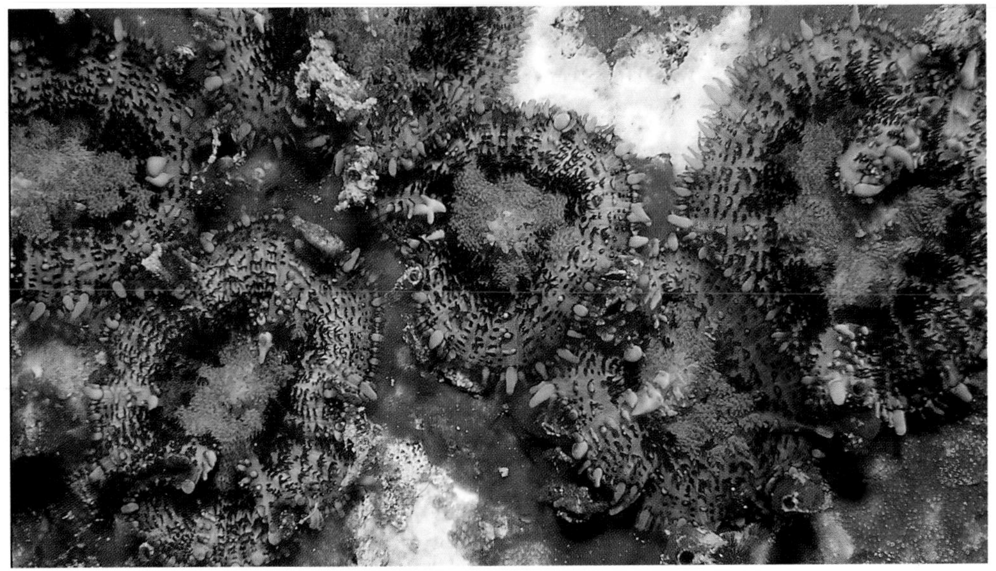

Stony corals

Features: A coral reef may be comprised of many hundreds of coral species, some similar in shape while others are singularly characteristic. They live for the greater part from intertidal level down to, and a little beyond 50 metres. Colonies may vary from several millimetres in size to massive monoliths five to 10 metres across. The low tide fossicker sees only a minor fraction of these, for the majority live subtidally. It is the snorkeller or scuba diver who has the greatest opportunity to observe the true living reef. Most coral polyps are nocturnal and shun the light of day, but when the skies are overcast many feed during the daylight hours.

There are around 250 species of stony corals recorded from the Maldives. Of these the staghorn corals (*Acropora*) are by far the most dominant group with 47 species identified. Although Warty corals (*Pocillopora*) have nowhere near the same number of species (only six) they are also very fast growing and in some areas appear very common.

In general, the more robust corals live on the exposed situations, or grow smaller and stouter than their counterparts in deeper water or sheltered lagoons. The polyp of stony corals has six tentacles or is made up of multiples of six and the tentacles are simple, not pinnate (branched), as are the soft corals (*Alcyonarians*). The majority of tropical corals are colonial, building their massive structures by budding or splitting (asexual reproduction) in a cloning-like manner. Others are solitary, some of the largest solitary corals are the mushroom corals (*Fungia* and *Heliofungia*). Due to its nature of extending its feeding tentacles during the day, *Heliofungia actiniformis* is often thought to be a sea anemone, and although it does look like one, it has a hard coral skeleton.

Lifestyle: The majority of reef-building corals are colonial. Even though each polyp acts independently it is linked to its relations by common flesh. So, even though a coral clump may be a single object, it is made up of thousands of connected polyps all contributing to the colony as a whole. The food caught and eaten by each polyp helps to sustain the entire group. The general life history of the more common corals is well known throughout the world, and the Maldivian forms differ little from these.

The colours of the stony reef-building corals are living colours and are only contained within the tissues of the polyps themselves. There is also another factor which accounts for the colour of coral animals: embedded in the coral's flesh are thousands of minute single-celled marine plants called zooxanthellae. During the daylight hours these algae provide extra supplies of oxygen as well as contributing around 98% of the nutrients required by the corals. At night, when corals feed,

the polyps obtain oxygen directly from the water passing over, or through, the tissues.

Every type of coral is a carnivore feeding on planktonic organisms which either drift or are directed towards the tentacles. Each tentacle is armed with batteries of nematocyst pods. These pods resemble minute oval balloons filled with venom and contain a small coiled spring, tipped with a barbed dart. The instant a small animal brushes past the tentacle, it is transfixed by these poisonous darts. The tentacles then move the prey towards the mouth which enlarges and engulfs the animal. Digestion begins immediately and when the meal is finished, refuse is exuded from the mouth.

The best time to see corals is during night dives as they all have their tentacles out feeding on plankton. One of the most brilliantly-coloured coral polyps is Faulkner's coral (*Tubastrea*) which grows on the roofs and sides of caves and under ledges in small fist-sized clumps. Sometimes these can be seen out feeding on overcast days or incoming tides.

Reproduction: Upon reaching maturity, coral polyps produce both sperm and eggs. At certain times of the year, when conditions are right the sperm and egg bundles are released into the surrounding water. Sometime later, after fertilisation has occurred, small gourd-shaped larvae emerge from the eggs and join the many millions of other minute organisms, called plankton, drifting along with the currents. Capable of some directive movement, motivation of the larvae is controlled by the backward and forward lashings of hair-like cilia which cover their external surface.

After several days to a week of drifting, the larvae settles to the bottom. The site chosen for settlement must be on hard, solid substrate and must be found within a short period of time otherwise the cycle is interrupted and the larvae will die. Anchoring itself with a glue-like secretion, the larvae gradually alters its shape to finally resemble a minute polyp. The polyp grows rapidly, lime begins to form in the tissues and a new coral colony is born.

Different types of corals form colonies in various ways. One of the most common methods of increasing the colony is by budding, this is where smaller corallites form at the sides of the larger ones, such as with staghorn corals. Another method is by division; here the corallite splits, forming separate polyps and as growth proceeds, separate corallites.

Associations: Besides the crown of thorns sea star which is an active predator, stony corals support a large number of associations including sponges, worms, molluscs, crustaceans, echinoderms and fish in a myriad different manners and lifestyles. (See specific species texts for details).

Identification: One of the easiest methods of telling corals from sea anemones, corallimorphs, zoanthids and soft corals is to touch them. Corals have hard stony skeletons which can be felt; the other groups are various degrees of soft, squelchy or firm. If the polyps are out, the easiest method to separate stony corals from soft corals is by close examination of the polyps. On stony corals the polyp tentacles are arranged as six tentacles or in multiples of six and the tentacles are smooth and unbranched (not pinnate) whereas the Alcyonarians (Octocorals) have eight tentacles (only) and these always have some form of branching appendages.

Although visual identification of living corals has advanced with general knowledge over the past 30 years there is still a long way to go and some species remain difficult to separate on their living characteristics alone. Scientists still require small samples of the skeleton which has been cleaned of all tissue before they can give an accurate identification of a species by studying the characteristics of the skeleton under a microscope.

In the field, specific identification on visual characteristics to species are often complicated due to the colonies environmental situation. The choice of habitat chosen by the settling larvae determines the growth patterns and structure as the growing colony skeleton is subjected to the forces around it. Specific corals which live in turbulent, high-energy areas such as the reef edge will most likely produce shorter, stouter low profile colonies in contrast to the more extravagant delicate forms living in the sheltered deeper water of a lagoon. There are colour variations between colonies of the same species depending on depth and other relevant factors.

With a little familiarisation and practice is's not too difficult to determine most living corals to at least genus level and many to species.

POCILLOPORIDAE

Warty coral

Pocillopora damicornis

Coral reefs, rocky reefs

Lt to 10 metres (0 to 33 ft)

300 mm (12 in) across colony

Common across the entire Indo-Pacific area this genus is readily recognised due to its wart-like growths on the branches. Colours range from brown to yellow and green to pink with growth differences depending on the location. Fine branches in sheltered water, compact and low profile branches in situations of high wave action.

Recorded from the Maldives across to the Pacific this is not a common species. It grows along the tops of reef slopes and may be brown, cream or pink in colour.

POCILLOPORIDAE

Meandering coral

Pocilliopora meandrina

Coral reefs, rocky reefs

Lt to 10 metres (0 to 33 ft)

170 mm (6.8 in) across colony

Well known from the Red Sea to the southern Pacific this species is generally compact and low profile and seems to prefer reef rims and the tops of reef slopes as a preferred habitat. Colour forms include pink, cream or blue and the nodules on the branches have red-brown stalks.

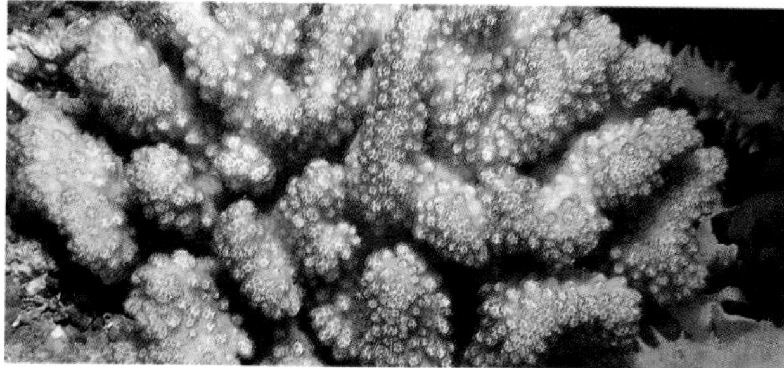

POCILLOPORIDAE

Verrucose Pocillopora coral

Pocilliopora verrucosa

Coral reefs, rocky reefs

Lt to 10 metres (0 to 33 ft)

160 mm (6.4 in) across colony

Ranging from East Africa to Samoa, needle coral can have long slim pointed branches in protected water or shorter double spiked branches in unprotected waters. Colour ranges from cream to blue and pink and this colony shown is in the process of ejecting its zooxanthellae due to rising sea surface temperatures.

POCILLOPORIDAE

Needle coral

Seriatopera hystrix

Coral reefs, rocky reefs

Lt to 10 metres (0 to 33 ft)

200 mm (8 in) across colony

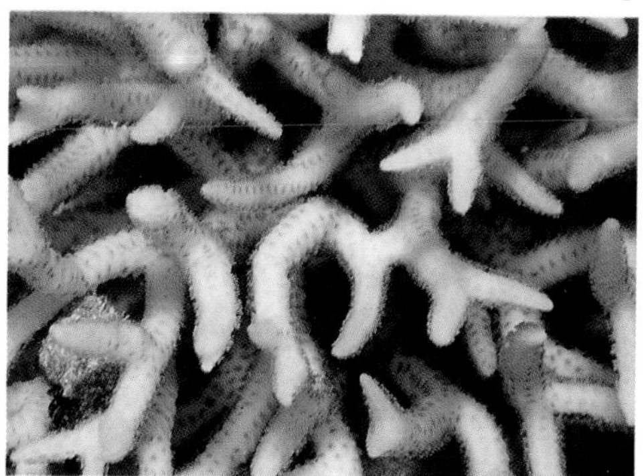

Colour variation, Great Barrier Reef.

POCILLOPORIDAE
Pistillate coral
Stylophora pistillata
Coral reefs, rocky reefs
Lt to 10 metres (0 to 33 ft)
200 mm (8 in) across

Found across the entire Indo-Pacific this species can be extremely common in some areas. Colonies are generally short and stocky with blunt forked branches; colours range from cream to blue green or pink.

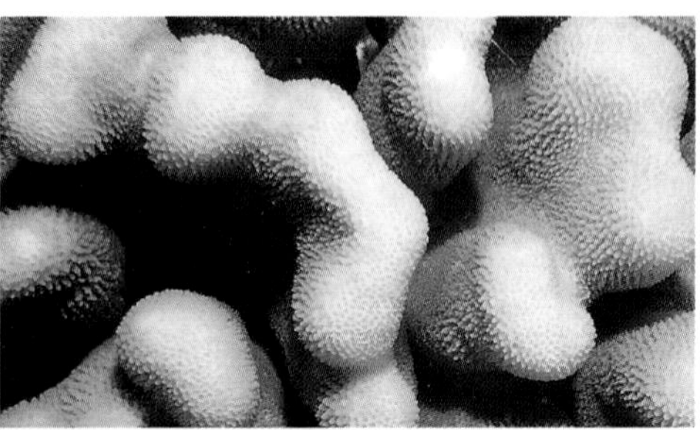

Maldivian form growing in an exposed habitat.

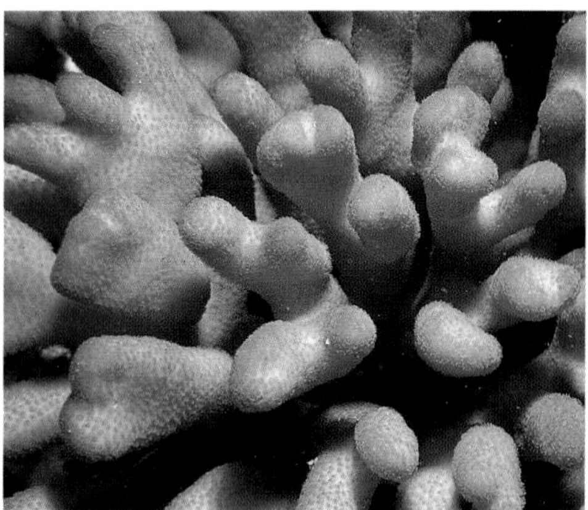

POCILLOPORIDAE
Undate coral
Montipora undata
Coral reefs, rocky reefs
Lt to 35 metres (0 to 115 ft)
170 mm (6.8 in) across photo

Recorded for the first time in the Maldives the picture shows a typical colour formation with highly developed fused tuberculae.

ACROPORIDAE
Verrucose Montipora coral
Montipora verrucosa
Coral reefs, rocky reefs
5 to 20 metres (16 to 66 ft)
170 mm (6.8 in) across photo

Living along the tops of reef slopes and the edges of lagoons and channel walls this species ranges from the Red Sea to the Pacific. The colonies may be submassive or encrusting and grow up to two metres across. It has very well developed tuberculae on the surface which are reasonably uniform in growth. Colours include brown or purple and the polyps are blue or green.

Close up of uniform tuberculae structure, Great Barrier Reef.

ACROPORIDAE
Lattice coral
Acropora clathrata
Coral reefs, rocky reefs
5 to 10 metres (16 to 33 ft)
170 mm (6.8 in) across photo

Growing in large horizontally radiant table-like colonies the lattice coral lives on fringing reefs along upper reef slopes usually in sheltered areas. Colours may be brown or green and its distribution stretches from Madagascar to the Tuamotu Archipelago.

ACROPORIDAE
Neat coral
Acropora latistella
Coral reefs, rocky reefs
10 to 20 metres (33 to 66 ft)
170 mm (6.8 in) across photo

This coral was mostly seen as small rounded tables 200 to 300 mm (12 in) across and brown in colour with white tips. The branchlets are very evenly spaced and it ranges from the Maldives to Samoa.

ACROPORIDAE
Nosey coral
Acropora nasuta
Coral reefs, rocky reefs
5 to 15 metres (16 to 49 ft)
170 mm (6.8 in) across photo

Distributed from the Red Sea to Tahiti this common species was named for its neat rows of upside down radial polyps which resemble "noses". It generally prefers shallow water and can be brown or cream with pink or mauve branch tops.

Zooxanthellae rejection, Maldives.

ACROPORIDAE

Samoan coral

Acropora samoensis

Coral reefs, rocky reefs

3 to 15 metres (16 to 49 ft)

170 mm (6.8 in) across photo

Recorded from the Maldives for the first time this species is relatively uncommon and is known in Australia from the Dampier Archipelago to the Great Barrier Reef. Most colonies observed were small, up to 300 mm (12 in) across and some smaller ones. Pink seemed to be the stable colour.

Shallow water form showing stubby branches and rounded colony shape, Maldives.

ACROPORIDAE

Solitary Islands coral

Acropora solitaryensis

Coral reefs, rocky reefs

8 to 20 metres (26 to 66 ft)

170 mm (6.8 in) across photo

A new record for the Maldives this species generally prefers reefs in lower latitudes and is common on the east and west coasts of Australia around 30°. It can be dark brown or green and forms large circular colonies up to 1 metre (3.3 ft) across.

This species ranges from Mauritius to the South Pacific and can be easily recognised by its evenly spaced branches with wide-lipped radial corallites which give it a rosette look. Colours may be brown or pink.

ACROPORIDAE
Thin coral
Acropora tenuis
Coral reefs, rocky reefs
5 to 20 metres (16 to 66 ft)
200 mm (8 in) colony

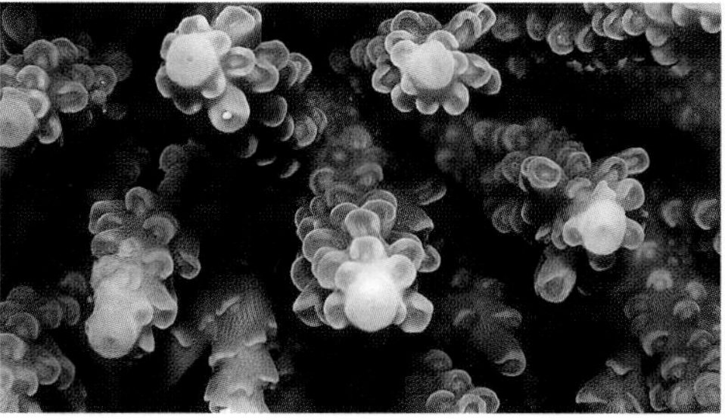

Example of wide-lipped corallites, Maldives.

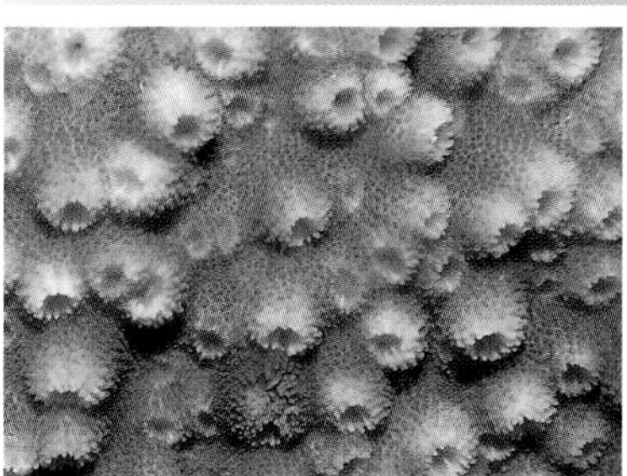

This species grows as small round coral heads in cream, blue or yellow and the conical corallites are evenly spaced and round in shape.

ACROPORIDAE
Many corallites coral
Astreopora myriophthalma
Coral reefs, rocky reefs
5 to 20 metres (16 to 66 ft)
300 mm (12 in) colony

Known from Madagascar to Tonga in the Pacific this easily identified branching species inhabits lagoons and reef tops. Yellow seems to be the dominant colour but colonies can be cream, blue or green.

PORITIDAE
Cylinder coral
Porites cylindrica
Coral reefs, rocky reefs
Lt to 10 metres (0 to 33 ft)
1 metre (3.3 ft) colony

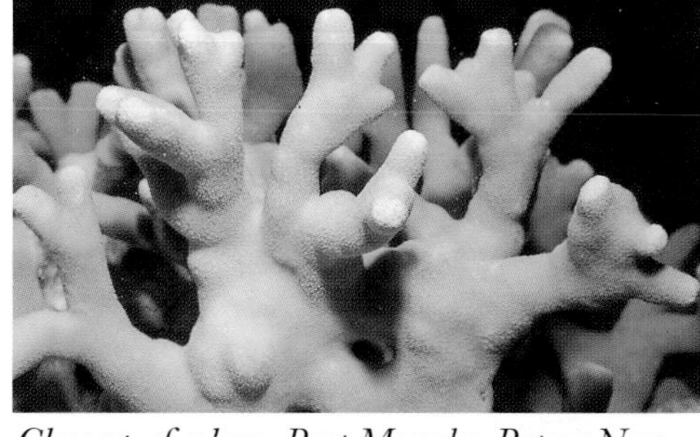

Close up of colony, Port Moresby, Papua New Guinea.

PORITIDAE

Evermann's coral

Porites evermanni

Coral reefs, rocky reefs

5 to 10 metres (16 to 33 ft)

170 mm (6.8 in) across pic

Mostly seen in small colonies this new record for the Maldives was only observed as being ochre in colour. It has very characteristic angular nodules and is not considered common.

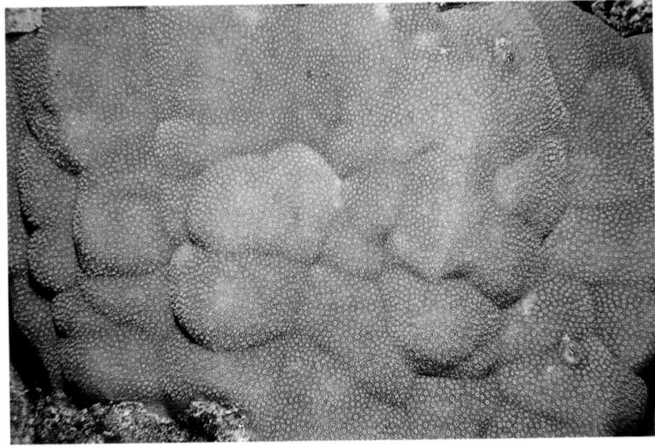

PORITIDAE

Flame coral

Porites rus

Coral reefs, rocky reefs

5 to 20 metres (16 to 66 ft)

170 mm (6.8 in) across photo

Found from the Red Sea to Hawaii and the Great Barrier Reef this species has very small corallites separated into groups by converging ridges which suggest a pattern of flames. Colour may be brown with lighter branch tips, or yellow.

Unidentified species of Porites, *Maldives.*

PORITIDAE

Warrior coral

Goniopora sp.

Coral reefs, rocky reefs

5 to 20 metres (16 to 66 ft)

170 mm (6.8 in) across photo

A very aggressive coral that extends very long sweeper tentacles (up to 400 mm) which will attack any other corals in range. Colonies often measure some metres across. The polyps have 24 tentacles and the genus flourishes from the Red Sea to the Tuamotu Islands in the Pacific.

Close up of polyp tentacles, Maldives.

AGARICIIDAE

Duendend's coral

Pavona duendeni

Coral reefs, rocky reefs

10 to 20 metres (33 to 66 ft)

450 mm (20 in) height

Recorded here for the first time in the Maldives this species was very uncommon and appeared to favour the tops of reef slopes on outer reefs. Brown was the only colour observed.

AGARICIIDAE
Maldivian coral
Pavona maldivensis
Coral reefs, rocky reefs
5 to 10 metres (16 to 33 ft)
170 mm (6.8 in) across photo

Although this coral has been named in honour of the Maldives (being the "type locality" of the original colony described) the species ranges from Madagascar to Lord Howe Island in the South Pacific. Colours are variable and include brown, grey, green and orange.

AGARICIIDAE
Explanate coral
Leptoseris explanata
Coral reefs, rocky reefs
10 to 35 metres (33 to 115 ft)
170 mm (6.8 in) colonies

Found on rock walls and beneath caves and ledges this species is not common in the Maldives. The two colonies shown have grown (fused) together which seems to be a feature in some areas. Colour ranges from dark brown to light brown and yellow and most colonies have a white growing edge (margin).

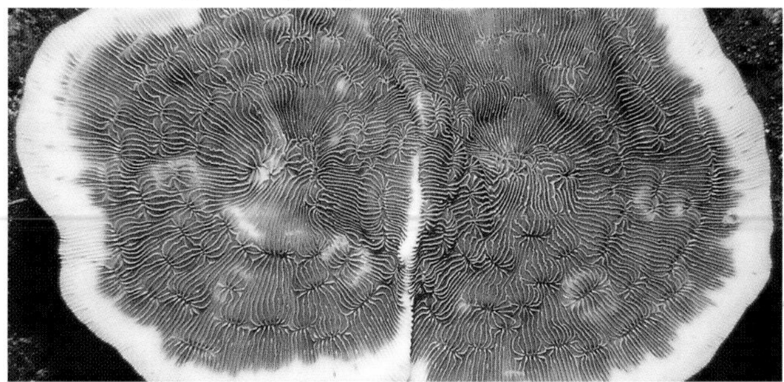

AGARICIIDAE
Hawaiian coral
Leptoseris hawaiiensis
Coral reefs, rocky reefs
10 to 35 metres (33 to 115 ft)
150 mm (6 in) colony

An uncommon species found almost exclusively on drop offs and vertical walls this species may be mottled brown or green. The white margin always appears to be thin and the tissue striations are very well defined.

Speciose coral has a dish-like shape with horizontal, reasonably uniform ridges and cannot be confused with its known relatives. It ranges from the Red Sea to Tahiti, and is either brown or grey.

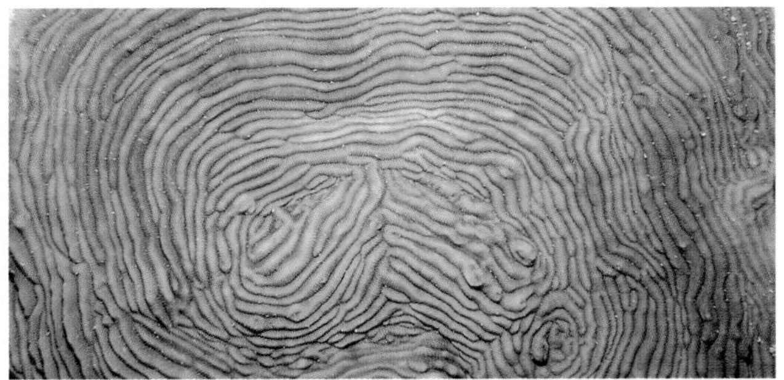

AGARICIIDAE

Speciose coral

Pachyseris speciosa

Coral reefs, rocky reefs

5 to 30 metres (16 to 98 ft)

170 mm (6.8 in) across

This Maldivian coral was only able to be identified to genus. It was solid and robust in form and suggests a very characteristic pattern. However, until a piece can be collected and forwarded to a coral taxonomist it remains a mystery.

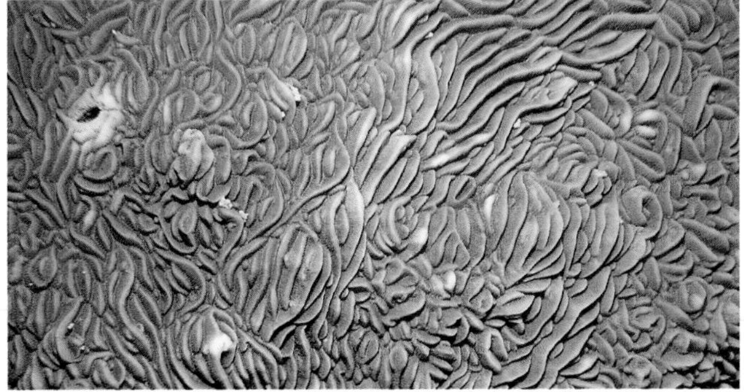

AGARICIIDAE

Terrace coral

Pachyseris sp.

Coral reefs, rocky reefs

5 to 10 metres (16 to 33 ft)

170 mm (6.8 in) across photo

A common easily recognised species, it has very prominent septal teeth and only one mouth. It ranges from the Red Sea to Samoa and is common over most of its range.

FUNGIIDAE

Hedgehog mushroom coral

Ctenactis echinata

Rubble, dead reef slopes

5 to 10 metres (16 to 33 ft)

250 mm (10 in)

FUNGIIDAE

Common mushroom coral

Fungia fungites

Rubble, coral reefs, rocky reefs

Lt to 20 metres (0 to 66 ft)

125 mm (5 in)

These very common mushroom corals have highly developed triangular septal teeth. Colours can be brown, grey, yellow or white and range extends from the Red Sea to French Polynesia.

FUNGIIDAE

Scuted mushroom coral

Fungia scutaria

Coral reefs, rocky reefs, rubble

3 to 20 metres (10 to 66 ft)

170 mm (6.8 in)

A common easily recognised form found across the entire Indo-Pacific it is generally seen on reef tops and along the edges of slopes. It is always elongate in shape and heavy set with prominent tentacular lobes (usually green). Colour may be yellow or brown.

FUNGIIDAE

Paumotu mushroom coral

Fungites paumotensis

Rubble, dead reef

5 to 10 metres (16 to 33 ft)

200 mm (8 in)

This coral was first found in the Paumotu Islands sometime before 1849 and is now known to range from Madagascar to French Polynesia.

Common across the entire Indo-Pacific these long, round-ended colonies may grow up to one metre (3.3 ft) in length. They can be brown, green or yellow and are found on reef tops, slopes and sandy bottomed lagoons. Often referred to as canoe corals.

FUNGIIDAE

Slug-like mushroom coral

Herpolitha limax

Coral reefs, rocky reefs, rubble, lagoons

Lt to 10 metres (0 to 33 ft)

300 mm (10 in)

A free-living colonial coral this species with its easily recognised shape and texture occurs from East Africa to Samoa where it is considered uncommon. Honey brown in colour the edges (margins) may be pink or purple.

FUNGIIDAE

Cap-like mushroom coral

Halomitra pileus

Coral reefs, rocky reefs, rubble

10 to 20 metres (33 to 66 ft)

300 mm (12 in)

Common across the entire Indo-Pacific where it often forms large colonies up to 3 metres (10 ft) across. Colour can be green, red, brown or yellow with a number of growth forms; the corallites are generally well formed with blade-like septa.

OCULINIDAE

Bristle coral

Galaxea fascicularis

Coral reefs, rocky reefs

5 to 20 metres (16 to 66 ft)

170 mm (6.8 in) across photo

MUSSIDAE
Tear-lobed coral
Cynarina lacrymalis
Coral reefs, rocky reefs
20 to 30 metres (66 to 98 ft)
80 mm (3.2 in)

Seen on deeper walls and drop offs this solitary coral has highly developed polyp walls. At night these are retracted and its feeding tentacles are extended. The species ranges across the Indo-Pacific.

MUSSIDAE
Diminutive coral
Lobophyllia dimiduta
Coral reefs, rocky reefs
5 to 10 metres (16 to 33 ft)
180 mm (7 in) across photo

A very rare species, this form is new to the Maldives. The colonies are white or yellow, are fairly regular in pattern and have well developed septal spines.

MUSSIDAE
Radiant coral
Symphyllia radians
Coral reefs, rocky reefs
10 to 20 metres (33 to 66 ft)
170 mm (6.8 in) across photo

Known from the Maldives to Fiji radiant coral is found in areas of upper reef slopes. Most colonies are round or flat and colours include grey, green, yellow and brown.

MUSSIDAE
Intestinal coral
Symphyllia recta
Coral reefs, rocky reefs
5 to 10 metres (16 to 33 ft)
200 mm (8 in) across photo

Most colonies are domed in shape with very sinuous septa often having colours of red, green, brown or grey or combinations of these. It is found from the Maldives to Samoa and is common along the edges of reef slopes.

In its plate form this species is easily determined but it has many different growth forms, several of which may occur on the same colony depending on its situation. Most colonies are pink or brown with bright greenish yellow in between. It ranges from the Maldives to Lord Howe Island and often forms large multi-tiered colonies up to 3 metres (10 ft) across in lagoons.

MERULINIDAE

Loud coral

Merulina ampliata

Coral reefs, rocky reefs

5 to 20 metres (16 to 66 ft)

400 mm (16 in) across photo

Uncommon over most of its Indo-Pacific range colonies of this species may be flat or rounded with larger colonies being quite massive. They have a very characteristic series of plated nodules (called hynophores) evenly distributed across the surface area and may be green, cream or brown in colour.

MERULINIDAE

Small-coned coral

Hydnophora microconus

Coral reefs, rocky reefs

8 to 20 metres (26 to 66 ft)

350 mm (14 in) colony

Although this colony is only small it represents a new record for the Maldives and was found growing on a loose piece of rubble on a reef slope.

FAVIIDAE

Dan's coral

Favia danae

Coral reefs, rocky reefs

5 to 10 metres (16 to 33 ft)

150 mm (6 in) colony

FAVIIDAE

Honeycomb coral

Favia favus

Coral reefs, rocky reefs

5 to 10 metres (16 to 33 ft)

1 metre (3.3 ft) colony

A very common species spread across most of the Indo-Pacific it grows in massive colonies which may be dark green, grey or brown in colour and reach 2 metres (6.6 ft) in size.

FAVIIDAE

Secret coral

Favites abdita

Coral reefs, rocky reefs

5 to 10 metres (16 to 33 ft)

Up to 1 metre (3.3 ft)

Common on reefs from the Red Sea to Lord Howe Island, this species forms massive colonies with thick walls centred by a bright green colour around the polyp mouth.

FAVIIDAE

Angular coral

Favites halicora

Coral reefs, rocky reefs

8 to 15 metres (26 to 49 ft)

170 mm (6.8 in) across photo

The growth forms in the Maldives are fairly distinctive with angular corallites and thick walls in a massive colony. It ranges from the Red Sea to Samoa.

FAVIIDAE

Russell's coral

Favites russelli

Coral reefs, rocky reefs

5 to 20 metres (16 to 66 ft)

100 mm (4.4 in) colony

Although this new record for the Maldives is generally seen as a massive encrusting form in the Pacific, those observed in the Maldives were only small colonies.

Brain-like colonies with a characteristic ragged appearance to the septa. This species is common from the Red Sea to Lord Howe Island and may have brown walls and septa with green or white valleys in between.

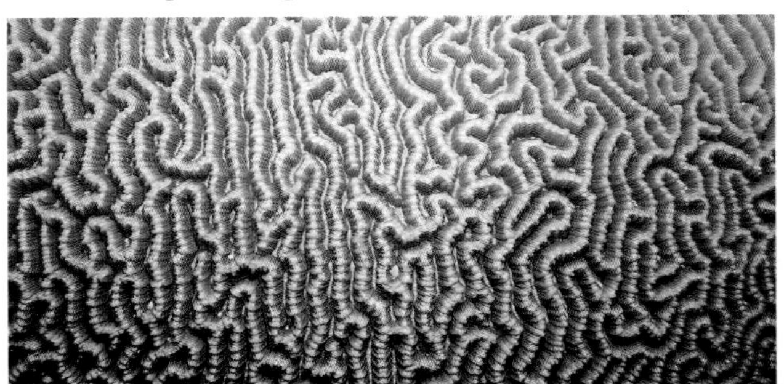

FAVIIDAE

Artistic coral

Platygyra daedalea

Coral reefs, rocky reefs

5 to 20 metres (16 to 66 ft)

1 metre (3.3 ft)

A delicately designed, attractively patterned species, this small colony was one of several observed. Larger colonies may be massive but the septa have characteristic easily distinguished cross sections on the ridges. The species is uncommon across its Indo-Pacific range.

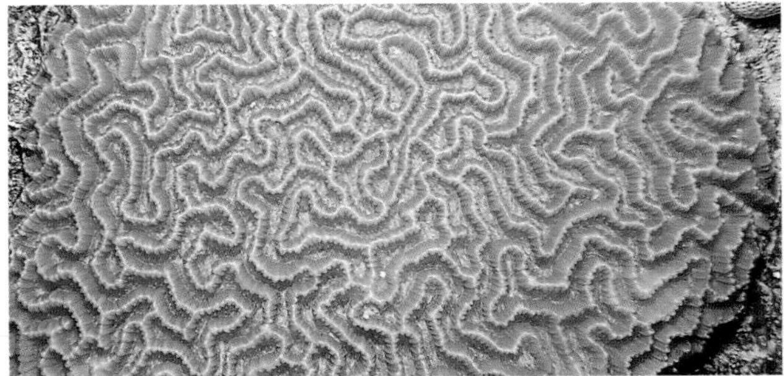

FAVIIDAE

Sinuous coral

Platygyra sinensis

Coral reefs, rocky reefs

3 to 20 metres (9 to 66 ft)

170 mm (6.8 in) across

Ranging from the Red Sea to Tahiti, this fairly common massive growing colony has very uniform septa with bright yellow or green valleys. Most colonies observed in the Maldives were up to 1 metre (3.3 ft) across.

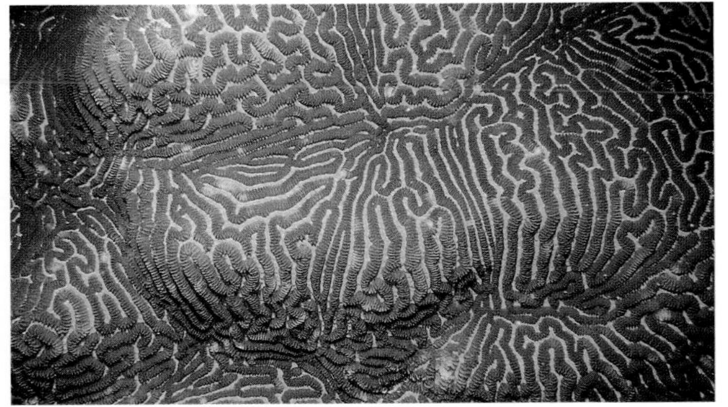

FAVIIDAE

Uniform coral

Leptoria phrygia

Coral reefs, rocky reefs

5 to 20 metres (16 to 66 ft)

Up to 2 metres (6.6 ft)

FAVIIDAE

Crested coral

Oulophyllia crispa

Coral reefs, rocky reefs

5 to 20 metres (16 to 66 ft)

250 mm (10 in) across

Massive round colony growth, deep widely-spaced shaped valleys and ragged septa with conspicuous mouths, these colonies are generally brown, green or cream. This species ranges from the Red Sea to Samoa.

FAVIIDAE

Sun coral

Diploastrea helipora

Coral reefs, rocky reefs

8 to 20 metres (26 to 66 ft)

170 mm (6.8 in) across photo

One of the most easily identifiable corals there is only one species in the genus. The colonies are massive and dome-shaped with a very even surface pattern. Colours range from green to brown or cream and the species is known from the Red Sea to Samoa.

CARYOPHYLLIIDAE

Bald-tipped coral

Euphyllia glabrescens

Coral reefs, rocky reefs

10 to 30 metres (33 to 98 ft)

180 mm (7.2 in) colony

With its polyps out night and day, this species is one of the unique *Euphyllias* which can only be separated to species by comparison of the polyps. The typical Maldivian form (pictured) is found from the Red Sea to Samoa.

Named for the anchor-shaped tips on its polyps, this species is a new record for the Maldives. It was found on a reef undercut at 22 metres and extends its range out to Norfolk Island in the South Pacific.

CARYOPHYLLIIDAE
Anchor coral
Euphyllia ancora
Coral reefs, rocky reefs
15 to 30 metres (49 to 98 ft)
100 mm (4 in) colony

Looking remarkably like a bunch of grapes, this bubble-tentacled coral is easy to identify and can be extended day or night depending on depth and shade. This species is distributed from the Red Sea to the South Pacific.

CARYOPHYLLIIDAE
Sinuose coral
Plerogyra sinuosa
Coral reefs, rocky reefs
20 to 30 metres (66 to 98 ft)
100 mm (4 in) colony

Polyps partially withdrawn, Maldives.

Common across the Indo-Pacific this easily identified coral is found on deeper walls and beneath underhangs in the Maldives. Its grape-like bubble vesicles are expanded during the day but these are somewhat hidden by the longer feeding tentacles seen out at night.

CARYOPHYLLIIDAE
Lichtensteins' coral
Physogyra lichtensteini
Coral reefs, rocky reefs
20 to 30 metres (66 to 98 ft)
170 mm (6.8 in) colony

Feeding tentacles are expanded at night, Maldives.

DENDROPHYLLIIDAE
Graceful coral
Dendrophyllia gracilis
Coral reefs, rocky reefs
10 to 20 metres (33 to 66 ft)
170 mm (6.8 in) across photo

Generally restricted to a habitat beneath ledges, overhangs and in caves, this very attractive coral grows in small bushy colonies and the large polyps are self-pigmented and only expand in shaded areas of moderate current during late afternoon or at night.

Polyps retracted in daylight, Maldives.

DENDROPHYLLIIDAE
Faulkner's coral
Tubastraea faulkneri
Coral reefs, rocky reefs
10 to 20 metres (33 to 66 ft)
170 mm (6.8 in) colony

Living beneath caves and overhangs this coral genus is recorded from the Red Sea to the Sea of Cortez (Mexico). It grows in small compacted clumps. The skin may be pink or bright orange and the large polyps are generally only extended at night.

Colony shape with polyps retracted, Maldives.

Close up of polyps, Maldives.

Found on deeper terraces on some southern atolls, this species lives in areas of strong currents lining the tops of drop offs and taking advantage of the up-welling water to bring planktonic food.

DENDROPHYLLIIDAE
Midnight coral
Tubastraea micrantha
Coral reefs, rocky reefs
25 to 40 metres (82 to 133 ft)
Up to 1 metre (3.3 ft) colony

Polyps fully extended at night, Maldives.

Seen as huge stands (resembling giant convoluted cabbages), this species is found from the Red Sea to the South Pacific. Only small colonies were observed in the Maldives.

DENDROPHYLLIIDAE
Membraneous coral
Turbinaria mesenterina
Coral reefs, rocky reefs
10 to 20 metres (33 to 66 ft)
250 mm (10 in) across

This species remains identified; it was found on a reef edge and only seen in one colour. The polyps were always bright yellow and had 12 tentacles whereas *T. frondens* (recorded from the Maldives) has grey or bluish polyps with around 36 tentacles.

DENDROPHYLLIIDAE
Nipple coral
Turbinaria sp.
Coral reefs, rocky reefs
8 to 20 metres (26 to 66 ft)
170 mm (6.8 in) across photo

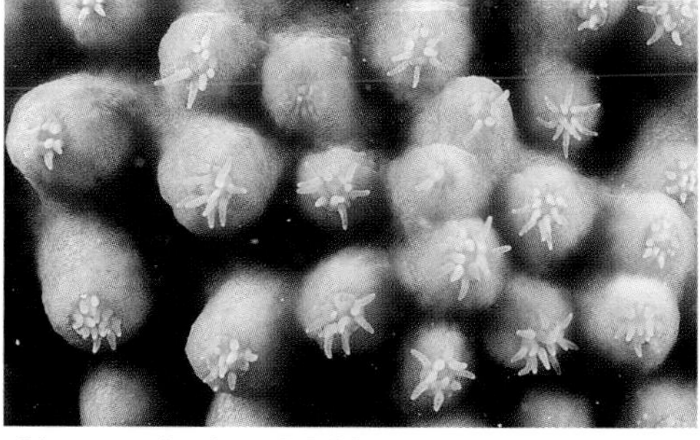

Close up of polyps, Maldives.

Flatworms

Chapter 4

Flatworms

PHYLUM: PLATYHELMINTHES

CLASS: *Turbellaria*

Features: The greater number of marine flatworms are grouped in the Order Polycladida. (The term "flatworm" includes the turbellarians, or free-living flatworms, parasitic flukes and tapeworms, but is used here to refer to the turbellarians.)

Flatworms are for the most part wafer-thin, bilaterally symmetrical creatures that appear to glide over the substrate. There is a head with simple sense organs, including simple tentacles and eye spots, visible under a microscope.

Flatworms have no external gills (unlike most nudibranchs) but some have marginal tentacles sensory folds at the "head" end which may contain eyes, and other species may have dorsal tentacles issuing from the back near the "head".

The development of a head and bilateral symmetry is closely related to the evolution of forward locomotion. The body is made up of three layers of cells and contains a gut which opens via the mouth on the underside. The pharynx may be eversible and is sometimes extruded to engulf whole prey. There is no anus and no circulatory system. Respiration is achieved by the diffusion of oxygen into the body from outside; carbon dioxide escapes by the reverse process.

Lifestyle: Few divers see flatworms and, if they do, they generally see only the more brightly coloured species. Even then they may confuse them with nudibranchs (shell-less molluscs). Flatworms live intertidally down to and beyond 40 metres (131 ft) and can be found on coral reefs, rocky reefs, rubble, sand and mud. Some are diurnal and others may be strictly nocturnal and have only ever been seen in the open during the night. Many species live beneath stones because their prey also lives under stones and dead coral slabs.

Most species living in the sea are predatory and carnivorous with digested food being distributed around the body by diffusion. In the author's experience many flatworms feed on colonial ascidians. Only a few species show any specific body colour patterns that relate to the markings of the species on which they may prey.

The gliding motion that flatworms possess is produced by a combination of minute, beating cilia on the underside of the flatworm and muscular contraction. At times some flatworms can also swim by undulating their body margins. Swimming is thought to be an escape response but may also be a means of locomotion. Swimming flatworms have been observed taking off from a high reef and being carried along by the current for up to 20 or 30 metres (65–100 feet).

Reproduction: Flatworms are hermaphrodites, having complex male and female sex organs. Mating and cross fertilisation occur between two individuals. Eggs are laid on the substrate in spirals, similar to an open-ended circle. Remarkably, some flatworm egg ribbon spirals are very similar to those of some nudibranchs.

Associations: Apart from prey predator associations flatworm relatives can be found on soft corals, gorgonians and hard corals.

Identification: Flatworms are very difficult to identify if not preserved properly (a complicated process). Disposition of the eyes and structures on the head are all-important in laboratory identification using a microscope. It had been thought that variation in the colours and patterns of flatworms prevented their identification with any degree of accuracy, but experience has shown that most patterned species from warmer waters, especially in the genus *Pseudoceros*, can be visually identified once accurate identification has been made by a trained taxonomist on a properly preserved specimen and cross-referenced with a colour slide.

Suzanne's flatworm, Maldives

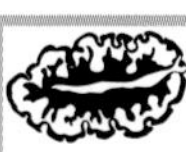

PSEUDOCEROTIDAE

Orsak's flatworm

Maiazoon orsaki

Coral reefs, rocky reefs

Lt to 10 metres (0 to 33 ft)

35 mm (1.4 in)

Recorded from the Maldives to the Marshall Islands it lives on the reef flats intertidally and has also been found in deeper water beneath coral slabs, rocks and rubble during the day. An easily recognised species there doesn't appear to be much colour variation in the Maldivian forms.

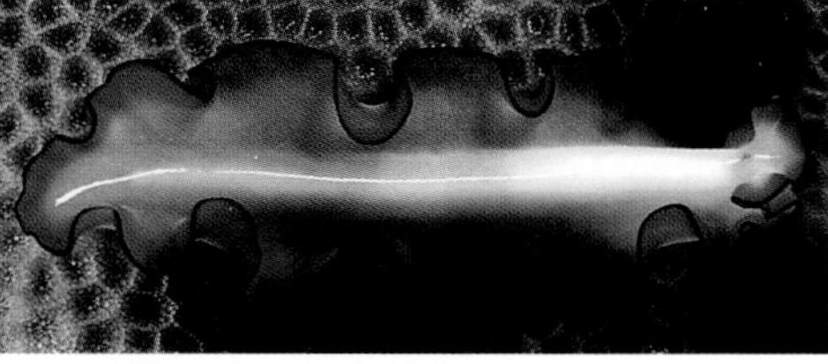

Juveniles have the same colour pattern, Maldives.

Mosaic flatworm

Eurylepta fuscopunctatus

Coral reefs, rocky reefs

5 to 20 metres (16 to 66 ft)

35mm (1.4 in)

Occurring from the Maldives to the Great Barrier Reef this flatworm appears very distinctive but the dorsal mosaic pattern may be very faint in some forms. The mosaic flatworm can be seen out in the open during the day.

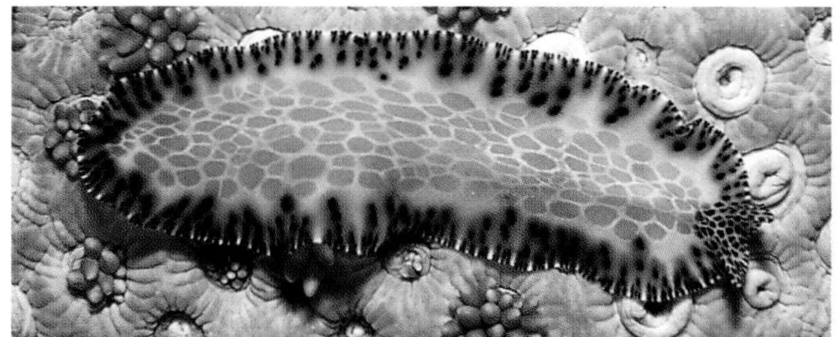

PSEUDOCEROTIDAE

Lightning flatworm

Pseudobiceros fulgor

Coral reefs, rocky reefs

5 to 15 metres (16 to 49 ft)

30 mm (1.2 in)

This Indian Ocean species has been recorded across to Australia, the Great Barrier Reef and down to Lord Howe Island. It is a daytime resident and can be seen moving along in the open being ignored by predatory fish. This behaviour assumes it has noxious characteristics.

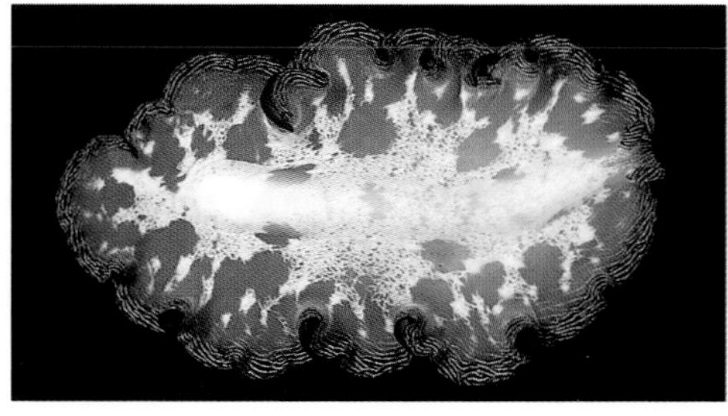

Variation, Lord Howe Island, South Pacific.

PSEUDOCEROTIDAE
Glorious flatworm
Pseudobiceros gloriosus
Coral reefs, rocky reefs, rubble
5 to 20 metres (16 to 66 ft)
70 mm (2.8 in)

Although mostly black in colour this species has a very easily-recognised tri-coloured margin of orange, pink and burgundy on the outer edge. Not as common as some other species it ranges from the Maldives to Fiji in the Pacific where it crawls around in the open during daylight.

PSEUDOCEROTIDAE
Bird-wing flatworm
Pseudobiceros sp.
Coral reefs, rocky reefs
5 to 10 metres (16 to 33 ft)
40 mm (1.6 in)

A fast-moving diurnal species seen out in the open on reef slopes and under ledges this Indo-Pacific species has a remarkable resemblance to Bedford's flatworm *Pseudobiceros bedfordi* but even allowing for a large amount of colour and pattern variation it appears different.

Close relative, Pseudobiceros *sp., Bargara, Queensland.*

Bedford's flatworm, Milne Bay, Papua New Guinea.

Close up Bedford's flatworm, Pseudobiceros bedfordi, *Heron Island, Great Barrier Reef.*

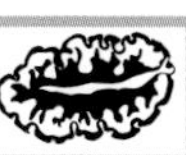

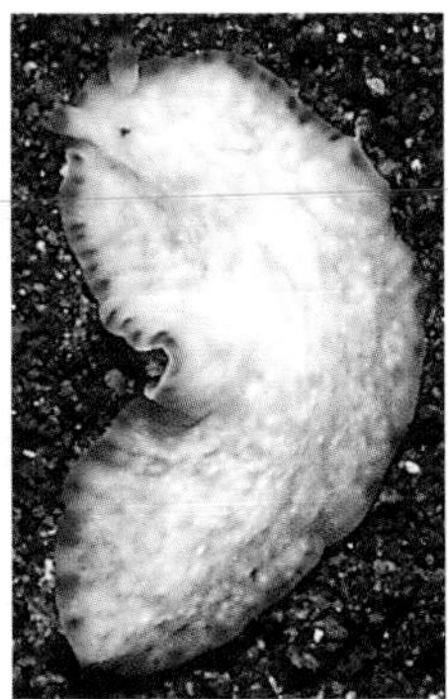

Named after Dr Terry Gosliner (who collected the type species) in 1994 this species is known from the Maldives by several photographic records. It ranges across the Indian Ocean to Indonesia, Madang and the Great Barrier Reef. It is not considered common anywhere in its range and the mottled cream background is subject to colour variation.

PSEUDOCEROTIDAE
Gosliner's flatworm
Pseudoceros goslineri
Coral reefs, rocky reefs, sand
Lt to 30 metres (0 to 98 ft)
60 mm (2.4 in)

Found from the Maldives to Australia this easily identified species does not appear to vary much across its range. It can be seen out in the open or found beneath coral rocks. (Photo: Jorg Aebi)

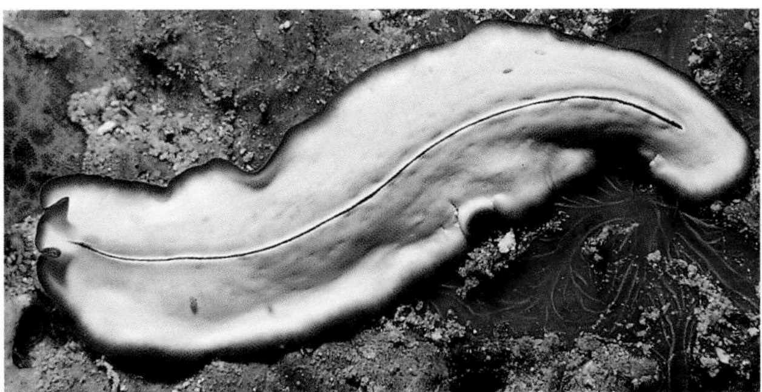

PSEUDOCEROTIDAE
Fine-lined flatworm
Pseudoceros monostichos
Coral reefs, rocky reefs
5 to 10 metres (16 to 33 ft)
40 mm (1.6 in)

Widely distributed, this species ranges from the Maldives to Papua New Guinea with a sibling species discovered by the author at Norfolk Island in the South Pacific in 1988 where it is quite prolific.

PSEUDOCEROTIDAE
Suzanne's flatworm
Pseudoceros suzzanae
Coral reefs, rocky reefs
5 to 20 metres (16 to 66 ft)
30 mm (1.2 in)

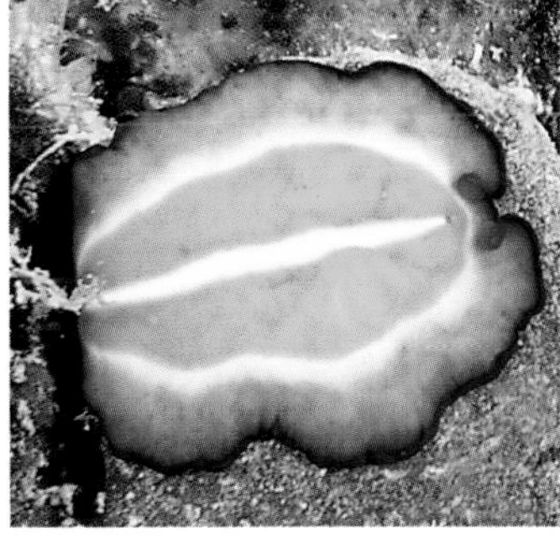

Feeding on an ascidian, Maldives.

PSEUDOCEROTIDAE

Tri-lined flatworm

Pseudoceros sp.

Coral reefs, rocky reefs, rubble

8 to 20 metres (26 to 66 ft)

50 mm (2 in)

A new record for the Maldives this species was discovered out in the open during night dives. Previously, it was known from Papua New Guinea and the Great Barrier Reef. A relatively rare species it was not found at all during the day. It feeds on ascidians and there is some variation in colour across its distribution.

The sapphire flatworm is a close relative seen here feeding on ascidians. Heron Island, Great Barrier Reef.

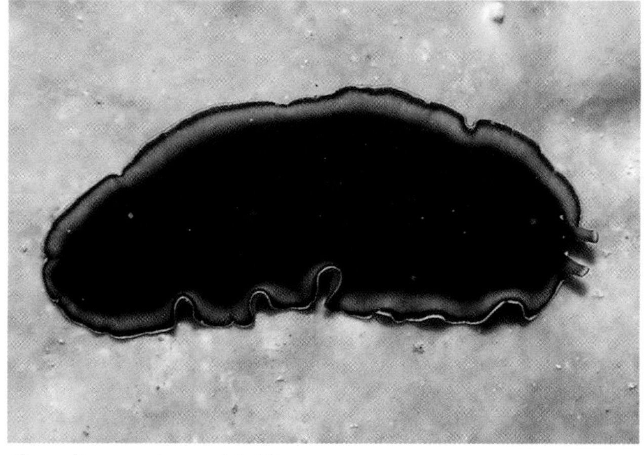

Crawling specimen, Maldives.

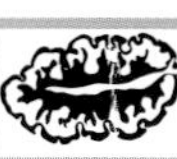

Known from the Maldives to the Great Barrier Reef this spectacular flatworm is seen out in the open both day and night and unlike previous species has studs of raised papillae on its back. When disturbed it executes an immediate escape response by swimming up into the water column by undulating movements of its mantle edge.

PSEUDOCEROTIDAE

Yellow Papillae flatworm

Thysanozoan nigropapillosum

Coral reefs, rocky reefs, rubble

Lt to 20 metres (0 to 66 ft)

70 mm (2.8 in)

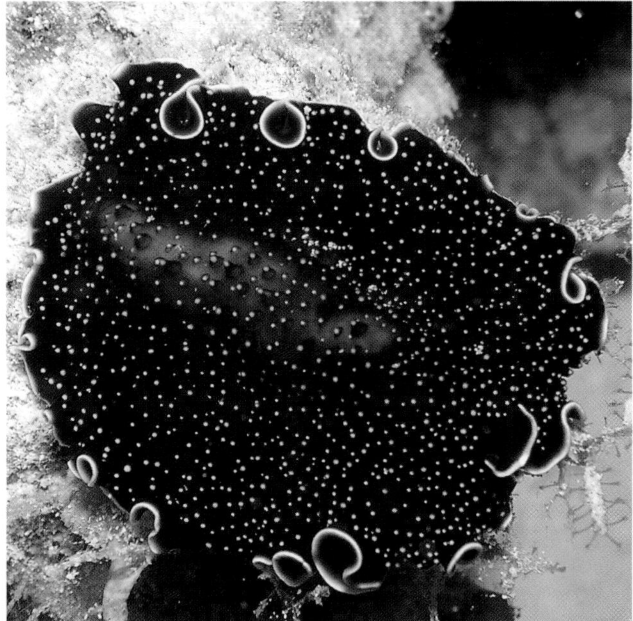

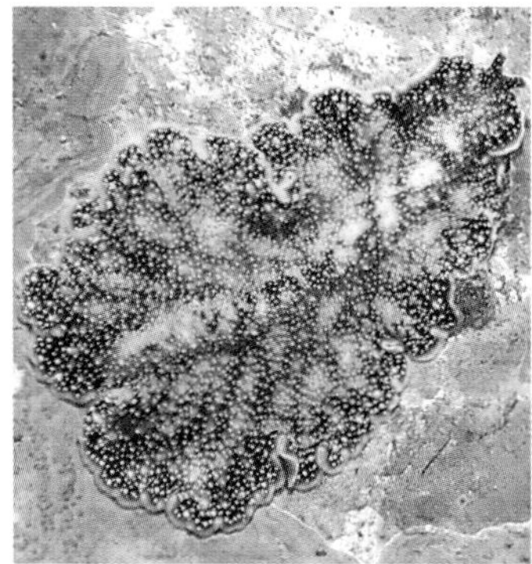

Colour variation, Port Moresby, Papua New Guinea.

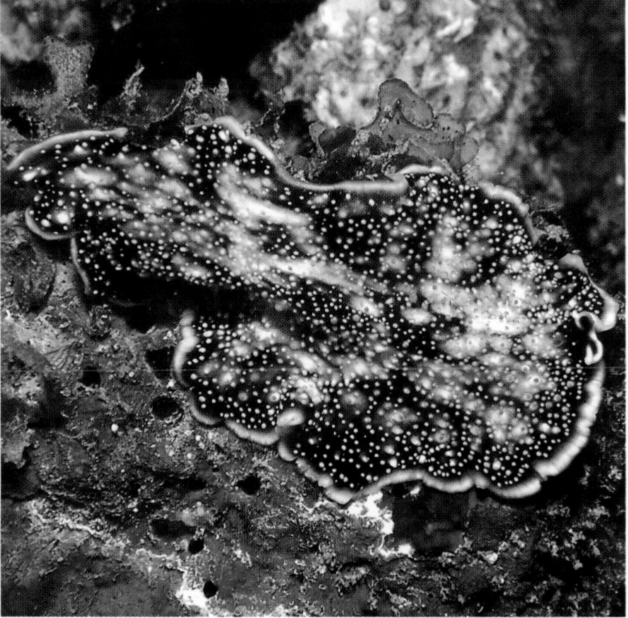

Colour variation, Port Moresby, Papua New Guinea.

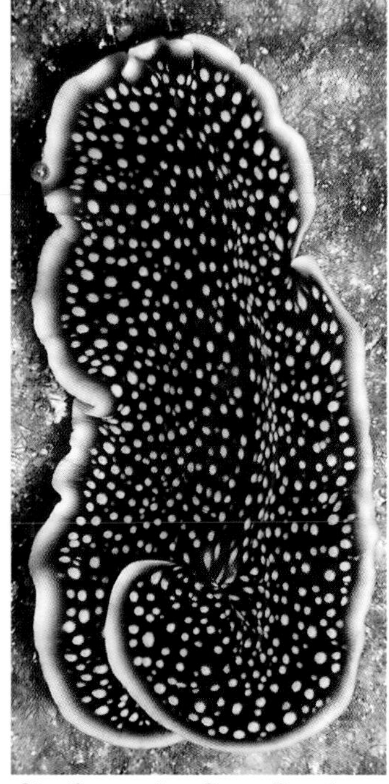

Similar species, Great Barrier Reef.

Segmented worms

Chapter 5

Segmented worms

PHYLUM: ANNELIDA

CLASS: *Polychaeta*

Features: The phylum Annelida, the segmented worms, is one of the major groupings of the animal kingdom. It demonstrates a successful evolutionary pattern of animals constructed from three cell layers. It shows bilateral symmetry, development of a body cavity between the body wall muscles and the gut muscles and, most important, a segmented body. The basic anatomical features of each segment can have different specialised functions. This is best seen in the head segments of some annelids where quite sophisticated organs are borne on different segments for different functions. Of the four or so classes of the Annelida only the Polychaetes are really abundant in the sea.

There are more than 12,000 species and 70 families worldwide and comparatively little is known of the natural history or distribution of this diverse group. Ecologically they are of two types: the active, mobile, foraging Polychaetes, and the sedentary burrowing or tube-dwelling suspension or detrital feeders.

Lifestyle: Polychaetes can be found in almost every subtidal habitat. The various forms may be rock boring, tube dwelling, free roving, symbiotic, mud burrowing and even pelagic. They inhabit intertidal areas down to abyssal depths, and in many soft bottom areas are the most common forms of life.

As worms are very vulnerable to predation, many have evolved lifestyles and armour to enhance their chances of survival. Some sedentary species construct tubes of calcium carbonate, sand grains, or mucus in which to live; others bore into coral. The free-living, non-tubiculous

Molluscs

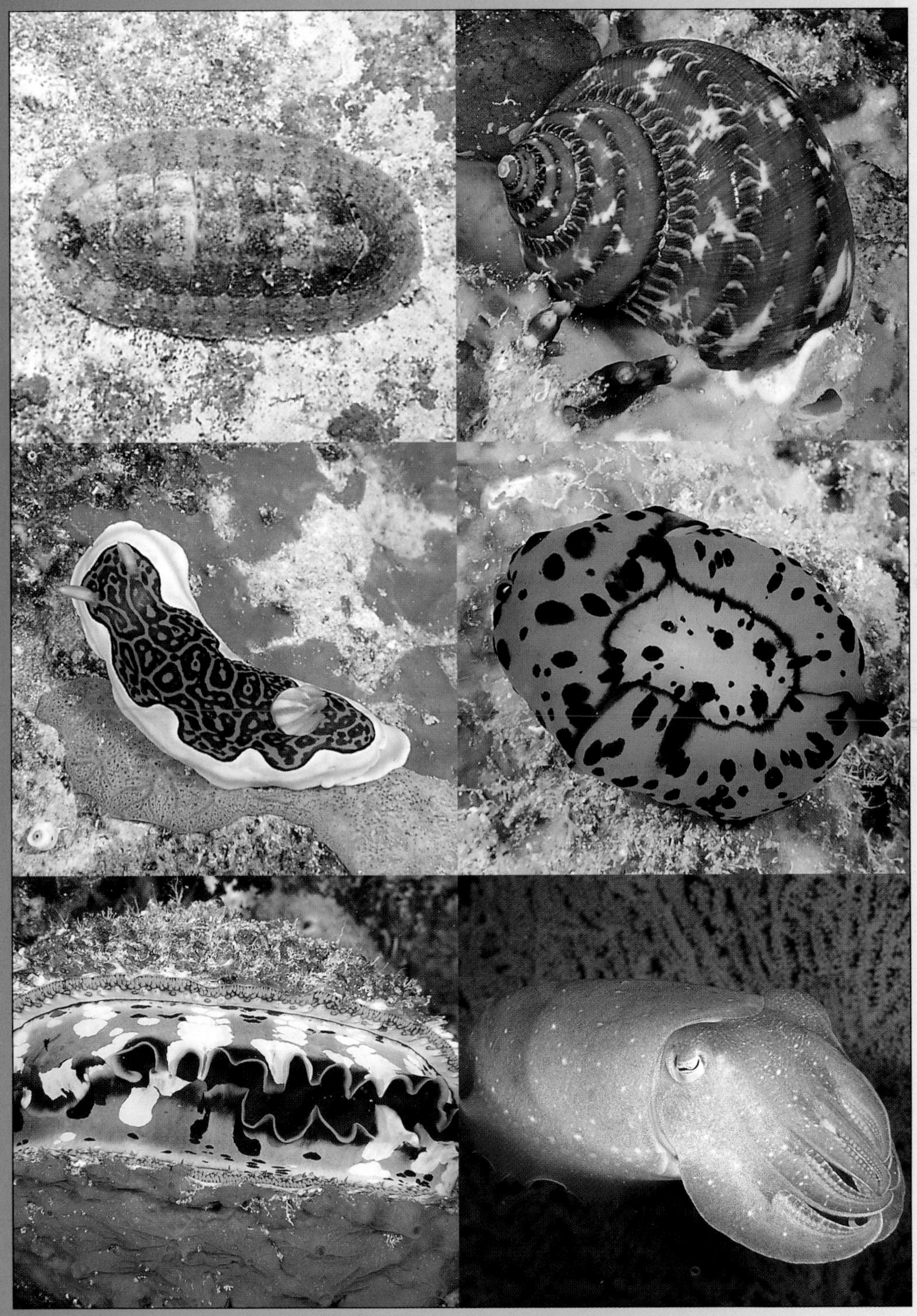

Chapter 6

Molluscs

PHYLUM: MOLLUSCA

CLASSES: *Polyplacophora* (Chitons)
Gastropoda (Univalves)
Bivalvia (Bivalves)
Cephalopoda (Cuttles, Squid, Nautilus, Octopus)

Features: Besides the four classes described here, there are three other classes of the phylum Mollusca. These are, Monaplacophora, Aplacophora and Scaphopoda, whose living representatives are rarely seen. The first class includes small, limpet-like animals that live hundreds to thousands of metres down in the deep ocean trenches. The second class consists of small, worm-like molluscs without shells that live in bottom sediments or among algae and sedentary invertebrates. The third class are shell-shaped tusks which live beneath the sand.

Like the segmented worms, the molluscs make up a major part of the world's marine invertebrate faunas. At least 112,000 species of molluscs are known and probably many more remain to be discovered. Oysters, mussels, scallops and squid are served at restaurants and seafood shops. Besides their importance as a source of food, the shells themselves are highly prized for their beauty, myriad shapes, intricate designs, patterns and colours. As calcium carbonate structures that may exist for thousands of years after the death of the animal that formed them, they are truly a wonder of nature.

CYPRAEIDAE

Carnelian cowry

Cypraea carneola

Coral reefs, rocky reefs

Lt to 8 metres (0 to 26 ft)

50 mm (2 in)

Throughout most of its Indo-Pacific range the carnelian cowry can be located beneath rocks and dead coral at low tide. This mollusc illustrated was found on a night dive. The shell of this species can be easily identified by its purple aperture and teeth.

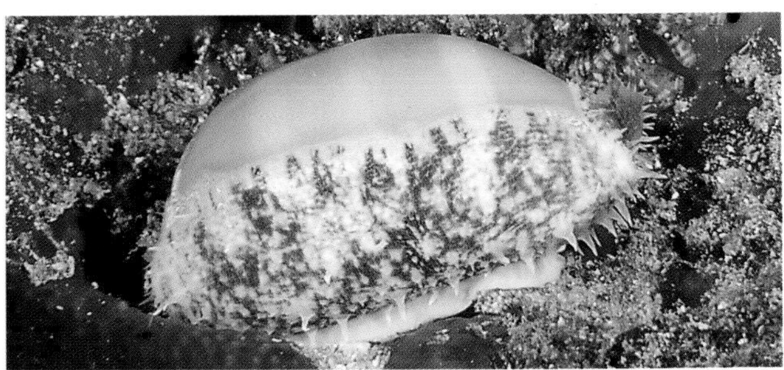

CYPRAEIDAE

Eroded cowry

Cypraea erosa

Coral reefs, rocky reefs

Lt to 10 metres (0 to 33 ft)

50 mm (2 in)

Named for the thick roughened shell edge and very coarse aperture teeth the eroded cowry is a very common shallow water species in the harbours, break waters and lagoons in the Maldives with a range extending each way across the Indo-Pacific. Breeding is in September/October.

Close up of eggs.

On Australia's east coast the mantle papillae of this species are extremely long.

With its mantle fully extended the eroded cowry is extremely difficult to see.

Chapter 6

Molluscs

PHYLUM: MOLLUSCA

CLASSES: *Polyplacophora* (Chitons)
Gastropoda (Univalves)
Bivalvia (Bivalves)
Cephalopoda (Cuttles, Squid, Nautilus, Octopus)

Features: Besides the four classes described here, there are three other classes of the phylum Mollusca. These are, Monaplacophora, Aplacophora and Scaphopoda, whose living representatives are rarely seen. The first class includes small, limpet-like animals that live hundreds to thousands of metres down in the deep ocean trenches. The second class consists of small, worm-like molluscs without shells that live in bottom sediments or among algae and sedentary invertebrates. The third class are shell-shaped tusks which live beneath the sand.

Like the segmented worms, the molluscs make up a major part of the world's marine invertebrate faunas. At least 112,000 species of molluscs are known and probably many more remain to be discovered. Oysters, mussels, scallops and squid are served at restaurants and seafood shops. Besides their importance as a source of food, the shells themselves are highly prized for their beauty, myriad shapes, intricate designs, patterns and colours. As calcium carbonate structures that may exist for thousands of years after the death of the animal that formed them, they are truly a wonder of nature.

Each class of the phylum Mollusca is relatively easy to distinguish, but no one class shows the overall plan of molluscan architecture well. This is difficult to describe briefly. In essence the basic mollusc consists of a head with sense organs and a mouth, a visceral mass comprising the gut and associated structures, reproductive and excretory organs, and a muscular foot for creeping or digging. The body is formed of three cell layers. There is a small body cavity and the animal is not divided into segments. The visceral hump may be twisted and/or coiled and covered by a shell. A special area of body well, the mantle, secretes the shell and this often encloses a mantle cavity which may house the gills, reproductive and excretory openings.

Lifestyles: As the second largest group of aquatic animals molluscs live in almost every habitat and may be seen at the surface of the ocean swimming in the water column or on coral reefs, rocky reefs, rubble, sand and mud. However, as most of them are edible to other marine species such as fish, crabs, sea stars, brittle stars, mantis shrimps and other molluscs even though they may appear as very common washed up on beaches, in their natural habitat they are not always easy to see or find. Most are nocturnal and only come out at night so that during the day they hide away beneath rocks and dead coral, in holes, crevices, under the sand or rubble. Those that live exposed on the reef are generally very overgrown with encrusting marine life and difficult to see even in the day. Molluscs prey on many other animal forms. Different types eat sponges, cnidarians, worms, other molluscs, crustaceans, echinoderms, bryozoans and fish.

Reproduction: Molluscs may be hermaphroditic or have separate sexes, but cross fertilisation is the rule. In many marine species there is a planktonic larval phase. However, some species release juveniles which have undergone development inside their parents' bodies, and others have direct development.

Associations: Many animals have evolved both casual and obligate relationships with molluscs including sponges, sea anemones, worms, crabs, shrimps, amphipods, barnacles and fish.

Identification: Whereas in the past it was necessary to have the dead specimen to identify most molluscs it is now possible to identify several thousand species from good colour photographs or from good colour reproduction in field guides. However, where species are heavily overgrown it's best to have a record of both the dorsal and ventral (underside) aspect, or a specimen shell illustration.

CHITONS

CLASS: POLYPLACOPHORA

Features: Chitons have eight separate valves held together by a tough, leather-like girdle and due to this are often called 'coat-of-mail' shells because of their resemblance to the armour worn by soldiers in early European history. There are around 300 species described. Australia has the largest numbers.

Lifestyles: All chitons are marine and most species exist in the littoral and shallow subtidal zones of the rocky seashore. Most avoid light and during the day are found beneath stones and dead coral. A few species can be seen in the open in cracks, fissures or holes in the reef. The majority are slow-moving, active herbivores that feed on minute algae scraped off rocks by a wide, many-toothed, ribbon-like feeding organ called a radula. This works rather like a rasping tongue.

Reproduction: Reproduction occurs in several ways. The males have no penis and simply release sperm into the water, which in turn triggers the female of the species to emit eggs or enables the sperm to be taken into the female's mantle cavity by way of currents in the water set up to bring in oxygen for respiration. Several species of temperate water chitons are known to brood their young and others lay egg strings attached to the substrate.

Associations: There are specific recorded associations on red encrusting algae and seagrass.

Identification: Owing to their cryptic habits, many chitons are not well-known and though many species have been recorded, few have been illustrated in colour. Colour variations within species are far from being recorded photographically and in some regions most identifications rely on fine anatomical features which are best resolved by a specialist from a specimen.

Found beneath a jumbled pile of breakwater stones, this chiton is unable to be identified. However, it serves the purpose to define the class and record it to the Maldives.

UNIVALVES

CLASS: GASTROPODA

Features: The class Gastropoda contains more species than any other within the phylum Mollusca and up to 90,000 species are thought to exist worldwide.

Species are fairly well known and numerous colour guides to identification for collectors, naturalists, beachcombers, students and scientists have been published since the eighteenth century. Books with scientific descriptions are also available. This diverse class requires listing to subclass level to simplify description.

SUBCLASS: **PROSOBRANCHIA** (Shells snail-like, generally coiled: cones, cowries, helmets, tritons, murex, winkles, whelks, top shells, etc.)

Features: The molluscs of this subclass have gills and anus in front of their visceral mass, which is sometimes referred to as the visceral hump. In general they have a single shell coiled into a tube, similar to a snail. The tube is open at one end and may be partly sealed by a trapdoor (operculum). The head is well formed, with two eyes, each set at the base of a tentacle and may have a retractable proboscis, or 'trunk', containing a well-developed radula.

Lifestyles: Most species have a mobile lifestyle and are able to move over the substrate in search of food or mates. Univalves occupy almost every habitat with the exception of mid-water. Most rely on their shells for protection and, in general, they appear more active at night feeding on algae, sponges, cnidarians, worms, molluscs, echinoderms, ascidians and fish. A few live sedentary lives as filter and suspension feeders. Little work has been published on Maldivian species and accumulative data is still being established.

Reproduction: In most species the sexes are separate, with the male impregnating the female with a penis that issues from the right side of the neck. External fertilisation is also known. Eggs are laid on the substrate, on a food source or held within the body. In many cases, the female sits on the eggs and protects them until hatching.

Associations: There are few established commensal relationships known except in regards to sponges, cnidarians, crabs and bryozoans.

Identification: Most of the larger species are fairly well known and thousands can now be identified visually without requiring the shell. Smaller species and close relatives may still require a shell until our knowledge becomes more complete.

The Asse's ear abalone can be found at low water on late afternoon incoming tides. The shell itself is shaped like an elongated ear and is very shiny and smooth due to extended mantle which almost envelops the entire shell. At some localities a small pea crab lives in the animal's gill cavity.

HALIOTIDAE

Asse's ear abalone

Haliotis asinina

Coral reefs, rocky reefs

Lt to 5 metres (0 to 16 ft)

150 mm (6 in)

Close up of the mouth.

Almost covered by the animal's mantle there is only a fine slit in the centre that reveals any presence of a shell. This species lives beneath rocks and dead coral and is known from a number of areas in the Indo-Pacific. It has a very characteristically marked animal and is easy to recognise once the identity has been established.

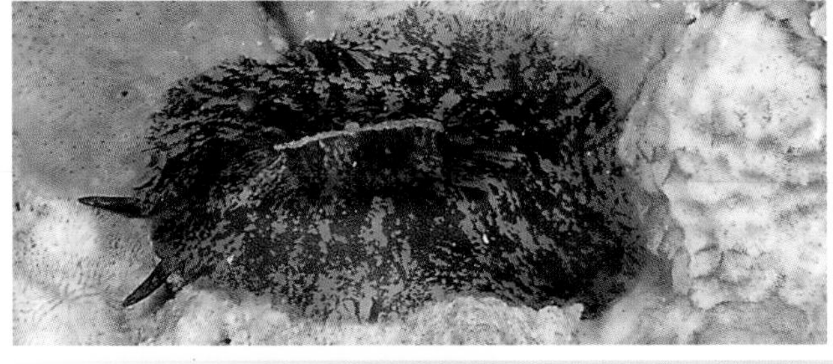

FISSURELLIDAE

Toe-nail limpet

Scutus unguis

Coral reefs, rocky reefs

Lt to 5 metres (0 to 16 ft)

50 mm (2 in)

Well known across the Indo-Pacific the maculated top shell can be found beneath dead coral slabs and rocks on intertidal reef and out in the open feeding on algae-covered rock in deeper water at night.

TROCHIDAE

Maculated top

Trochus maculatus

Coral reefs, rocky reefs

Lt to 10 metres (0 to 33 ft)

60 mm (2.4 in)

TURBINIDAE

Tapestry turban

Turbo petholatus

Coral reefs, rocky reefs

Lt to 20 metres (0 to 66 ft)

60 mm (2.5 in)

Distributed across the Indo-Pacific, it doesn't appear common in the Maldives. The beauty of the animal's shell is further enhanced by the naturally high polish. Found beneath dead coral and rocks during the day; at night, it comes out to feed on algae.

TURBINIDAE

Silvermouth turban

Turbo argyrostoma

Coral reefs, rocky reefs

Lt to 10 metres (0 to 33 ft)

70 mm (2.8 in)

A coarsely ribbed species with a characteristic colour patch on the operculum (trapdoor) the silvermouth turban inhabits the undersides of dead coral and rocks in shallow water across the Indo-Pacific.

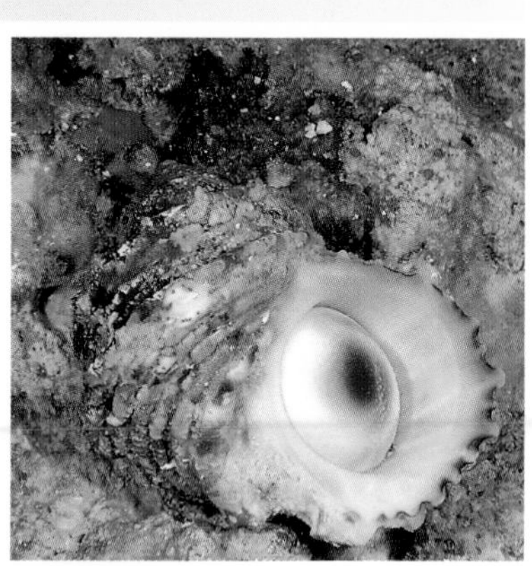

VERMETIDAE

Large worm shell

Dendropoma maxima

Coral reefs, rocky reefs

3 to 20 metres (10 to 66 ft)

10 mm (0.4 in) diameter

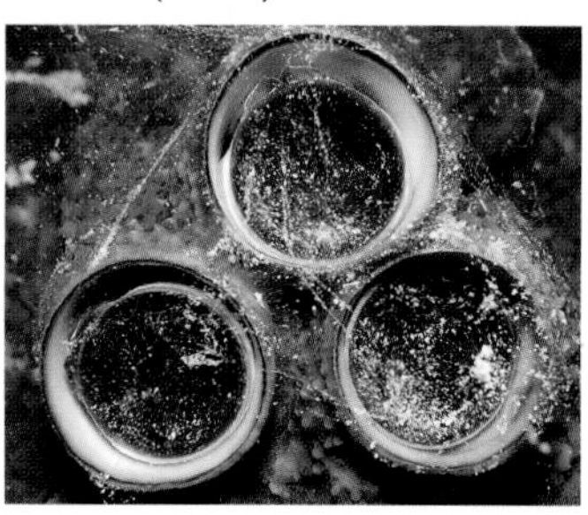

Close up of the large worm shells mucous net which it uses to snare plankton and detritus. At various intervals the mucous net is sucked back in and redigested along with the organic content, then it is cast out again, helped by ciliary currents.

Especially common in the Maldives this species is found burrowed into live and dead coral rock, sometimes in large numbers. The mollusc is easy to identify due to the presence of a black operculum (trapdoor) at the aperture.

VERMETIDAE
Grand worm shell
Serpulorbis grandis

Coral heads, dead coral

2 to 20 metres (6.6 to 66 ft)

20 mm (0.8 in) diameter

The largest non-operculumed worm shell which in larval forms settles onto a site with good current movement and proceeds to build a shell which stays anchored forever. The foot is very distinctively marked and varies from yellow and brown to yellow and black. It feeds by catching plankton on strands of mucus sent out by ciliary currents produced by its gill. This species is found throughout the Indo-Pacific.

Shell shape of the grand worm shell, Great Barrier Reef.

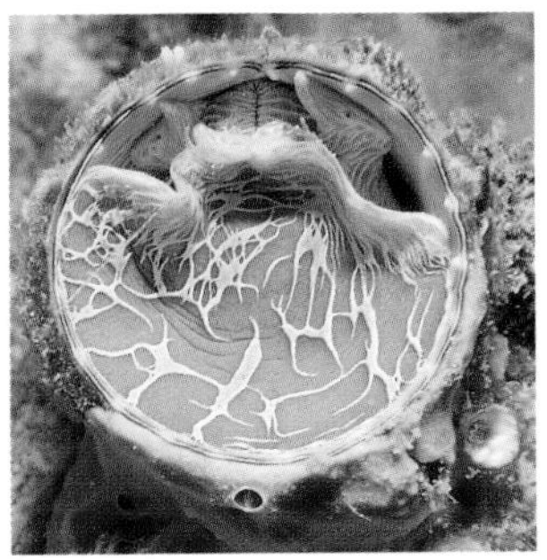

Variation of animal from Lizard Island, Queensland.

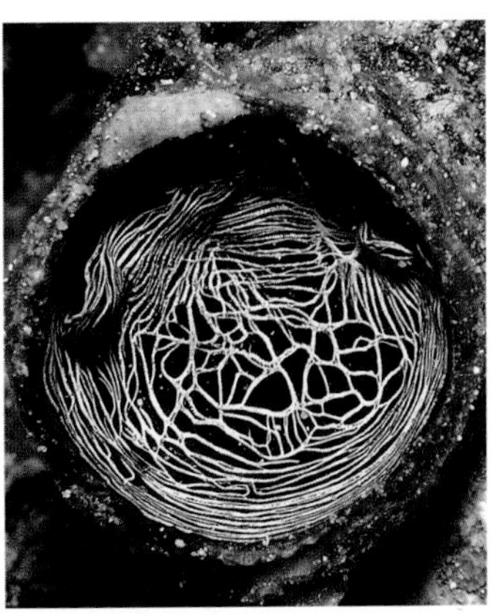

STROMBIDAE
Arthritic spider shell
Lambis chiragra arthritica

Rubble, dead coral reef, hard bottom

8 to 25 metres (26 to 82 ft)

150 mm (6 in)

Specific to the West Indian Ocean this subspecies ranges from South Africa to the Maldives where it lives on broken bottom and rubble on reef. The shell is quite solid, covered by a periostracum (skin) and usually eroded or covered by algae.

Underside of Maldivian form shows the very dark colouration and dark teeth along the aperture.

A juvenile spider shell.

STROMBIDAE

Common spider shell

Lambis lambis

Sand, rubble, seagrass meadows, mud

Lt to 20 metres (0 to 66 ft)

228 mm (8.5 in)

Common across the Indo-Pacific only a few molluscs were encountered in the Maldives. They are herbivores and feed on filamentous algae growing on dead coral. Spider shell animals have excellent vision and if uprighted are able to turn themselves back over by way of their clawed (operculum) foot.

Dorsal aspect of a common spider shell, Port Moresby, Papua New Guinea.

STROMBIDAE

Scorpio spider shell

Lambis scorpio

Rubble, coral reef, rocky reef, mud

8 to 20 metres (26 to 66 ft)

170 mm (6.8 in)

This species is extremely difficult to see. Some forms have long delicate shell extensions and others living in rougher conditions have shorter shell extensions. However, the radial black and white lines across the underside are stable features.

Underside of shell, Port Moresby, Papua New Guinea.

STROMBIDAE

Truncate spider shell

Lambis truncata truncata

Sand, rubble, dead reef

10 to 30 metres (33 to 98 ft)

350 mm (14 in)

This giant spider shell is only found in the Indian Ocean from East Africa to the Maldives and is the largest known form in its family. It generally inhabits deeper water and the underside of the lip and aperture is white with a tinge of yellow. Old shells are heavier and have shorter lip extensions.

Underside of a truncate spider shell, Seychelles.

Side-on aspect of the shell.

CYPRAEIDAE

Ringed money cowry

Cypraea annulus

Coral reefs, rocky reefs, rubble, seagrass meadows

Lt to 5 metres (0 to 16 ft)

30 mm (1.2 in)

An integral part of the Maldivian economy for many hundreds of years the ringed money cowry was used as currency throughout the Indo-Pacific. A common intertidal species it lives beneath rocks and around algae covered rubble during the day. Ringed money cowries feed on algae and breed during summer.

Colour variation from Moreton Bay, Queensland, Australia.

Colour variation from Port Moresby, Papua New Guinea.

CYPRAEIDAE
Carnelian cowry
Cypraea carneola
Coral reefs, rocky reefs
Lt to 8 metres (0 to 26 ft)
50 mm (2 in)

Throughout most of its Indo-Pacific range the carnelian cowry can be located beneath rocks and dead coral at low tide. This mollusc illustrated was found on a night dive. The shell of this species can be easily identified by its purple aperture and teeth.

CYPRAEIDAE
Eroded cowry
Cypraea erosa
Coral reefs, rocky reefs
Lt to 10 metres (0 to 33 ft)
50 mm (2 in)

Named for the thick roughened shell edge and very coarse aperture teeth the eroded cowry is a very common shallow water species in the harbours, break waters and lagoons in the Maldives with a range extending each way across the Indo-Pacific. Breeding is in September/October.

Close up of eggs.

On Australia's east coast the mantle papillae of this species are extremely long.

With its mantle fully extended the eroded cowry is extremely difficult to see.

CYPRAEIDAE

Isabel cowry

Cypraea isabella

Coral reefs, rocky reefs

Lt to 5 metres (0 to 16 ft)

40 mm (1.6 in)

With its fawn colour, three orange bands and bright orange shell pustulations at front and rear this species is very easy to identify. It has a long range across the Indo-Pacific and in most localities has black specks in lines along the dorsal surface.

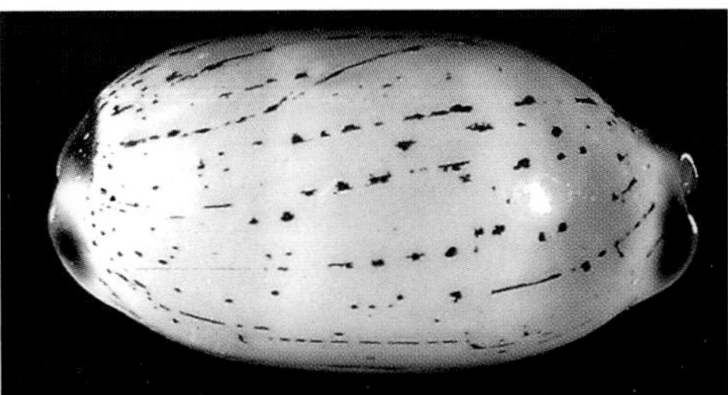

Variation, Coral Sea.

CYPRAEIDAE

Lynx cowry

Cypraea lynx

Coral reefs, rocky reefs

Lt to 10 metres (0 to 33 ft)

50 mm (2 in)

Found beneath dead coral slabs and rocks in the intertidal zone across the Indo-Pacific specimens found in the Maldives were located living in caves below low tide level. Females are bigger than males and a white egg mass is laid beneath a rock usually in July/August.

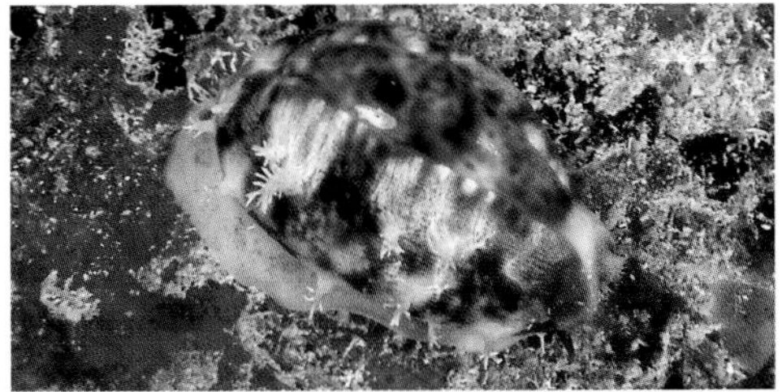

Colour variation with partly raised mantle, Great Barrier Reef.

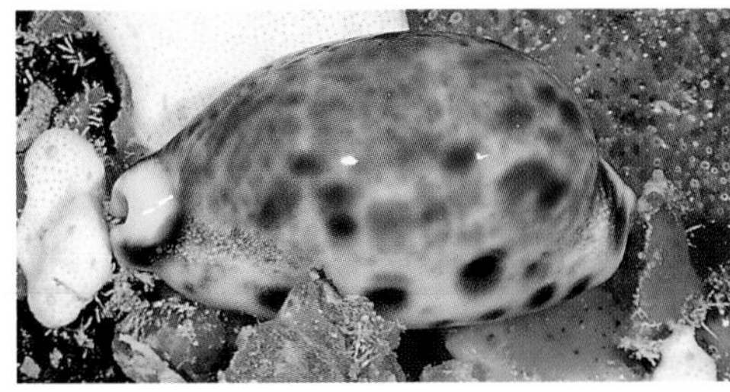

CYPRAEIDAE

Reticulated cowry

Cypraea maculifera

Coral reefs, rocky reefs

2 to 5 metres

60 mm (2.2 in)

A solid chunky shell with black spots at each end, a large reticulated dorsal pattern and a black animal. This species is generally only found in shallow water intertidally, along the sea walls or amongst boulders on the tops of reefs. Food is mainly algae scraped from reef or rocks.

CYPRAEIDAE
Money cowry
Cypraea moneta
Coral reefs, rocky reefs, rubble
Lt to 10 metres (0 to 33 ft)
30 mm (1.2 in)

Any successful species which has a large habitat spread across many thousands of kilometres is going to be variable, yet as can be seen by the illustrations the colours of the shells and the animals may be more or less, but all quite relative to each other.

Juvenile, Maldives.

Large adult money cowry with extended mantle, Dampier, Western Australia.

Bright yellow shells were once highly prized in the shell money trade. This form from the Great Barrier Reef shows variation in shell colour and mantle.

CYPRAEIDAE
Pustulose cowry
Cypraea staphlea
Coral reefs, rocky reefs
Lt to 8 metres (0 to 26 ft)
33 mm (1.4 in)

A very easily recognised species which feeds on encrusting wine coloured sponges the pustulose cowry is a relatively common shallow water mollusc found beneath dead coral and rocks in the central Maldives and throughout the Indo-Pacific.

Dorsal aspect from the Maldives showing the wine coloured mantle and white papillae.

One of the larger cowry shells this species is not regarded as common; it is recorded from the extreme low tide level living beneath dead coral rocks but seems more prevalent in deeper water. Maldivian shells do not appear significantly different to those living in the Pacific Ocean.

CYPRAEIDAE
Mole Cowry
Cypraea talpa
Coral reefs, rocky reefs
Lt to 20 metres (0 to 66 ft)
90 mm (3.6 in)

A female mole cowry with mantle and foot fully expanded sitting on a clutch of eggs. She will protect them until they hatch.

Fairly common in the Maldives and across its Indo-Pacific range the tiger cowry is nocturnal, the shallow water forms living beneath dead coral rocks and deeper water ones living in caves and beneath ledges.

CYPRAEIDAE
Tiger cowry
Cypraea tigris
Coral reefs, rocky reefs
Lt to 20 metres (0 to 66 ft)
130 mm (5 in)

A living tiger cowry at night showing the mantle almost fully extended.

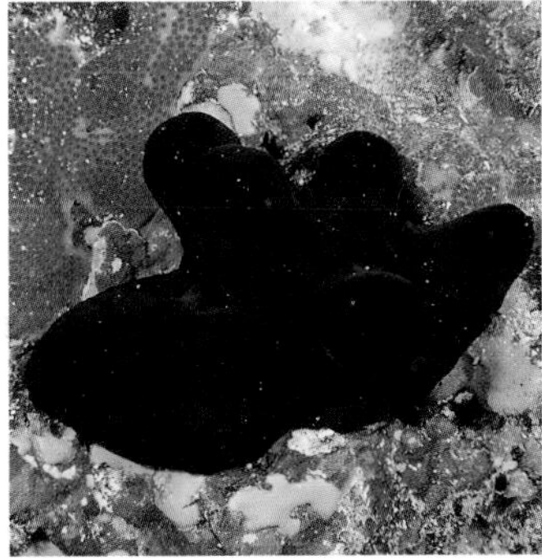

Varying in colour between brown and dark blue this species of lamellarid has a number of black spots on the body and to date is only known from the Maldives. Many species of lamellarids feed on ascidians.

LAMELLARIIDAE
Hiby's lamellarid
Coriocella hibyae
Coral reefs, rocky reefs
10 to 20 metres (33 to 66 ft)
40 mm (1.6 in)

NATICIDAE
Dark-marked moon snail
Polinices melanotomoibes
Sandy sea floor, lagoons
2 to 15 metres (6.6 to 49 ft)
40 mm (1.6 in)

With a brown blotched shell and a pure white animal this species lives beneath the sand where it makes foraging trails in the sand as it hunts down bivalve molluscs. It drills holes in the bivalve shells with its radula and proceeds to shred up the mollusc within, leaving only the empty shell.

A bivalve shell showing a hole drilled by a moon snail.

A moon snail egg case.

CASSIDAE
Giant helmet
Cassis cornuta
Sand
5 to 30 metres (16 to 98 ft)
355 mm (14 in)

Vulnerable to over-collecting for the tourist trade, in many areas of their Indo-Pacific distribution they have been fished out, or are fully protected by law. Small numbers are fished in the Maldives where they are not considered common. Giant helmets feed on heart urchins they dig out of the sand and will also hunt regular urchins on flat reef.

BURSIDAE

Giant frog shell

Bursa bubo

Coral reefs, rocky reefs

5 to 25 metres (16 to 82 ft)

180 mm (7 in)

Most giant frog shells are heavily encrusted with coralline algae and other encrusting marine life making them difficult to see on the reef slopes and terraces. They are very well known from a number of atolls in the Maldives. Females are bigger than males and they lay long upright capsules which they sit on and protect until they hatch.

A distinctive aperture enables easy identification, Maldives.

BURSIDAE

Blood-stained frog shell

Bursa cruenta

Coral reefs, rocky reefs

5 to 20 metres (16 to 66 ft)

40 mm (1.5 in)

Regularly observed on reefs across the Indo-Pacific this species is not uncommon in the Maldives living in caves or beneath dead coral and rocks. Shells are heavily encrusted and identification is generally made by the presence of a number of red or black marks on the inside of the aperture.

BURSIDAE
Lamarck's frog shell
Bursa lamarcki
Coral reefs, rocky reefs
8 to 20 metres (16 to 66 ft)
50 mm (2 in)

A very difficult species to find Lamarck's frog shell hardly resembles a shell it is so encrusted with other marine life. It is not considered to be common anywhere throughout its Indo-Pacific range and is rare in the Maldives.

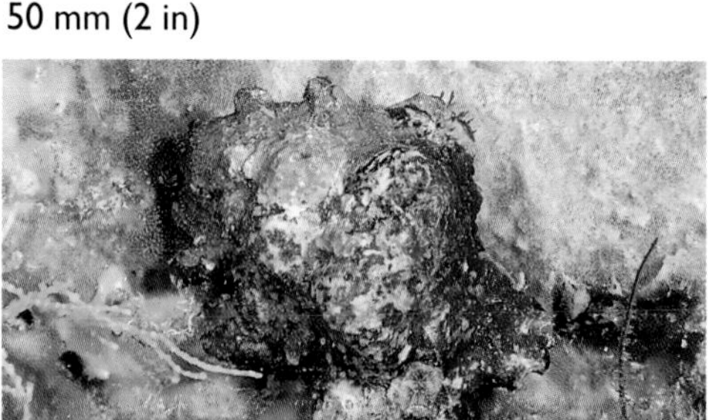

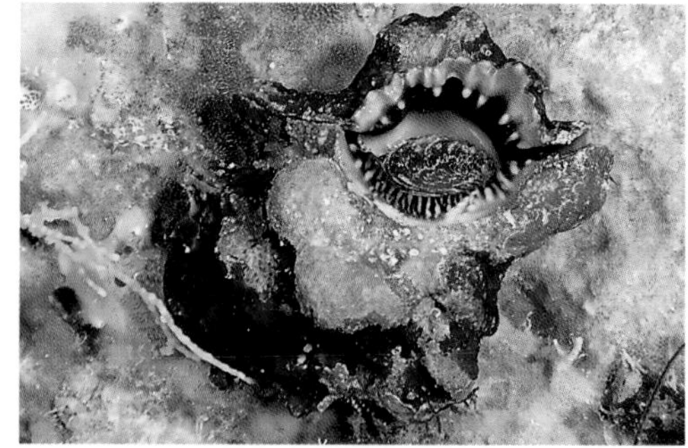

This shell has a very distinctive black band in the aperture and white teeth.

RANELLIDAE
Robin-redbreast triton
Cymatium rubeculum
Coral reefs, rocky reefs
Lt to 20 metres (0 to 66 ft)
40 mm (1.6 in)

Living as it does beneath dead coral slabs and rocks this species is only seen out in the open during the night. The very attractive shell colouration is natural and the shell is protected by a periostracum or skin which is why there are few encrustations. Although it is recorded throughout the Indo-Pacific, it is not commonly observed.

The very distinctive aperture.

RANELLIDAE
Black-banded triton
Cymatium hepaticum
Coral reefs, rocky reefs
5 to 20 metres (16 to 66 ft)
50 mm (2 in)

Similar to the robin-redbreast triton this species has very definite black bands in the sutures running around the shell. The black-banded triton ranges throughout the Indo-Pacific but is not regarded as common at any one location.

RANELLIDAE

Giant triton, triton's trumpet

Charonia tritonis

Coral reefs, rocky reefs

5 to 30 metres (16 to 98 ft)

457 mm (18 in)

Giant tritons eat many kinds of echinoderms. A crown-of-thorns sea star may be almost 450 mm (18 in) across; the stomach of a giant triton is quite small by comparison and could not hold a crown-of-thorns (even minced up) in a two or three hours eating session. Published statements on giant tritons "completely swallowing the poisonous mass of spines" are somewhat exaggerated, not based on facts, and completely misleading.

The very characteristic aperture on the giant triton has teeth on the lip to hold prey down and stop it from escaping while feeding is in progress.

Giant triton shell feeding on a small crown-of-thorns. It stayed in this position for three days and nights without consuming the sea star.

TONNIDAE

Partridge tun

Tonna perdix

Sand, coral reefs, rocky reefs

Lt to 20 metres (0 to 66 ft)

150 mm (6 in)

Although the partridge tun buries in the sand during the day, at night it hunts across the flats and up onto the reef. It feeds mostly on sea cucumbers.

EPITONIIDAE

Golden wentletrap

Epitonium billeeanum

Coral reefs, rocky reefs

8 to 20 metres (26 to 66 ft)

15 mm (0.6 in)

With a distribution ranging from South Africa to the Sea of Cortez in Mexico the golden wentletrap is a very well documented species. It is found in the vicinity of *Tubastraea* corals which live in caves under ledges and on drop-off walls in current areas. The golden wentletraps feed on the coral polyps and lay their eggs on them. Female golden wentletraps can be twice the size of the males.

Female golden wentletrap with eggs, Seychelles.

Male and female golden wentletraps with developing eggs, Heron Island, Great Barrier Reef.

MURICIDAE

Scorched murex

Chicoreus microphyllus

Coral reefs, rocky reefs

5 to 20 metres (16 to 66 ft)

120 mm (4.8 in)

Due to the encrusting bright orange commensal sponge which grows on scorched murex shells they are easy to find underwater and as such are well recorded across the Indo-Pacific. However, other closely-related species of murex are also encrusted with sponge and many people (including some shell book authors) think that it is the true colour of the shell. This has led to a great deal of confusion. The scorched murex has fine brown and white bands, short varice fronds and a yellow aperture.

Specimen shell showing the identification features.

MURICIDAE
Rose-fronded murex
Chicoreus palmarosae
Coral reefs, rocky reefs
5 to 30 metres (16 to 98 ft)
150 mm (6 in)

Shaped very similar to other species of *Chicoreus* spp. murex shells, the rose-fronded murex has a beautiful pink or mauve colouration on the insides of the fronds, jet black teeth on the outer aperture lip and black teeth on the inner aperture lip. The frond opposite the top of the aperture is usually very well developed. This species occurs from Sri Lanka throughout the Maldives and across into the Pacific regions.

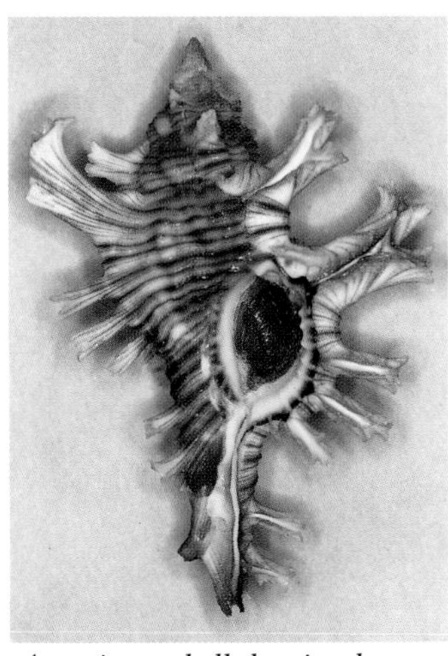

A specimen shell showing key identification features, Great Barrier Reef.

Underside view of the rose-fronded murex, Maldives.

MURICIDAE
Stout murex
Chicoreus sp.
Rocky reef
3 to 10 metres (6.6 to 33 ft)
100 mm (4 in)

This is a very solid chunky shell with simple fronding. The outer edge of the aperture lip has very well developed teeth stained black or dark red and the inner side (columellar) of the aperture lip is white and smooth. So far as is known this species has only been found under the rocks and pods of the sea walls. The orange colour is from a commensal encrusting sponge.

Underside view of the Stout murex, Maldives.

MURICIDAE
Giant murex
Chicoreus ramosus
Coral reefs, rocky reefs, rubble, sand
10 to 40 metres (33 to 131 ft)
300 mm (12 in)

Often seen on drop offs and caves drilling holes in giant thorny oysters, this is the largest species of murex shell and it is found throughout the entire Indo-Pacific region. The giant murex lives in a variety of habitats and seems equally at home on soft bottom as hard. The inside of the aperture (columellar) is pink. Females are larger than males.

Close up of giant murex egg capsules. The central spot is a "soft spot" escape hatch that the small veligers will break open when they emerge.

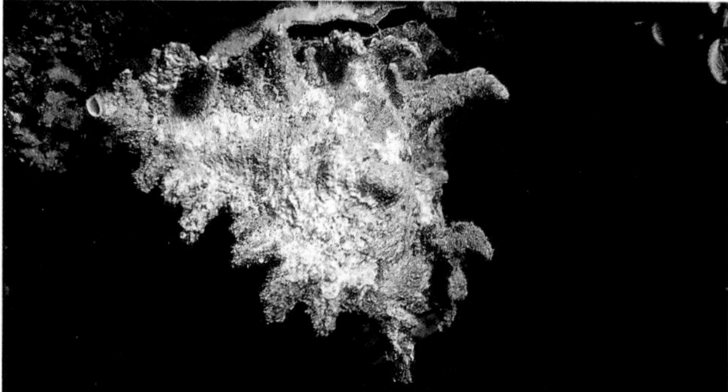

Giant murexes laying eggs on a large rock.

MURICIDAE
Anatomical murex
Homalocantha anatomica

Coral reefs, rocky reefs

5 to 20 metres (16 to 66 ft)

60 mm (2.4 in)

Extremely well camouflaged in its habitat the anatomical murex is almost invisible at a distance. They inhabit the tops of dead coral heads and dead table corals where they feed on tube worms. The Maldivian specimens have very well developed varices and are larger than those from other areas in the Indo-Pacific.

Underside view illustrating that the previous picture really is a shell.

CORALLIOPHILIDAE
Violet-mouthed coral shell
Coralliophila neritoidea

Coral reefs

3 to 20 metres (10 to 66 ft)

35 mm (1.4 in)

Always found on live corals this species has a particular affinity with *Porites* sp. corals upon which they feed. Shells generally congregate in hollows or crevices where they are protected and are usually heavily encrusted by coralline algae. Females are larger than males and lay oval transparent egg capsules half-filled with pink eggs. These capsules are kept within the shell and brooded. The young are released after hatching. Very common throughout the Indo-Pacific.

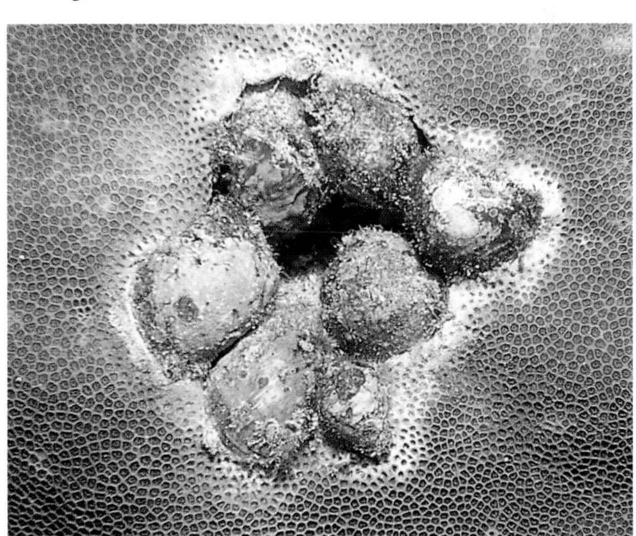

Underside of the violet-mouthed coral shell showing the brooded egg capsules.

FASCIOLARIIDAE

Filamentose spindle shell

Pleuroploca filamentosa

Coral reefs, rocky reefs

Lt to 20 metres (0 to 66 ft)

120 mm (5 in)

A common Indo-Pacific species the filamentose spindle shell is variable in colour ranging from light to dark brown bands across the shell. It lives beneath dead coral slabs during the day and comes out at night to hunt other non-operculum (trap-doored) molluscs (trochoids) which are attacked through their open non-protected aperture and smothered.

FASCIOLARIIDAE

Many-angled spindle shell

Latirus polygonus

Coral reefs, rocky reefs

Lt to 10 metres (0 to 33 ft)

70 mm (2.6 in)

Hardly resembling anything but a piece of encrusted dead coral adult many-angled spindle shells are always heavily overgrown. This Maldivian form is laying eggs out in the open on the reef and appears to be adapted to living in the open, whereas most of these molluscs live beneath dead coral and rocks during the day.

Specimen shell showing its identifying features, Great Barrier Reef.

OLIVIDAE

Ringed olive shell

Oliva annulata

Sand

Lt to 10 metres (0 to 33 ft)

60 mm (2.2 in)

Found in tracks under the sand during the day this species comes up on incoming tides in the late afternoon and at night. Although variable across its Indo-Pacific range the illustration depicts a typical Indian Ocean form. Inside the aperture is bright orange.

MITRIDAE

Giant mitre

Mitra mitra

Sand

Lt to 20 metres (0 to 66 ft)

180 mm (6.6 in)

Fairly common in shallow water lagoons in the Maldives and throughout the Indo-Pacific this very easily identified species is found in sand tracks both day and night. The giant mitre has an extremely long white proboscis which is used to hunt out tube worms.

MITRIDAE

Butterfly mitre

Neocancilla papilio

Sand

5 to 15 metres (16 to 49 ft)

60 mm (2.4 in)

A fairly common well known species distributed throughout the Indo-Pacific; the Indian Ocean forms appear richer in colour than those in the Pacific. Mitrids are known to prey on worms but this species also eats the eggs of other mitre shells.

COSTELLARIDAE

Grainy mitre

Domiporta granitina

Sand

5 to 10 metres (16 to 33 ft)

25 mm (1 in)

Common in a number of Maldivian lagoons the grainy mitre lives in colonies and during the day can only be located in trails beneath the sand. It has been recorded from many other Indo-Pacific locations.

CONIDAE
Sand-speckled cone
Conus arenatus
Sand
Lt to 10 metres (0 to 33 ft)
40 mm (1.6 in)

Very common throughout the Maldives this cone inhabits many shallow water lagoons. During the day it lives under the sand and can be found in trails. At night it is often seen crawling along the sandy bottom. The shell has coronations on the shoulder and the animal has a red tip on the siphon.

CONIDAE
Princely cone
Conus aulicus
Sand, coral reef
Lt to 20 metres (0 to 66 ft)
140 mm (5.6 in)

Although its distribution stretches from East Africa to the Pacific this species is by no means common. It lives in sand under dead coral during the day and comes out at night to hunt other univalves and small fish. They should not be handled.

CONIDAE
Tiger cone
Conus canonicus
Sand, rubble, coral reef, rocky reef
Lt to 10 metres (0 to 33 ft)
60 mm (2.4 in)

The tiger cone is superficially similar to the textile cone but the markings are finer, the tent pattern is often larger, the shell has a less developed shoulder and the aperture is narrower. This venomous species lives beneath rocks on hard bottom and rubble and feeds on other univalves.

Extremely common in some Maldivian lagoons the ivory cone lives buried in the sand during the day and comes up on the surface at night to hunt prey. It is very variable in the size of its black spots but the spots are all in concentric bands around the shell.

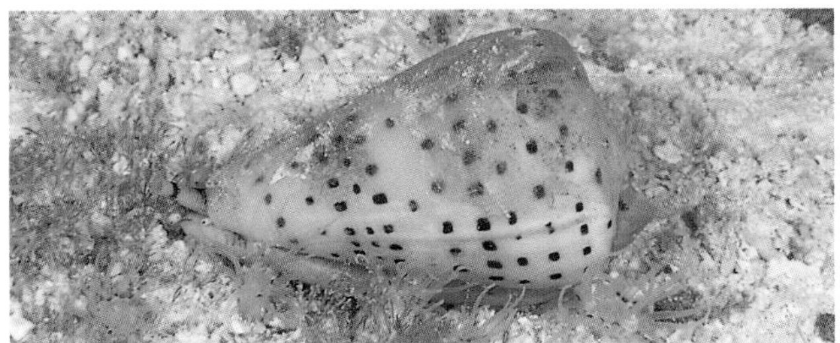

CONIDAE
Ivory cone
Conus eburneus
Sand
Lt to 20 metres (0 to 66 ft)
50 mm (2 in)

Living in the open on reef it has an easily recognisable pattern somewhat similar to the captain cone; the shell of the weasel cone is much slimmer. The outer shell skin (periostracum) in the illustrated Maldivian form has been grazed on by an unknown animal. The weasel cone occurs throughout the Indo-Pacific where it is considered uncommon.

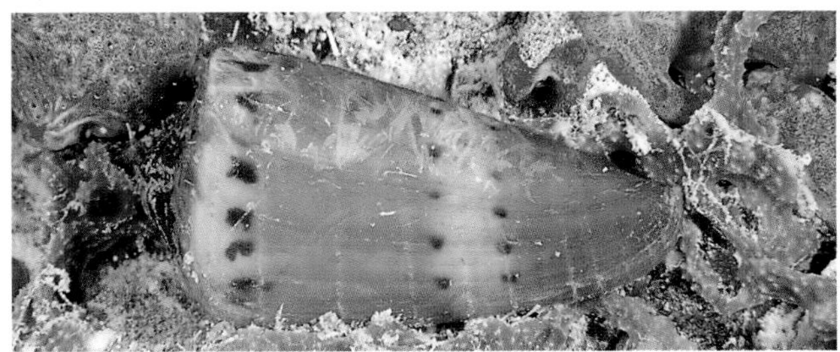

CONIDAE
Weasel cone
Conus mustelinus
Coral reefs, rocky reefs
5 to 25 metres (10 to 82 ft)
60 mm (2.4 in)

A very common species seen in coarse sand and rubble habitats it feeds on worms and is not considered harmful to humans. It has two broad light and dark bands of colour, fine concentric lines and the periostracum (skin) is usually intact. The planorbis cone is encountered across the Indo-Pacific.

CONIDAE
Planorbis cone
Conus planorbis
Sand, rubble
Lt to 10 metres (0 to 33 ft)
45 mm (1.8 in)

CONIDAE

Tessellated cone

Conus tessellatus

Sand

Lt to 40 metres (0 to 120 ft)

45 mm (1.8 in)

A very attractive subsand dwelling species only coming to the surface on late afternoon incoming tides or at night. The tessellated cone is not commonly encountered but has been recorded from South Africa to Mexico. It feeds on worms and is generally covered by a yellow periostracum.

CONIDAE

Zonated cone

Conus zonatus

Rubble

10 to 20 metres (33 to 66 ft)

65 mm (2.5 in)

Known from the Indian Ocean the zonated cone is not considered common but is certainly not rare in the Maldives. It favours deeper water and lives buried on rubble slopes amongst reef during the day coming out only at night. This species is believed to feed on other univalve molluscs.

TEREBRIDAE

Lance auger

Hastula lanceata

Sand

Lt to 10 metres (0 to 33 ft)

65 mm (2.5 in)

A clean shiny shell with fine-lined dashes down its full length this species is quite common across the Indo-Pacific and the Maldivian form illustrated differs little to other forms thousands of kilometres away.

Recorded from East Africa across to the Pacific this very common auger is generally restricted to shallow water lagoons. Colour is variable but the smooth shell and patterned lines are good distinguishing features.

TEREBRIDAE
Similar auger
Terebra affinis
Sand
Lt to 10 metres (0 to 33 ft)
50 mm (2 in)

A solid, thick, heavy shell which leaves massive tracks in the sand as it drags itself along searching for prey. It is very easy to recognise as no other species is as large or has similar markings. It is distributed across the entire Indo-Pacific to Lord Howe Island.

TEREBRIDAE
Marlin spike auger
Terebra maculata
Sand
Lt to 40 metres (0 to 131 ft)
228 mm (9 in)

Common across the Indo-Pacific the smooth shell and squarish blotches enable simple identification. Similar to most augers this species lives under the sand creating trails as it moves around in search of worms, its staple diet.

TEREBRIDAE
Subulate auger
Terebra subulata
Sand
Lt to 20 metres (0 to 66 ft)
130 mm (5 in)

SUBCLASS: *Opisthobranchia* (Nudibranchs, Pleurobranchs, Bubble shells, Sea hares)

Features: Entirely marine, the opisthobranchs are the 'butterflies' of the sea and are among the most beautiful and spectacular underwater creatures. Over 3000 species have been described across the world with new undescribed species being discovered on a regular basis.

These molluscs may have reduced external shells, internal shells, or no shells at all in their adult form. They may have gills behind or beside their visceral mass, or they may have no gills at all, depending on the respiratory functions of the skin, or on the other parts of the body (such as pustules or cerata). Many have a well-defined head, one pair of eyes and at least one pair of tentacles. The eyes are reduced, or non-existent in some species, with most only acting as light receptors.

Lifestyle: They are generally active, mobile animals, and some are even able to swim. With specific plant or animal diets many are seasonal in their appearance and live in almost every habitat available in the sea. Some are easy to see and advertise their presence with blatantly brilliant colours hiding their repugnant and bad tasting properties. The bright colours and patterns serve as a warning to visual predators. However, they may still be preyed upon by others of their own group who cannot see them.

Many are cryptically coloured and blend into their habitat or food source so well that it's almost impossible to see them. Opisthobranchs range in size from several millimetres up to 300 mm (1 ft) and live intertidally down to and beyond 182 metres (300 ft).

Reproduction: Almost all species are hermaphrodites with each individual in a mating pair transferring and receiving sperm, though some (such as sea hares) may form groups, or mating chains, each fertilising individual laying its own egg mass or string which is mostly spiral and may contain a million eggs. Most species have planktonic larvae dispersal. Some are born male and as they grow develop into females.

Associations: Some species are used by shrimps and crabs for protection and transport and other species are parasitised by copepods. Very little has been recorded in this area.

Identification: Most species (wherever known) can be identified from a good colour photograph or colour reproduction. However, due to their wide distribution numbers of colour variations exist which sometimes makes identification difficult without comparative illustrations or previous knowledge.

AGLAJIDAE

Blue-edged Philinopsis

Philinopsis cyanea

Sand

Lt to 20 metres (0 to 66 ft)

45 mm (1.8 in)

Although this species is variable in the amount of yellow or orange stripes on the body the blue line around the mantle edge and a flat nose are good identifying features. Distributed from South Africa across to Australia this slug lives in a coarse sand habitat.

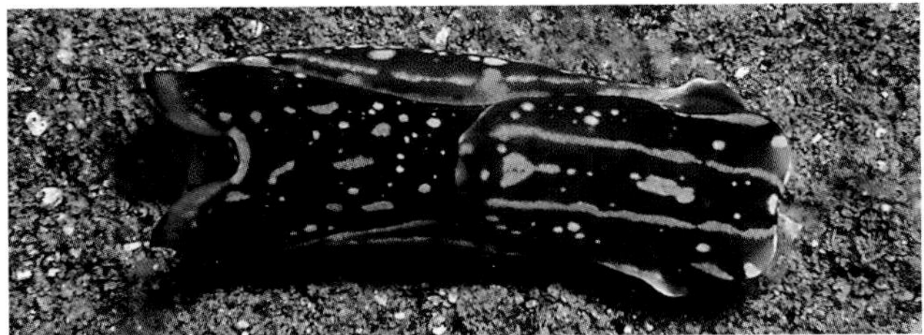

AGLAJIDAE

Gardiner's Philinopsis

Philinopsis gardineri

Sand, rubble

Lt to 20 metres (0 to 66 ft)

65 mm (2.6 in)

Known from the Maldives to the Great Barrier Reef this species varies little across its distribution, though the yellow band at the rear of the head shield may be present or absent. It feeds on worms and bubble shells.

APLYSIIDAE

Eared sea hare

Dolabella auricularia

Seagrass meadows, mud, sand, rubble

1 to 30 metres (3 to 98 ft)

300 mm (12 in)

Ranging from South Africa to the South Pacific the eared sea hare is fairly common in some areas. During the day it may be found on hard coral substrates beneath dead coral or in seagrass meadows in a sleeping position. It feeds on green algal turf and seagrass and will squirt out large amounts of purple dye if disturbed.

APLYSIIDAE

Long-tailed sea hare

Stylocheilus longicauda

Coral reefs, rocky reefs

Lt to 35 metres (0 to 115 ft)

60 mm (2.4 in)

Recorded from South Africa to Mexico this sea hare has fine lines running down the length of the body and iridescent blue spots. In many cases, this species forms aggregations to spawn. The eggs are laid in an irregular tangle of spaghetti-like strands.

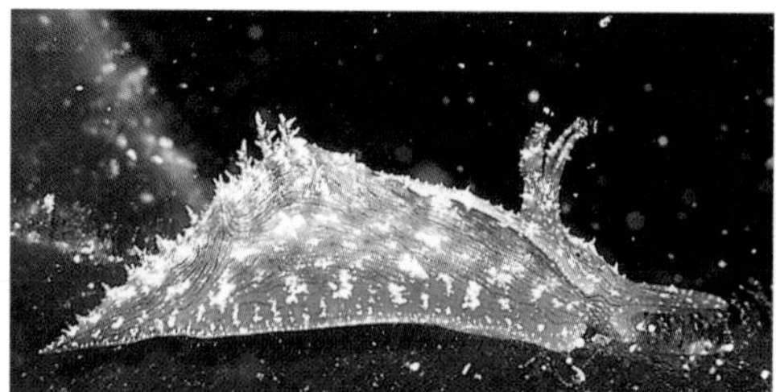

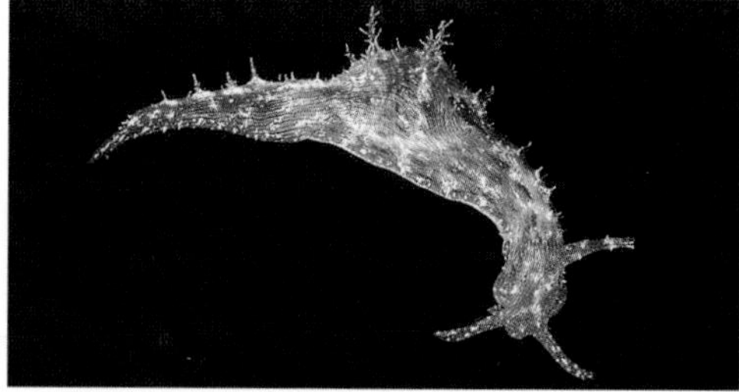

Variation, Lord Howe Island, South Pacific.

PLAKOBRANCHIDAE

Ornate Elysia

Elysia ornata

Coral reefs, rocky reefs

Lt to 18 metres (0 to 59 ft)

40 mm (1.6 in)

This species feeds on algae and ranges across the Indo-Pacific. Colour can vary from green with white and black specs on the side of the body to green with black and white specks on the side of the body. However, the black margin line bordered by a lower line of orange, or orange and white, appears stable.

PLAKOBRANCHIDAE

Neon Thurdilla

Thurdilla neona

Coral reefs, rocky reefs

5 to 20 metres (16 to 66 ft)

20 mm (0.8 in)

Known to occur from the Maldives across the Indo-Pacific to Lord Howe Island this species is very variable. Some forms have deep brown undulating saddles and others have shallow brown saddles.

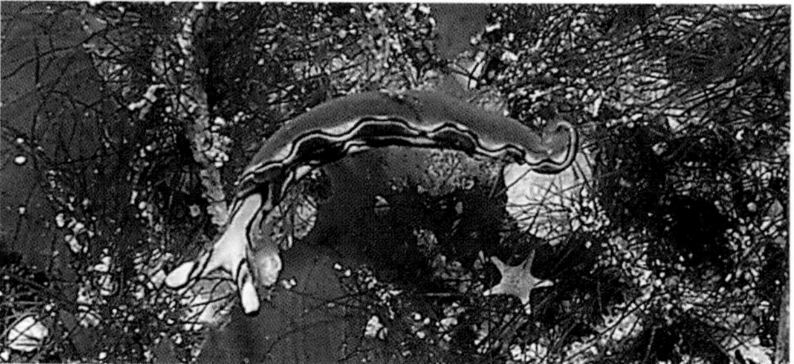

POLYBRANCHIIDAE
Black and gold Cycerce
Cycerce nigricans

Coral reefs, rocky reefs

Lt to 10 metres (0 to 33 ft)

50 mm (2 in)

An easily identified species ranging from South Africa to eastern Australia this delicate flamboyant slug moves its cerata when it is crawling and can actually swim by flapping them backwards and forwards. However, if harassed the cerata atonomise (are cast off) and will continue to wave even when separated from the slug.

PLEUROBRANCHIDAE
Marten's side-gilled slug
Berthella martensi

Coral reefs, rocky reefs

Lt to 25 metres (0 to 82 ft)

60 mm (2.4 in)

Ranging from Mauritius across the entire Indo-Pacific to Panama in South America this side-gilled slug is a well-known species. It is variable in colour and can be dark brown, cream, white, orange or black with brown spots, black spots, yellow spots or white spots or specks.

Colour variation, Maldives.

PLEUROBRANCHIDAE

Lemon side-gilled slug

Berthellina citrina

Coral reefs, rocky reefs

Lt to 40 metres (131 ft)

50 mm (2 in)

A very common well-known species recorded from South Africa to New Zealand this species lives beneath rocks and dead coral during the day and only comes out at night. It feeds on sponges and lays an orange spiral egg mass.

Colour variation, Seychelles.

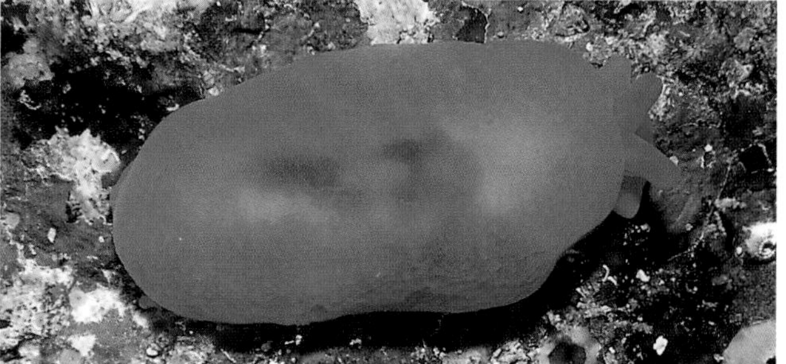

Colour variation, Norfolk Island.

POLYCERIDAE

Kubary Nembrotha

Nembrotha kubaryana

Coral reefs, rocky reefs

3 to 20 metres (10 to 66 ft)

110 mm (4.4 in)

There is a lot of colour variation in this species, with the Indian Ocean form having many red pustules which often blend, and the Pacific form having green pustules larger and more separated. This species lives in the open during the day.

POLYCERIDAE
Olive Tambja
Tambja olivaria
Coral reefs, rocky reefs
8 to 25 metres (26 to 82 ft)
60 mm (2.6 in)

Endemic to the Maldives this characteristic nudibranch may be seen out in the open in the day time. Similar to other species within this genus the olive Tambja feeds exclusively on the blue bryozoan *Bugula* sp. (Photo: Musthag Hussain)

AEGIRIDAE
Gardiner's Notodoris
Notodoris gardineri
Coral reefs, rocky reefs
Lt to 20 metres (0 to 66 ft)
77 mm (3 in)

The body of this nudibranch is very rigid and quite firm to the touch. It feeds on sponges particularly *Pericharax heterorhaphis* the volcano sponge (in the Pacific). It ranges from the Maldives to Lord Howe Island is fairly common across its distribution.

Colour variation, Great Barrier Reef.

Egg ribbon of Gardiner's Notodoris nudibranch.

GYMNODORIDIDAE

Ceylon Gymnodoris

Gymnodoris ceylonica

Sand, rubble

Lt to 20 metres (0 to 66 ft)

60 mm (2.4 in)

Known as a predator on sea hares (Coleman, 1981) and other opisthobranchs this species has been recorded from many areas in the Indo-Pacific. It lays orange egg strings and a number of animals may congregate to mate and lay eggs.

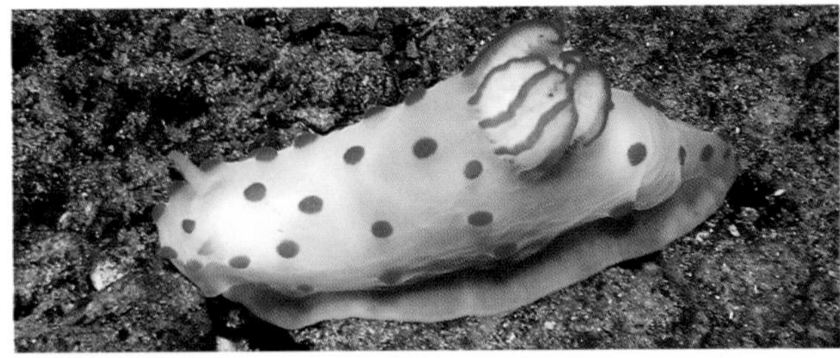

GYMNODORIDIDAE

Red papulose Gymnodoris

Gymnodoris rubropapulosa

Sand, rubble, dead coral

5 to 10 metres (16 to 33 ft)

50 mm (2 in)

Found from the Maldives to Australia the red papulous Gymnodoris is not considered common across its distribution. Colour varies from solid orange pustules or orange circles. (Photo: Wally Rowlands)

Juvenile, Port Moresby, Papua New Guinea.

DORIDIDAE

Tessellated Halgerda

Halgerda tessellata

Coral reefs, rocky reefs

Lt to 20 metres (0 to 66 ft)

30 mm (1.2 in)

Fairly rare across most of its Indo-Pacific range this species can be seen on reef in the open or found beneath dead coral slabs. Although it may vary in its predominant colour from red to orange the small white dots on black in the body depressions are constant.

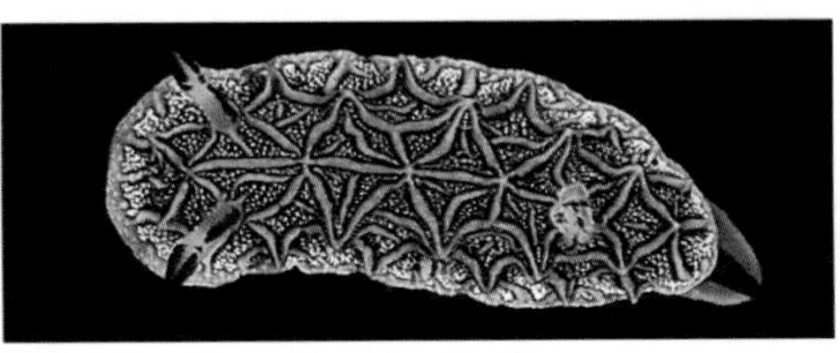

Juvenile, Great Barrier Reef.

A very distinctive nudibranch distributed throughout the Indo-Pacific. This species appears to mature sexually at a fairly small size as very large forms and small forms have been seen to congregate together during mating and spawning sessions.

DORIDIDAE

Funeral Jorunna

Jorunna funebris

Coral reefs, rocky reefs

Lt to 25 metres (0 to 82 ft)

80 mm (3.2 in)

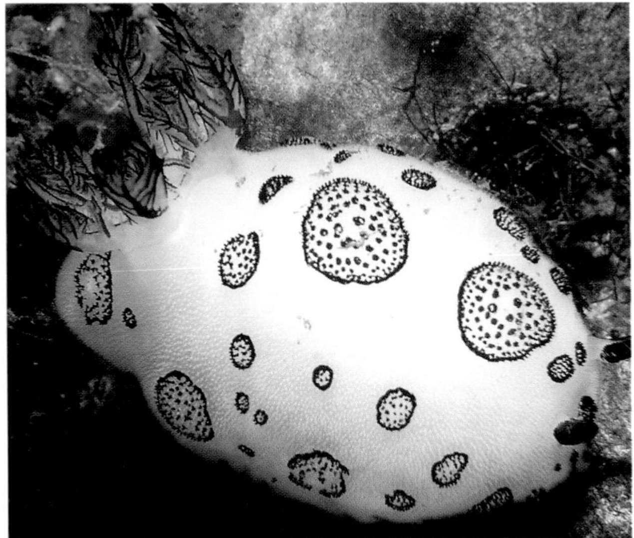

Spawning on food sponge showing newly laid eggs, Kimbe Bay, Papua New Guinea (right).

Unique and distinctive in its overall appearance the red-lined Kentrodoris is rarely encountered across its Indo-Pacific range though it has been recorded from a number of areas. It is found in the open during the day (generally on sand) and lays a pink crenulated egg ribbon.

DORIDIDAE

Red-lined Kentrodoris

Kentrodoris rubescens

Sand, rubble, dead reef

Lt to 18 metres (0 to 59 ft)

170 mm (6.8 in)

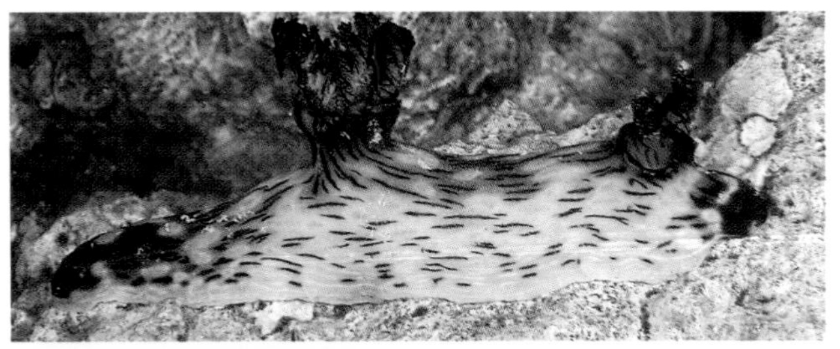

Colour variation, Bali, Indonesia.

DORIDIDAE
Magnificent Ceratosoma
Ceratosoma magnifica
Coral reefs, rocky reefs
Lt to 30 metres (0 to 98 ft)
80 mm (3.2 in)

An extraordinary nudibranch this species ranges across the Indo-Pacific and with such a distinctive shape and colour pattern can hardly be mistaken for any other species. It lives in the open, feeds on sponges and has a very firm body.

Tweed Heads, New South Wales, Australia.

DORIDIDAE
Netted Ceratosoma
Ceratosoma sp.
Coral reefs, rocky reefs
Lt to 20 metres (0 to 66 ft)
50 mm (2 in)

Although this nudibranch ranges across the Indo-Pacific it is very rarely seen due to its pustuled body and indistinctive colour pattern which blends into the surrounding reef. However, it is easily recognised by its crenulated mantle edge and network pattern. It appears to be an undescribed species. (Photo: Jorg Aebi)

DORIDAE

Dotted Platydoris

Platydoris sp.

Coral reefs, rocky reefs

10 to 20 metres (33 to 66 ft)

70 mm (2.8 in)

This very distinctive Maldivian species is unable to be identified to date. It lives beneath dead coral slabs during the day and has not been encountered before. It has minute, evenly spaced raised dots inside white circular patches.

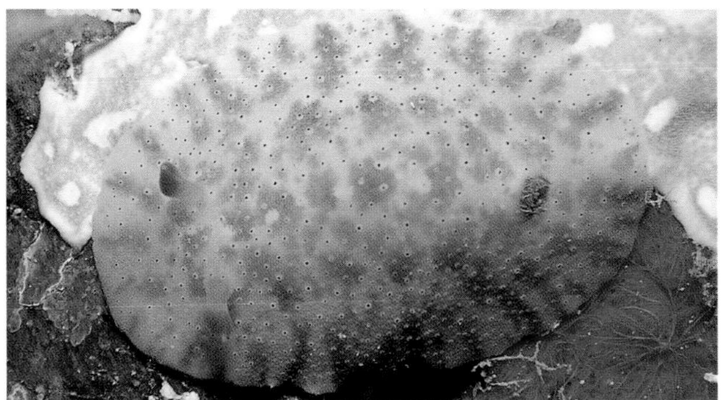

CHROMODORIDIDAE

Bouchet's Chromodoris

Chromodoris boucheti

Coral reefs, rocky reefs

10 to 30 metres (33 to 98 ft)

30 mm (1.2 in)

Found at a number of Indian Ocean localities this species is especially common throughout the Maldives. Quite often a number may be seen feeding on blue sponges which grow in caves.

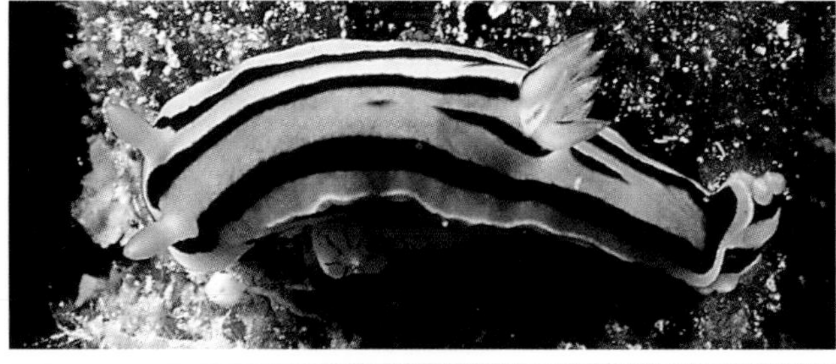

CHROMODORIDIDAE

Elisabeth's Chromodoris

Chromodoris elisabethina

Coral reefs, rocky reefs

Lt to 25 metres (0 to 82 ft)

45 mm (1.8 in)

Found across the Indo-Pacific this nudibranch is largely light blue on the dorsal surface with a narrow white line at the outer edge of the mantle. It is seen out in the open during the day and feeds on sponges.

CHROMODORIDIDAE
Geometric Chromodoris
Chromodoris geometrica
Coral reefs, rocky reefs
Lt to 20 metres (0 to 66 ft)
25 mm (1 in)

Although the Geometric Chromodoris is found across the Indo-Pacific and at times could be confused with other species superficially similar in colour it has a very soft body and its gills and rhinophores are greenish. When moving, the mantle edge is continually flexed; it feeds on sponges and lays an orange egg mass.

CHROMODORIDIDAE
Glenie's Chromodoris
Chromodoris gleniei
Coral reefs, rocky reefs
5 to 25 metres (16 to 82 ft)
45 mm (1.8 in)

A very distinctive nudibranch endemic to the Indian Ocean, this species appears to be more common in the Maldives than it does in the Seychelles or at other locations. It lives in lagoons as well as on open reef and along drop offs; it feeds on sponges.

Colour variation, Maldives.

CHROMODORIDIDAE
Strigate Chromodoris
Chromodoris strigata
Coral reefs, rocky reefs
10 to 20 metres (33 to 66 ft)
15 mm (0.6 in)

Seen out in the open on reef during the day this nudibranch does not appear to be common in the Maldives. Over its Indo-Pacific range colour does vary but the pattern stays definite.

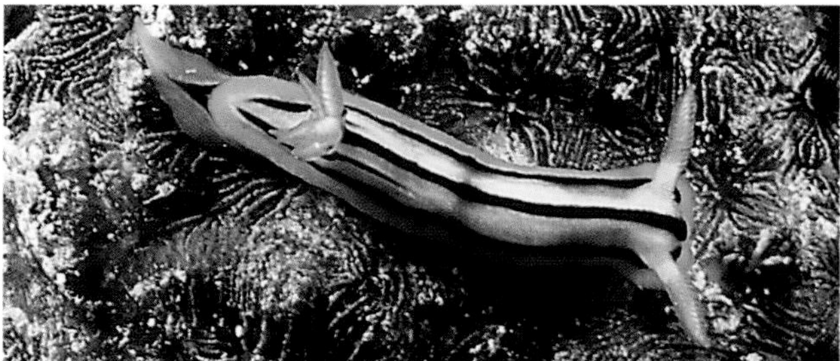

Endemic to the Indian Ocean this species lives in the open on reefs and terraced drop offs in the Seychelles but seems to be more prevalent in the Maldives where it can be seen in small groups (prelude to mating) around October.

CHROMODORIDIDAE
Tritos Chromodoris
Chromodoris tritos
Coral reefs, rocky reefs
10 to 30 metres (33 to 98 ft)
45 mm (1.8 in)

Distributed from East Africa to Fiji, the Indian Ocean form shown here is feeding on the black sponge *Hyritos* sp. upon which it also lays its egg ribbons.

Variation, Kimbe Bay, Papua New Guinea.

CHROMODORIDIDAE
Girdled Glossodoris
Glossodoris cincta
Coral reefs, rocky reefs
Lt to 25 metres (0 to 82 ft)
55 mm (2.2 in)

Ranging from the Maldives to eastern Australia, Emm's Hypsellodoris feeds on sponges and lays an undulated, coiled egg mass. This species discharges a white foul-smelling liquid when aggravated.

CHROMODORIDIDAE
Emm's Hypselodoris
Hypselodoris emmae
Coral reefs, rocky reefs
8 to 20 metres (26 to 66 ft)
30 mm (1.2 in)

CHROMODORIDIDAE

Maridad Hypselodoris

Hypselodoris maridadilus

Coral reefs, rocky reefs, seagrass meadows

2 to 10 metres (6.6 to 33 ft)

25 mm (1 in)

With a range extending from the Maldives to the north-western Australian coast, the Maldivian forms (pictured) were found in seagrass meadows feeding on a sponge. All forms have bright red gills and rhinophores and mauve lines on the dorsal surface and sides of the body.

CHROMODORIDIDAE

Variable Noumea

Noumea varians

Coral reefs, rocky reefs

Lt to 15 metres(0 to 49 ft)

25 mm (1 in)

An attractive smaller species the Variable Noumea is sometimes seen out in the open during the day where it crawls along searching out its choice of sponges by chemoreception. This nudibranch ranges across the Indo-Pacific and was first recorded from the Maldives in 1994.

PHYLLIDIIDAE

Painted Fryeria

Fryeria picta

Coral reefs, rocky reefs

Lt to 20 metres (0 to 66 ft)

50 mm (2 in)

Only described in 1993 this species extends from the Maldives into the Pacific areas and similar to many other phyllids is variable in colour. Members of the *Fryeria* genus differ by having their anus towards the rear. This species is seen out in the open on reef day and night.

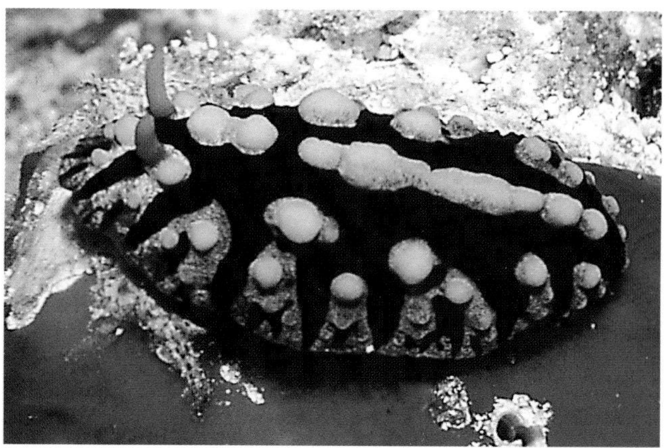

The Elegant Phyllidia is sometimes difficult to identify across its Indo-Pacific range as the basic colours and design vary, but the rhinophores always remain yellow. The Maldivian form shows a lot more pustules. It feeds on sponges and is seen out in the open both day and night.

PHYLLIDIIDAE
Elegant Phyllidia
Phyllidia elegans
Coral reefs, rocky reefs
Lt to 30 metres (0 to 98 ft)
50 mm (2 in)

Variation, Mooloolaba, Queensland, Australia.

Colour variation, Solomon Islands.

Active in the open both day and night across its Indo-Pacific range this species is common in the Maldives but is highly variable. The dorsal ridge of this species has no gaps, the pustules are capped with gold and there is a definite stripe on the sole of the foot. It eats sponges and is able to extract their toxins to protect itself.

PHYLLIDIIDAE
Varicose Phyllidia
Phyllidia varicosa
Coral reefs, rocky reefs
Lt to 30 metres (0 to 98 ft)
115 mm (4.6 in)

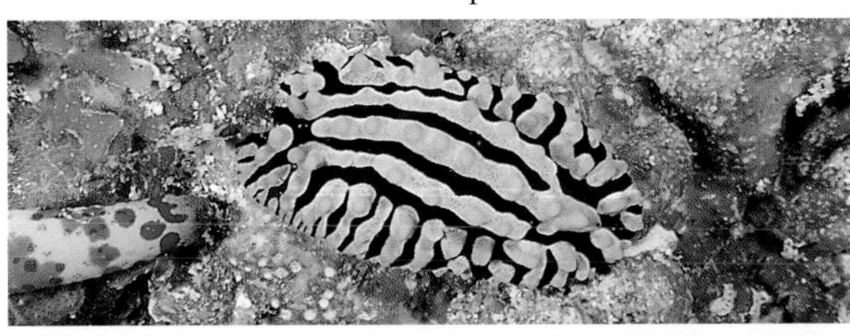

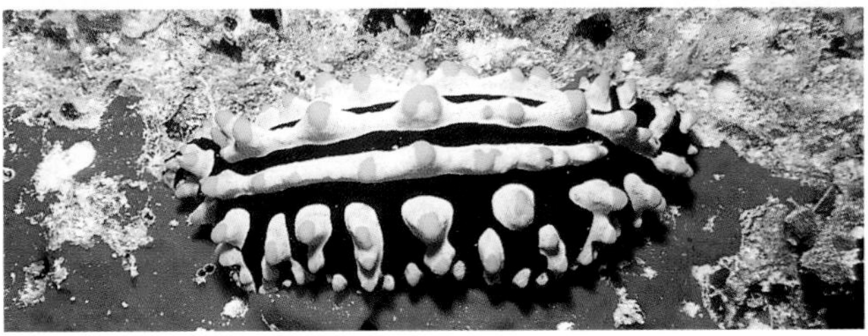

Colour variations, Maldives.

PHYLLIDIIDAE
Rose Phyllidiella
Phyllidiella rosans

Coral reefs, rocky reefs

15 to 30 metres (49 to 98 ft)

35 mm (1.4 in)

Commonly observed in the Seychelles and the Maldives this species ranges from east Africa to the Pacific. Although the lines of pustules on the back and sides sometimes have gaps there are always six lines running down the body. Rose Phyllidiellas feed on sponges and are seen in the open on reefs both day and night.

Variation, Seychelles.

PHYLLIDIIDAE
Rudman's Phyllidiella
Phyllidiella rudmani

Coral reefs, rocky reefs

5 to 30 metres (16 to 98 ft)

50 mm (2 in)

Rudman's Phyllidiella occurs in the open on reefs from the Maldives across the Great Barrier Reef and can be recognised by its pale pink colour and one black line down each side. It is known to feed on sponges *Phakellia* sp.

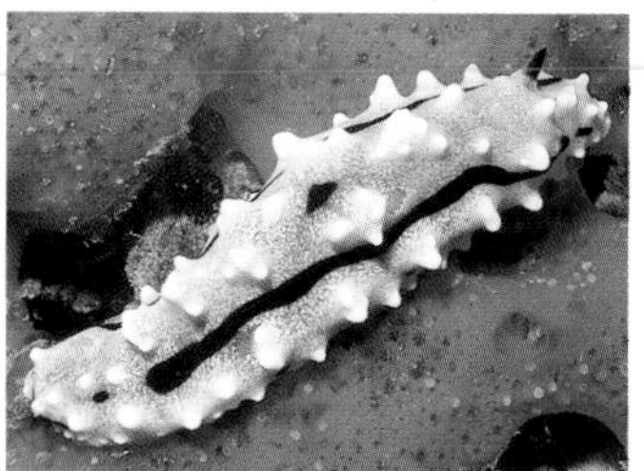

Colour variation, Bali, Indonesia.

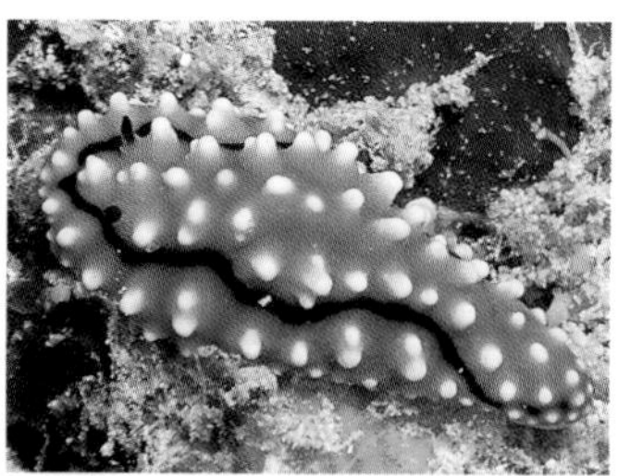

Colour variation, Great Barrier Reef.

Colour variations, Maldives.

Highly variable, this species is known from South Africa to Australia and, at this point in time, appears to be an Indian Ocean species. It feeds on sponges and lives in the open on reef both day and night.

PHYLLIDIIDAE
Zeylan Phyllidiella
Phyllidiella zeylanica
Coral reefs, rocky reefs
5 to 20 metres (16 to 66 ft)
60 mm (2.4 in)

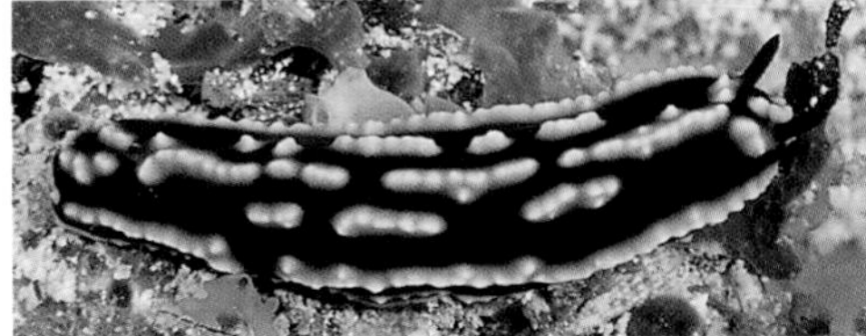

Colour variation, Maldives.

A high profile triangular nudibranch this species is very firm-bodied and from the Maldives to the Solomon's shows little variation. Shirin's Phyllidiopsis lives in the open on reef day and night feeding on sponges.

PHYLLIDIIDAE
Shirin's Phyllidiopsis
Phyllidiopsis shirinae
Coral reefs, rocky reefs
10 to 25 metres (33 to 82 ft)
110 mm (4.4 in)

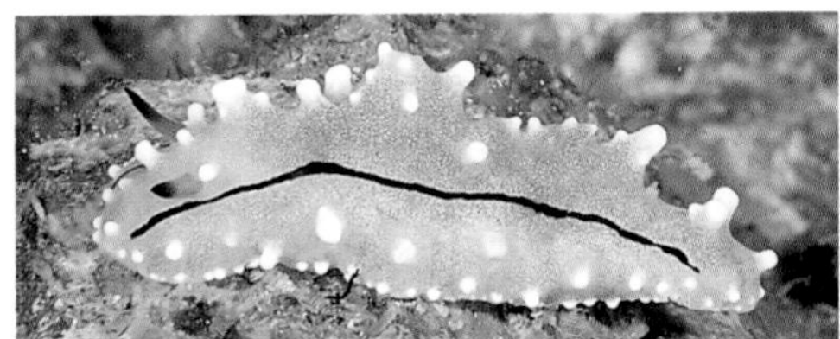

Variation, Kimbe Bay, Papua New Guinea.

With very long widely-spaced cerata on its back decorated with double bands this nudibranch is simple to identify. It ranges from East Africa to the northern Pacific, feeds on hydroids and does not appear to be common anywhere throughout its distribution.

FLABELLINIDAE
Bilas Flabellina
Flabellina bilas
Coral reefs, rocky reefs
5 to 25 metres (16 to 82 ft)
25 mm (1 in)

FLABELLINIDAE

Much-desired Flabellina

Flabellina exoptata

Coral reefs, rocky reefs

Lt to 40 metres (0 to 131 ft)

30 mm (1.2 in)

This species is distributed from the Maldives to the Great Barrier Reef. It feeds and lays its eggs strings on the hydroid *Halocordyle disticha*.

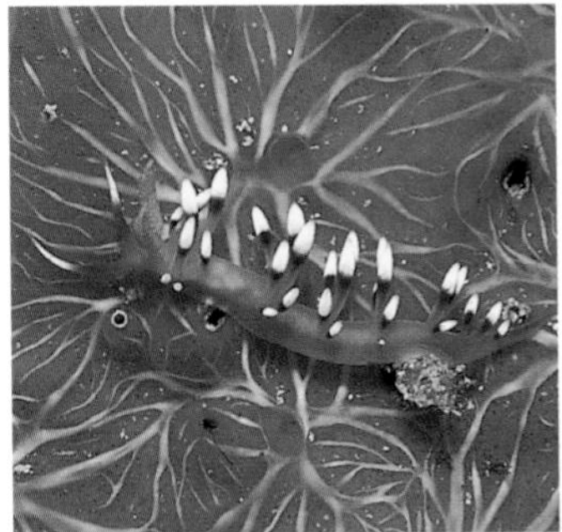

Colour variation, Bali, Indonesia.

Colour variation feeding on hydroids, Maldives.

Colour variation, laying eggs on its food source, Great Barrier Reef.

FACELINIDAE

Brock's Phidiana

Phidiana brockii

Coral reefs, rocky reefs

5 to 25 metres (16 to 82 ft)

35 mm (1.4 in)

Brock's Phidiana is not considered common across its Indo-Pacific range; it can be seen in the open at night or beneath dead coral and stones during the day. The colour is fairly stable and the white "T" bar in the centre of the head is featured on all specimens observed.

With an Indian Ocean distribution that extends to Fiji this species is commonly observed on reefs during the day where it feeds on the hydroids *Halocordyle disticha* and *Salacia tetracythara*. Its colour can be variable.

FACELINIDAE

Indian Ocean Phidiana

Phidiana indica

Coral reefs, rocky reefs

5 to 20 metres (16 to 66 ft)

50 mm (2 in)

This extremely common distinctively-shaped nudibranch occurs from East Africa to Fiji. It feeds on stinging hydroids and stores the stinging cells in the cerata on its back enabling the nudibranch to sting humans who touch it. Regardless of very variable body colours the tentacles always carry white and purple bands.

Maldivian form feeding on hydroids growing out of an encrusting sponge.

FACELINIDAE

Violet Pteraeolidia

Pteraeolidia ianthina

Coral reefs, rocky reefs

Lt to 30 metres (0 to 98 ft)

190 mm (7.6 in)

Colour variation, Papua New Guinea.

BIVALVES

CLASS: *Bivalvia*

Features: Bivalves can be easily recognised because most have two shell valves. Each valve is hinged at the dorsal margin; the animal inside is laterally compressed and can open or close the shell valves by contracting or relaxing the adductor muscles attached to the inside of each value.

Bivalves do not have a head but a well-developed mantle that lines the shell and builds its valves; the gills and the viscera are also enclosed in the mantle cavity. The mantle lobes are often fused and may extend as two siphons through which water is pumped in and out to provide respiration and food in the form of plankton and suspended sediment.

The harvesting and farming of bivalves (aquaculture) is a very important commercial industry throughout the world. There are about 15,000 species of bivalves known throughout the world.

Lifestyle: Many bivalves are attached or fixed to the substrate, either permanently like oysters, or temporarily like mussels; others are free living. Some scallops can swim and are propelled by water jetted out of the mantle cavity but this mobility is rare. Most burrowers can move along and dig by means of a well-developed foot.

Bivalves that live exposed on reefs may be completely overgrown with other marine life such as algae, hydroids or barnacles. Free-living forms living in sand or mud may only be located by telltale holes in the substrate where their siphons show, or by marks made by their shell movements.

Reproduction: Most bivalves have separate sexes, though hermaphroditic species do occur. Fertilisation is external by shedding eggs and sperm into the water. The young hatch as free-swimming larvae (veligers).

Associations: There are a number of known bivalve associations including many species of shrimps and crabs. Pearl shells, pen shells, oysters, giant clams, window pane shells, thorny oysters and mussels all house commensals. The pearlfish *Carapus* sp is also found in pearl shells.

Identification: Bivalves with colour patterns, designs, or other distinguishing features such as shape, spines, ridges, bumps, or nodules are fairly easy to recognise to species level. Many others with less individual features require the assistance of an experienced taxonomist for accurate identification.

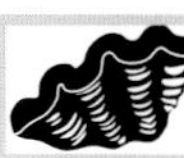

ARCIDAE
Giant ark
Arca ventricosa
Coral reefs, rocky reefs
5 to 30 metres (16 to 98 ft)
80 mm (3.2 in)

This bivalve is extremely common in the Maldives and across the Indo-Pacific where it occupies holes in the walls of caves and drop-offs and dead coral heads. Any water disturbance or direct light causes it to withdraw into the hole. The red colour on the specimen pictured is due to a sponge growth.

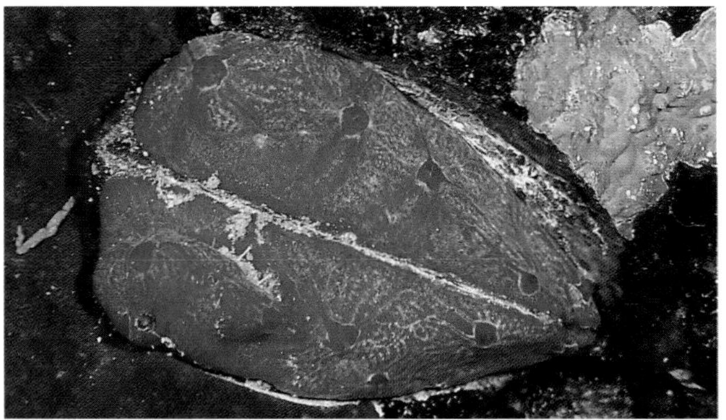

MYTILIDAE
Philippine mussel
Modiolus philippinarum
Coral reefs, rocky reefs
5 to 20 metres (16 to 66 ft)
100 mm (4 in)

Known from South Africa to Papua New Guinea this species is a crevice-dwelling form seen mostly in live or dead coral heads. Although solitary animals are commonly encountered, occasionally several may be seen together. The valves are covered by a thick brown periostracum.

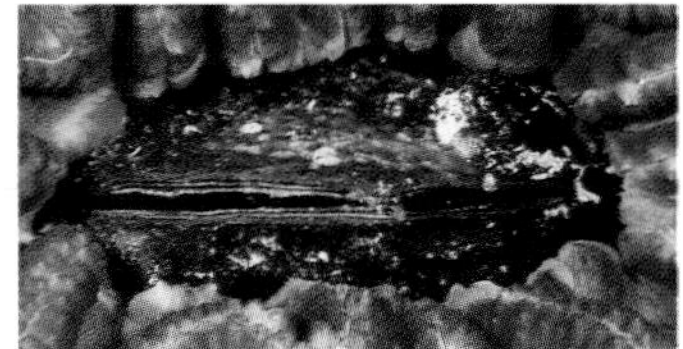

Fully adult specimen, Kimbe Bay, Papua New Guinea.

GASTRODINIDAE
Double-barrelled bivalve
Gastrochaena sp.
Coral reefs, rocky reefs
2 to 20 metres (6.6 to 66 ft)

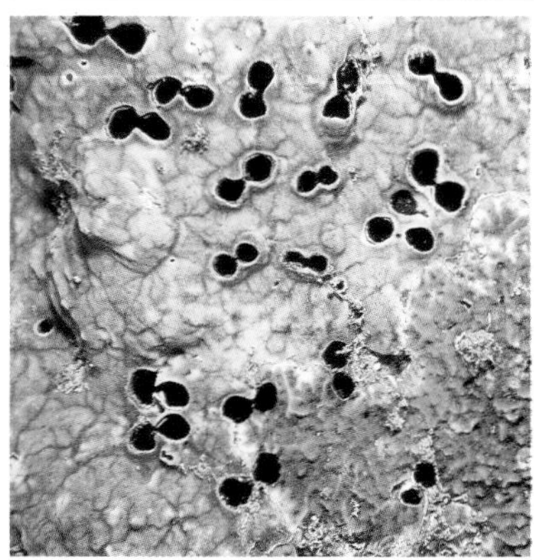

Buried deep in the substrate these bivalves are hidden to view. Only their calcareous siphons can be seen to advertise their presence. The species is very common in the Maldives.

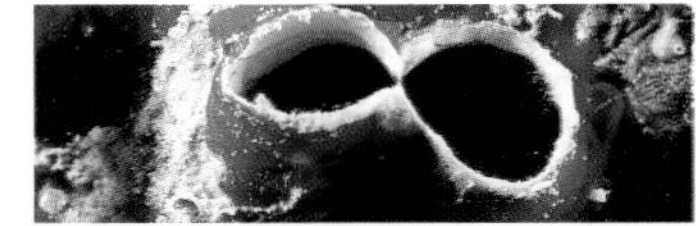

Close up of calcareous siphons.

PTERIIDAE
Penguin wing oyster
Pteria penguin
Coral reefs, rocky reefs
20 to 40 metres (66 to 132 ft)
250 mm (10 in)

Attached to gorgonians and black corals this species is very common in the Maldives. Younger oysters have a pronounced "wing" absent in large oysters. In some areas (Seychelles) theses oysters are cultivated to produce black pearls.

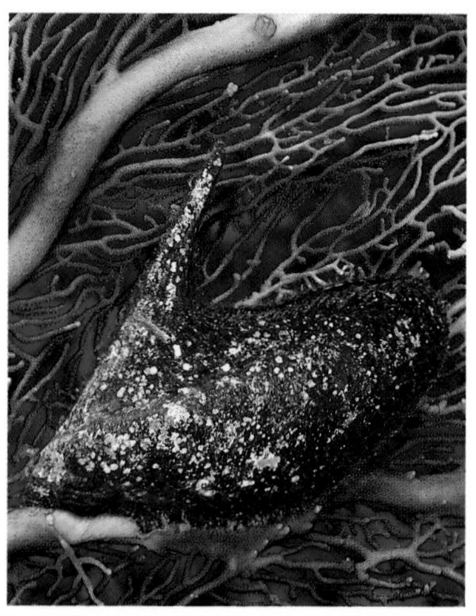

PECTINIDAE
Coral scallop
Pedum spondyloidum
Coral reefs
3 to 20 metres (33 to 66 ft)
50 mm (2 in)

Buried deep in the recesses of their coral fortress these beautiful bivalves are well protected from predators and consequently have very thin, fragile shell valves. Some specimens have bright blue mantles edged with red "eyes" (which can detect shadow and movement). Others may have brown and white animals with red "eyes". This species is relatively common throughout the Maldives.

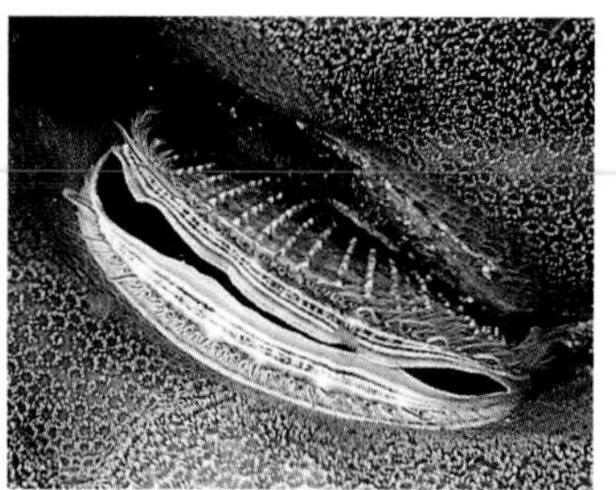

Colour variation, Kimbe Bay, Papua New Guinea.

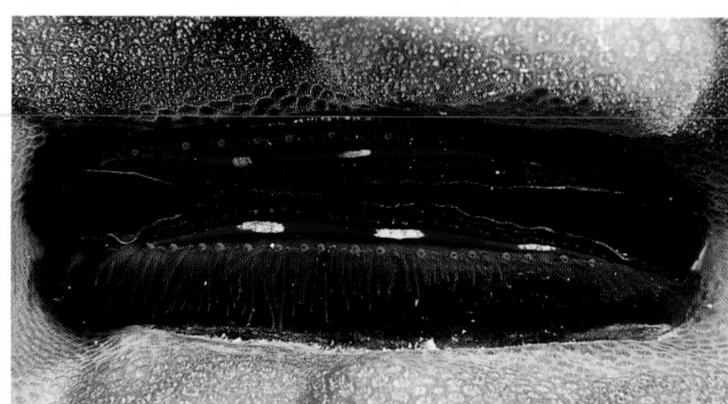

PECTINIDAE
Scaly scallop
Chlamys sp.
Coral reefs, rocky reefs
Lt to 10 metres (0 to 33 ft)
50 mm (2 in)

Living beneath rocks and dead coral this scallop has very well developed scales on the upper valve and is generally light brown in colour with a darker brown pattern.

SPONDYLIDAE
Black-banded thorny oyster
Spondulus nicobaricus
Coral reefs, rocky reefs
Lt to 10 metres (0 to 33 ft)
100 mm (4 in)

Found attached to the undersides of dead coral and rocks this species is one of the most delicately-spined thorny oysters. It may be seen in two colour forms, white with black patches (in bands) or pink with black patches. It is not common in the Maldives.

Colour form, Kimbe Bay, Papua New Guinea.

SPONDYLIDAE
Variable thorny oyster
Spondylus varians
Coral reefs, rocky reefs
15 to 40 metres (49 to 131 ft) ✓
200 mm (8 in)

Mostly seen attached to back walls of caves, underhangs, crevices and ledges this species is the largest thorny oyster in the Indo-Pacific. The colour and pattern of the animal is highly variable; of six molluscs in one cave each had a different pattern. Very common in the Maldives this very attractive bivalve is sensitive to water movement and light.

Colour variation, Maldives.

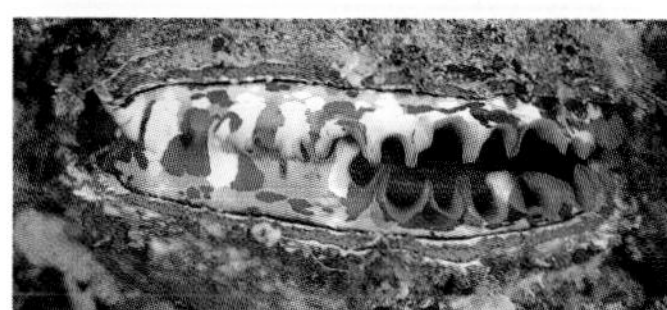

Colour variation, Maldives.

Colour variation, Maldives.

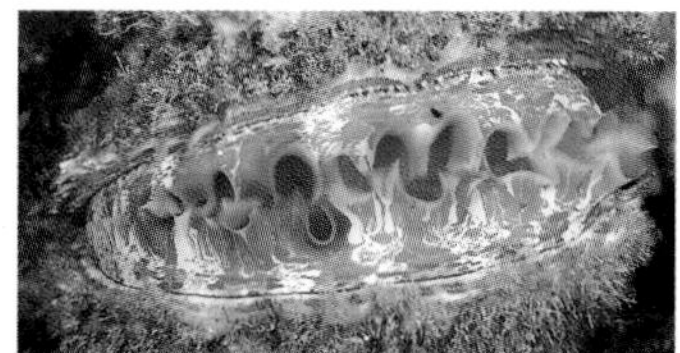

Colour variation, Maldives.

SPONDYLIDAE
Scoop-spined thorny oyster
Spondulus sp.
Coral reefs, rocky reefs
10 to 30 metres (33 to 98 ft)
110 mm (4.4 in)

Whereas the variable thorny oyster grows its shell out at an angle from the substrate this species grows flat and has few distinguishing features other than scoop-shaped spines. It lives in caves at around 20 metres.

SPONDYLIDAE
Fork-spined thorny oyster
Spondylus sp.
Coral reefs, rocky reefs
8 to 25 metres (26 to 82 ft)
100 mm (4 in)

Occurring in many areas of the Indo-Pacific this species appear rare in the Maldives where it lives in caves and under ledges. It grows flat on the substrate and the double-forked spines are quite noticeable in all specimens observed. The shell is pure white.

OSTREIDAE
Crenulated oyster
Alectryonella plicatula
Coral reefs, rocky reefs
5 to 20 metres (16 to 66 ft)
110 mm (4.4 in)

Seen commonly attached to coral heads across the Indo-Pacific this very distinctively-shaped oyster has a series of very well defined teeth around the shell edges. It is almost always overgrown with encrusting marine life but rarely attracts sponge growth.

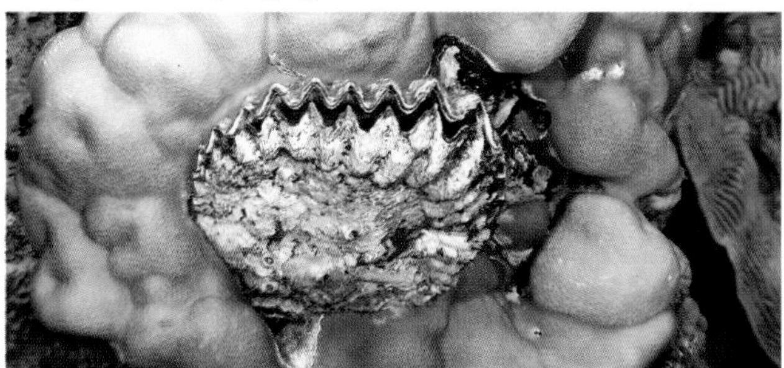

A veritable giant of an oyster this species is found across the entire Indo-Pacific and is common in the Maldives. It has a very thick, heavily overgrown calcified shell and acutely angled triangular "teeth" along the aperture. The animal is black and the valves can be agape day and night.

OSTREIDAE

Honeycomb oyster

Hyotissa hyotis

Coral reefs, rocky reefs

2 to 30 metres (6.6 to 98 ft) ✓

250 mm (10 in)

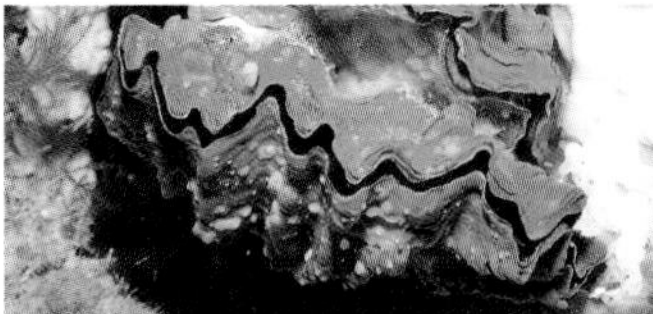

Juvenile forms covered in commensal orange sponge, Maldives.

A well known common species found throughout the Indo-Pacific the cock's comb oyster has a very light delicate shell and strong angular teeth along the edges of valves. It has a special relationship with a number of different encrusting sponge species. On some occasions a number may be seen together in a cluster.

OSTREIDAE

Cock's comb oyster

Lopha cristagalli ✓

Coral reefs, rocky reefs

5 to 30 metres (16 to 98 ft)

90 mm (3.5 in)

Sponge associate, the northern Great Barrier Reef.

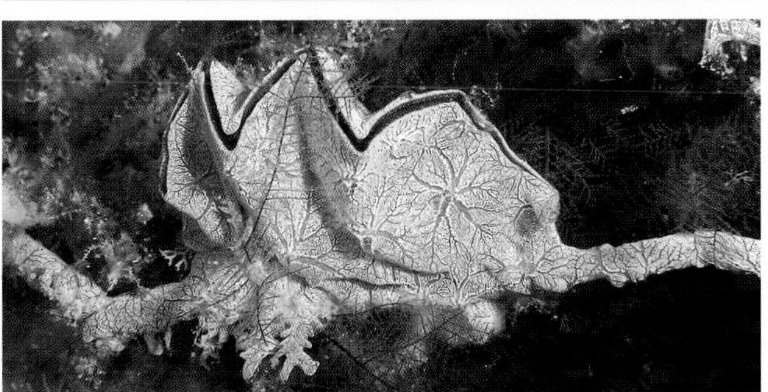

Sponge associate, Kimbe Bay, Papua New Guinea.

Sponge associate, Heron Island, southern Great Barrier Reef.

LIMIDAE

Fragile file shell

Limaria fragilis

Rubble, dead coral

Lt to 10 metres (0 to 33 ft)

35 mm (1.4 in)

This species inhabits the undersides of rocks and dead coral. It has extremely long red-striped tentacles which are very sticky. Should the tentacles break off they continue to twist and turn like small worms.

LIMIDAE

Maldivian file shell

Limaria sp.

Rubble, dead coral

Lt to 5 meters (0 to 16 ft)

25 mm (1 in)

File shells generally live in pairs in hollows beneath dead coral slabs on rubble or sand. This Maldivian form had very little scalloping on the shell, was almost smooth and the animal had very short tentacles.

GALEOMMATIDAE

Crawling bivalve

Amphilepida sp.

Coral reefs, rocky reefs

Lt to 5 metres (0 to 16 ft)

20 mm (0.8 in)

A strange little mollusc which lives under stones and dead coral rock in shallow water. It does not like light and when exposed will use its long prehensile foot to drag itself back to the dark side of the rock. This Maldivian form was seen in several areas.

Using its prehensile foot.

TRIDACNIDAE

Crocus giant clam

Tridacna crocea

Coral reefs, rocky reefs

Lt to 20 metres (0 to 66 ft)

100 mm (4 in)

Living in cracks and fissures in live coral heads and rocky reefs this is the smallest species of giant clam in the Indo-Pacific region. The mantle colours are variable and the shell has very short concentric sculpture.

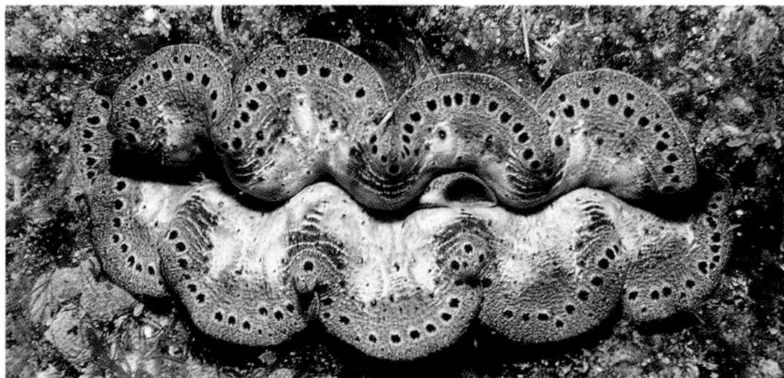

Colour variation, Maldives.

Colour variation, Port Moresby, Papua New Guinea.

TRIDACNIDAE

Necklace giant clam

Tridacna derasa

Coral reefs, rocky reefs, sand, mud

8 to 20 metres (26 to 66 ft)

500 mm (20 in)

The second largest giant clam living in the Indo-Pacific region this species prefers sheltered waters such as back reefs and lagoons where it is frequently seen on soft bottom. It has a more triangular shape than other species and the shell edges are wavy rather than convoluted. Colour is generally dark blue with yellow and green edging to the mantle.

Variation showing shell edges, Great Barrier Reef.

TRIDACNIDAE
Large giant clam
Tridacna maxima
Coral reefs, rocky reefs
Lt to 10 metres (0 to 33 ft)
300 mm (12 in)

A common species across the Indo-Pacific this species has an elongate shape, well developed concentric sculpture (scales) on the shell valves and lives anchored to the reef usually between coral heads or in depressions. The animal's mantle can be varied in colour but, in general, blue is the most common.

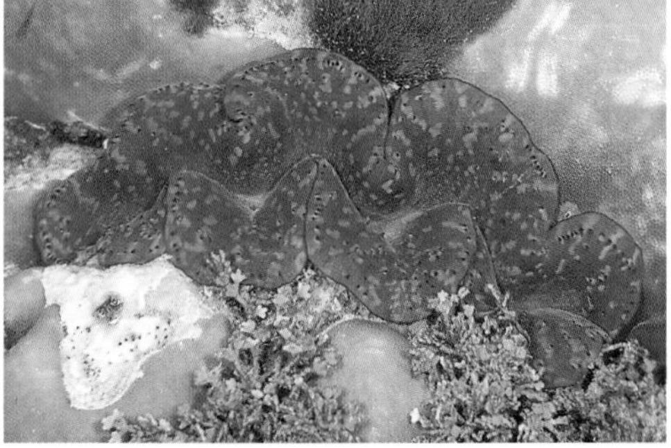

Maldivian form showing shell.

TRIDACNIDAE
Fluted giant clam
Tridacna squamosa
Coral reefs, rocky reefs
2 to 20 metres (6 to 66 ft)
400 mm (16 in)

Although the fluted giant clam animal has a range of colours and patterns it can be easily recognised by the extremely well developed leaf-like scutes on the sides of the shell. It ranges from South Africa to the South Pacific.

Juvenile fluted giant clam, Maldives.

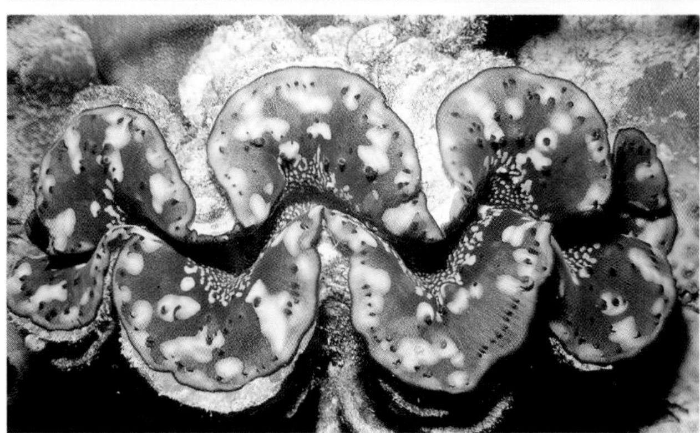

Mantle pattern of one of the more common Maldivian forms.

Living beneath the sand in shallow water lagoons the lettered venus is locally common across many areas of the Indo-Pacific. Whereas in most places the shell is fairly variable in pattern, Maldivian forms have very pronounced black blotches which is unusual.

VENERIDAE
Lettered venus
Tapes litteratus
Sand
2 to 10 metres (6.6 to 33 ft)
90 mm (3.5 in)

Colour variation, Port Moresby, Papua New Guinea.

Not often encountered the embossed venus is a subsurface dweller living in coarse sandy shell grit substrate on slopes and in deeper lagoons. The species has been recorded across the Indo-Pacific region and is more well known in the Pacific areas.

VENERIDAE
Embossed venus
Globivenus toreuma
Sand
5 to 20 metres (16 to 66 ft)
60 mm (2.5 in)

CUTTLES, SQUID, NAUTILUS, OCTOPUS

CLASS: *Cephalopoda* ("head-footed" molluscs)

Features: By far the most advanced of all molluscs, cephalopods could be said to represent the ultimate invertebrate. They have a well-developed brain, a highly responsive nervous system, and eyes which compare favourably with those of many of the higher vertebrates.

Apart from the ram's horn squid, nautiluses, and argonauts, the cephalopods in general do not produce shells. Octopods have no shell at all and almost all the squids have but a thin rudimentary internal "pen" or gladius. In the cuttles this "pen" is a much heavier structure and cuttle bones from dead animals are one of the most familiar objects in the flotsam cast ashore by the waves.

All cephalopods except pearly nautiluses have arms studded with powerful suckers. These suckers have horny, circular rims with soft pliable walls and a piston-like centre. The suckers displace air or water and once the vacuum seal is made the suckers adhere so tightly to an object that they may be torn from the arm of an octopus before they lose their grip. Within the suckers are chemical receptors which enable the octopus to test objects for edibility.

The mouth is positioned at the centre of the arms where a parrot-like beak is used for biting and holding prey while it is rasped away by the radula and digested. Another unique feature in nearly all cephalopods (but not the pearly nautilus) is the ink sac. This interesting organ is purely a defence mechanism and is connected to the siphon. When hard pressed by a predator, the mollusc can direct the contents of the ink sac in the direction of the attacker, leaving a confusing "smoke" screen while it jets away. Octopuses in shallow tide pools will often spray ink, or a jet of water as much as 1 metre in height. They have excellent aim, as anyone who has had a cold spurt up the leg of their shorts can vouch. Cephalopod ink has been used for writing; it flows easily from the pen and has a brown or sepia look when dry.

Cephalopod colouration is regulated by pigment cells called chromatophores in the skin. These cells can be expanded or contracted by the cephalopod at will. By rapid condensing and dispersing of the pigment cells the animal can cause instant colour changes to take place. Although stimulation of substrate colouration

can be assumed by octopods, squids and cuttles seem to use definite inherent patterns. Each pattern has a particular purpose, and these include warning patterns, sex patterns, mating patterns, hunting patterns, and escape patterns. Cephalopods range in size from the giant deep-water squid which reaches over 15 metres, down to the 25 mm pygmy squid.

Lifestyle: Strictly marine, cephalopods are mostly mobile, voracious carnivores, which live from the littoral zone down to the night-like depths of the abyss.

Squids are mostly pelagic and swim in schools for protection, most octopuses are bottom dwellers and, except briefly during the mating season, seem to prefer a solitary existence.

Cuttles and squids are jet-propelled hunters, relying on the speed and accuracy of their hunting tentacles to capture food. The hunting tentacles are housed in pouches in the cheeks below the eyes and can be shot out at amazing speed. The ends of the tentacles are studded with suckered pads, or hooks, and when a fish or crab is captured it is swiftly pulled into the mass of shorter tentacles encircling the mouth. By holding the prey with the tentacles, the octopus can use its beak to kill the prey. Fish are usually eaten head first, held by the beak and rasped away by the radula.

Because cephalopods are mostly very active, their need for oxygen is greater than that of the less active classes. To maintain their oxygen supplies they use their muscular mantle to pump large quantities of water through the mantle cavity and over the gills. Jet propulsion in cephalopods is achieved by the expulsion of this water from a siphon which is situated on the ventral, or underside, of the head. At the same time this exhalant current disposes of excretory and respiratory wastes. The siphon is very manoeuvrable and can be directed at will, enabling the cephalopod to move by means of controlled propulsion in almost any direction.

Not only can cephalopods alter their colours, but they also have the power to alter their skin texture. When fleeing, cuttles are smooth and streamlined, but when they are in hiding their skin erupts, and these filaments, pustules, and knobs present a less definitive shape and tend to blend in with the surrounding terrain. It is these instant body and colour changes which have made cephalopod identification so difficult in the past, especially field identification.

The pearly nautilus is devoid of many of the features other cephalopods display. It has a unique, many-chambered external shell, the many tentacles are without suckers, it has no ink sac, and is relatively lacking in eyesight. It lives in deep water close to the bottom near reef walls where it depends on smell to find crabs and sleeping fish upon which it feeds.

Reproduction: Cephalopods are separately sexed and in many species the male is the smaller. Copulation is achieved by means of a special organ on the end of one of the male's arms. This organ is called a hectocotylus. A spermatophore or packet of sperm is conveyed from the body along the arm to the tip of this organ, where it is contained. During mating, the male inserts the arm tip and organ into the mantle cavity of the female. Often the tip of the arm with the hectocotylus will detach from the male's body and stay inserted in the female. Mass mortality often follows mating and egg laying by some species of squids and cuttlefish.

Octopus lay various numbers of gelatinous capsules in a nest or lair. Smaller species often occupy shells, tins and bottles. The female octopus is a capable, defensive, and determined mother and will only desert her eggs under extreme duress.

Many octopods seem to lay eggs of the same size, even though some animals may be 25 to 30 times larger than adults of other species. Certainly the larger species lay greater numbers of eggs.

Associations: None known.

Identification: Whereas in the past visual identification without the aid of a specimen has been difficult, recent advances by scientific workers in Australia over the last 20 years have got most of the Indo-Pacific forms worked out. However, due to the large number of new species, many are still awaiting scientific description.

Broad-stripe cuttle.

NAUTILIDAE

Pearly nautilus

Nautilus pompilius

Coral reefs, rocky reefs

20 to 250 metres (66 to 825 ft)

200 mm (8 in)

A very deep water dweller during the day this species lives at the base of deep water drop offs and reefs and during the night engages in vertical migration up into the shallows 20 metres (66 ft) or less in search of food in the form of crabs or sleeping fish. The buoyant shell is known from washed up specimens found throughout the Indo-Pacific.

Head on aspect with the siphon fully expanded, Vanuatu.

Sectioned shell showing the compartment-like construction.

SEPIIDAE

Broad-stripe cuttle

Sepia latimanus

Coral reefs, rocky reefs

10 to 25 metres (33 to 82 ft)

300 mm (12 in)

Known from the Red Sea to Fiji and New Caledonia this species is active during the day and may often be seen in pairs. It generally hovers just above the bottom on reefs and has a number of colour patterns. However, as it's the only large cuttle throughout its distribution recognition is simple.

Newly laid cuttle eggs, Heron Island, Great Barrier Reef.

Baby cuttles ready to hatch, Great Barrier Reef.

Side-on aspect, Port Moresby, Papua New Guinea.

Colour variation, Bali, Indonesia.

SEPIOLIDAE

Long-finned squid

Sepioteuthis lessoniana

Water column above reefs

Surface to 100 metres (surface to 330 ft)

200 mm (8 in)

Spread across the Indo-Pacific from East Africa to Japan and down to New Zealand, this common, well known species is often seen when night diving. It feeds on fish and lays its eggs in coral or in rock crevices beneath gorgonians or black corals.

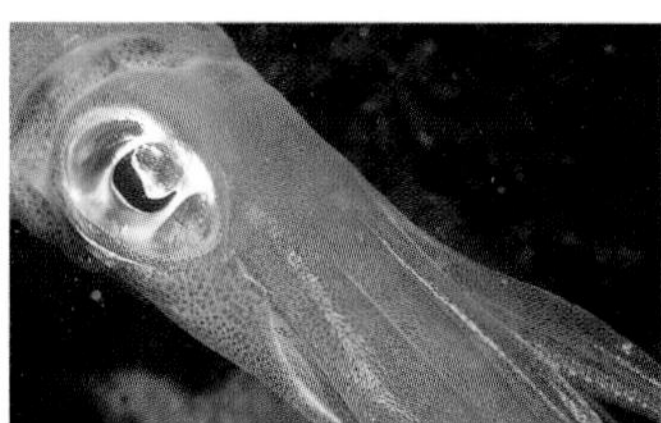

Close up of eye at night, Great Barrier Reef.

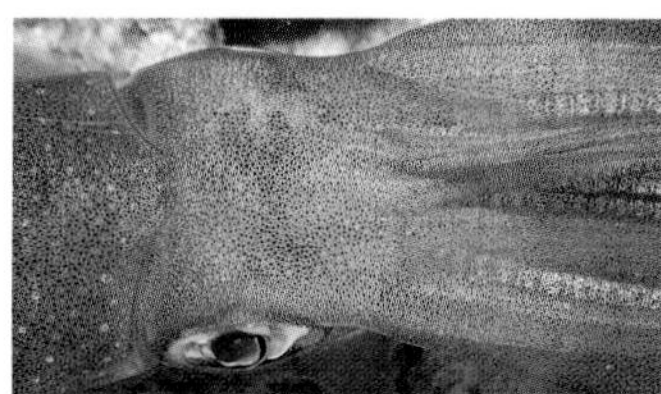

Close up of head at night, Great Barrier Reef.

Half grown specimen, Port Moresby, Papua New Guinea.

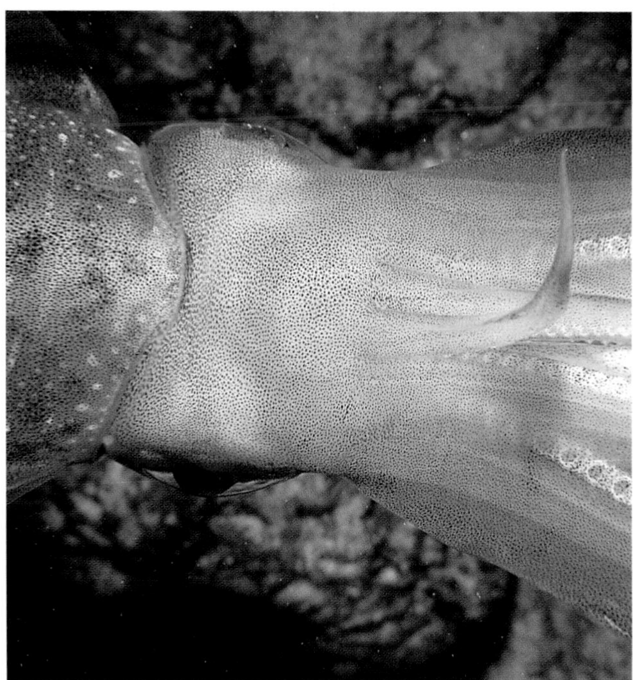

Close up of colour change at night, Great Barrier Reef.

Female depositing eggs in rocks around black coral, Kashiwajima, Shikoku Island, Japan.

Sun dried squid, Kashiwajima, Shikoku Island, Japan.

OCTOPODIDAE

Reef octopus

Octopus cyanea

Coral reefs, rocky reefs

5 to 20 metres (16 to 66 ft)

300 mm (12 in)

Although a common reef-dwelling octopus throughout the Indo-Pacific this species was not seen very often in the Maldives. It is active during overcast days and lives in a lair between rocks with pieces of coral "clinker" around the entrance.

Octopus at the entrance to its lair, Maldives.

Crustaceans

Chapter 7

Crustaceans – Insects of the Sea

PHYLUM: ARTHROPODA (Insects)

SUBPHYLUM: CRUSTACEA

Features: It is estimated that there may be over 3,000,000 insects on earth. Of these only a relative small number have been scientifically described. The crustaceans number around 35,000 to 45,000 species and these are made up of mostly marine species, some fresh water types, and those that live in rainforest leaf litter. Although crustaceans as a group may have different body forms they all have a jointed armour-like outer casing (exoskeleton), a protective carapace over the head and organs, jointed legs, a double set of antennae (insects only have one) and compound eyes which, in many cases, provide remarkably acute eyesight.

The exoskeleton is comprised of rigid segments of calcium carbonate and as most crustaceans are continually growing for most of their life cycles the animal outgrows the outer shell which is periodically shed or moulted. The new exoskeleton is soft and pliable and the animal pumps in water to expand it. Quite often individuals may eat part of their old casing to reabsorb its calcium which is used to harden the new shell. During moulting periods crustaceans are very vulnerable to predators and cannibalistic members of their own species and usually hide away until their new shell hardens.

The segmented body has a head end and an abdomen with jointed legs controlled by internal muscles. Other internally controlled appendages provide life-serving functions such as sight, locomotion, sensory perception, chemo-reception, feeding, respiration, communication and defence.

Lifestyle: As a group, crustaceans feed on a wide variety of organisms and may be herbivores, plantivores, carnivores or detritus feeders. Some are specialised (cleaner shrimps) and act as "fish doctors" setting up "cleaning stations" in caves where fish sleep or working from their symbiotic "home" in a sea anemone.

Most crustaceans are nocturnal and are only seen at night, or on overcast days. They have evolved nocturnal lifestyles in order to avoid the many day time visual predators such as fish. During the day they live beneath rocks deep in the coral, under ledges, in caves, holes in the rocks and reef.

Reproduction: Sexes are mostly separate, though in some classes (barnacles) hermaphrodic species do exist; most crustacean females are impregnated internally by the males. However, this is only generalised and specific behaviour and habits are detailed in the introductions to each class. Eggs are carried beneath the abdomen or on especially modified swimmerets under the abdomen. Once hatched, the larvae enter the plankton and progress through a number of stages before settling to the bottom as a juvenile of their adult form. Rock lobsters may go through over 10 stages, spending up to nine months in the plankton before settling onto a reef.

Associations: Quite a large number have developed commensal relationships with other marine creatures such as sea anemones, sea whips, soft corals, black corals, corals, echinoderms, sponges, sea squirts, fish and molluscs.

Identification: In general, identification can now be made on many living species especially where an accurate full colour photograph has been published and is available. However, the living taxonomy of crustaceans is not well published. Due to the painstaking work involved in trying to match pictures in colour to scientific drawings in black and white (when and if some willing crustacean taxonomist can be found with time and experience to do the work) there is still a long way to go. As 80 per cent of the crustacean pictures contained in the Australasian Marine Photographic Index are cross-referenced against actual specimens housed in museums in Australia identifications have been determined from the animal wherever possible.

CLASS: *Malacostraca* (Decapods – Mantis shrimps, Shrimps, Rock lobsters, Hermit crabs, Squat lobsters, Crabs)

Features: This is a very large and varied group of crustaceans. Many species are popular as food animals and those farmed commercially are fairly well known. The development and life histories of others remain a mystery and the animals themselves are known only to people familiar with the group.

As their name suggests the decapod crustaceans have ten legs (including the larger claws or pincers).

Lifestyles: With over 10,000 described species decapod crustaceans can be found in almost every habitat in the sea. They live in burrows in sand or mud among rubble, on reefs, in caves and under ledges and rocks. Some bury by day and emerge at night. Some carry shells over their heads and others live in them. Some are permanent swimmers in the vast ocean spaces. There are species only millimetres in size that are carried about in the water column as plankton, and giants weighing 15 kilograms (33 pounds) that crawl about on rocky reefs 100 metres (330 feet) below the surface. Most are free living and feed on a variety of organisms: bacteria, plankton, sediment, suspended particles, algae, molluscs, fish, worms and other crustaceans and carrion.

Reproduction: The sexes are generally separate and, after mating, the female lays eggs that are carried beneath the abdominal flaps of crabs, on the modified swimmerets (swimming feet) of rock lobsters and shrimps, and on the chests of mantis shrimps. On hatching, the larvae join the plankton and pass through a series of free-swimming stages before settling to the bottom where they metamorphose into juveniles of their particular species.

Associations: Some live commensally with other animals such as echinoderms, cnidarians, sponges, bryozoans and ascidians while smaller species may be obligate commensals or parasites with highly modified bodies.

Identification: Where there is a good colour reproduction available the larger and more distinctively patterned species can be identified whenever known. However, the smaller more obscure species and those where there is little colour shape or pattern to make visual identification possible still require a good taxonomist and a specimen before identity can be determined.

Mantis shrimps

Features: Superficially similar in appearance to large prawns, mantis shrimps have a long flat body with a short carapace and eight appendages, six legs and variously modified raptorial claws. These claws are reminiscent of preying mantis of the insect world and each species of mantis shrimp is armed with specific versions depending on their prey.

There are fish stabbing and grasping versions which have sharp points and rows of needle-sharp spines. Those that feed on bivalve and univalve shells have blunt swollen claws with bevelled edges designed for smashing hard-shelled prey. (These are called thumb splitters for obvious reasons).

Mantis shrimps have stalked, high profile compound eyes which can be rotated independently of each other, giving them excellent vision. Besides the raptorial claws they have an armoured, sharp, spined tail which is capable of injuring humans. Each species has a differently designed armament and their agility and effective use of front or back defences makes handling any species very foolhardy.

Lifestyles: All mantis shrimps have homing burrows or lairs beneath rocks or amongst coral rubble and rock where they hole up. While some species hunt from "home" others move out over a "territory" and actively hunt, bringing prey back to the burrow to eat.

The giant fish hunting species live in a home burrow tunnelled in the sand or rubble and ingeniously camouflaged with a thin sand-studded mucous edging which effectively camouflages the true nature of the hole and the deadly ambusher waiting below.

Reproduction: The sexes are separate, the male's penis is situated at the base of the back legs and the female's genital pores are on the underside chest area between the middle legs. Eggs are laid as a mass which the female carries around on her chest until hatching takes place after which the larvae enter the plankton until settling to the bottom some time later as juveniles.

Associations: Few associations have been recorded but it is known that at least four species of shrimps live in or around the burrows of the giant fish-eating mantis shrimps, *Stenopus tenuirostris*, *Thor amboinensis*, *Periclimenes tenuipes* and *Periclimenes imperator*. However, it is not known if these behaviours extend to the Maldivian forms.

Identification: Most mantis shrimps can now be identified in situ or by sight as they all have visually distinctive features.

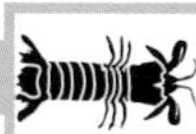

GONODACTYLIDAE
Chiragra mantis shrimp
Gonodactylus chiragra

Coral reefs, rocky reefs

Lt to 5 metres (0 to 16 ft)

100 mm (3.8 in)

This mantis shrimp is a "smasher" which feeds on univalve molluscs and hermit crabs by breaking open their shells with its modified raptorial claws. It lives in holes in coral and under rocks from the Maldives to the Great Barrier Reef.

Underside view.

Close up of swimmerets.

Close up of head, Vanuatu, South Pacific.

GONODACTYLIDAE
Flat-bodied mantis shrimp
Gonodactylus platysoma

Coral reefs, rocky reefs

Lt to 5 metres (0 to 16 ft)

100 mm (4 in)

Mostly seen in the shallows along reef flats during a flooding tide this species is a smasher; its prey, a cat's eye turban shell, can be seen beside it. It is more common to the Pacific but has been recorded from a number of locations throughout the Indian Ocean.

ODONTODACTYLIDAE

Green mantis shrimp

Odontodactylus scyllarus

Coral reefs, rocky reefs, rubble

Lt to 50 metres (0 to 164 ft)

180 mm (7.2 in)

Although this species lives in a burrow excavated from beneath a rock or in a reef hole, it leaves its lair to hunt univalve molluscs and crabs. Shells are carried back to the lair smashed, eaten and discarded at the entrance of the lair.

Green mantis shrimp with a captured cone shell, Bali, Indonesia.

Caught out in the open this specimen has adopted a threat posture, Papua New Guinea.

Green mantis shrimp at the entrance to its lair.

LYSIOSQUILLIDAE

Spotted mantis shrimp

Lissiosquillina maculata

Coarse sand, rubble

Lt to 20 metres (0 to 66 ft)

300 mm (12 in)

A large fish spearing species the spotted mantis shrimp has small spots or specks on its front parts while the body of the animal is distinctly banded. It lives in a burrow covered by a thin coating of mucus membrane and any fish which comes too close is impaled in a three millisecond strike.

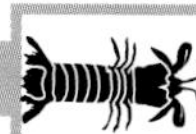

Variation, Port Moresby, Papua New Guinea.

Spotted mantis shrimp in the open showing the body banding. (Photo: Rudie H Kuiter)

LYSIOSQUILLIDAE

Red-knuckled mantis shrimp

Lissiosquillina sp.

Sand, rubble

8 to 35 metres (26 to 115 ft)

250 mm (10 in)

Found from the Maldives across to Papua New Guinea this very large interesting species is well known but as yet it not described. The knuckles of its raptorial claws are always held high up and have very distinctively-shaped plates. (Photo: Musthag Hussain))

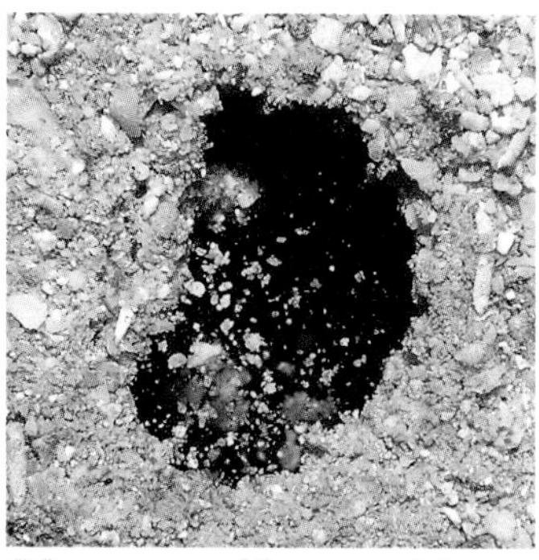

Mucus covered burrow with spy hole.

The burrows of this species are often inhabited by a pair of small cleaner shrimps Stenopus tenuirostris *(Indonesia).*

Variation, Port Moresby, Papua New Guinea.

Shrimps

Features: Caridean shrimps are found throughout the world with most of the 1000 known species living in tropical seas. They are generally smaller than prawns and have far more species in the tropics than in temperate waters. Due to their diversity this introduction is only basic and features will be given with each group in the species general remarks.

Lifestyle: These shrimps are all marine and live in a variety of habitats including coral reefs, rocky reefs, rubble, seagrass meadows and down burrows in sand, under rocks in caves, under ledges. With such a variety of lifestyles food ranges from algae, to detritus and may include plankton, mucous, copepods, fish tissue, sea stars and scavenged material.

Reproduction: Sexes are separate and males are generally smaller than females. Mating takes place and the female carries the eggs under the abdomen on modified swimmerets. In some species gravid females can be seen all year round.

Associations: Shrimps may live in specific micro-habitats in either as casual or obligate commensals. They can be found with algae, seagrass, sponges, corals, anemones, soft corals, sea fans, sea whips, black corals, sea pens, giant clams, nudibranchs, slugs, feather stars, sea stars, sea urchins, sea cucumbers, ascidians and many clean fish.

Identification: Colour patterns can be variable between males and females (sexual dichromatism) but as many pairs are found together identification is not difficult on known forms. Colours are also somewhat variable at different localities but, in general, the adult pattern remains characteristic. Juveniles of many species have less colours, and night time patterns may be different to day time ones. However, those with distinctive colour patterns can mostly be identified from a good picture once the species is published.

Anton Bruuni cleaner shrimp.

A very shy little boxer shrimp this species lives beneath ledges and in holes in the reef generally in association with sleeping fish (moray eels) which these shrimps actively clean at night. The red spots on the back are an excellent identification feature.

STENOPODIDAE
Devaney's boxer shrimp
Stenopus devaneyi
Coral reefs, rocky reefs
10 to 20 metres (33 to 66 ft)
60 mm (2.4 in)

Getting ready to clean a moray eel, Maldives.

Easily recognised by its long white antennae, red and white striped body and chelae, this species generally occurs in pairs. Cleaning stations are in coral, rock crevices, or under caves and ledges. It is active during the day and also cleans sleeping fish at night.

STENOPODIDAE
Banded boxer shrimp
Stenopus hispidus
Coral reefs, rocky reefs
Lt to 30 metres (0 to 98 ft)
70 mm (3 in)

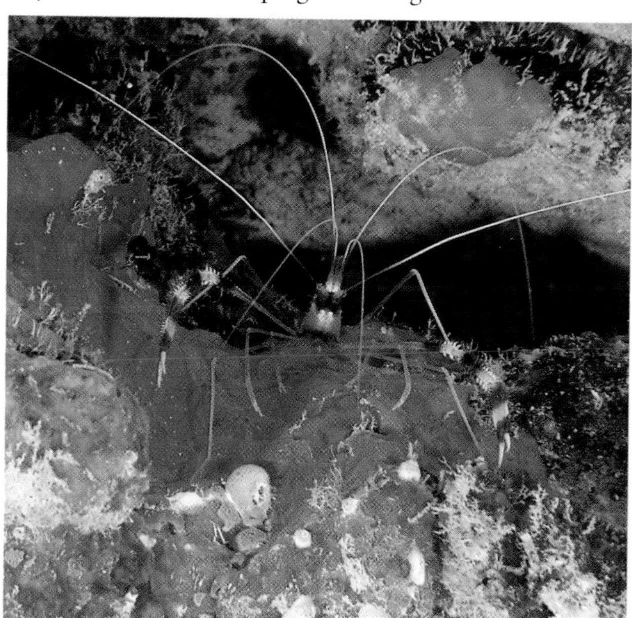

Juvenile Maldivian form.

STENOPODIDAE
Ghost boxer shrimp
Stenopus pyrsonotus
Coral reefs, rocky reefs
20 to 61 metres (66 to 200 ft)
30 mm (1.2 in)

Living in caves and under ledges along deep drop off walls this very secretive and shy shrimp is nocturnally active and cleans sleeping fish. Although it is well known from East Africa to Hawaii it is not often seen by divers. (Photo: Rudie H Kuiter)

Maldivian form. (Photo: Rudie H Kuiter)

STENOPODIDAE
Kuiter's boxer shrimp
new genus/new species
Coral reefs, rocky reefs
20 to 30 metres (66 to 98 ft)
50 mm (2 in)

Strictly nocturnal this unusual shrimp has very long legs and long chelipeds and appears to be undescribed. It lives beneath ledges and in caves in relatively deep water along walls and drop offs where there is a good current flow. The shrimp faces into the current and filters food from the water with its hairy well developed thoracic appendages. Rare in the Maldives, its distribution is unknown. (Photo: Rudie H Kuiter)

Ranging from South Africa to the South Pacific this very common hinge-beak shrimp lives under ledges, in wrecks, caves and beneath dead coral. They have been seen to wander over sleeping fishes at night as if cleaning but this may not be specific.

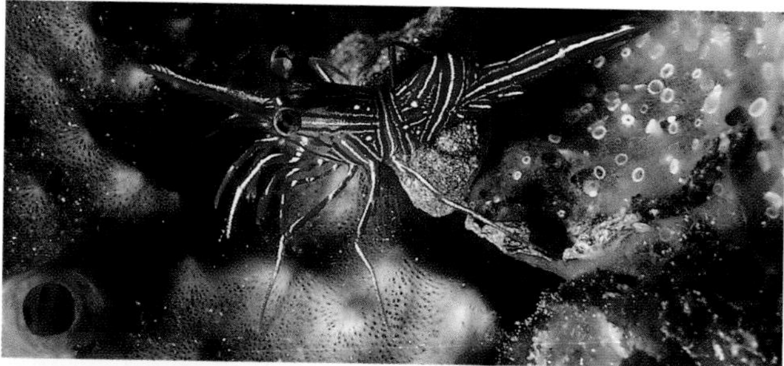

A group of juveniles, Port Moresby, Papua New Guinea.

RHYNCHOCINETIDAE

Durban hinge-beak shrimp

Rhynchocinetes durbanensis

Coral reefs, rocky reefs

8 to 25 metres (26 to 82 ft)

40 mm (1.6 in)

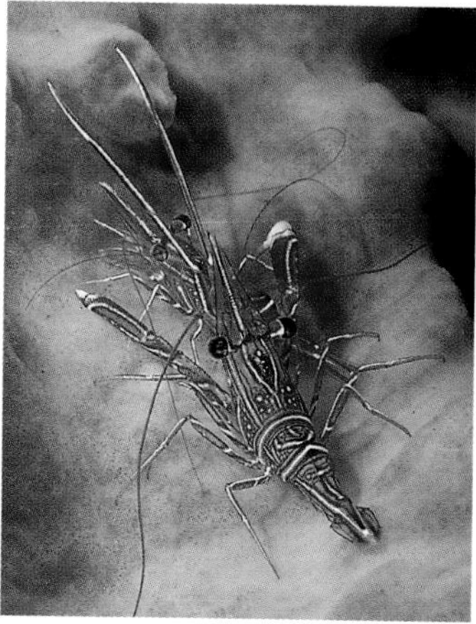

Male (thickly developed chelipeds) courting a female at night from Bali, Indonesia.

Commonly seen on night dives across the Maldives, this hinge-beak shrimp has a constant colour pattern across the Indo-Pacific. The males have long arms and extend them when walking; female chelipeds are much smaller.

RHYNCHOCINETIDAE

Mosaic hinge-beak shrimp

Rhynchocinetes sp.

Coral reefs, rocky reefs

8 to 20 metres (26 to 66 ft)

40 mm (1.6 in)

Female Maldivian form. (Photo: Rudie H Kuiter).

RHYNCHOCINETIDAE

Hawaiian hinge-beak shrimp

Cinethorhynchus hawaiiensis

Coral reefs, rocky reefs

10 to 20 metres (33 to 66 ft)

22 mm (0.8 in)

A new record for the Maldives this species has only been known from Hawaii up until 1999. Although not common in any of the visited sites it is strictly nocturnal and was not seen during dusk dives. It lives in holes in rubble banks and caves and showed a distinct dislike for bright lights.

GNATHOPHYLLIDAE

Harlequin shrimp

Hymenocera picta

Coral reefs, rocky reefs

Lt to 30 metres (0 to 98 ft)

50 mm (2 in)

Beneath the multi-coloured flared chelipeds lie strong razor sharp secondary nippers which can cut the plated skeletons of sea stars to shreds. Paired harlequin shrimps maintain a lair and hunt together dragging back small sea stars such as *Fromia* spp and *Nardoa* sp. Due to colour variations the Indian Ocean form and the Pacific form were once thought to be different species, however, at the present time, only one name is valid.

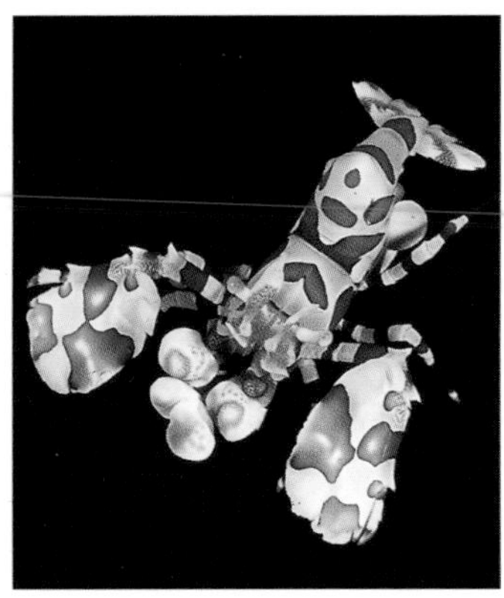

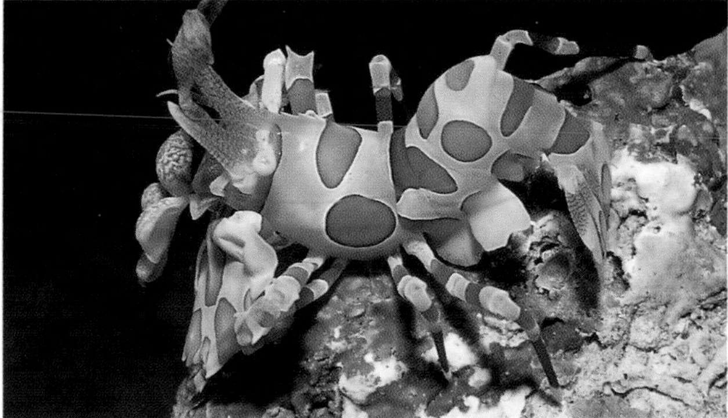

Colour variation (female), Port Moresby, Papua New Guinea.

Indian Ocean form with a captured sea star and feeding method.

Distinctly different, the plumed shrimp is unlikely to be confused with any other species. It has been recorded from the Maldives to Japan and New Caledonia in the Pacific where its patterns and colours are very similar.

PALAEMONIDAE

Plumed shrimp

Leander plumulosus

Coral reefs, rocky reefs

5 to 20 metres (16 to 66 ft)

30 mm (1.2 in)

This species is easy to identify as there are no other similar commensal shrimps. The female may often be twice the size of the male and has been observed with eggs during November. Relatively common in the Maldives they are shown here on the sea anemone *Cryptodendrum adhaesivum*.

PALAEMONIDAE

Short-head anemone shrimp

Periclimenes brevicapalis

Coral reefs, rocky reefs

Lt to 25 metres (0 to 82 ft)

40 mm (1.6 in)

Colour variation, Milne Bay, Papua New Guinea.

Exclusively associated with feather stars this little shrimp is generally similar in colour to its hosts arms. This species is well distributed throughout the Indo-Pacific from the Maldives across to the Great Barrier Reef.

PALAEMONIDAE

Horned feather star shrimp

Periclimenes cornutus

Coral reefs, rocky reefs

5 to 20 metres (16 to 66 ft)

15 mm (0.6 in)

PALAEMONIDAE
Holthuis's anemone shrimp
Periclimenes holthuisi
Coral reefs, rocky reefs
3 to 20 metres (10 to 66 ft)
25 mm (1 in)

The illustration here is the classic day time colour pattern for this species. The colour patch on the abdominal hump is boomerang-shaped and edged either front or back, or both, with a darker edging. This species is common from East Africa to the South Pacific.

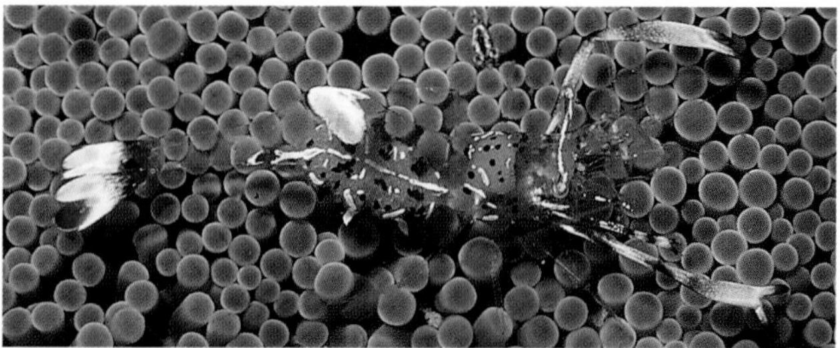

PALAEMONIDAE
Imperial shrimp
Periclimenes imperator
Coral reefs, rocky reefs
Lt to 30 m (98 ft)
25 mm (1 in)

Colour variation, Port Moresby, Papua New Guinea.

During its adult stage the imperial shrimp is found in commensal association with the Spanish dancer nudibranch (*Hexabranchus sanguineus*); it is also known to live on the sea cucumber (*Stichopus* sp.) and other species of sea cucumbers and opisthobranchs.

PALAEMONIDAE
Sibling sea star shrimp
Periclimenes soror
Coral reefs, rocky reefs
3 to 20 metres (10 to 66 ft)
15 mm (0.6 in)

A common Indo-Pacific species ranging from East Africa to South America this little shrimp is always associated with sea stars. There appear to be two main colour phases, red with small white specks and brown or red with a broad yellow or white stripe down the back. In the Maldives they are found on *Acanthaster planci*, *Choriaster* and *Culcita* spp.

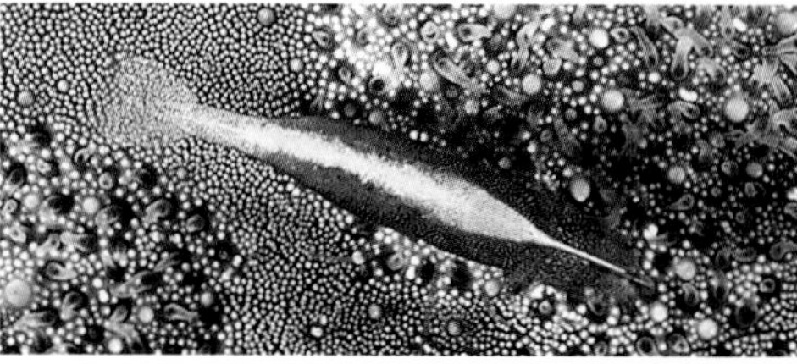

Variation, Kimbe Bay, Papua New Guinea.

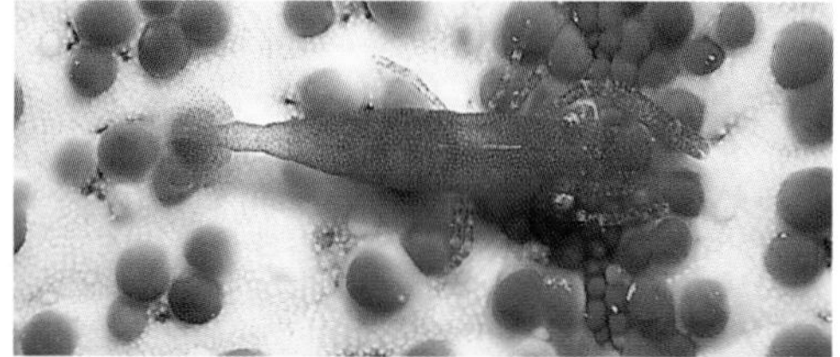

Colour variation or "true" P. soror, *Seychelles.*

PALAEMONIDAE

Thin-armed shrimp

Periclimenes tenuipes

Coral reefs, rocky reefs

Lt to 25 metres (0 to 82 ft)

35 mm (1.4 in)

A free-living species found in sandy floor caves, under ledges and sometimes in conjunction with other invertebrates such as sea anemones, sea fans and mantis shrimps. The body is transparent with white flecks at the chest area, a red stripe down the centre of the body and red brown or yellow on the pincers of its chelipeds.

Head on aspect, Maldives.

PALAEMONIDAE

Hidden sea whip shrimp

Pontonides sp.

Coral reefs, rocky reefs

5 to 60 metres (16 to 197 ft)

15 mm (0.6 in)

Found on several different species of black coral sea whips these small obligate commensals range across the Indo-Pacific and may prove to be several different species. They do not appear common in any one area but, in general, there are a male and female present on a single whip.

Variation, Kimbe Bay, Papua New Guinea.

PALAEMONIDAE

Anton Bruuni cleaner shrimp

Urocardiella antonbruunii

Coral reefs, rocky reefs

20 to 30 metres (66 to 98 ft)

30 mm (1.2 in)

Photographed at a depth of 25 metres this shrimp was one of a number that had set up a cleaning station in the branches of a gorgonian sea fan inside a cave. These shrimps clean receptive fish by swimming out from their launching site and clinging to the fish while it hovers.

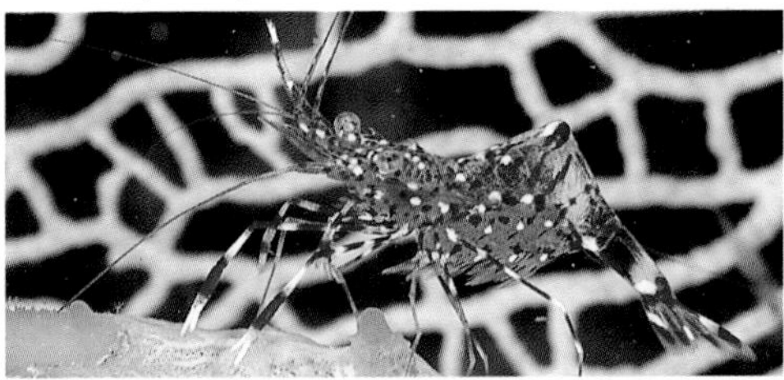

Female shrimp with eggs, Maldives.

ALPHEIDAE

Green-banded alpheid shrimp

Alpheopsis sp.

Coral reefs, rocky reefs

5 to 10 metres (16 to 33 ft)

20 mm (0.8 in)

Restricted to an under boulder and dead coral habitat this small shrimp has a similar banding pattern to other species in the Indo-Pacific but they have red bands. This species is not very common in the Maldives and, as such, has not been able to be identified.

ALPHEIDAE

Pretty snapping shrimp

Alpheus bellulus

Sand

10 to 30 metres (33 to 98 ft)

40 mm (1.6 in)

A very distinctive species with a clearly defined pattern and characteristic black or dark brown bands on its nippers, it is always associated with burrow-guarding gobies of the genus *Ambelyeleotris* and *Ctenogobiops*.

ALPHEIDAE
Djeddah snapping shrimp
Alpheus djeddensis
Sand
5 to 20 metres (16 to 66 ft)
40 mm (1.6 in)

Common to the Indo-Pacific this species lives in burrows which it digs in coarse sand. In almost all cases observed it has resident gobies standing guard outside the burrow to warn of any impending danger.

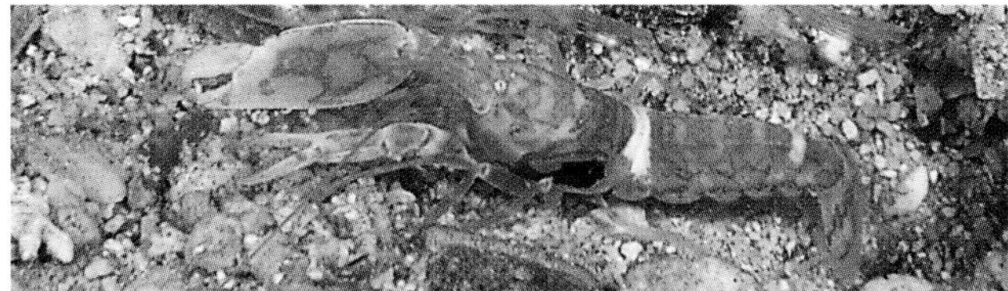

ALPHEIDAE
Randall's snapping shrimp
Alpheus randalli
Sand
5 to 40 metres (16 to 131 ft)
30 mm (1.2 in)

Named for the famous ichthyologist Dr Jack Randall this species is known from the Maldives to the Great Barrier Reef. Randall's snapping shrimp lives with *Amblyeleotris aurora*, *Flabelligobius latruncularis*, *Stenogobiops dracula* and *Vanderhorstia prealta* in the Maldives. (Photo: Toshikazu Kozawa).

Variation, Bali, Indonesia.

ALPHEIDAE
Stimpson's snapping shrimp
Synalpheus stimpsoni
Coral reefs, rocky reefs
10 to 30 metres (33 to 98 ft)
25 mm (1 in)

Found only on the dorsal body disc of feather stars Stimpson's snapping shrimp has many colour variations that don't always match their host's colours. However they have a very distinctive pattern of body stripes which, in most cases, allows recognition.

Colour variation, Dampier, Western Australia.

Colour variation, Exmouth, Western Australia.

HIPPOLYTIDAE

Amboin cleaner shrimp

Lysmata amboinensis

Coral reefs, rocky reefs

8 to 25 metres (26 to 82 ft)

60 mm (2.4 in)

An easily identified widespread species the Amboin cleaner shrimp is active both day and night and lives in caves and crevices in the reef in pairs or in colonies. It seems to attract fish by waving its brilliant white antennae and maxillipeds, which contrast vividly with the dark recesses of the station.

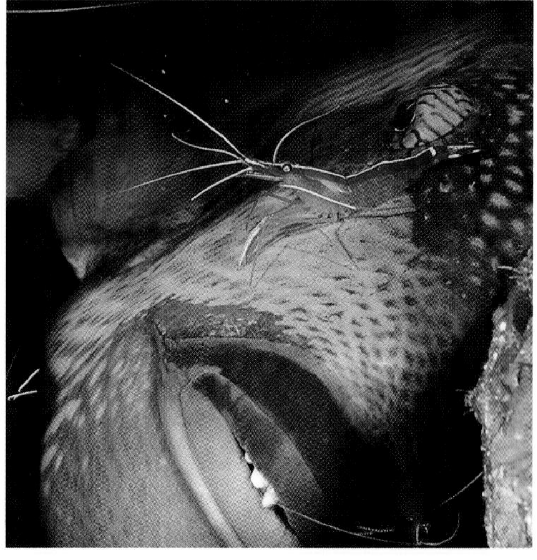

A triggerfish being cleaned at night. Bali, Indonesia.

HIPPOLYTIDAE

Marmorate marble shrimp

Saron marmoratus (male)

Coral reefs, rocky reefs

Lt to 10 metres (0 to 33 ft)

40 mm (1.6 in)

The Marmorate marble shrimp ranges from East Africa across the Indo-Pacific and is very common in Papua New Guinea and on the Great Barrier Reef where they live in shallow water beneath rocks or in coral reef. Maldivian forms live in rubble reef and under ledges.

Colour variation (or undescribed species) female, Lord Howe Island, South Pacific.

HIPPOLYTIDAE

Tapestry marble shrimp

Saron sp.

Coral reefs, rocky reefs

10 to 30 metres (33 to 98 ft)

60 mm (2.4 in)

A large, nocturnal or late overcast afternoon mover this shrimp has a very easily recognised colour pattern and is rarely seen during the day. As yet undescribed it is widely distributed over the Indo-Pacific and regularly seen in the Maldives.

Front on aspect showing the extensive toothbrush-like bristles which are indicative of the female of this species, Maldives.

HIPPOLYTIDAE

Amboin shrimp

Thor amboinensis

Coral reefs, rocky reefs, rocky shores

Lt to 30 metres (0 to 98 ft)

12 mm (0.5 in)

This commensal shrimp inhabits at least seven different species of sea anemones as well as the solitary mushroom coral (*Heliofungia actiniformis*). It holds its abdomen and tail in an almost vertical position and flicks it up and down which, together with a stable colour pattern, makes the species easily identified in the field.

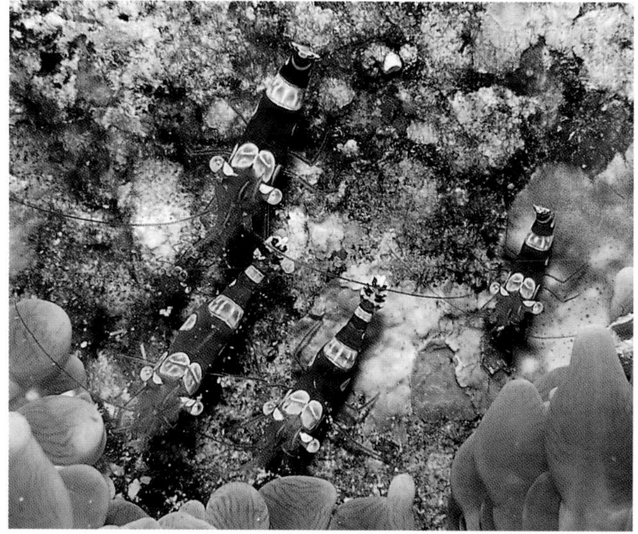

Rock lobsters and Slipper lobsters

Features: Spiny crayfish or rock lobsters are well known throughout most tropical seas where they form the basis of major fisheries. As adults these animals are fairly large (400 mm) with a cylindrical-shaped carapace, a pair of long spiny antennae and eyes which are high on the head and protected by large curved spines (rostral horns). The powerfully muscled abdomen has downward pointing curved spiny plates along the edges and the tail is broad and strong.

Lifestyle: Rock lobsters usually live in caves, under large coral heads or table corals. Nocturnal of habit they venture forth during the night to hunt prey. Tropical species are not caught in pots as they are not attracted to the bait generally used to catch temperate water species (offal). Some tropical species feed on hard-shelled molluscs. Rock lobsters in the Maldives are generally seen along drop offs in caves and ledges during the day.

Reproduction: The sexes are separate with the males being larger than the females. In all species the male has sperm pores at the base of the back legs and the female has genital pores at the bases of both third legs.

Painted rock lobsters may court for several hours with the male endeavouring to deploy the female into a receptive position. Once a chest to chest situation is achieved (usually in the back of a cave) the male rears up and squirts sperm onto the female's chest. This solidifies and is known as a "tar spot". (Other species carry male sperm patches on their legs). During spring and summer months the female painted rock lobster may lay up to 700,000 eggs using claws on the last pair of legs to scrape at the "tar spot" package on the chest thereby releasing the sperm to fertilise the eggs. The eggs are attached to the swimmerets under the abdomen taking three to nine weeks to hatch. Nine to eleven months later after going through several stages in the plankton they settle to the bottom resembling miniature versions of the adults.

The reef-dwelling slipper lobsters have similar natural history and life cycles.

Associations: There are some barnacles which only live on rock lobsters.

Identification: Most rock lobsters have been illustrated in popular books and these are adequate for identification as they all have unique colour patterns and bodily characteristics.

PANINURIDAE

Stripe-legged spiny lobster

Panulirus femorstriga

Coral reefs, rocky reefs

2 to 20 metres (6.6 to 66 ft)

250 mm (10 in)

Found from the Maldives throughout the Indo-Pacific, the young specimen illustrated has a white blaze from the eye to the bottom angle of the carapace which seems to be a feature of the Maldivian forms.
(Photo: Rudie H Kuiter)

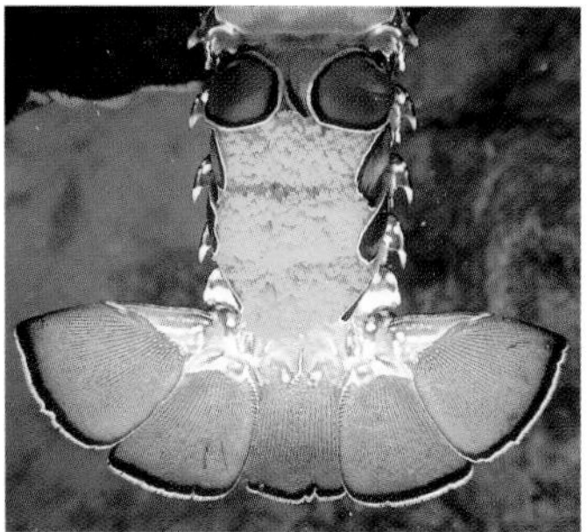

Female showing position of the eggs and the underside of the tail.

Variation from the Great Barrier Reef shows the characteristic white stripe on the legs.

Male and female courting, Lord Howe Island, South Pacific.

PANINURIDAE
Painted rock lobster
Panulirus versicolor
Coral reefs, rocky reefs
Lt to 40 metres (0 to 131 ft)
457 mm (18 in)

The painted rock lobster inhabits the more sheltered parts of coral reefs, lagoons and along back reefs and drop offs. Although they do not readily enter traps or pots the species is a predator, feeding on molluscs. It will also scavenge dead or dying animals.

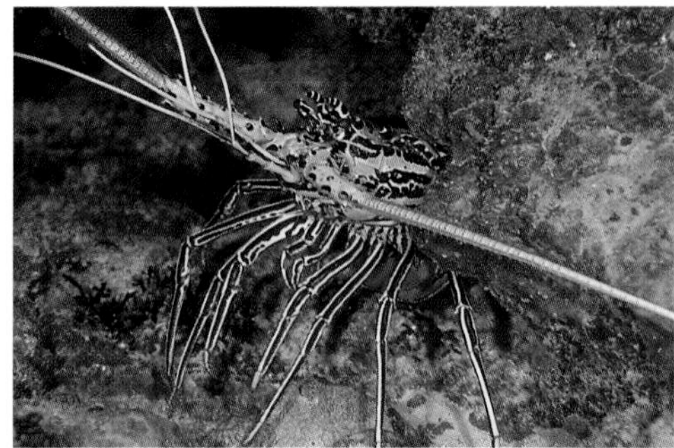

Sperm packet deposited by the male on the female's chest ("tar spot").

Painted rock lobster eggs may number 700,000.

Male and female during the lengthy courting procedure.

Special claw used by the female to scrape sperm from the solidified packet on her chest over her eggs.

Juvenile in coral, Port Moresby, Papua New Guinea.

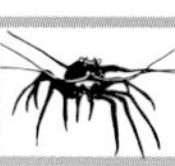

SCYLLARIDAE

Sculptured slipper lobster

Parribacus antarcticus

Coral reefs, rocky reefs

3 to 30 metres (10 to 98 ft)

95 mm (38 in)

Slipper lobsters have a special knack of being able to lever out the animals of turban shells with the flat spiny point on one of their back legs, absolutely ingenious to watch, as they do it beneath the body in the dark, just by touch.

Variation, the Coral Sea.

The female lays a huge mass of eggs which are protected by the flared sides of the carapace.

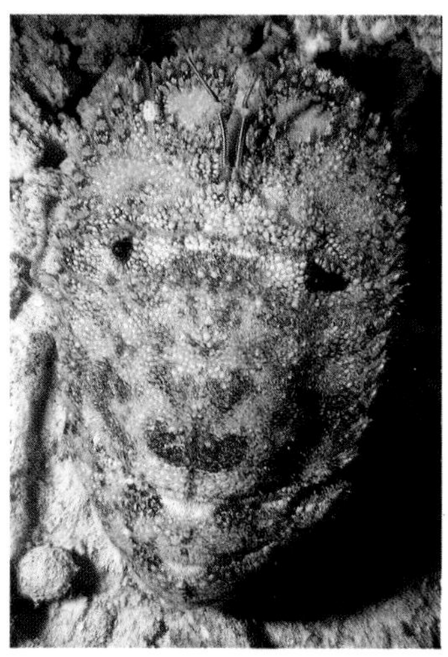

SCYLLARIDAE

Blunt-headed slipper lobster

Scyllarides squammosus

Coral reefs, rocky reefs

5 to 20 metres (16 to 66 ft)

350 mm (12 in)

Ranging from East Africa to the Pacific this nocturnal species lives on the roofs of caves and beneath ledges during the day. Colour varies a little but identification is fairly simple.

Close up of head features, Great Barrier Reef.

Hermit crabs

Features: Most hermit crabs have no protective shell for their abdominal soft parts, they utilise the shells of dead univalves in order to survive and as such are not true crabs. The giant land hermit crab known as the coconut crab (*Birgus latro*) only uses univalve shells at a juvenile stage developing a hardened "shell" for its soft parts as it grows. Most hermit crabs have short strong legs, long eye stalks with small eyes for diurnal kinds and bigger eyes in nocturnal species. The diogenids and coenobitids have larger left hand claws which they use to plug the aperture of the mollusc shell and pagurids have a larger right hand claw.

Lifestyle: Hermit crabs live on coral reef, rocky reef, rubble, sand, mud and feed on algae, other invertebrates and each other. Most will scavenge and many can feed by ciliary processes of their hairy antennae and flagellums. Many species are very colourful.

There are several species of land hermit crabs in the tropics and in some areas they can occur in large numbers crawling around at night amongst decaying leaf litter. Although these crabs spend their adult lives ashore they rarely venture too far from the sea shore and after mating the females go back to the sea to release hatching larvae.

Reproduction: In some species the males may be larger than the females but not always. Sexes are separate and after fertilisation the female lays her eggs along the side of the abdomen attached to small tendril like pleopods. They stay in this position inside the shell until they hatch and the larvae are released.

Identification: Visual identification can be made using leg colour, claw shapes and eye stalks once a good colour reproduction is referenced.

Anemone hermit crab.

COENOBITIDAE

Variable land hermit crab

Coenobita variabilis

Shoreline to 100 metres inland

Lt (0)

50 mm (2 in)

Forms of this terrestrial hermit crab are found across the entire Indo-Pacific. Due to this there are quite a number of variations in colour, size and general morphology. They eat vegetation, scavenge, hunt insects or anything else in the leaf litter and in some areas the big ones eat the small ones.

Smaller versions occur in the Seychelles and the Maldives.

Close up showing how the specially adapted larger claw fits into the aperture as a protective trap door, Vanuatu.

DIOGENIDAE

Blue-spot hermit crab

Dardanus guttatus

Coral reefs, rocky reefs

5 to 20 metres (16 to 66 ft)

80 mm (3.2 in)

A very distinct and easily recognised species due to the circular green blue spot on all the walking legs. It occurs from east Africa throughout the Indo-Pacific to Samoa though it does not appear to be common anywhere within its range.

DIOGENIDAE
Hairy red hermit crab
Dardanus lagapodes
Coral reefs, rocky reefs
Lt to 40 metres (0 to 131 ft)
150 mm (6 in)

This active predator can be observed both day and night across the Indo-Pacific and is generally seen below low-tide level. The hairy red hermit crab is not specific in its food intake and, as an opportunist, will kill and eat fish, molluscs, echinoderms, and other hermit crabs; it is also a very efficient scavenger.

Colour variation museum specimen, Lord Howe Island, South Pacific.

Colour variation, Port Moresby, Papua New Guinea showing the typical dark phase and distinct white tips on its hairs. Antennae can be blue with a yellow streak as some forms in the Maldives or be entirely yellow.

DIOGENIDAE
Red hermit crab
Dardanus megistos
Coral reefs, rocky reefs, lagoons, seagrass meadows
Lt to 25 metres (0 to 82 ft)
250 mm (10 in)

The largest of the reef hermit crabs, the red hermit crab can be found from low-tide level into deep waters throughout many coral reefs of the world. Mainly predatory, red hermit crabs also scavenge and are also able to derive nourishment from detrital feeding. In the Maldives it can be recognised by its bright red orange colour, white antennae and white ocellated spots.

Living beneath dead coral slabs and rocks during the day this hermit crab is nocturnal (big eyes) and only seen out at night. Its shell is almost always "planted" with one or more commensal sea anemones (*Calliactis*) which protect the hermit crab from predators. Anemone hermit crabs are found from South Africa to the South Pacific.

DIOGENIDAE

Anemone hermit crab

Dardanus pedunculatus

Coral reefs, rocky reefs, sand

Lt to 40 metres (0 to 131 ft)

50 mm (2 in)

Nocturnal by nature (big eyes).

For a very common little intertidal hermit crab that occurs from Africa to the South Pacific, one would wonder at the name "secretive". Perhaps when it was described in 1840 it was. Greenish in colour, this species is relatively smooth with a characteristic purple band on each walking leg above the white tip. Claws are white.

DIOGENIDAE

Secretive hermit crab

Calcinus latens

Coral reefs, rocky reefs

Lt to 8 metres (0 to 26 ft)

15 mm (0.6 in)

Restricted to a habitat of live corals where it occupies discarded worm holes this small relation of true hermit crabs is not always easy to find in its coral abode. It feeds both day and night by twirling its long feather-like antennae around catching plankton. Widespread across the Indo-Pacific it has an easily identified pattern on its larger chelae.

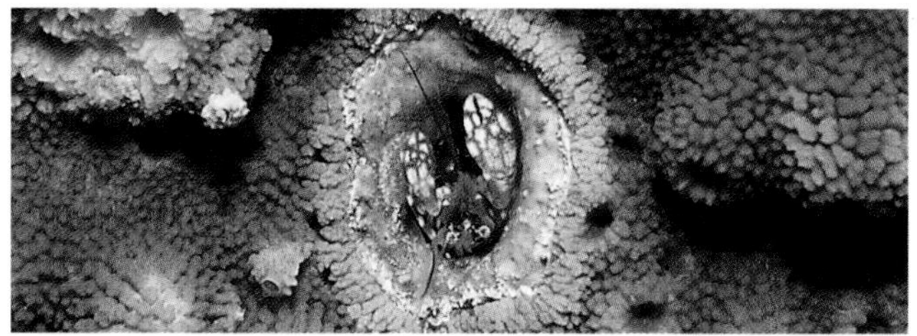

PAGURIDAE

Scott's coral hermit crab

Paguritta scottae

Coral reefs

8 to 20 metres (26 to 66 ft)

10 mm (0.4 in) across

Squat lobsters

Features: Small lobster-like crustaceans belonging to the family Galatheidae occur throughout the Indo-Pacific but as they are quite small (15 to 20 mm) few people notice them. They have a flattened carapace, a well-developed rostrum and a symmetrical abdomen which is curled beneath the body. Their large claws are elongated and the last pair of legs are generally under-developed stubs.

Lifestyle: These animals inhabit nooks and crannies in reef and at night climb up on sponges and the sides of tube anemones and put their hairy arms out into the current to catch plankton. There are many attractive species but little has been done to record them. During the day many live beneath dead coral slabs.

Reproduction: In some cases, females are bigger than males, mating is during summer and the females carry the eggs beneath the abdomen.

Associations: These unusual little creatures are often associated with other invertebrates such as corals, soft corals, tube anemones, sea pens, sea cucumbers and feather stars. Those that live in a commensal relationship with feather stars have the same basic colours as their hosts and can be singularly coloured or striped. Other obligate commensals may also have similar colours to their hosts.

Identification: Almost all species have distinctive shapes and colour patterns though few have been published in colour and a lot more remain undiscovered. They can be visually identified from a photograph but initial identity must first be confirmed by a taxonomist.

GALATHEIDAE

Elegant squat lobster

Allogalathea elegans

Coral reefs, rocky reefs

5 to 25 metres (16 to 82 ft)

10 mm (0.4 in)

Found living among the pinnate arms of several species of crinoids (feather stars), the elegant squat lobster has an ideal habitat, safe from most predators. Its colour tends to mimic that of its host. Although most individuals have longitudinal stripes of various thicknesses and colours, those living on red crinoids can be totally red.

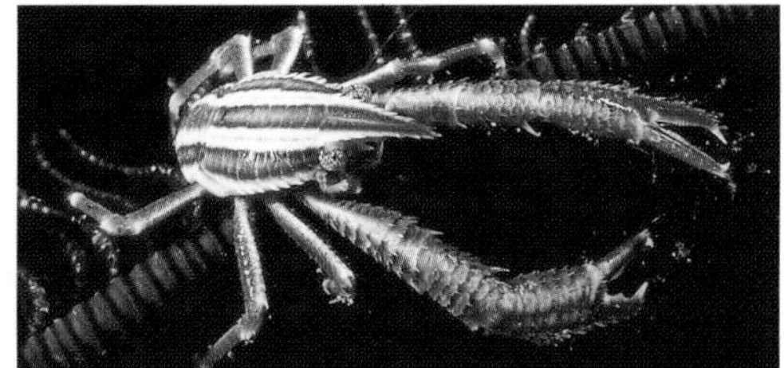

Structural details of exo-skeleton.

Crabs

Several thousand different kinds of crabs occur throughout world oceans. Crabs can walk, run, crawl, clamber, swim, dig, burrow and scurry depending on their type.

Although some species have evolved into incredibly bizarre examples they all retain the same basic body form. The body is encased in a carapace with a reduced abdomen folded under as an abdominal flap housing the sexual organs. Most have claws known as chelae, some are exaggerated in size and are used for defence, to capture prey, attract females and repulse other males.

Lifestyles: Crabs live from the shore down to the bottom of the deepest oceanic trenches and are found in most habitats between. There are spider crabs that grow gardens of algae, sponge or ascidians on their backs and legs as camouflage and sponge crabs that use pieces of live sponge as a hat to avoid predators.

The porcelain anemone crab is immune to its hosts' stinging nematocysts and on a rising tide comes out of hiding beneath the anemone's "skirt" and "fishes" for its meal of plankton.

There are so many interesting and peculiar lifestyles but crabs are difficult to study due to their secretive behaviour.

Reproduction: Crabs are singularly sexed and males must mate with a female from behind or from the front at a time when her new shell is soft (after a moult). Some of the smarter males actually carry a female around for some time before she moults, ensuring they achieve the purpose. Females lay their eggs and carry them beneath their abdominal flap until the eggs hatch and the larvae join the rest of the plankton.

Male and female crabs of the same species can be separated by their claws (males generally having the larger) or by their abdominal flaps. Males have narrow abdominal flaps and females have wider ones, to accommodate their eggs.

Associations: Many live in association with sponges, algae, sea anemones, corals, soft corals, black corals, tube anemones, sea whips, feather stars, sea stars, sea cucumbers and molluscs. In some cases the crabs are coloured and shaped to resemble their host (mimicry).

Identification: Due to their shapes and patterns the identification of some crab types is fairly simple and many can be determined to species once their colour images are available in popular books. The commensal species (wherever the association is well known) are also fairly easy to identify. However, unless there are easily recognised distinguishing features some species can only be separated to types by process of elimination in scientific papers.

PORCELLANIDAE
Marbled porcelain crab
Pachycheles sp.
Coral reefs, rocky reefs
3 to 10 metres (10 to 33 ft)
15 mm (0.6 in)

Found under dead coral and rocks in exposed shallow water areas this species has very thick chunky arms which seem too heavy for the size of its body. The pattern on the back doesn't show much variation on Maldivian forms.

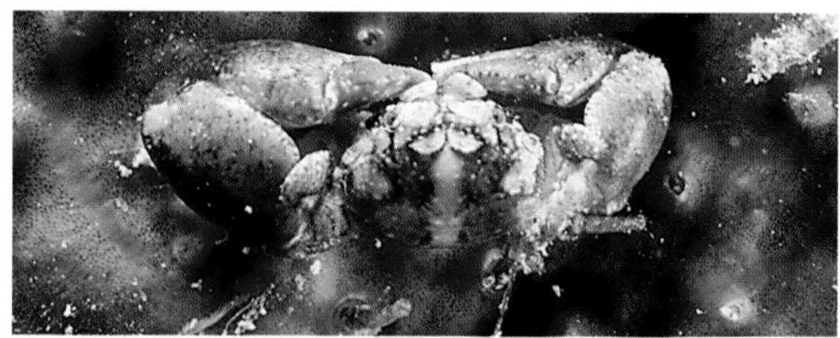

PORCELLANIDAE
Furry porcelain crab
Petrolisthes pubescens
Coral reefs, rocky reefs
Lt to 5 metres (0 to 16 ft)
15 mm (0.6 in)

This species ranges from the Maldives to the West Coast of Australia. There are distinctive purple markings on the flattened claws and back and the claws have well-developed spines on the inner sides.

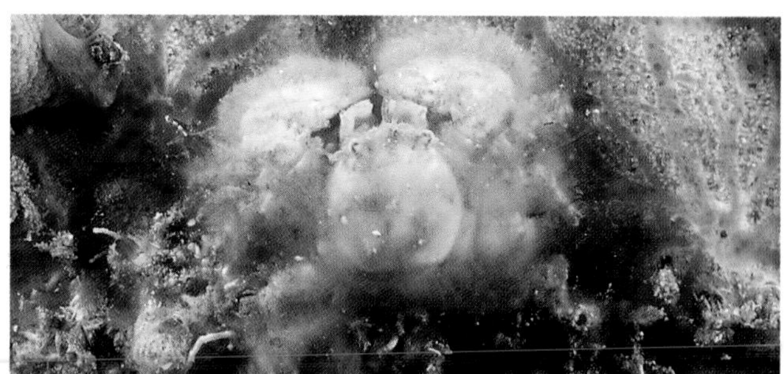

PORCELLANIDAE
Spotted porcellanid crab
Neopetrolisthes maculatus
Coral reefs, rocky reefs
Lt to 25 metres (0 to 82 ft)
35 mm (1.4 in)

Living with sea anemones, the spotted porcellanid crab is found throughout the Indo-Pacific. The feeding mechanism is two modified appendages (maxillipeds), which are alternately flung out and returned in a rhythmic procedure, catching plankton.

A similar species Neopetrolisthes oshmai from Port Moresby, Papua New Guinea showing the action of feeding in progress (above).

MAJIDAE

Low-eyed spider crab

Cyclax suborbicularis

Coral reefs, rocky reefs

Lt to 10 metres (0 to 33 ft)

25 mm (1 in) across

During the day this crab lives beneath rocks and dead corals and often has a light covering of filamentous algae on its body. There are small spines on the back (carapace) and legs and a distinctive pattern on the back. This species is recorded across the Indo-Pacific.

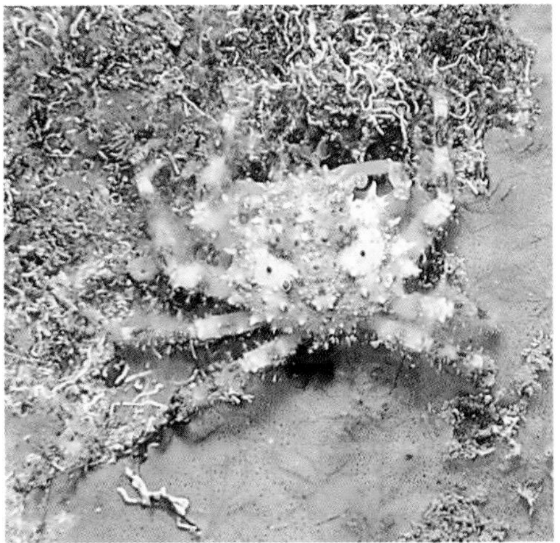

Colour variation with some sponge coating, Maldives.

MAJIDAE

Noduled spider crab

Cyclocoeloma tuberculata

Coral reefs, rocky reefs

Lt to 10 metres (0 to 33 ft)

25 mm (1 in) across

Recorded from the Maldives to Australia this little spider crab is often seen covered in algae, ascidians or sponges which it attaches to its back and legs in order to camouflage itself. The back (carapace) has very distinctive tubercules arranged in a pattern indicative of the species. During the day it lives beneath rocks and dead coral.

MAJIDAE
Oate's soft coral crab
Hoplophrys oatesii

Coral reefs, rocky reefs

5 to 15 metres (16 to 49 ft)

15 mm (0.6 in) across

One of the most difficult species of commensal crabs to find and even more so to photograph, the carapace, legs and claws are spiky and often tinged purple. The opaque white pattern on its back blends into the spicule pattern on the stems of soft corals. It is found from the Red Sea to the Maldives and across into the Pacific.

Side on aspect, Bali, Indonesia.

Dorsal aspect, Bali, Indonesia.

MAJIDAE
Long-horned spider crab
Naxiodes taurus

Coral reefs, rocky reefs

20 to 40 metres (66 to 131 ft)

30 mm (1.2 in) across

Living near black corals and gorgonians these crabs climb into the branches during the night and feed. They have long pointed horns on their heads and some have hydroids growing on their backs and legs. Males have much larger chelae (claws) than females. (Photo: Rudie H. Kuiter)

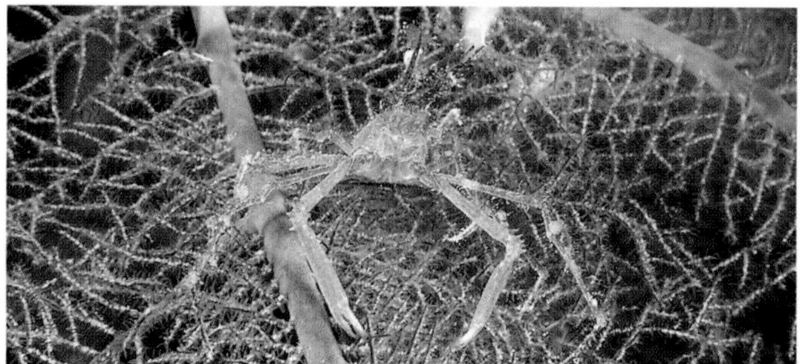

Common across the entire Indo-Pacific the rough spider crab was named for the rough shell texture on the back (carapace) and legs which provides a good surface for the planted garden of sponges on its back and legs.

MAJIDAE

Rough spider crab

Schizophrys aspera

Coral reefs, rocky reefs

Lt to 30 metres (0 to 98 ft)

25 mm (1 in) across

Museum specimen showing the crab's real colouration, pattern, well-developed spines and rough shell texture.

A young rough spider crab showing the tubercle design on the carapace.

Found on various species of *Antipathes* black coral trees that have yellow skin and tentacles the black coral spider crab with its similar body colouration and definite opaque white stripe down the back is simple to identify. The species is known from the Maldives to the Pacific.

MAJIDAE

Conical black coral spider crab

Xenocarcinus conicus

Coral reefs, rocky reefs

25 to 40 metres (82 to 131 ft)

20 mm (0.8 in) across

PARTHENOPIDAE

Elegant crinoid crab

Harrovia elegans

Coral reefs, rocky reefs

5 to 10 metres (16 to 33 ft)

15 mm (0.6 in) across

An obligate commensal the elegant crinoid crab is only found on crinoids of the genus *Comaster* and *Comanthus*. Colour varies from chocolate brown with yellow markings to black with white markings. The species is well known across the Indo-Pacific and easy to identify.

Colour variation with Comaster *sp. host, Great Barrier Reef.*

PORTUNIDAE

Anemone crab

Lissocarcinus laevis

Coral reefs, rocky reefs

5 to 25 metres (16 to 82 ft)

30 mm (1.2 in) across

Found in association with sea anemones and tube anemones this widely distributed species is well known throughout the Indo-Pacific. Although there is a degree of colour and design variation across its range the general pattern concept is maintained and is easily distinguished visually.

Colour variation, Port Moresby, Papua New Guinea.

PORTUNIDAE

Sea cucumber crab

Lissocarcinus orbicularis

Coral reefs, rocky reefs

Lt to 25 metres (0 to 82 ft)

30 mm (1.2 in) across

Mostly found on various sea cucumbers this small form was living on *Stichopus* sp. in 25 metres (82 ft) of water on a sand bottom. It's interesting to note that the crab is predominantly white whereas the sea cucumber is very dark. Sometimes the crabs live in the cloacal chamber (anus) of the sea cucumber.

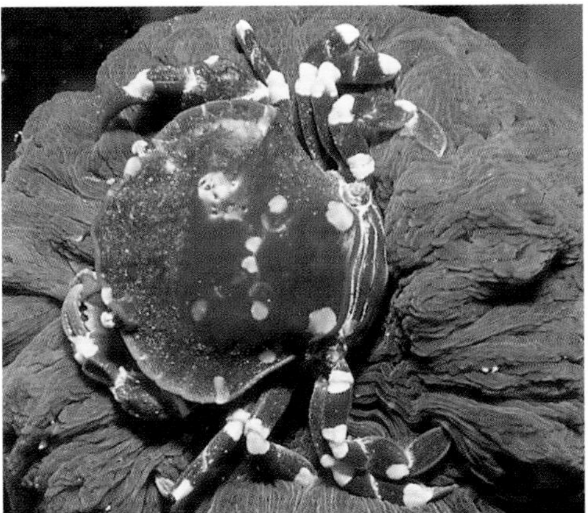

Colour variation, Exmouth, Western Australia.

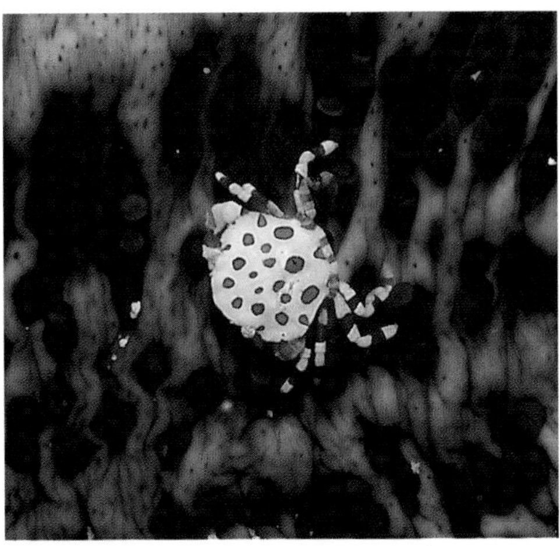

XANTHIDAE

Beaded crab

Actaea polyacantha

Coral reefs, rocky reefs

2 to 10 metres (6.6 to 33 ft)

15 mm (0.6 in) across

Spectacularly sculptured the beaded crab is a shallow water dweller that inhabits the undersides of rocks and dead coral during the day in areas of moderate wave action. There doesn't appear to be much colour variation in the Maldivian specimens observed and even those living in Japanese waters show little variation.

XANTHIDAE

Round-backed coral crab

Carpilius convexus

Coral reefs, rocky reefs

Lt to 30 metres (0 to 98 ft)

100 mm (4 in)

Sometimes seen beneath coral slabs in low-tide areas. When disturbed, the coral crab runs into a depression or hollow where it hangs on tightly. By presenting its very strong smooth carapace, the coral crab repels any potential predators trying to dislodge it. Its colour is variable ranging from an unpatterned orange to orange with red mottling.

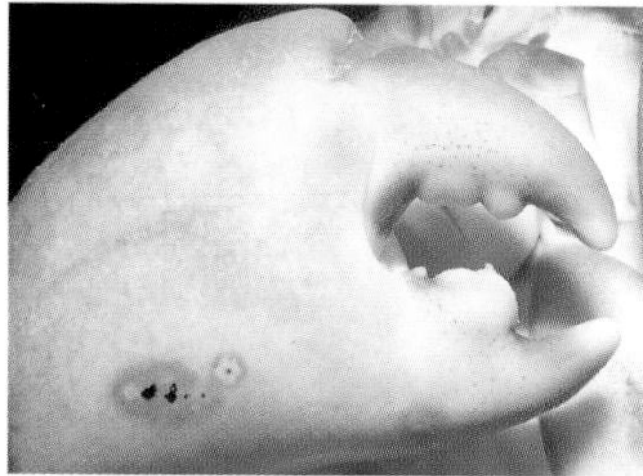

Specially adapted claw for breaking open univalve shells.

Colour variation, Lord Howe Island, South Pacific.

XANTHIDAE

Blood-spotted crab

Carpilius maculatus

Coral reefs, rocky reefs

Lt to 10 metres (0 to 33 ft)

90 mm (3.6 in)

A common nocturnal species known from the Red Sea to the South Pacific. The colour and pattern varies little throughout its distribution.

With such a distinctive-shaped carapace, white speckles, thorny legs and yellow eye stalks, this shallow water species would seem to be easily identified but like many other Maldivian species it proved difficult. During the day it hides beneath rocks and dead coral in exposed situations.

XANTHIDAE

Speckled crab

Estius sp.

Coral reefs, rocky reefs

2 to 10 metres (6.6 to 33 ft)

30 mm (1.2 in) across

This beautiful little crab has a remarkable association with minute *Boloceractis prehensa* anemones which it carries in its claws. Well known throughout the Indo-Pacific the female lays a batch of red eggs which are carried beneath the abdominal flap.

XANTHIDAE

Tessellated boxer crab

Lybia tessellata

Coral reefs, rocky reefs

2 to 20 metres (6.6 to 66 ft)

20 mm (0.8 in) across

Frontal aspect, Maldives.

This species inhabits the underside of rocks and dead coral on exposed reefs in the Maldives. Both the carapace and the claws are noduled and the pattern on the back did not appear to bear much variation on those observed.

XANTHIDAE

Ungulate crab

Phymodius ungulatus

Coral reefs, rocky reefs

Lt to 5 metres (0 to 16 ft)

20 mm (0.8 in)

TRAPEZIIDAE

Granulose black coral crab

Quadrella granulosa

Coral reefs, rocky reefs

15 to 50 metres (49 to 164 ft)

20 mm (0.8 in) across

Occurring at a number of localities throughout the Maldives, this very attractive little crab lives inside the bottlebrush black coral (*Antipathes*) which grows from the bottom and sides of caves near deep water drop offs. Most observations show that there is a male and female crab present in each black coral colony and both are of the same proportions and similar colours.

Colour variation is unusual in that its legs are the same colour and pattern as the darker form, Maldives.

TRAPEZIIDAE

Red-dotted coral crab

Trapezia cymodoce

Coral reefs, rocky reefs

Lt to 10 metres (0 to 33 ft)

20 mm (0.8 in) across

Common across the Indo-Pacific wherever shallow water corals occur these commensal coral crabs are totally dependant on their hosts for living quarters and protection. During the day they hide deep in the coral. At night they climb up to the edges, spread their arms and feed on plankton.

Close up, Indian Ocean form.

Night time, showing spread-armed feeding behaviour, Kimbe Bay, Papua New Guinea.

TRAPEZIIDAE
Spotty-legged coral crab
Trapezia guttata
Coral reefs, rocky reefs
Lt to 10 metres (0 to 33 ft)
20 mm (0.8 in) across

Mostly found amongst the fronds of the coral *Seriotopora hystrix* this little crab has a dark chocolate-coloured underside, a white dot on the inside of each arm when it's extended during feeding and dark spots on its legs. The carapace is ivory white; these colours remain similar across the crab's extensive Indo-Pacific range.

Dorsal aspect, Lord Howe Island, South Pacific.

EUMEDONIDAE
Adam's urchin crab
Zebrida adamsii
Coral reefs, rocky reefs
3 to 15 metres (10 to 49 ft)
25 mm (1 in) across

Inhabiting the Indian Ocean across to the Coral Sea this easily identified uniquely-shaped commensal crab is only found on various species of sea urchins. It occurs on tropical species *Toxopneustes pileolus*, *Asthenosoma ijimai* and on *Heliocidaris erhthrogramma* in the southern Indian Ocean. The crab has modified hooks on the end of each leg which is used to hang onto the urchin's spines.

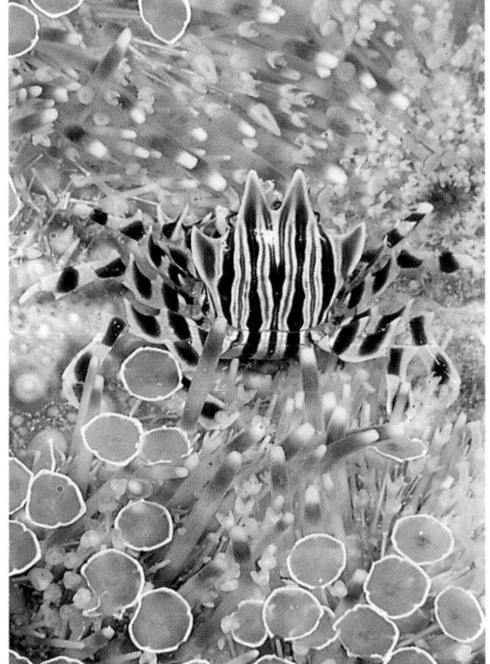

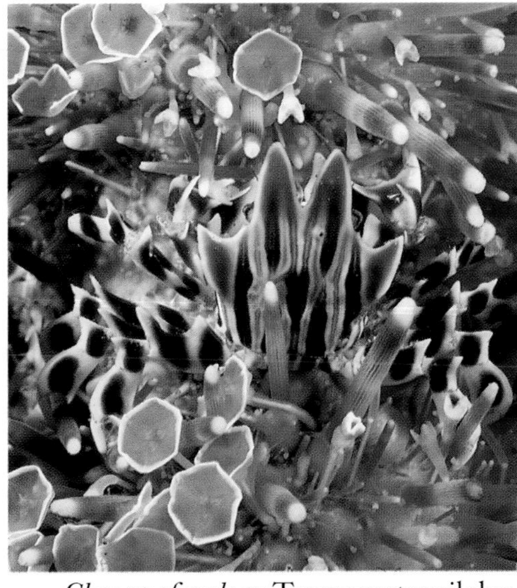

Close up of male on Toxopneustes pilolus, *Kashiwajima, Shikoku Island. Japan.*

GRAPSIDAE

Swift-footed rock crab

Grapsus albolineatus

Coral reef rocks, rocky reefs, rocky shores

Intertidal

200 mm (8 in)

The swift-footed rock crab inhabits beach rock, rock walls, boat ramps and jetties across the Indo-Pacific. Its body is coloured in a multitude of greens, blues, oranges and blacks which may vary throughout its range. This species feeds on algae and detritus from rock walls as well as preying on small invertebrates.

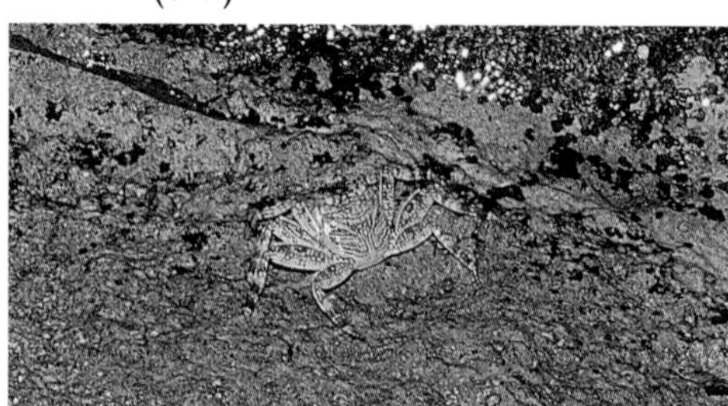

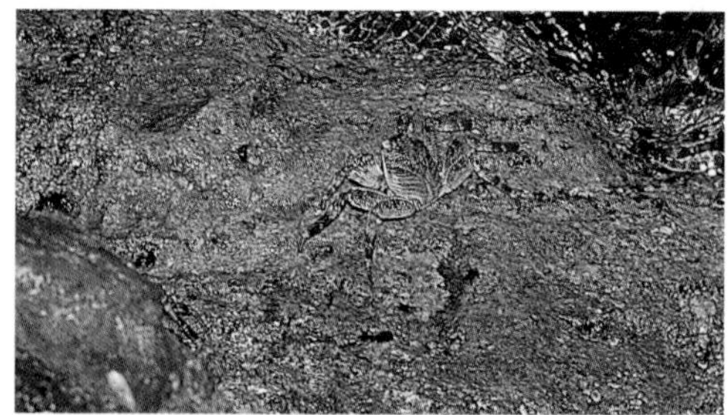

Typical Maldivian colour pattern.

Colour variation, dorsal aspect, Indian Ocean.

Colour variation, frontal aspect (male), Heron Island, Great Barrier Reef.

OCYPODIDAE

Stalk-eyed ghost crab

Ocypode ceratophthalma

Sandy beaches, cays

Intertidal

200 mm (8 in)

This crab is the largest of the tropical ghost crabs and can be distinguished by the pointed stalks that protrude above the eyes of adult specimens, the two dark red blotches on its back and the dark red on the underside of the body and legs. Stalk-eyed ghost crabs live down burrows dug deep into the sand during the day and are mostly seen only at night.

Large male cannibalising a small ghost crab. Carnarvon, Western Australia.

OCYPODIDAE

Little ghost crab

Ocypode cordimana

Sandy beaches

Intertidal

20 mm (0.8 in) (carapace)

Widespread across tropical beaches, the little ghost crab has unarmed eyes and tends to be whitish in colour with a few grey blotches; colour has been observed to alter from grey to pinkish red during the night-and-day changeover. It feeds at the tide line on animal and vegetable flotsam and also devours terrestrial insects.

Colour variation at night, Shark bay, Western Australia.

Echinoderms

Chapter 8

Echinoderms

PHYLUM: ECHINODERMATA (Spiny skinned animals)

CLASSES: *Crinoidea* (Feather stars)
Asteroidea (Sea stars)
Ophiuroidea (Brittle stars, Serpent stars, Snake stars, Basket stars)
Echinoidea (Sea urchins, Heart urchins, Sand dollars)
Holothuroidea (Sea cucumbers)

Features: Echinoderms, more than any other marine invertebrates, are perhaps the most often seen underwater. They are large, simple in external design, attractively coloured and in some cases have sharp spines. Rarely would an ocean dive be completed without seeing or touching an echinoderm.

They are exclusively marine and occur in every major habitat from the intertidal zone down to the bottom of the deep sea trenches, and within that range inhabit every type of bottom terrain, from soft mud to rugged coastline constantly pounded by surf.

The typical echinoderm is pentamerous (with five sides, five parts, or five arms), a design unique in the animal kingdom. Although they appear to be very varied in structure, there are two features which unite them all. One character is called radial symmetry, whereby the body is divided into separate but similar sections. The other unique feature is the possession of tentacle-like structures called tube feet. These tube feet are hydraulically controlled by a water vascular system which, when used in conjunction with powerful suction pads situated at their extremities, allow most echinoderms to move around on almost any surface, even upside down.

They have no heart, brain, nor eyes, yet although it isn't always apparent, a top and bottom or back and front exists. In general, all classes except feather stars and sea cucumbers and some sea urchins have their mouth on the underside and their anus on top.

Echinoderms can regenerate missing limbs, arms, spines – even intestines – in response to wounding. Some brittle stars and sea stars can reproduce asexually by breaking a ray or arm or by deliberately splitting the body in half, each of which then generates a whole new body.

With so many lifestyles, the evolution of feeding mechanisms has played a large part in the success of this phylum. Various forms may be carnivorous, omnivorous or herbivorous. There are also detrital foragers and planktonic and suspended sediment feeders.

Lifestyles: Although their jointed exoskeleton and spiny skins protect them in numerous ways, echinoderms are preyed upon by other sea creatures, including numbers of their own phylum and class. Sea stars are eaten by triton shells, fish, other sea stars and shrimps. Brittle stars face predation from fish, sea stars and crabs. Sea urchins are hunted by fish, triton shells, helmet shells and sea stars; while sea cucumbers fall prey to triton shells and tun shells.

Many echinoderms only show themselves at night (nocturnal), therefore reducing the threat from the more numerous day time predators.

Humans use the roe of sea urchins and the specially prepared outer body walls of sea cucumbers for food. A small "trepang" fishing industry exists in the Maldives as dried sea cucumber is widespread as a food additive in Asia.

Reproduction: Reproduction is carried out by the release of sperm and eggs into the sea, though some species may be hermaphrodites. The majority produce pelagic planktonic larvae. These larvae are bilaterally symmetrical, unlike their parents. The juveniles develop typical echinoderm features when they settle to the bottom. Some echinoderms give birth to live young and brood them in special chambers. This is peculiar to cold water species.

Associations: Creatures from many diverse phyla inhabit echinoderms. Some are non-specific associations, others are very specific, and still others so modified that they are host-reliant parasites found nowhere else.

Besides epiphytes such as sponges, hydroids, and ascidians which are only incidental associations there are univalve molluscs, crabs, shrimps, squat lobsters, barnacles, brittle stars and fish which have obligate associations with echinoderms.

Identification: Although through books like this is it now possible to visually identify many living species by external features in their natural habitats there is still a long way to go. Each species must be researched, observed and photographed over their entire range of distribution so that all forms and colour variations are recorded. Until that time many species can only be illustrated as examples of what exists and hope that by doing so it will encourage a greater participation in the study and understanding of Maldivian echinoderms.

CLASS: *Crinoidea* (Feather stars)

Features: Very common in ancient seas (over 400 million years ago) the stalked sea lilies are still present in modern oceans but are restricted to deep waters, or in the cold depths beneath the ice in Antarctica. Whereas the stalked sea lilies are anchored in the bottom sediments and do not move around, the feather stars can crawl, roll, walk and even swim.

The body of a typical feather star is cup-shaped, supported on a circular arrangement of jointed appendages known as cirri which cling to the substrate and are attached to a base on the underside of the cup. The sides of the cup extend up into five many-jointed arms which then (depending on the species) fork at various intervals and produce multiple branches, or arms.

Both the cup and the arms have an internal skeleton of close fitting calcareous plates which give the feather star its jointed yet very rigid form. The arms bear the side branches or pinnules which in turn bear suckerless tube feet rich in mucus-secreting glands which trap plankton and suspended sediment working together as net. Food is trapped by the "net" incorporated into a mucus strand which is passed down food grooves in each arm to the mouth.

Unlike any other class of echinoderm, feather stars have both their mouth and their anus on the upper surface. On many species the anus can be extended to form a long tube which exudes waste products away from the mouth.

Lifestyle: Although many feather stars can be seen with their arms extended and feeding during the day, at night many more come out of the reef to move around and feed. On some reefs there are extensive populations while others have less, depending on the current movement. Feather stars do not appear to have many predators. If damaged they can replace their arms at will.

Reproduction: The sexes are separate; sperm and ova are released into the sea where fertilisation occurs. A brief (1 to 5 days) planktonic larval phase follows after which the larvae settle, attach to the substrate and grow a stalk (a reminder of their sea lily ancestors). Sometime later the juveniles break free from their stalked existence and start life as feather stars.

Associations: A number of other sea creatures have formed close relationships with feather stars, including cling fish gobies, snapping shrimps, pontonine shrimps, squat lobsters, worms, brittle stars and crabs. Small parasitic molluscs also live on them.

Identification: Most feather stars are not easily identified in the field and require a specimen and a trained taxonomist. However, with more information becoming available together with increased photographic coverage some will become easier in the future.

COLOBOMETRIDAE

Pretty feather star

Cenometra bella

Coral reefs, rocky reefs

10 to 50 metres (33 to 164 ft)

140 mm (5.5 in)

Recorded from the Bay of Bengal to New Caledonia, this species is commonly seen attached to black coral sea whips *Cirripathes anguinus* and gorgonian sea whips *Junceella* sp. (which may be grey, orange, or red). It appears expanded both day and night and frequents areas of strong current, such as channels between reefs.

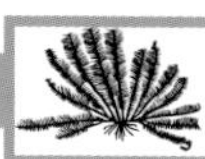

The feather star genus *Colobometra* is widespread across the Indo-Pacific and into the South Pacific. In general, this species has 10 arms and has long cirri by which it hangs onto gorgonians and black coral sea whips.

COLOBOMETRIDAE
Spinose feather star
Colobometra perspinosa
Coral reefs, rocky reefs
15 to 40 metres (49 to 131 ft)
200 mm (8 in)

With only ten arms the Maldivian form of this delicate species appears a lot easier to define than many of its relations. It is always found on sea fans and ranges to the west coast of Australia.

COLOBOMETRIDAE
Ten-armed feather star
Oligometra serripinna
Coral reefs, rocky reefs
20 to 30 metres (66 to 98 ft)
170 mm (6.8 in)

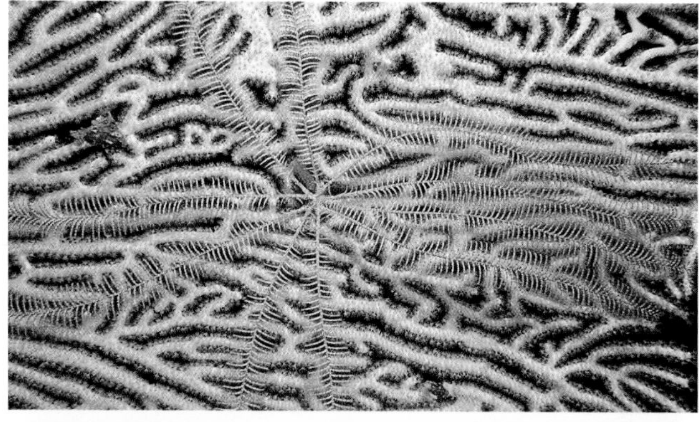

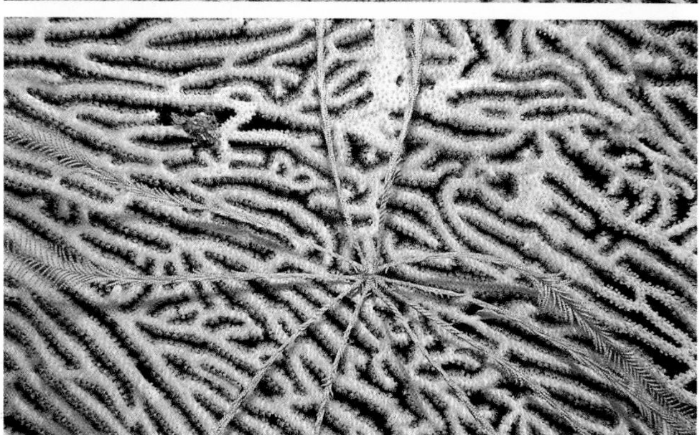

Same individual with closed pinnules, Maldives.

COMASTERIDAE
Noble feather star
Comanthina nobilis
Coral reefs, rocky reefs
5 to 25 metres (16 to 82 ft)
400 mm (16 in)

Common in many areas throughout the Indo-Pacific, the noble feather star has two main colour forms: bright yellow; and black with white, green and yellow colourings. It is found in situations such as high coral outcrops and ledges directly in the current flow and is inhabited by commensal shrimps and squat lobsters.

COMASTERIDAE
Bennett's feather star
Oxycomanthus bennetti
Coral reefs, rocky reefs
10 to 20 metres (33 to 66 ft)
200 mm (8 in)

With over 100 arms and a range of colour variations Bennett's feather star is difficult to identify visually from similar species. However, unlike the *C. nobilis* or *schlegeli* its attachment cirri are more developed and it generally doesn't hang on by its arms.

Strictly nocturnal of habit this feather star is never seen out in the open. It lives in a hole or crevice and only extends a few arms to catch plankton. Most specimens were orange.

COMASTERIDAE

Long-arm feather star

Comissa sp.

Coral reefs, rocky reefs

5 to 20 metres (16 to 66 ft)

170 mm (6.8 in) across photo

Common across the Indo-Pacific, the robust feather star may be seen feeding during the day on incoming tide. When observed as such the animal appears red all over, however, the underside of the arm's central stem may be bright yellow, white or grey.

HIMEROMETRIDAE

Robust feather star

Himerometra robustipinna

Coral reefs, rocky reefs

5 to 30 metres (16 to 98 ft)

300 mm (12 in)

Resting position, Great Barrier Reef.

MARIAMETRIDAE

Indian feather star

Stephanometra indica

Coral reefs, rocky reefs

Lt to 20 metres (0 to 66 ft)

250 mm (10 in)

The Indian feather star is known to range from East Africa to the South Pacific. This species is nocturnal; at night it crawls out of its protective cranny deep within the rubble bank, spreads out its arms and feeds.

Feeding position, Great Barrier Reef.

MARIAMETRIDAE

Palm-frond feather star

Stephanometra sp.

Coral reefs, rocky reefs

5 to 20 metres (16 to 66 ft)

170 mm (6.8 in) across photo

Only seen out at night this genus is common across the entire Indo-Pacific and in many cases individuals have a very indicative pattern.

Colour variation, or another form, Maldives.

Only seen out at night these common Maldivian feather stars present a spectacular sight at some locations with over 20 individuals occupying positions within a small area.

MARIAMETRIDAE

Regal feather star

Stephanometra sp.

Coral reefs, rocky reefs

5 to 20 metres (16 to 66 ft)

200 mm (8 in) across

Close up of closed pinnules, Maldives.

Colour variation, or another species, Maldives.

Side on aspect, Maldives.

CLASS: *Asteroidea* (Sea Stars)

Features: All sea stars have the same basic star shape and most have five arms. There is a mouth on the underside; the anus (where present) is at the centre of the disc together with the water intake (madreporite) on the dorsal surface. The body is covered by plates which may be large or small depending on the species. While some kinds appear soft, others given the impression of being quite rigid and cannot be bent even under pressure. Many will break before they yield. These plates are often spiny, or modified in some way. In the case of the crown of thorns sea star, the plates are extremely modified and the spines have acquired venomous properties, and as such are serious threats to careless divers.

Between the plates (which are embedded in the body walls) are soft tissue and small gills which are retractable. When these gills are extended they tend to give the sea star a soft velvety appearance. On the body surface there are other small organs peculiar to sea stars and sea urchins. These devices are known as pedicellariae of which there are three different types; simple, pincer-like and scissor-like. On sea stars all pedicellariae are sessile, while on sea urchins they are stalked. These pedicellariae act as cleaning and defence organs.

Beneath each arm there is an ambulacral groove which contains two rows of mobile tube feet except in some Echinasteridae which have 4 rows. These locomotory tube feet are operated by water pressure and have suckers at the tips in reef-dwelling sea stars, or end in points for digging purposes on sand-dwelling sea stars. Reef-dwelling sea stars are sometimes found on sand and soft bottom, but sand-dwelling forms are unable to climb on rocky reefs and would have difficulty finding food. They can all regenerate damaged or missing parts.

Lifestyle: The majority of sea stars are carnivorous though different species may be herbivorous, carnivorous, omnivorous and/or detritus feeders, or scavengers, depending on what's available. Food is generally absorbed outside of the mouth by way of extruding the stomach over the prey or, in the case of some sand stars, the prey is swallowed, or half swallowed (when too big) and eaten gradually. Food includes detritus, algae, seagrass, sponges, corals, worms, bryozoans, molluscs, crustaceans, echinoderms, ascidians, and almost anything dead. In turn, they are preyed upon by fish, molluscs, crustaceans and other sea stars.

Reproduction: Sea stars have separate sexes (male and female) and although some (sand sea stars) actually participate in close contact external fertilisation, most just shed their reproductive products (egg and sperm) into the surrounding water at dusk during breeding season, or at night.

Although large numbers of eggs are released, planktonic larval dispersal is often lengthy and few survive.

Some species (*Linckia multiflora*) reproduce asexually. Either juveniles or adults cast off an arm (autotomy) which then grows other arms eventually growing into a complete but often lopsided sea star.

Associations: Many other animals live with or on sea stars including parasitic limpets (*Thyca* sp.), small ulimid molluscs (also parasitic), scale worms, crabs, shrimps and creeping ctenophores.

Identification: External identification by location, habitat, shape, colour and pattern is possible on the majority of sea stars but there are some which due to unavailable knowledge, information and photographic reproductive comparison remain difficult and uncertain. Eventually with books such as this available for reference the unknown factors will become common knowledge.

ASTROPECTINIDAE

Comb sea star

Astropecten polyacanthus

Sand

3 to 30 metres (10 to 98 ft)

260 mm (10 in)

Ranging from the Red Sea throughout the Indo-Pacific region to New Zealand, the comb sea star spends most of the time beneath the substrate. At the turn of the tide it breaks cover to hunt for small gastropods and bivalves, ingesting up to five at once.

ASTROPECTINIDAE

Bordered sea star

Astropecten monacanthus

Sand

10 to 60 metres (33 to 197 ft)

100 mm (4 in)

Distributed from East Africa to the north western coast of Australia the bordered sea star is not as commonly found as some of its sand-dwelling relations. The colour varies a little depending on the location but the short spines along the arms and the distinctive border are fairly stable characteristics. It feeds mostly on bivalves.

OREASTERIDAE

Juvenile sea star

Bothriaster primigenius

Coral reefs, rocky reefs

5 to 50 metres (16 to 164 ft)

80 mm (3 in)

Generally nocturnal, this species ranges in colour from red to purple and green, however, its basic shape, plates along the arms, rigid body form and pentagonally-shaped centre are stable features.

This picture represents a new record for the Maldives.

Colour variation of a juvenile sea star, Port Moresby, Papua New Guinea.

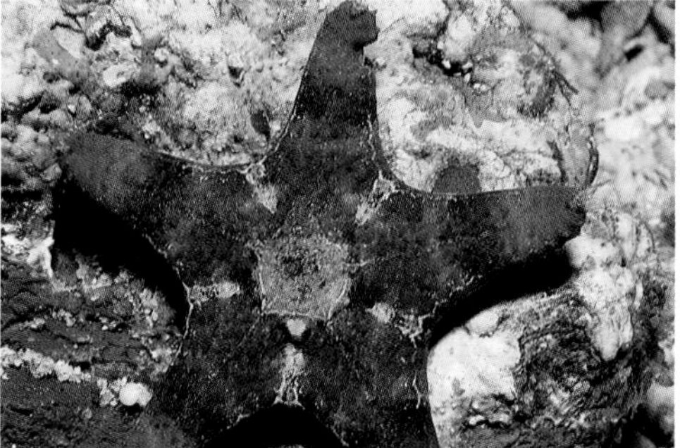

Quite a rare species, this colour form is from Milne Bay, Papua New Guinea.

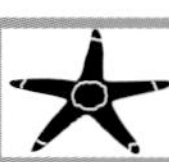

ORIEASTERIDAE

Granulated sea star

Choriaster granulatus

Rubble slopes, reef

5 to 40 metres (16 to 131 ft)

270 mm (11 in)

As the only species within the genus *Choriaster*, the granulated sea star is unique enough in shape and stable pinkish colour to be easily recognised on visual features throughout its Indo-Pacific distribution. The commensal shrimp *Periclimenes soror* has been observed on it in the Maldives.

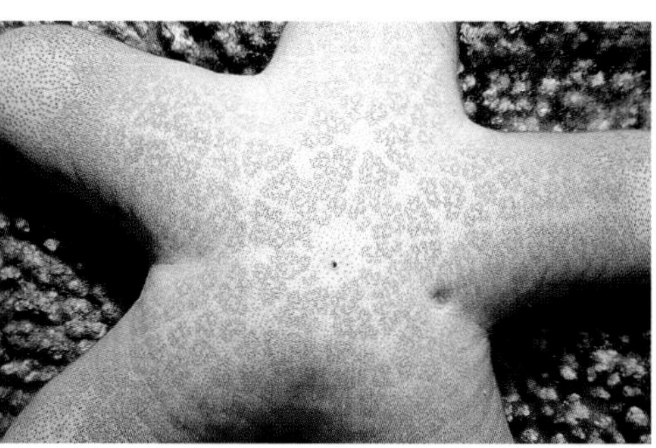

Close-up of the granulated sea star showing the dorsal pattern.

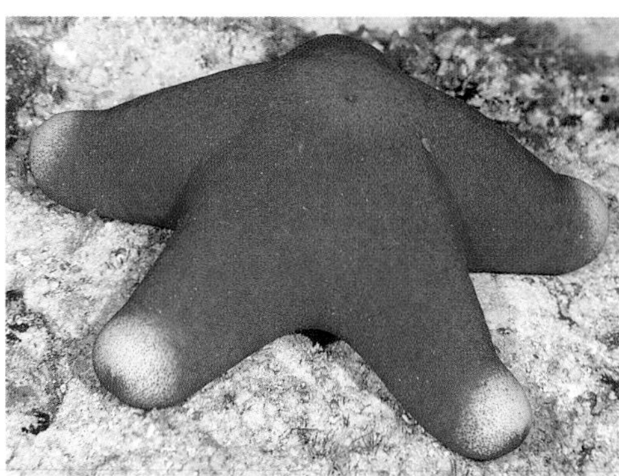

OREASTERIDAE

Schmedelian pin-cushion sea star

Culcita schmedeliana

Coral reefs, rocky reefs, rubble

Low tide to 30 metres (0 to 98 ft)

250 mm (10 in)

This sea star is moderately common in deeper waters to 30 metres (100 ft) across the Indian Ocean. The pin-cushion sea star feeds on a variety of organisms including algae, bottom detritus and the polyps and flesh of some corals. Occasionally, the small commensal shrimp *Periclimenes soror* may be seen living on the underside of the sea star.

Close-up of underside area showing the mouth plates.

The extruded stomach digests its food outside of its body.

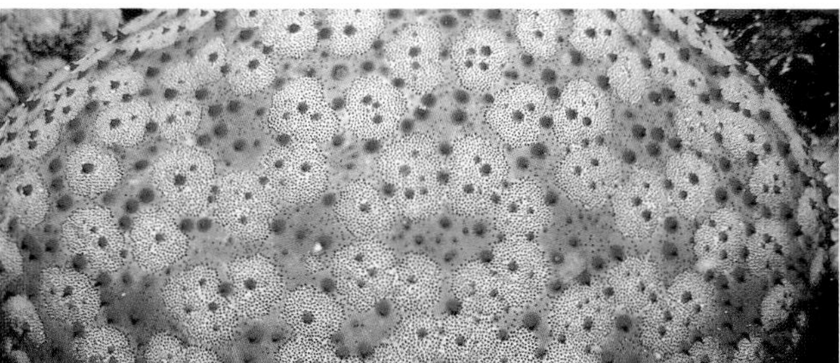

Dorsal pattern of one Maldivian colour form, showing colour variation

OREASTERIDAE

Regular sea star

Pentaceraster regulus

Sand, rubble

Low tide to 115 metres (0 to 377 ft)

300 mm (12 in)

The regular sea star is a soft bottom dweller which feeds on organic detritus. Colours range from those of the specimen pictured through to pink and dark red. Small commensal crabs *Lissocarcinus polyboides* may be found on the underside, and the parasitic limpet *Thyca* sp. is sometimes seen on the dorsal surface.

Colour variation, Pacific Ocean.

Juvenile colour forms have larger tubercules on the arms, Great Barrier Reef.

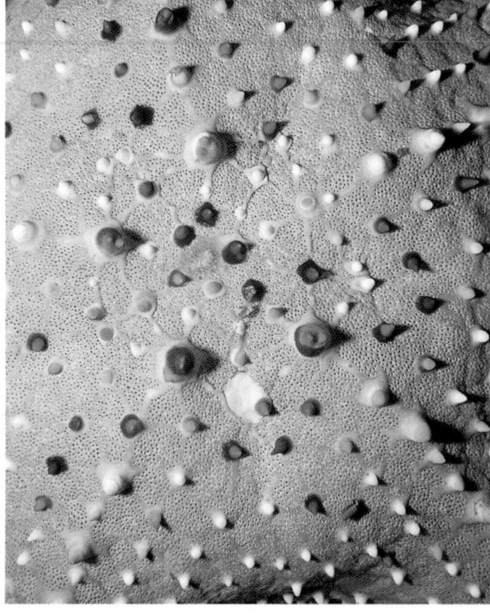

The dorsal surface and tubercules of this adult show a pronounced difference in pattern, size and colour, Moreton Bay, Queensland, Australia.

One of the most common *Fromia* in the Maldives, most specimens observed have had five arms, although others may have four, or even six. When damaged by predators they can grow new arms. The dancing shrimp *Hymenocera picta* is a voracious predator on this species.

OPHIDIASTERIDAE

Indian sea star

Fromia indica

Coral reefs, rocky reefs, rubble

Low tide to 40 metres (0 to 131 ft)

50 mm (2 in)

Pattern variation, Lady Elliot Island on the Great Barrier Reef.

This form has shorter and stockier arms and is of a lighter colour than others.

Damaged by a predator this sea star is in the process of growing three new arms.

A regular six-armed form, Great Barrier Reef.

Four-armed forms are not very common.

This male sea star is spurting sperm out of genital pores on its dorsal surface.

OPHIDIASTERIDAE

Thousand pores sea star

Fromia milleporella

Coral reefs, rocky reefs

3 to 10 metres (10 to 33 ft)

50 mm (2 in)

Although this distinctive little sea star ranges from the Seychelles to the Great Barrier Reef, it is by no means a commonly observed species. It lives in the open and is easily recognised by its orange to brown colouration and large dark pore openings scattered across the dorsal surface.

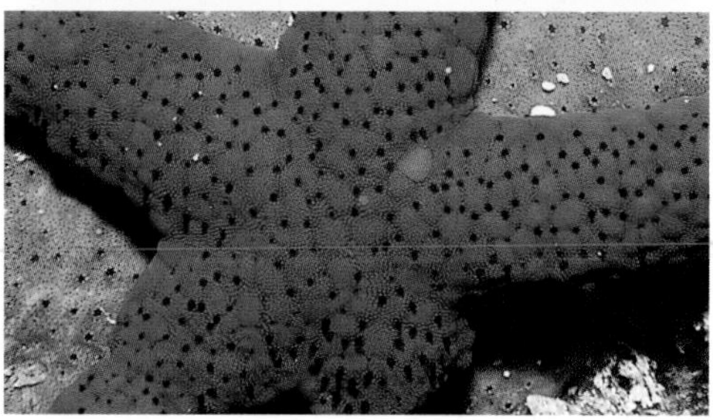

Close up of the dorsal surface showing the distinctive pore patterning, Maldives.

This species may have four or six arms.

Many sea stars were found with one or more arms eaten off, suggesting the close presence of the harlequin shrimp Hymenocera picta, *Maldives.*

OPHIDIASTERIDAE

Noduled sea star

Fromia nodosa

Coral reefs, rocky reefs

10 to 40 metres (33 to 131 ft)

70 mm (3 in)

There are a number of different species. Although they appear easy to identify even the experts have difficulty. The noduled sea star occurs from the Seychelles to the Maldives and within this range the enlarged nodules along the sides of the arms appear to be a stable characteristic.

Variation showing a different central disc pattern, Maldives.

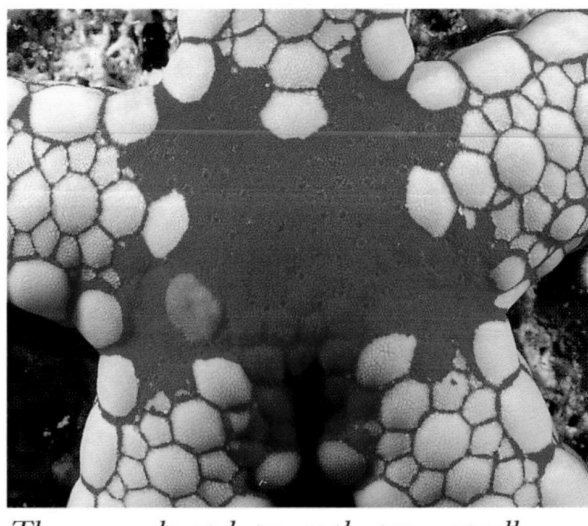

The orange lump between the two centrally positioned plates is the madroporite through which the sea star breathes, Maldives.

Juvenile form showing gaps between the plates on the sides of the arms, Maldives.

Juvenile from the Seychelles showing the same gaps.

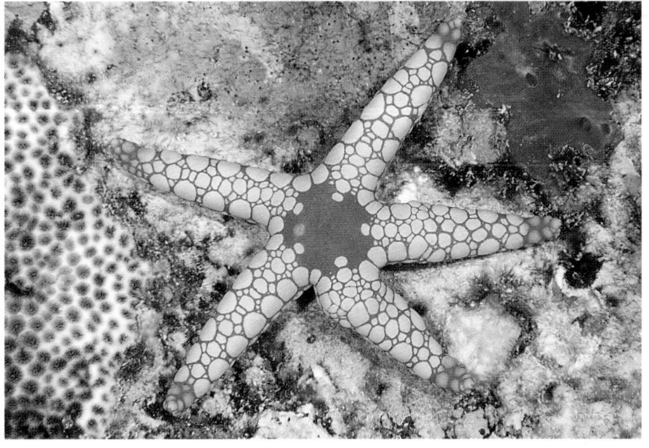

In contrast, this necklace sea star Fromia monilis *from the Seychelles is relatively smooth, with few raised nodules.*

OPHIDIASTERIDAE
Egeri's sea star
Gomophia cf. egeriae
Coral reefs, rocky reefs
5 to 20 metres (16 to 66 ft)
160 mm (6.4 in)

Common throughout the Maldives, especially at night, this species is widespread across the Indo-Pacific reefs.

Colour variation, Maldives.

OPHIDIASTERIDAE
Egyptian sea star
Gomophia egyptiaca
Coral reefs, rocky reefs
5 to 30 metres (16 to 98 ft)
200 mm (8 in)

Widespread throughout the Indo-Pacific the Egyptian sea star is a fairly common resident on the Maldivian reefs, though due to its nocturnal habits, observations by divers are rare. Maldivian forms are extremely variable in colour and pattern but the sharp-pointed tubercules with a dark circle around base is a reliable identification feature.

This unusual six-legged form from the southern atolls shows extreme variation in colour and was the largest encountered, Maldives.

OPHIDIASTERIDAE

Leach's sea star

Leiaster leachi

Coral reefs, rocky reefs

Low tide to 50 metres (0 to 164 ft)

455 mm (18 in)

Ranging from East Africa across to Lord Howe Island this large, mostly nocturnal sea star hides in the reef during the day and is not observed on a regular basis. However, in deeper water (30 metres) it may be seen out feeding during the day. There does not seem to be a great deal of colour variation from the Indian to Pacific Oceans.

South Pacific colour form, Lord Howe Island.

This juvenile has had three of its arms chewed off by a predator, Lord Howe Island.

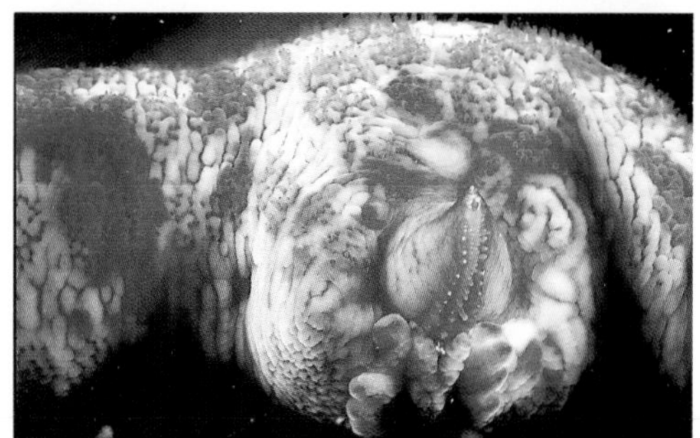

Close-up showing a new arm tip regrowing from a chewed off stump, Lord Howe Island.

Close-up of coloured papillae and pore pattern on the side of an arm, Lord Howe Island.

OPHIDIASTERIDAE

Guilding's sea star

Linckia guildingi

Coral reefs, rocky reefs

5 to 20 metres (16 to 66 ft)

300 mm (12 in)

Although Guilding's sea star appears to have a fairly stable colour form in the Maldives (pictured) and Seychelles, across its distribution and into the Pacific it can be brown, light green, khaki or grey.

Sperm can be seen issuing from genital pores in the arms (November, Seychelles).

Close-up showing raised groups of pores, Maldives.

OPHIDIASTERIDAE

Blue sea star

Linckia laevigata

Coral reefs, rocky reefs, rocky shores

Low tide to 60 m (0 to 197 ft)

400 mm (16 in)

Commonly encountered intertidally throughout the Indo-Pacific coral reefs, this well-known sea star is generally only recognised in its blue form (its commonest colour). However, on some reefs other colour forms exist and may be blue-green with orange underside, pink, or yellow. It may be inhabited by a small blue or black scale worm, blue copepod or a parasitic blue limpet.

Dark blue colour forms usually inhabit deeper water, Great Barrier Reef.

 only 1 at Bandos

Colour variation, Papua New Guinea/Fiji.

A small juvenile (12 mm) Great Barrier Reef.

(continued)

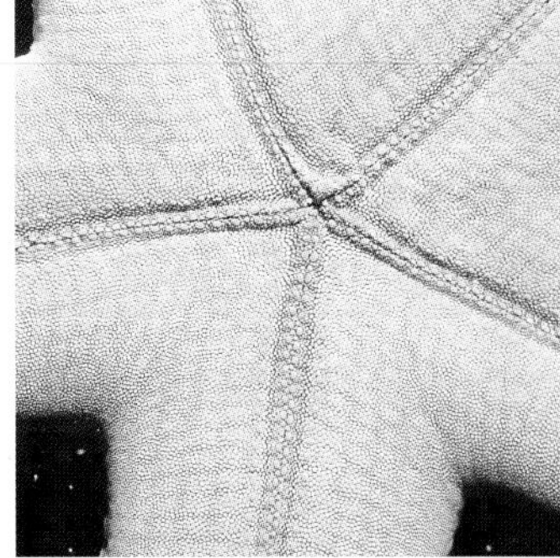

Light-coloured Indian Ocean form showing underside pattern.

Rarely seen juvenile colour variation, Papua New Guinea.

Normal juvenile colour pattern, Papua New Guinea

OPHIDIASTERIDAE

Multi-pore sea star

Linckia multifora

Coral reefs, rocky shores, rocky reefs

Low tide to 46 metres (151 ft)

100 mm (4 in)

Occurring on Indo-Pacific reefs, this species is the most common sea star in the Maldives. It feeds both night and day on a diet of filamentous algae and detritus. Small parasitic limpets may be seen on the undersides of the arms and some are deformed by gall-forming parasitic molluscs (*Stilifer* sp.) burrowing into their bodies.

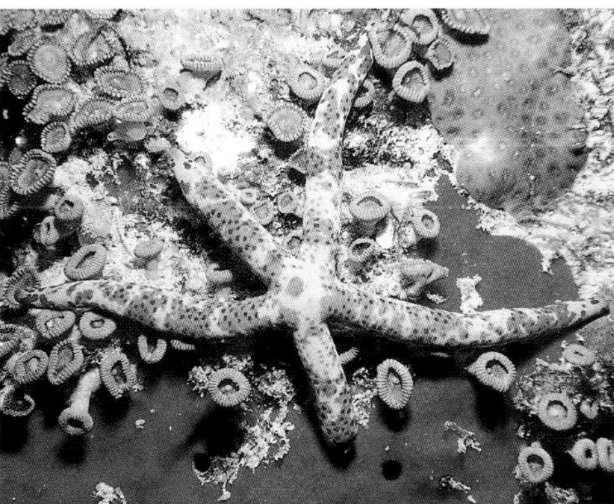

Maldivian colour form.

(continued)

Maldivian colour form.

This distinctive colour form was encountered in the southern atolls, Maldives.

Typical colour form from the Coral Sea this specimen has grown from an autonomised arm.

Growing four arms from one which has been autonomised (asexual reproduction), Great Barrier Reef.

This eight-legged form is very rare, Maldives.

OPHIDIASTERIDAE

Rose sea star

Nardoa rosea

Coral reefs, rubble

8 to 25 metres (26 to 82 ft)

140 mm (5.5 in)

A resident of inshore and offshore reefs of the Indo-Pacific, this very attractive sea star is certainly not commonly seen on Maldivian reefs. It lives in the open on reef slopes and broken bottom and feeds on algae and detritus.

This form from Queensland, Australia shows little variation but has shorter arms.

OPHIDIASTERIDAE

Galathea sea star

Nardoa galatheae

Rubble, rocky reefs, sand

5 to 10 metres (16 to 33 ft)

160 mm (6 in)

A resident of reef flats and lagoon shallows, it is usually found in sheltered waters. Colour is restricted to browns and all specimens found were free from damage. No predators of fully grown adults have yet been observed. A small commensal worm can often be found on the underside of this sea star near the tube feet furrows.

Colour variation from 8 metres on sand, Bali, Indonesia.

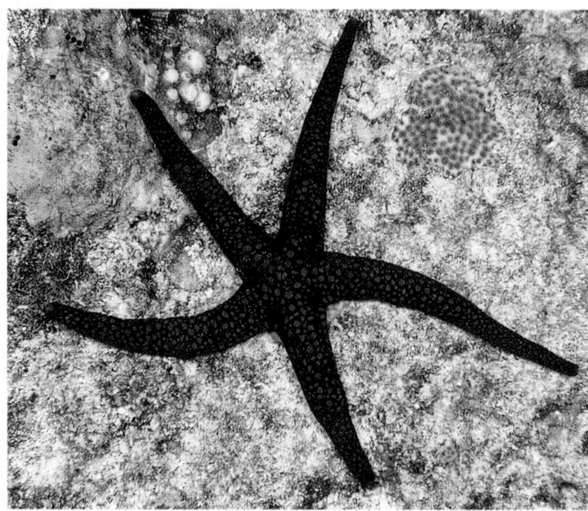

OPHIDIASTERIDAE

Pimpled sea star

Nardoa variolata

Rubble, rocky reef

2 to 8 metres (6.6 to 26 ft)

120 mm (5 in)

Shallow water dwelling members of this genus are usually prolific in some areas of lagoons or reef shallows but this does not seem to be the case in the Maldive locations visited.

OPHIDIASTERIDAE

Cuming's sea star

Neoferdina cumingi

Coral reefs, rocky reefs

8 to 25 metres (26 to 82 ft)

65 mm (2.5 in)

Found in isolated areas across the Indo-Pacific this species lives under ledges or beneath dead coral slabs during the day. Cuming's sea star is variable in the number and distribution of purple spots down the arms.

OPHIDASTERIDAE
Offret's sea star
Neoferdina offreti
Coral reefs, rocky reefs
15 to 25 metres (49 to 82 ft)
60 mm (2.4 in)

Usually found in deeper water on rubble or broken bottom, Offret's sea star is by no means common across the Indo-Pacific range. It appears to be a new record for the Maldives.

OPHIDIASTERIDAE
Hemprich's sea star
Ophidiaster hemprichi
Coral reefs, rocky reefs
8 to 20 metres (26 to 66 ft)
90 mm (4 in)

Rarely seen underwater this species is relatively unknown to divers and is generally found beneath dead coral slabs during daylight hours, yet it has been recorded right across the Indo-Pacific from Madagascar to the South Pacific. Colours and pattern are not highly variable.

ASTEROPIDAE
Double-spine sea star
Asteropsis carnifera
Coral reefs, rocky reefs
5 to 25 metres (16 to 82 ft)
70 mm (3 in)

The flat profile and the thorny double spines along the edges of the arms make this species relatively easy to identify. It is strictly nocturnal, seen on late night dives or found beneath dead coral during the day. It is distributed across the entire Indo-Pacific and is not common anywhere.

Juvenile colour form, Bali, Indonesia.

(continued)

Colour form, Lady Elliot Island, Great Barrier Reef.

Juvenile colour form, Milne Bay, Papua New Guinea.

ASTERINIDAE

Burton's sea star

Asterina burtoni

Coral reefs, rocky reefs

2 to 8 metres (6 to 26 ft)

40 mm (2 in)

A shallow water species, Burton's sea star lives beneath rocks and dead coral during the day. It feeds on algae and detritus, has a range of colour variations and its arms are narrower and do not have the flattened edging as does the next species.

Colour variation, Maldives.

ASTERINIDAE

Skirted sea star

Asterina cepheus

Coral reefs, rocky reefs

1 to 8 metres (3 to 26 ft)

30 mm (1 in)

Another new record for the Maldive area this small distinctive species lives beneath stones and dead coral slabs in shallow water and although its colours are variable the flat skirt around the edges of the arms distinguish it from any similar species.

Variation, Lady Elliot Island, Great Barrier Reef.

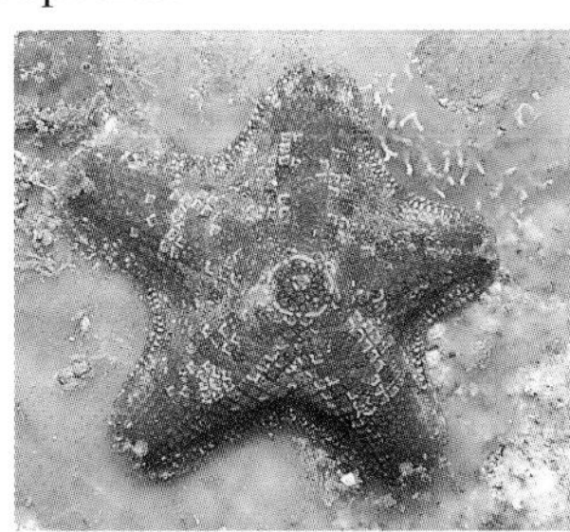

Variation, Lady Elliot Island, Great Barrier Reef.

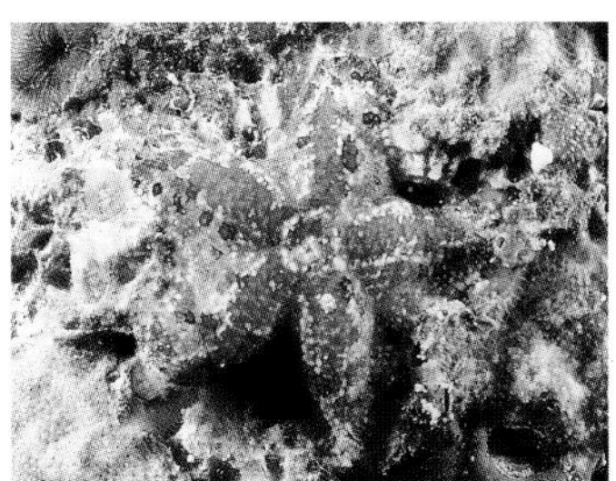

ACANTHASTERIDAE

Crown-of-Thorns sea star

Acanthaster planci

Coral reefs, rocky reefs

Low tide to 30 metres (98 ft)

400 mm (16 in)

Acanthaster planci and its relations in the Sea of Cortez and the Red Sea, should be avoided at all times as their spines are capable of causing severe injuries. The small shrimp, *Periclimenes soror*, is a resident commensal. Known predators include the puffer fish *Arthron hystrix* and the giant triton *Charonia tritonis*, but there is little evidence that these animals are more than opportunist predators.

Crown-of-thorns walking across open bottom between reefs searching for live corals to eat. Notice how the spines are lowered so as not to cause drag, Seychelles.

This juvenile is only 30 mm (1 in) across. It was found beneath dead coral, Seychelles.

MITHRODIIDAE

Nail-armed sea star

Mithrodia clavigera

Coral reefs, rocky reefs

8 to 40 metres (26 to 131 ft)

400 mm (16 in)

Widespread from Madagascar to Lord Howe Island, this species is at night in deep water caves; juveniles may be found under dead coral slabs. It feeds on algae, sponges, and detritus and in some areas has a yet undiscovered predator (triton shell?) which eats the insides of its arms.

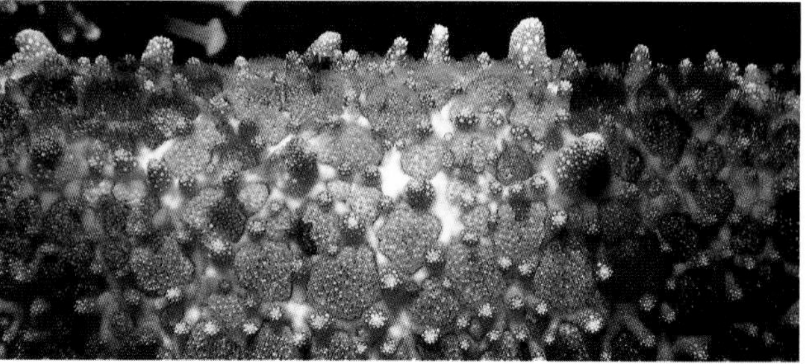

Close-up of adult spinelets, Lord Howe Island, South Pacific.

This species engages in autonomy during its juvenile stage casting off arms that grow into new sea stars, Papua New Guinea.

(continued)

Giant adults are rarely ever seen. This monster (530 mm, 21 in) was discovered at Ball's Pyramid south of Lord Howe Island in the South Pacific. (Notice the reduction in spine length).

Adult arm tip and tube feet.

ECHINASTERIDAE

Dove sea star

Cistina columbiae

Coral reefs, rocky reefs

3 to 15 metres (10 to 49 ft)

25 mm (1 in)

A new record for the Maldives this interesting but rarely seen species can be found in the open, or beneath rocks. Up until 1971 it was only recorded from the islands around Mauritius. However, it definitely occurs in the Maldives, Papua New Guinea and on several reefs in the Coral Sea. It feeds on algae and detritus growing on dead coral and is preyed on by harlequin shrimps.

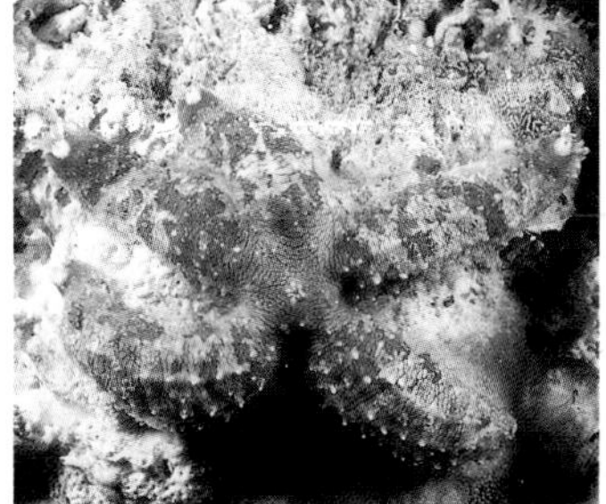

Colour variation Port Moresby, Papua New Guinea.

Variation Port Moresby, Papua New Guinea showing damaged arm.

CLASS *Ophiuroidea* (Brittle stars, Snake stars, Serpent stars, Basket stars)

Features: A basic brittle star is comprised of a central disc-like body from which five snake-like arms protrude. The body disc generally appears quite soft in brittle stars and serpent stars, but may be heavily armoured, with well developed plates in basket stars. The arms have no ambulacral grooves on the underside and may be plated, ridged, knobbed,spined or grooved depending on the species. These arms and their particular arrangements are most important to the brittle star as they perform both locomotion (brittle stars are the most active and fastest moving echinoderms) and feeding functions. The tube feet situated along the arms play no part in brittle star mobility, but instead are primarily used for feeding. Close up, the mouth and teeth of a brittle star is an amazing sight, certainly a formidable arrangement.

Lifestyle: Brittle stars inhabit most of the major ocean zones with the exception of the open sea. Although brittle stars are very common, most are cryptic, nocturnally active bottom dwellers. Unless being sought after they are generally only seen during the day as a few arms sticking out of the rocks or coral, or as basket stars and snake stars wrapped around sessile invertebrates (sponges, black corals) which they use as feeding platforms.

Brittle stars feed on plankton, suspended detritus, coral-shed mucus, bottom detritus, molluscs and worms. They also scavenge. Basket stars are strictly nocturnal or dark-water plankton netters, spreading their finely meshed medusa-like arms up into the water column while anchored on some lofty pinnacle by the lower arms. Serpent stars feed mostly on small invertebrates including molluscs, worms and crustaceans and are generally found beneath loosely positioned rocks. The snake stars live out their entire lives entwined in the branches of antipatharian black corals where they feed on the rich mucus of the host, in turn performing cleaning functions for the black coral colony.

Reproduction: On the underside of the body disc there is a split-like opening at the base of each side of each arm (two per space). These 10 openings are breathing and reproductive outlets, taking in water for oxygen and shedding eggs or sperm into the sea. Brittle stars are also known to brood young within the body, lay eggs, and to reproduce asexually by self-division (cleaving, fission). Most species split in half and some self-divide at the juvenile stages, later growing into two separate, fully functional adults. They also have the power to regenerate damaged or missing arms.

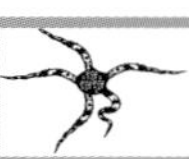

Associations: They are found associated with many different animals and sedentary colonies, to which they can be specific. They live on or in sponges, bryozoans, worm tubes, corals, soft corals, sea fans, hydroids, hydrozoans, sea anemones, ascidians, or on sea stars, sea urchins, feather stars and other brittle stars. Their predators include fish and sea stars, while commensal scale worms, amphipods, parasitic shells and other brittle stars have been found living on them. Yet for all their interesting features, very little is known about the living animals themselves.

Identification: With enough references on habitat, colour, patterns and close-up photography it is possible to identify quite a number of brittle stars. However, most require a specialist taxonomist to identify them from a preserved specimen, for as yet we do not have enough photographic evidence of species, colour forms or localised variants.

OPHIOMYXIDAE

Southern serpent star

Ophiomyxa australis

Coral reefs, rocky reefs, rocky shores, rubble

Low tide to 300 metres (984 ft)

240 mm (9 in)

Found throughout the Indian and Pacific oceans this species is remarkably diverse in colour and pattern, appearing in browns, yellows, red and olives with large, small and erratic spots, dashes and daubs. It is secretive, has smooth skin on its arms which are devoid of plates and during the day hides beneath rocks, dead coral slabs.

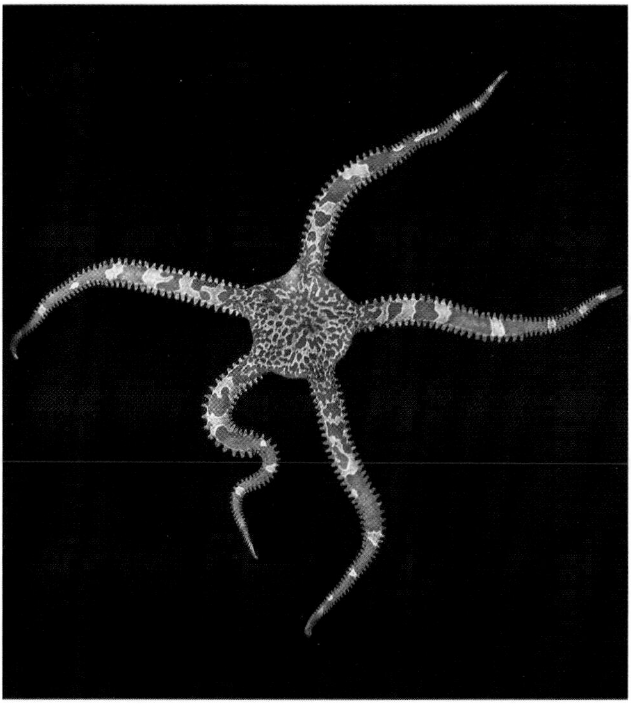

AMPHIURIDAE

Savigny's brittle star

Ophiactis savignyi

Rocky reefs, coral reefs

Low tide to 500 metres (lt to 1640 ft)

50 mm (2 in)

As the most widely distributed species in the world, Savigny's brittle star is also the most common with colour combination of greens, blacks, and white found in the Indian Ocean and the South Pacific forms. Although it breeds in a normal fashion (males and females producing sperm and eggs) this species often reproduces asexually, with some juveniles splitting into two – each part having three arms. The missing parts are then regenerated.

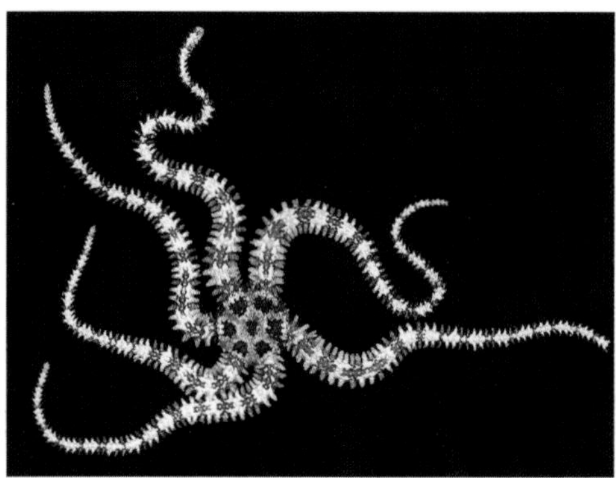

One Maldivian colour form.

OPHIOTRICHIDAE

Long-armed brittle star

Macrophiothrix longipeda

Sand and rubble

Low tide to 10 metres (0 to 33 ft)

800 mm (31 in)

A common shallow water brittle star living in holes in reef flats, under coral and beneath dead coral slabs, this species has extremely long arms which it extends across the bottom entrapping food in the form of settling plankton and organic detritus. It has Indo-Pacific distribution and is quite difficult to determine to species in the field without considerable experience.

Close-up showing the soft central disc.

A juvenile about to disappear down a small hole.

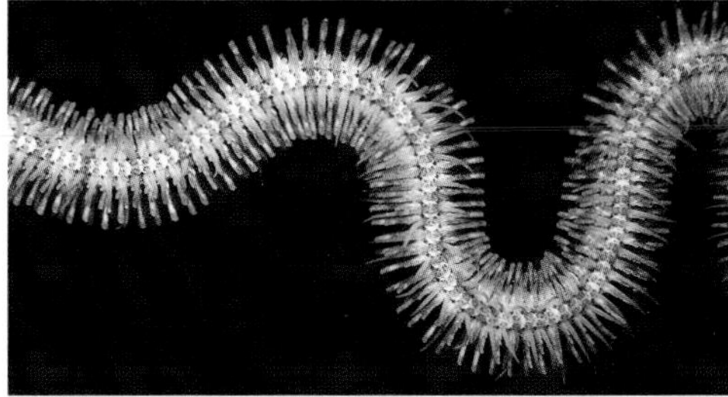

Close-up of arm of a closely-related species from the Seychelles.

A long-armed brittle star from Port Moresby, Papua New Guinea.

OPHIOTRICHIDAE

Dana's brittle star

Ophiothela danae

Coral reefs, rocky reefs

5 to 60 metres (180 ft)

20 mm (0.7 in)

Very common throughout the Indo-Pacific, Dana's brittle star is a small, beautifully patterned, colourful commensal, which is only found attached to, or on, other invertebrate animals. Its hosts include sea urchins, hydroids, gorgonians, soft corals, sponges, sea whips and bryozoans. Large specimens have six arms while small ones generally have three. It therefore seems probable that Dana's brittle star reproduces by fission.

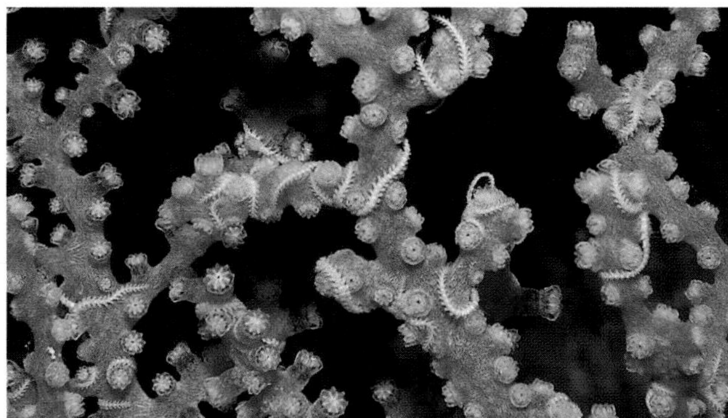

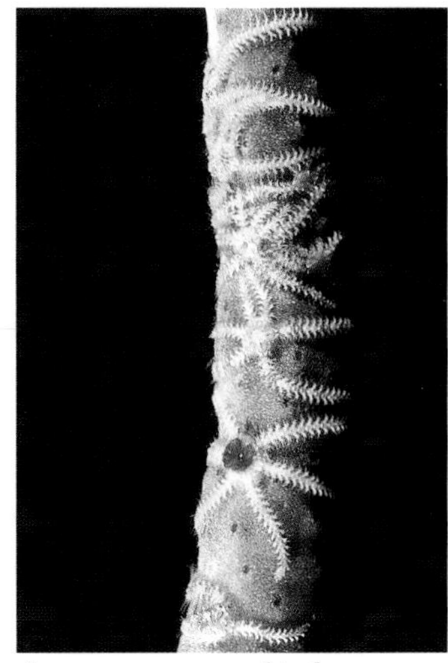

In contrast a sea whip has several different colour variations, Papua New Guinea.

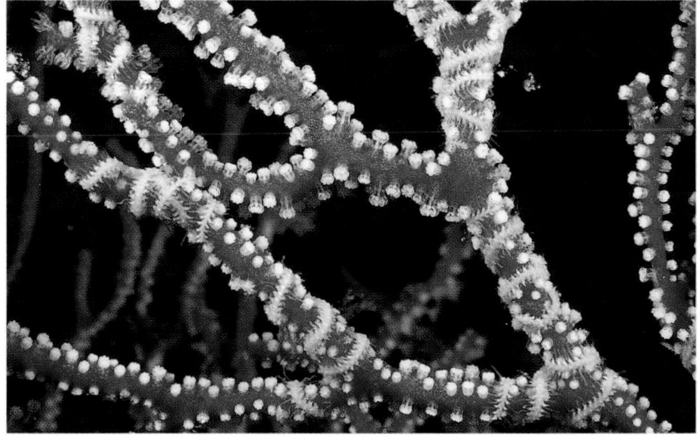

A thousand kilometres away a different species of sea fan is inhabited by yellow colour forms, Papua New Guinea.

OPHIOTRICHIDAE
Soft coral brittle star
Ophiothrix foveolata
Coral reefs, rocky reefs
8 to 25 metres (26 to 82 ft)
80 mm (3.2 in)

This species has a wide distribution from Madagascar across to the South Pacific and when found it is always associated with a species of soft coral. During the day it hides away in the folds or amongst the fronds of its host, only coming out at night. It feeds on plankton.

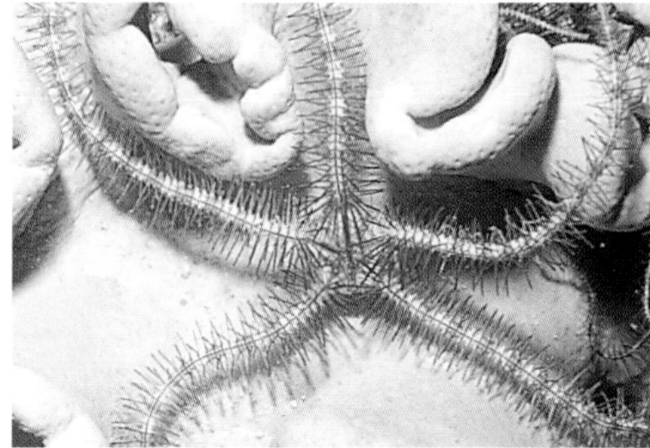

The colour in this species appears fairly constant, Port Moresby, Papua New Guinea.

OPHIOTRICHIDAE
Sea fan brittle star
Ophiothrix (Acanthophiothrix) purpurea
Coral reefs, rocky reefs
10 to 60 metres (33 to 197 ft)
150 mm (6 in)

Found throughout the Indo-Pacific region, the sea fan brittle star lives on gorgonian sea fans, soft corals or sponges of at least 8 different species. Its colouration can be yellow, pink, mauve or purple, and its spines are extremely long. A line of spots runs down the length of the arm and in some specimens this is bordered by another line each side of the central one.

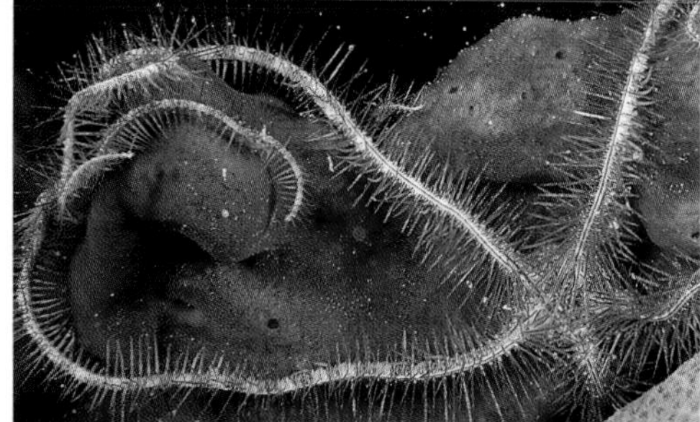

Colour form, Port Moresby, Papua New Guinea.

Colour form, northern Great Barrier Reef.

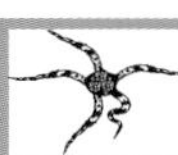

OPHIOTRICHIDAE

Sea nymph brittle star

Ophiothrix (Keystonia) nereidina

Coral reefs, rocky reefs

8 to 25 metres (26 to 82 ft)

120 mm (4.8 in)

This extremely attractive brittle star has very distinctive dark pink banding on the arms and up to three bright blue dots next to the bands. However, the pattern on the disc is variable. The sea nymph brittle star is found from East Africa throughout the Indian Ocean and into the Pacific.

Variation, Port Moresby, Papua New Guinea.

Variation, Milne Bay, Papua New Guinea

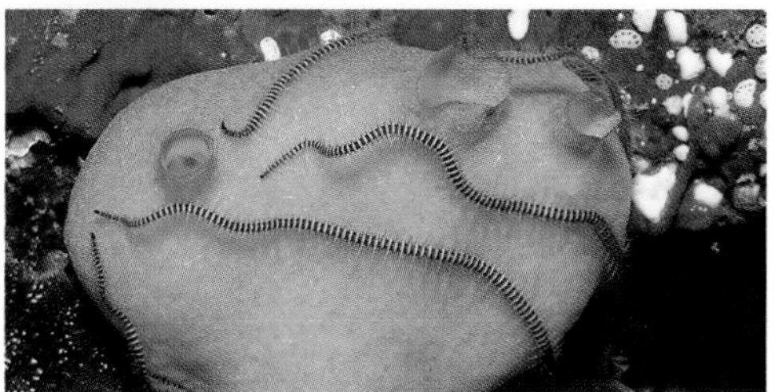

This brittle star can be seen with its feeding arms out during the day. Here it is utilising currents caused by the sponge to steal plankton from its host.

OPHIOCOMIDAE

Arm-band brittle star

Ophiocoma dentata

Sand and rubble

3 to 20 metres (10 to 66 ft)

120 mm (4.8 in)

A common species, the arm-band brittle star lives beneath rubble and dead coral. The disc has a fine netted pattern which often has a pentagonal design. This species feeds on organic debris and plankton.

Colour variation Moreton Bay, Queensland, Australia.

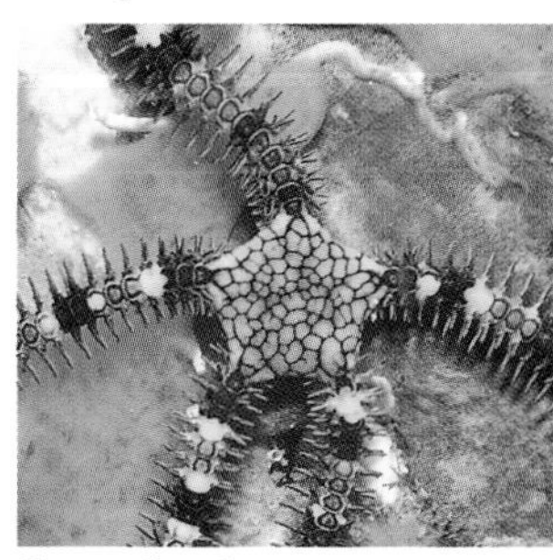

Juvenile colour variation, Norfolk Island, South Pacific.

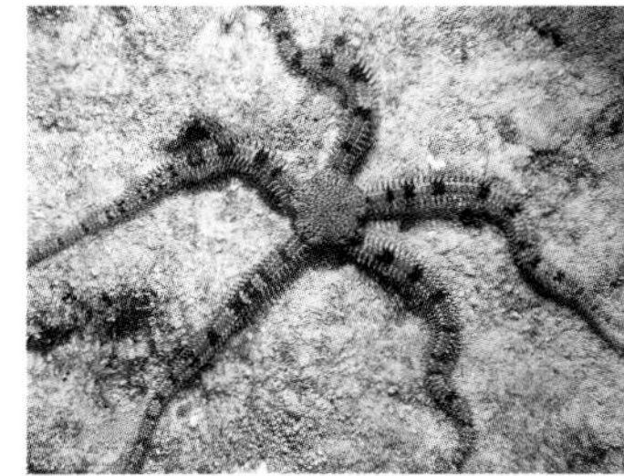

OPHIOCOMIDAE

Hedgehog brittle star

Ophiocoma erinaceus

Sand and rubble

2 to 20 metres (6 to 66 ft)

110 mm (4.4 in)

Always black or dark brown in colour the hedgehog brittle star has very well-developed spines on the sides of the arms and is very active when disturbed from beneath its shelter of dead coral or rock. It usually prefers a silty, sandy or even muddy substrate in lagoons or harbours. This species is found across the entire Indo-Pacific.

OPHIOCOMIDAE

Brown and gold brittle star

Ophiocoma pica

Coral reefs, rocky reefs

3 to 20 metres (10 to 66 ft)

200 mm (8 in)

Known from Zanzibar to the South Pacific, the brown and gold brittle star lives in holes and crevices in coral from which it holds out several arms to catch food. It can be black or brown in base colour with a gold-lined pattern on the disc; there may be a double row of gold spots running down the arms, or these may be joined to give the impression of bands.

There is very little variation in this species. This one from the Coral Sea is almost identical to the Maldivian form in the previous picture.

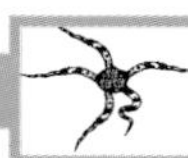

OPHIOCOMIDAE
Six-armed brittle star
Ophiocomella sexradiata
Coral reefs, rocky reefs
3 to 10 metres (10 to 33 ft)
20 mm (0.8 in)

Found beneath rocks and dead coral during the day the six-armed brittle star is distributed from the Maldives to the South Pacific. However, it may not have been seen from other parts of the Indian Ocean due to its small size. Those specimens observed have all had green markings on the disc and green bands on the arms.

OPHIOLEUCIDAE
Chain-link brittle star
Ophiomastix annulosa
Coral reefs, rocky reefs
2 to 20 metres (6 to 66 ft)
250 mm (10 in)

Found from the Indian Ocean, to the Great Barrier Reef, this large brittle star is very common and occurs beneath coral slabs and in holes and crannies within the reef. At night it can be seen out crawling but most times only its long arms with their characteristic chain-like patterns are noticed. This species is reported to have toxic mucus which causes death in small animals.

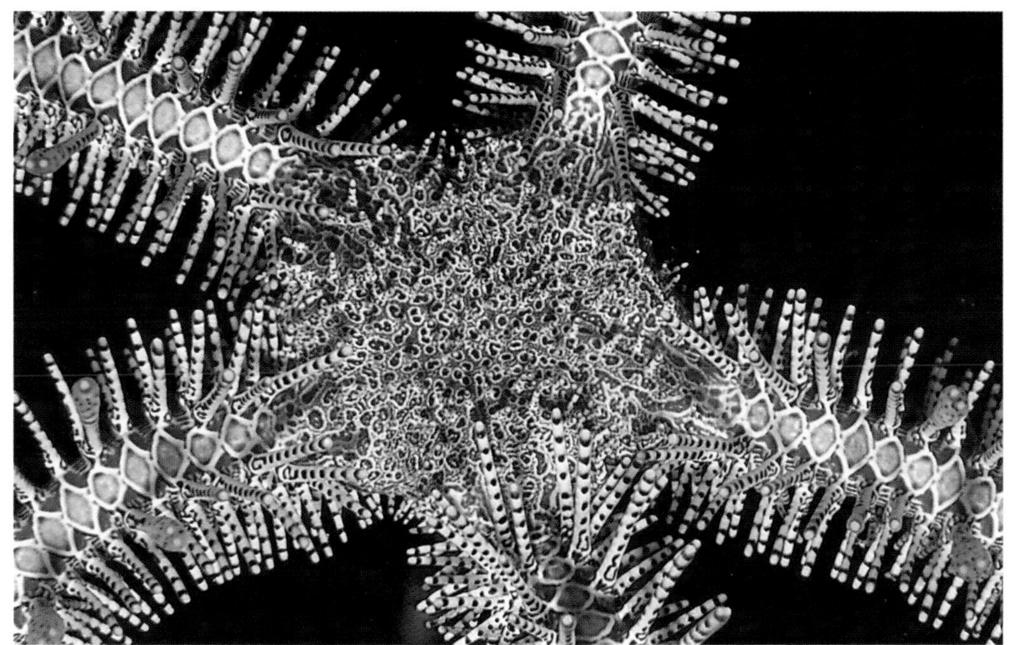

OPHIODERMATIDAE

Green serpent star

Ophiarachna incrassata

Sand flats, coral reefs

Low tide to 10 m (33 ft)

200 mm (8 in)

A large ophiuroid inhabiting many coral reefs, the green serpent star avoids light during the day hiding beneath coral slabs and crevices. The "green" common name is warranted, as its colour varies little throughout its entire Indo-Pacific range.

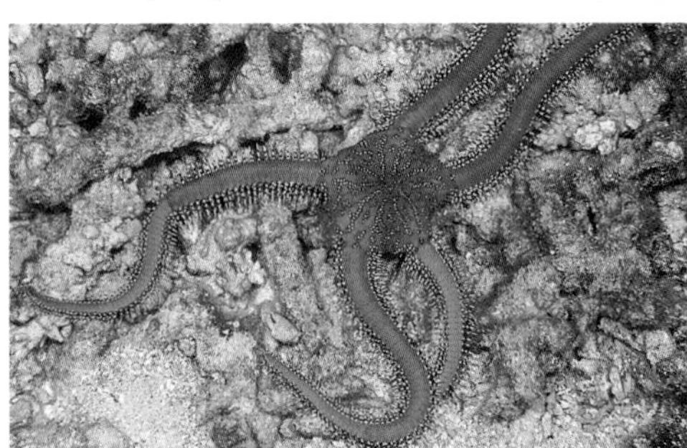

Juvenile colour variation, Port Moresby, Papua New Guinea.

OPHIODERMATIDAE

Seven-spined brittle star

Ophiarachnella septemspinosa

Coral reefs, rocky reefs

3 to 20 metres (10 to 66 ft)

110 mm (4.4 in)

A fairly distinctive species the seven-spined brittle star has yellow bands on the arms and two black dots on the disc opposite each arm. It's recorded across the Indo-Pacific living beneath dead coral slabs or rocks but does not appear to be common.

Variation, Port Moresby, Papua New Guinea.

OPHIURIDAE

Superb serpent star

Ophiolepis superba

Coral reefs, rocky reefs

Low tide to 20 m (66 ft)

100 mm (4 in)

The superb serpent star is very distinct. The pattern on the disc and the stripes on the legs can be chocolate, green or red. This species lives beneath dead coral slabs that are on, or close to sand.

CLASS: *Echinoidea* (Sea urchins, Heart urchins, Sand dollars)

Features: Sea urchins are mostly recognised as such by their spines, which in many species are sharp, pointed and, in some cases, venomous. The skeleton of a sea urchin is made up of small plates of calcium carbonate fused together to form a body shell or test covered by thin skin. In regular sea urchins the test may be circular in shape (like an inflated ball with the top and bottom flattened) or in the case of irregular sea urchins such as heart urchins or sand dollars (which live beneath the sand) the shape is modified for movement within this habitat.

In general, the spines work on a ball and socket principle. At the attachment end of the spine there is a small socket which fits over a tubercle on the test. Movement is controlled by a number of sinew-like attachments around the spine connecting it to the body. In some groups (slate pencil sea urchins) the spines can be locked into position by flattened secondary spines situated around the base of each spine. Double rows of tube feet protrude through the test at the ambulacral divisions from top to bottom. Locomotion is achieved by combination of tube feet and mobile spine movement.

The anus and madreporite are situated at the centre of the top on regular urchins and the mouth containing the unique fine-toothed chewing mechanism, called "Aristotle's lantern" is at the centre of the underside. Stalked pedicellariae are present and there are three valved types which, in the case of the flower urchin, are known to be deadly.

Lifestyle: Some species feed on sponges, some on algae and seagrasses, and others are detrital deposit feeders. Irregular urchins (sea biscuits) are known to gather numbers of living foraminifera (forams) which they store in the concave area below their mouth. Although observations show that many broken spines are not repaired at the ends, sea urchins can grow new spines.

Reproduction: The sexes are separate and the young are formed indirectly by the fusion of sperm and eggs released into the water (generally around dusk). The larvae feed on plankton for several weeks before changing into juveniles similar to the adult form, or by direct development (no larval stage present).

Associations: Many kinds of invertebrates and fish live amongst the spines of sea urchins, including gobies, cardinalfish, shrimps, crabs, worms, ctenophores, and molluscs (usually as parasites). Their major enemies are fish, triton shells, helmet shells and humans.

Identification: Most tropical sea urchins can now be identified from a good colour slide especially if information is available on habitat and locality

CIDARIDAE
Pillar sea urchin
Eucidaris metularia
Coral reefs, rocky reefs
2 to 20 metres (6 to 66 ft)
50 mm (2 in)

Although small and secretive this species has a very decorative pattern on the dorsal surface and the thick column-like spines are grooved at the tips with rows of tubercules running lengthways down the spines.

CIDARIDAE
Imperial sea urchin
Phyllacanthus imperialis
Coral reefs, rocky reefs
Low tide to 15 metres (0 to 49 ft)
170 mm (7 in)

Known from the Red Sea, and throughout the Indo-Pacific region, the imperial sea urchin is a nocturnal species which remains in hiding in holes and hollows in coral and rocks, during the day, venturing out to feed under the cover of darkness. Due to this secretive behaviour they appear a lot less common than realised.

Younger example from the Seychelles shows the distinctive banding on the arms.

CIDARIDAE
Thorn-spined sea urchin
Prionocidaris baculosa
Rubble, mud, seagrass meadows, reef
30 to 200 m (98 to 656 ft)
200 mm (8 in)

The thorn-spined sea urchin inhabits soft-bottom or low profile reef, sitting in the open both night and day.

Savigny's sea urchin has a black anal cone and no white on the body. Living in small pockets in reef, or around rocks, Savigny's sea urchin ranges across the Indo-Pacific.

DIADEMATIDAE
Savigny's sea urchin
Diadema savignyi
Coral reefs, rocky reefs, rubble, sand
Low tide to 25 metres (0 to 82 ft)
230 mm (9 in)

Juvenile colour example, Bali, Indonesia.

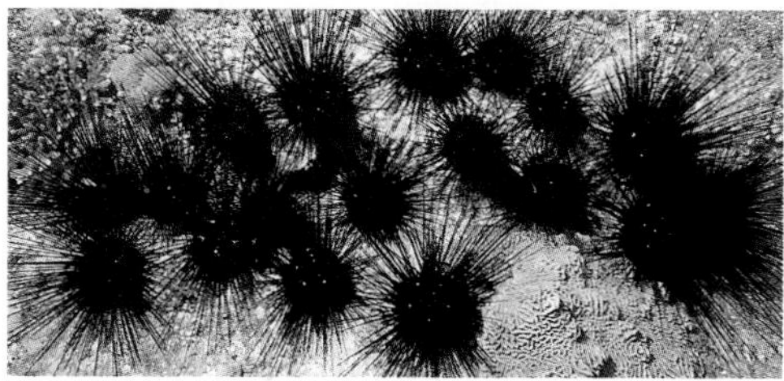

When moving across open areas this species forms groups for protection against fish.

Extremely common in lagoons and coral pools along barrier and continental reefs throughout the Indian and Pacific Oceans, the spiny sea urchin is a conspicuous and easily identified species. The main distinguishing factor between this urchin and its nearest relative *D. savignyi*, is the orange, or light coloured ring around the anal cone at the centre of the animal's dorsal surface.

DIADEMATIDAE
Spiny sea urchin
Diadema setosum
Coral reefs, rocky reefs, rubble
Low tide to 20 metres (0 to 66 ft)
200 (8 in)

Juvenile colour example, Seychelles.

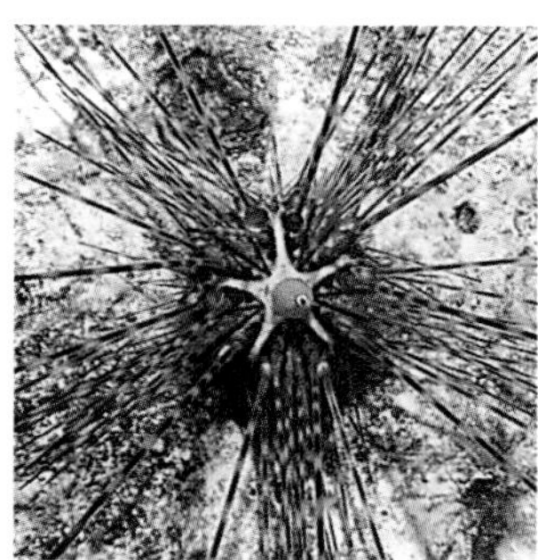

Juvenile colour example, Maldives

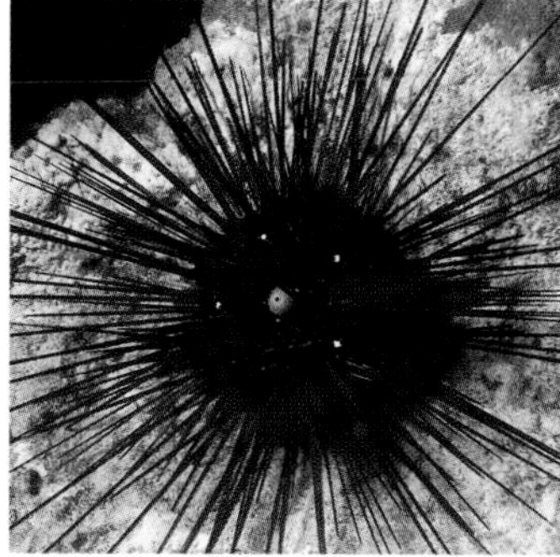

DIADEMATIDAE
Banded sea urchin
Echinothrix calamaris
Coral reefs, rocky reefs
Low tide to 15 metres
(0 to 49 ft)
250 mm (10 in)

From the Indian Ocean down to Tahiti, this urchin moves out of hiding at night to feed on algae and detritus deposits. The banded sea urchin should be avoided as its venomous intermediate spines are extremely fine and needle sharp. The commensal shrimp *Stegopontonia commensalis* lives among its spines, as do small cardinal fish *Siphamia* sp.

DIADEMATIDAE
Diadem sea urchin
Echinothrix diadema
Coral reefs, rocky reefs
Low tide to 25 metres
(Lt to 82 ft)
230 mm (9 in)

Not commonly seen on reefs during daylight hours, these relatively large velvet-black urchins hide under ledges and in caves along the reef edges. This species appears to be more prevalent at locations in the Indian Ocean than it does in the Pacific. Diadem Sea Urchins should never be handled (even with gloves) as their fine needle-sharp intermediate spines produce a painful sting.

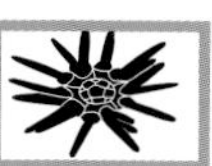

TOXOPNEUSTIDAE

Flower urchin

Toxopneustes pileolus

Coral reefs, rocky reefs, rubble, sand

0 to 30 metres (0 to 98 ft)

120 mm (5 in)

Although known to have caused the death of three divers in Japan there are no records of other injuries to divers in the southern hemisphere. These urchins can be common in sandy rubble areas and are well established in the Maldives. This is a very distinctive species and easily recognised in the field by its beautiful flower-like pedicillariae. It should never be touched with bare hands.

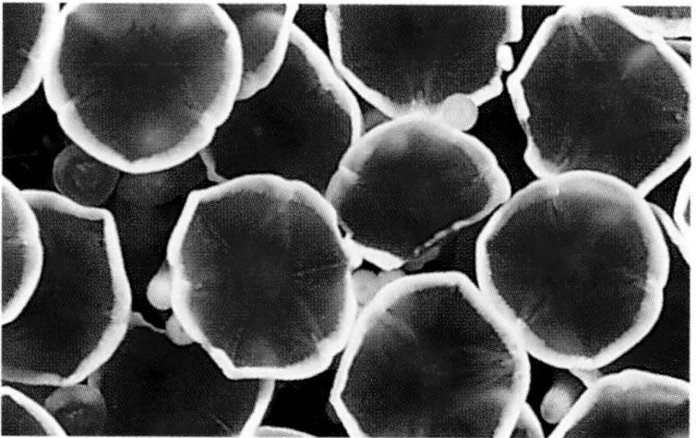

Close up of the venomous pedicillariae can be seen concealed (three pincer-like jaws) beneath the innocent flower-like petals, Kashiwajima, Japan.

Disturbance of the flower-like petals allows the distinctive red stripes on the body shell to be seen.

TOXOPNEUSTIDAE

Cake urchin

Tripneustes gratilla

Rocky reefs, coral reefs, rocky shores, rubble, seagrass meadows

Lt to 25 metres (0 to 82 ft)

150 mm (6 in)

This species is widespread throughout the Indo-Pacific region and has a number of colour variations throughout its distribution. The pattern of wider body spaces (5) between the spines is a reliable visual feature. Colour of the papillae in the five wider body spaces and the five smaller ones may be purple, black, brown, red, or green.

Colour variation, Lady Elliot Island, Great Barrier Reef.

ECHINOMETRIDAE
Mathae's sea urchin
Echinometra mathaei
Coral reefs, rocky reefs
Lt to 5 metres (0 to 16 ft)
85 mm (3 in)

Ranging from the Red Sea to the South Pacific, Mathae's sea urchin is a rock boring species which thrives in the rugged conditions. Mathae's sea urchin can be brown, pink, green, or purple, but the spines always appear to have a white circle of beaded tubercules around the base.

ECHINOMETRIDAE
Burrowing sea urchin
Echinostrephus molaris
Coral reefs, rocky reefs
5 to 20 metres (16 to 66 ft)
30 mm (1.2 in)

Exclusive to the Indian Ocean, this species is only found burrowed into coral or limestone reef so it is simple to identify from this habit. The spines on the sides are worn down by continual abrasion to fit the hole while those on the dorsal surface are long and act as a defence.

LAGANIDAE
Lesueur's sand dollar
Peronella lesueuri
Sand, mud
Lt to 40 metres (0 to 131 ft)
150 mm (6 in)

Found from the Maldives to Australia, this species is the largest of its genus, and though specimens from the same locality show a tendency to be similar in form, other geographically separated colonies may produce their own shapes and sizes. Colours range from rusty brown to pink, orange or purple. Like other sand-dwelling echinoids, Lesueur's sand dollar is a detrital feeder.

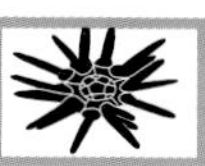

SPATANGIDAE

Fine-spined heart urchin

Maretia planulata

Sand

20 to 40 metres (66 to 131 ft)

70 mm (2.8 in)

Extremely common is some deeper sandy lagoons and sandy bottom across the Maldives this species is widespread throughout the Indo-Pacific. The longer spines over the animal's dorsal surface are very long and fragile yet they have the ability to climb over each other when coming out of the sand in large numbers to breed. (Photo: Rudie H Kuiter)

Mating aggregation of fine-spined heart urchins, Maldives. (Photo: Rudie H Kuiter).

LOVENIIDAE

Elongate heart urchin

Lovenia elongata

Sand

Lt to 88 metres (0 to 289 ft)

90 mm (3.5 in)

The elongate sea urchin is a far-ranging species found throughout the Indo-Pacific region. It lives in colonies and feeds on organic matter from minute animals, sand and detritus passed through its internal organs. When on the surface of the sand it erects long, sharp dorsal spines for defence.

CLASS: *Holothuroidea* (Sea cucumbers)

Features: The majority of holothurians are shaped like cucumbers or sausages and, although some (when alive) feel firm to the touch, their bodies are comprised of soft tissue which is somewhat supported by the presence of minute spicules of calcium carbonate embedded in the body walls. These spicules are used in the taxonomy of this group, as each species has a suite of characteristic patterns.

Sea cucumbers may have tube feet either covering their entire bodies, or in rows along their underneath side to aid in locomotion or attachment, or have entirely naked or smooth bodies. While other echinoderms have a radial symmetry, holothurians have bilateral symmetry with a distinct dorsal and ventral side.

Lifestyle: More commonly seen in the shallow lagoonal areas of tropical reefs than in temperate seas, sea cucumbers are represented from minute species only a few centimetres in length to long worm-like types which may stretch up to two metres.

At one end is the mouth, around which there are numbers of food collecting tentacles. These tentacles are actually modified tube feet whose design differs depending on the species and its method of feeding. The tentacles may be fine, many-branching networks designed to trap plankton in the water column, or bunches of sticky pads of the bottom-feeding detritus gatherers. The detritus gatherers pass bottom sediments through their intestines where the organic matter (plankton and bacteria) is digested and the "cleaned" sediment passed out through the anus at the opposite end of the sea cucumber's body. The respiratory trees are situated internally and water for breathing is drawn in through the anus (sea cucumbers actually breathe through their bums). Damage to the body can be regenerated and this includes the entire gut and respiratory tree which are able to be extruded as defence mechanisms. Some species can exude white sticky threads called *Cuvierian* organs which are toxic and would tend to dissuade any potential predator except triton and tun shells.

Reproduction: Some species may have separate sexes, or be hermaphroditic. Sperm and eggs are released into the sea on the rising tide at dusk, and many species have a planktonic larval dispersal. Others have direct development and some brood their young either internally or externally.

Associations: Sea cucumbers are inhabited by pearlfish which live inside the body by way of the anus. Externally, they provide food, transport and shelter for scale worms, shrimps and crabs. Small molluscs (ulimids) live on some sea cucumbers as parasites.

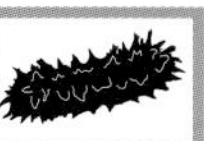

Identification: Traditional identification is by microscopic study of the various shaped spicules in each sea cucumber's body walls. However, once a good colour photograph (or series) showing the animal in its habitat is available for comparison, field identification for many species is achievable to an experienced eye.

Although this species is recorded in various places across the Indo-Pacific it is a new record for the Maldives. This sea cucumber lives in deep water on rubble and sand slopes and is by no means common anywhere throughout its range. The example pictured has similar colouring to others recorded from Port Moresby, Papua New Guinea.

HOLOTHURIIDAE
Crass sea cucumber
Actinopyga crassa
Sand, rubble
25 to 40 metres (82 to 131 ft)
400 mm (16 in)

Fairly common across its Indo-Pacific distribution this species lives in relatively exposed situations on coral and rocky reefs. It is quite firm to touch and can be variable in colour ranging from the one shown to all over brown with white underside. A detrital feeder it has 25 or more mouth tentacles and the outer body is densely covered with tube feet.

HOLOTHURIIDAE
Mauritian sea cucumber
Actinopyga mauritania
Coral reefs, rocky reefs
5 to 20 metres (16 to 66 ft)
300 mm (12 in)

HOLOTHURIIDAE

Black sea cucumber

Actinopyga miliaris

Sand, rubble, sandy reef

Lt to 10 metres (0 to 33 ft)

280 mm (11.2 in)

Common across the entire Indo-Pacific this species is well known to Trepang fishermen who refer to it as "black fish". It lives in shallow water around back reefs on a rubble or sand substrate and is often seen with a coating of sand on the back. (The sides are clean of sand). Although firm, it is soft to touch and only has a small number of papillae on the upper surface.

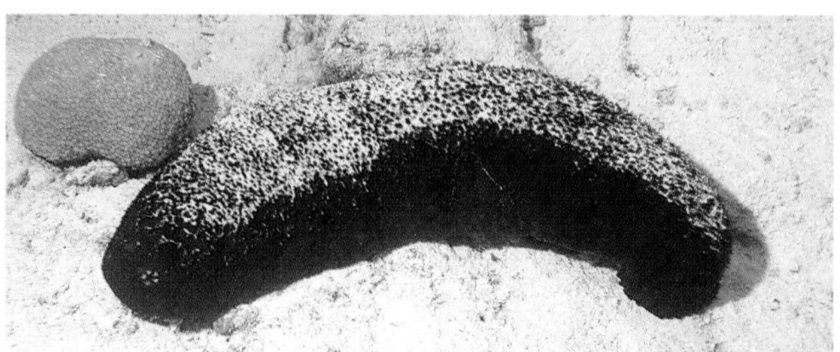

HOLOTHURIIDAE

Eyed sea cucumber

Bohadschia argus

Sand, rubble

Lt to 20 metres (0 to 66 ft)

450 mm (18 in)

The eyed sea cucumber is found throughout the Indo-Pacific region and collected for the Trepang industry as the "leopard fish". Although its colour may vary the pattern remains fairly constant. It is a suctorial feeder (specialised for suction) and when disturbed it will eject sticky, white threads (Cuvierian organs) from its anus.

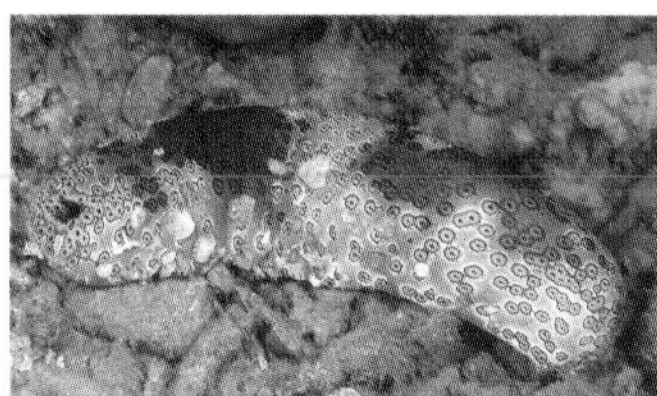

Variation, Kimbe Bay, Papua New Guinea.

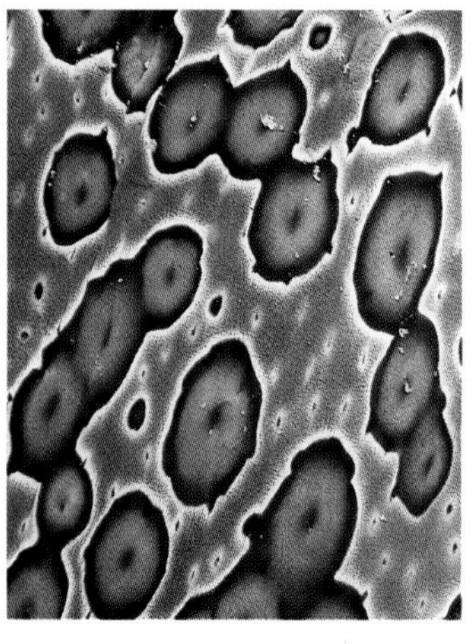

Close up of eyed pattern and papillae distribution.

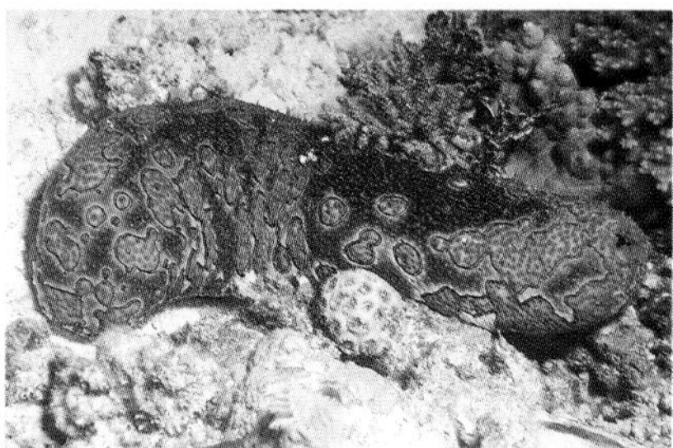

Variation, Kimbe Bay, Papua New Guinea showing Cuvierian organs.

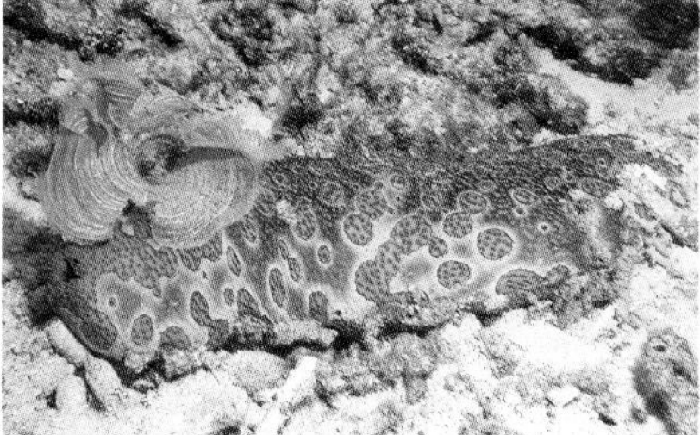

Colour variation, the Coral Sea.

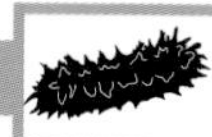

HOLOTHURIIDAE
Marmorate sea cucumber
Bohadschia marmorata

Sand, rubble, seagrass meadows

Lt to 20 metres (0 to 66 ft)

240 mm (9.6 in)

Known as the "chalky fish" to Trepang fishers this common species is spread across most of the Indo-Pacific and ranges in colour from light tan with white patches to the Maldivian example (which is a new record) illustrated. It may be seen out in the open or partially buried in the substrate.

Specimen extruding its sticky defensive Cuvierian organs. Milne Bay, Papua New Guinea.

Close up of Cuvierian organs. Milne Bay, Papua New Guinea.

HOLOTHURIIDAE
Edible sea cucumber
Holothuria (Halodeima) edulis

Sand, rubble, reef

Lt to 20 metres (0 to 66 ft)

200 mm (8 in)

Regardless of its wide-ranging distribution, from East Africa to the South Pacific this species has a very distinct colour pattern; a black or brown back and a bright pink sides and underside. However, this Maldivian form is pink all over with black specks. It is known as the "pink fish" to Trepang gatherers.

Normal colour combination, Kimbe Bay, Papua New Guinea.

HOLOTHURIIDAE

Impatient sea cucumber

Holothuria (Thymiosycia) impatiens

Sand, rubble, seagrass meadows

Lt to 10 metres (0 to 33 ft)

200 mm (8 in)

A common intertidal species this sea cucumber is widely distributed throughout the Indo-Pacific where it can be seen in the open during the day or found beneath rocks. Soft to touch the brown body is covered in conical warts with emerging papillae giving it a very knobbly appearance.

HOLOTHURIIDAE

Noble sea cucumber

Holothuria (Microthele) nobilis

Coral reefs, rocky reefs, sand

3 to 10 metres (10 to 33 ft)

250 mm (10 in)

Black, hard to touch and covered with a fine coating of sand the noble sea cucumber seems to prefer sand covered hard substrate rather than just sand. This species has been recorded throughout the Indo-Pacific and is known to the Trepang gatherers as the "mammy fish" or "teat fish" due to the very characteristic teat-like protuberances along the edges of the ventral surface.

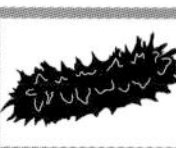

Found on reefs across the Indo-Pacific, Graeffe's sea cucumber varies in colour from a basic light green to a light brown. Its feeding behaviour involves the intake of sediments and small animals caught up in the soft, sticky 'catching pads' of its feeding tentacles. This species is active during the day.

HOLOTHURIIDAE

Graeffe's sea cucumber

Pearsonothuria graeffei

Coral reefs, rocky reefs sand, rubble

5 to 20 metres (16 to 66 ft)

250 mm (10 in)

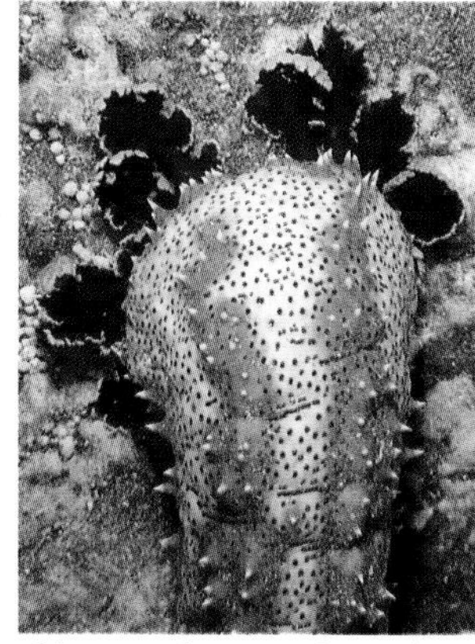

Close up showing the sticky mouth pads at work gathering up detritus.

Juvenile (15 mm). It is thought that some juvenile sea cucumbers mimic nudibranchs.

A distinctive, shallow-water species inhabiting the Indo-Pacific area, this sea cucumber can be seen on reef flats or in lagoons during the day. Colour is stable over its entire range, although occasionally the orange tips on the quadrangularly positioned papillae may often be missing. Feeding is by way of extensible mouth tentacles tipped with soft, sticky pads which pick up bottom detritus.

STICHOPODIDAE

Dark green sea cucumber

Stichopus chloronotus

Sand, rubble

Lt to 10 metres (0 to 33 ft)

300 mm (12 in)

STICHOPODIDAE

Horrid sea cucumber

Stichopus horrens

Rubble, sand, broken reef

Lt to 10 metres (0 to 33 ft)

250 mm (10 in)

The horrid sea cucumber is yet to be recognised in many Indian Ocean localities though it is fairly well known from northern Australia to Japan and into the South Pacific. Its colour varies from a mottled dark green to mottled grey; the body is firm to touch and covered with irregular-sized warts tipped by pointed papillae.

Variation, Exmouth, Western Australia.

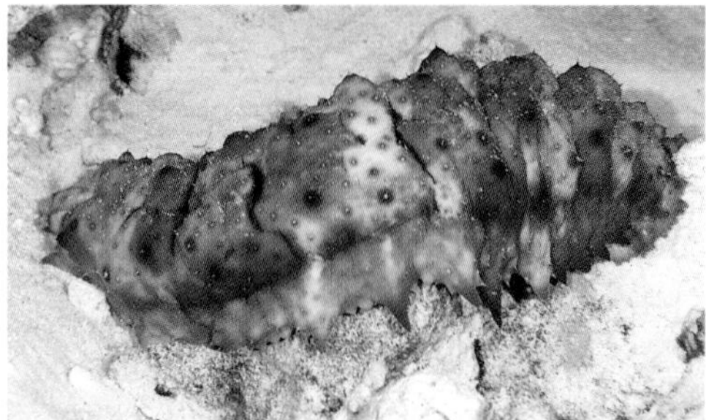

Variation, Kimbe Bay, Papua New Guinea.

STICHOPODIDAE

Netted sea cucumber

Stichopus sp.

Sand

20 to 35 metres (66 to 115 ft)

400 mm (16 in)

Only known from relatively deep water this undescribed species of sea cucumber lives on sand slopes and sandy bottoms around some of the southern atolls. It is quite distinctive in appearance with a netted design pattern and one individual had several imperial shrimps and a small sea cucumber crab living on it.

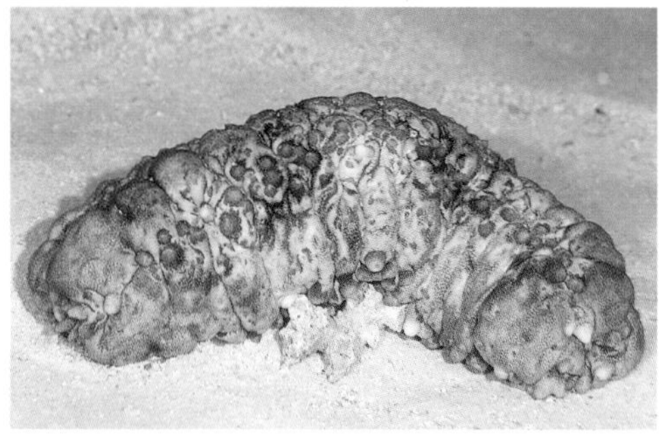

The Imperial shrimp
Periclimenes imperator *on* Stichopus *sp.*

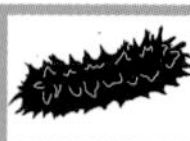

STICHOPODIDAE
Pineapple sea cucumber
Thelonota ananas
Coral reef, sand, rubble
5 to 40 metres (16 to 131 ft)
750 mm (30 in)

The pineapple sea cucumber with its firm pointed dorsal papillae is without doubt the most easily recognised sea cucumber. Its colour can be bright orange in deep waters, to pink, red, or brown in shallow waters. Several scale worms (*Gastrolepidia clavigera*) may be present on the one animal and are generally situated on the underside. This species is highly prized by trepang fishermen and known as "red fish".

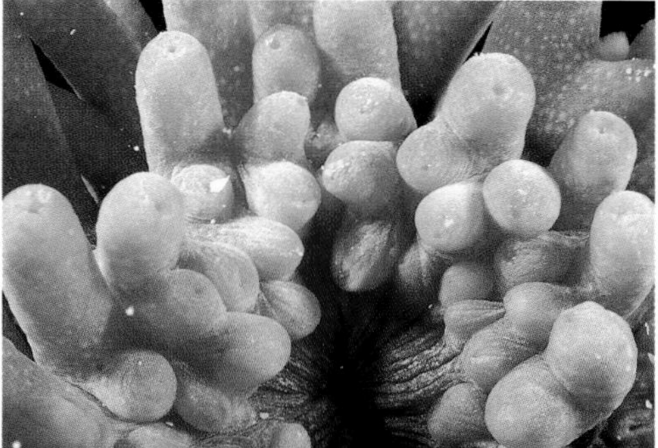

Close up of underside mouth area.

Close up of large modified "cockscomb" papillae on the dorsal surface.

Close up of dorsal papillae at the front end.

STICHOPODIDAE

Royal sea cucumber

Thelenota anax

Sand, sandy hard substrates

10 to 50 metres (33 to 164 ft)

600 mm (24 in)

A deeper water Indo-Pacific species, the royal sea cucumber is quite massive and with its red reticulated pattern is fairly simple to identify. Imperial shrimps *Periclimenes soror* and the commensal scale worm *Gastrolepidia clavigera* are known associates.

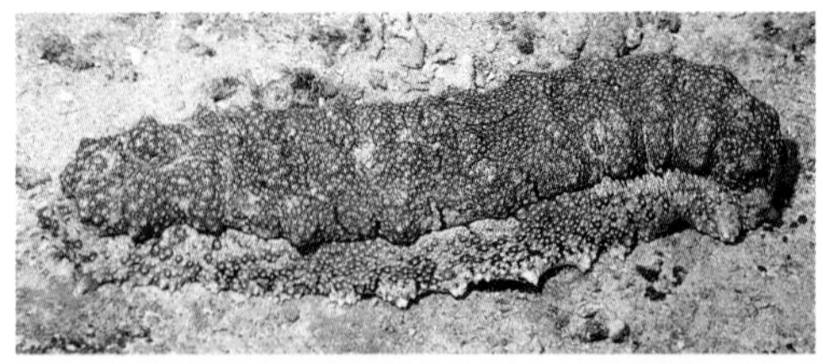

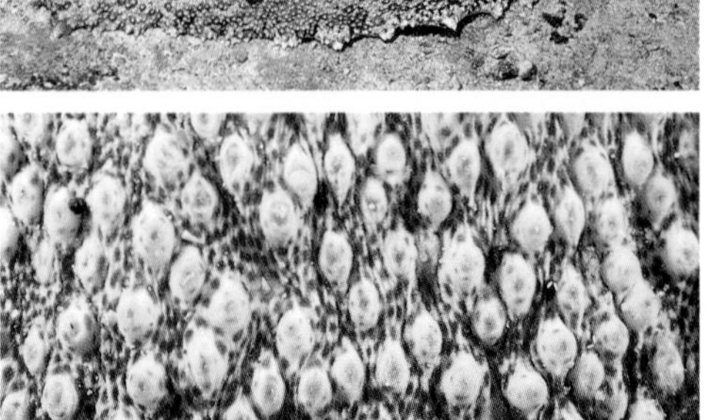

Extreme close up showing small parasitic ulimid shells burrowed into the skin and many minute copepods on the skin and at the papillae entrances.

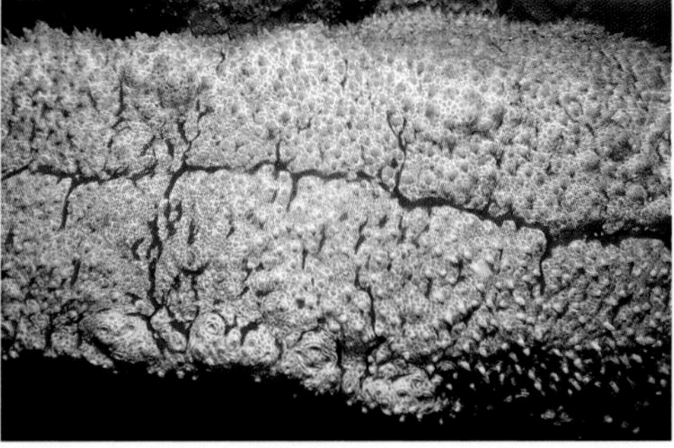

Close up of side wall area showing the red line bisecting the upper and lower areas.

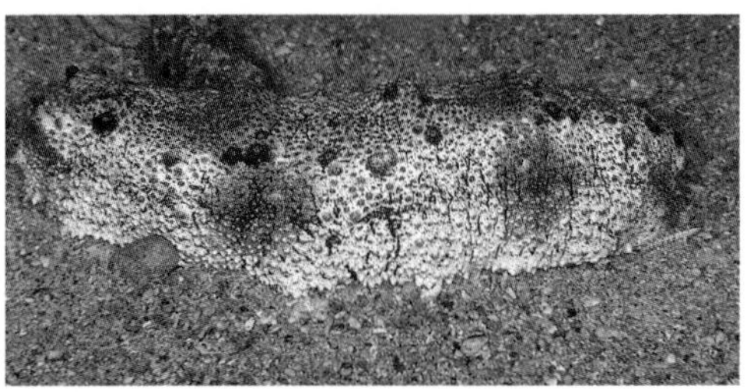

Variation, Kimbe Bay, Papua New Guinea.

SYNAPTIDAE

Spotted sea cucumber

Synapta maculata

Sand, rubble, seagrass/algae meadows

Lt to 30 metres (0 to 98 ft)

1 m (3 ft) to 2 m (6 ft)

Known in the tropical parts of the Indo-Pacific, this species is common in shallow water lagoons, harbours and amongst seagrass meadows. The animal is extremely soft and flabby, and has a "sticky" feeling when touched. It has no tube feet but moves by the extension and contraction of its body and feeds night and day, using its branched mouth tentacles.

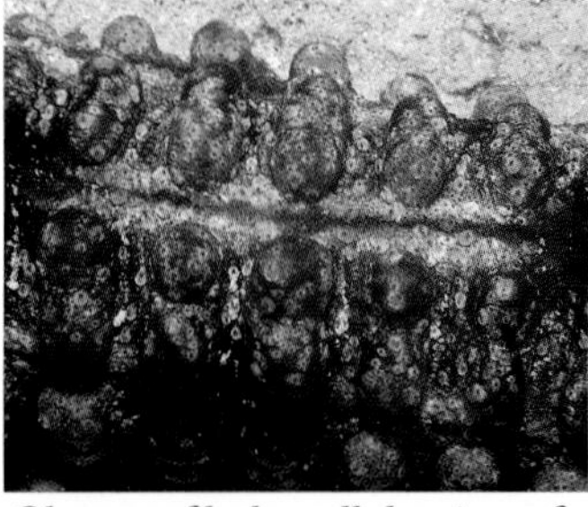

Close up of body wall showing soft bubble-like tubercules, Maldives.

SYNAPTIDAE
String-of-beads sea cucumber
Synapta sp.
Sand, mud
1 to 8 metres (3 to 26 ft)
400 mm (16 in)

Found in shallow water on sandy and muddy substrate this species is unable to be identified to date. However, the visual features showing two dorsal lines running the length of the body bisecting evenly displaced bead-shaped spots appear to be good external characteristics. The feeding mouth tentacles are active during the day.

SYNAPTIDAE
Gut-like sea cucumber
Synaptula recta
Coral reef, sponges
8 to 20 metres (26 to 66 ft)
150 mm (6 in)

With very few general records from the Indian Ocean locations this sea cucumber is well known from the Bay of Bengal to the South Pacific. Strictly nocturnal this species can be seen out in the open feeding on plankton and detritus swept up by its constantly moving mouth tentacles moving across the surface of sponges.

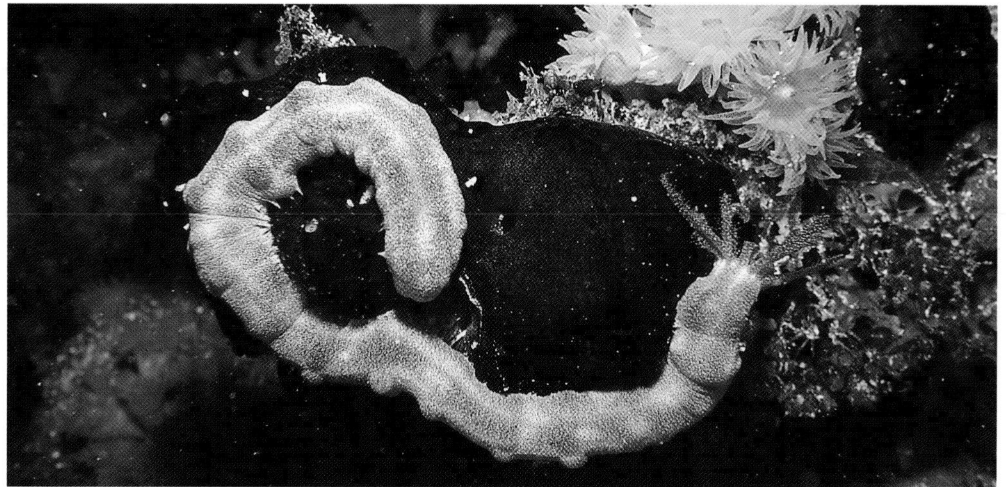

Ascidians

Chapter 9

Ascidians – Sea squirts

PHYLUM: CHORDATA

CLASS: *Ascidiacea* (Tunicates, Sea squirts, Colonial ascidians, Compound ascidians)

Features: Sea squirts, or ascidians, may not be the most well-known underwater creatures yet they are the most advanced of invertebrates. The basic tunicate or sea squirt is round or sac-like, and is permanently anchored to the substrate. The body is enclosed in a tunic of cellulose (a rare substance in the animal kingdom) which is the source of its name. Each individual has two body openings; one is an inlet for water which brings in oxygen for respiration and suspended plankton and detritus for food; the other is an exhalant siphon (usually at the higher end of the body) through which water-bearing carbon dioxide and waste is pumped out of the body. The inhalant siphon is generally larger and towards the bottom of the body. The large internal gills are ciliated and act as the pump.

The name sea squirt generally refers to solitary ascidians but some are colonial with many individuals either connected by a stalk to a common base or with the zooids embedded in a firm, jelly-like matrix, or as an investing sheet of tissue. Many are beautifully coloured. In some investing compound ascidians each zooid may have a small separate intake siphon but waste products are channelled out from larger communal exhalant siphons.

Lifestyle: There are about 1350 types of ascidians in the world's oceans. Ascidians are entirely marine and live wherever they can find their preferred settlement area; some species are specific in their choice of substrate, others are not. They can be found on reefs, rubble, algae, seagrasses, shells or rocks, in caves and under ledges and in sand and mud. There are even pelagic ascidians that drift in ocean currents and have complex life histories.

Reproduction: Most species of ascidians are hermaphrodites. Eggs are released from the exhalant siphon and fertilised by free-swimming sperm in open water, or are held in the exhalant siphon and fertilised by sperm taken in through the inhalant siphon. The embryos in many species develop quickly, often in a few hours. This may be important in enabling them to settle and develop in suitable situations near their parents. They have also been of great value to embryologists and because of their rapid development have been very useful in experimental studies. The larvae are distinctly tadpole-like and have a notochord or rudimentary backbone. It is the presence of the notochord in the larvae that indicates sea squirts to be related to animals with backbones (vertebrates).

Associations: Very few commensal associations have been recorded for ascidians though it is known that they are inhabited by amphipods, shrimps and the pear pearl fish *Carapus* sp. (see *Australian Fish Behaviour* 1993: Coleman).

Identification: Visual recognition to species level has come a long way over the past 30 years and quite a number of ascidians can be recognised from a good photograph. However, there are many different colours and patterns within many of the investing species and until there is enough photographic evidence cross-referenced with taxonomically identified preserved specimens, many will remain mysteries.

Leach's ascidian, Maldives.

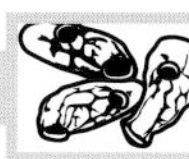

Mostly found beneath the edges of loose dead coral slabs in shallow water this species forms thick investing mats up to 250 mm (10 in) across. The texture is quite firm and it did not appear to be very common. The zooid free area is wider in relation to the next species.

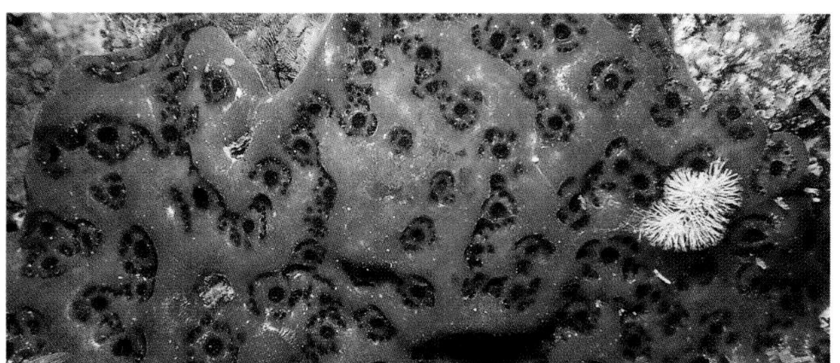

POLYCLINIDAE
Blue Aplidium
Aplidium sp.
Coral reefs, rocky reefs
5 to 10 metres (16 to 33 ft)
120 mm (4.8 in) colony

Very firm to touch and somewhat thicker in growth than the previous species, the green Aplidium zooids appear much closer in arrangement and the smaller inlet siphons are at a further distance around the larger outlet siphon. This genus is known throughout the Indo-Pacific.

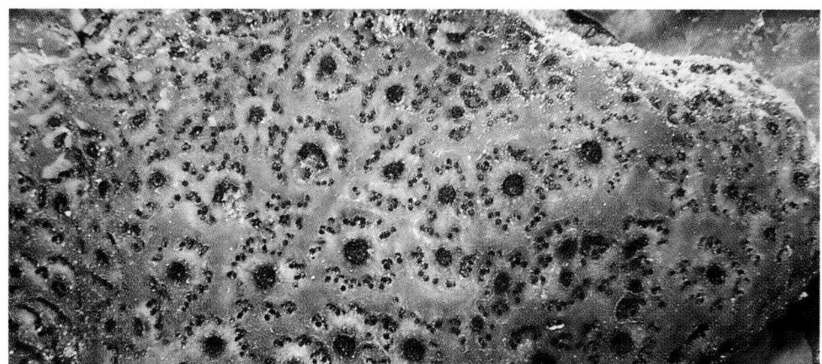

POLYCLINIDAE
Green Aplidium
Aplidium sp.
Coral reefs, rocky reefs
5 to 10 metres (16 to 33 ft)
120 mm (4.8 in) colony

The inlet siphons on this semi-transparent bulbous ascidian are located at the bottom of the bulb and are marked by small dots around the edge while the exhalant siphons have white circles around the rims.

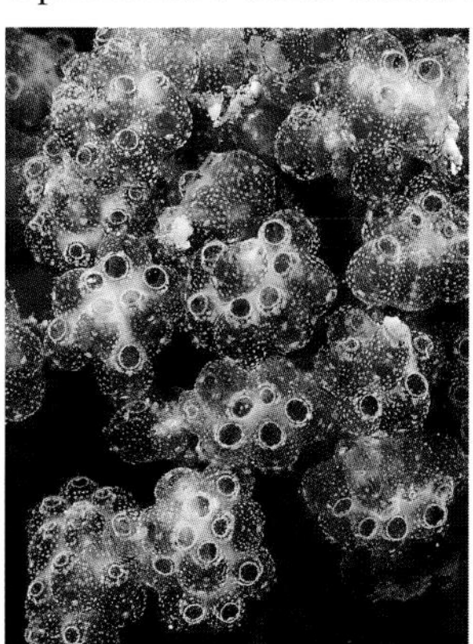

POLYCITORIDAE
Green transparent Eudistoma
Eudistoma sp.
Coral reefs, rocky reefs
10 to 20 metres (33 to 66 ft)
35 mm (1.4 in) (photo)

Colour variation, Maldives.

POLYCITORIDAE
Purple Eudistoma
Eudistoma sp.
Coral reefs, rocky reefs
8 to 30 metres (26 to 98 ft)
35 mm (1.4 in) (photo)

Very common on walls and drop offs during summer this attractive little ascidian grows in stalked clumps and forms in small patches over the reef. Although there are a number of other forms of *Eudistoma* this one does not appear similar to other species in its shape or colour pattern. The white openings are the outlet siphons and the purple speckled edged siphons are the inlet siphons.

Close up of zooid openings and growth pattern, Maldives.

Close up of zooid openings colour variation, Maldives.

DIDEMNIDAE
Soft Didemnum
Didemnum molle
Coral reefs, rocky reefs
Lt to 20 metres (0 to 66 ft)
25 mm (1 in)

Common tropical species throughout the Maldives and the entire Indo-Pacific region, this ascidian prefers shallow sheltered waters where it is seen growing on dead coral slabs, usually in groups. The green colour within is the result of the animals being inhabited by masses of minute blue-green algae which live as symbionts in the ascidians cloacal cavity.

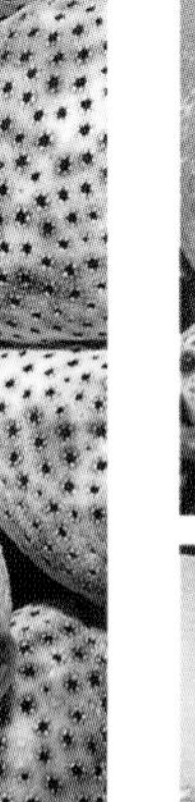

Close up of a colony group, Maldives.

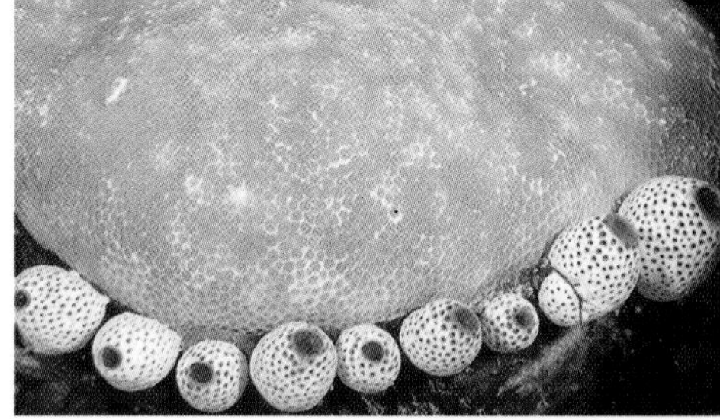

Colour variation, Maldives.

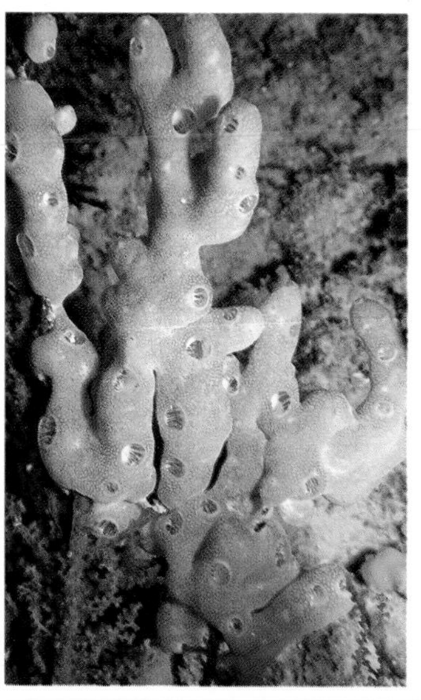

Living in deeper water this investing species has grown over gorgonian sea fan fronds and taken the shape of the sea fan. This is a distinct advantage to the colony as it is out in the water column, and is able to feed around its entire surface area. This species has light green cloacal apertures (largest outlets) and white oral apertures (smallest ones).

DIDEMNIDAE
Lobed Didemnum
Didemnum sp.
Coral reefs, rocky reefs
20 to 35 metres (66 to 115 ft)
200 mm (8 in) colony

With such a distinctive colour pattern this species is very easy to recognise in the field. The body test is white with bright orange highlighting the meandering paths of the smaller oral apertures (inlet siphons) while the larger fringed cloacal apertures (outlet siphons) are rimmed with orange; each one encircled by a ring of oral apertures.

DIDEMNIDAE
Meandering Didemnum
Didemnum sp.
Coral reefs, rocky reefs
10 to 20 metres (33 to 66 ft)
200 mm (8 in) colony

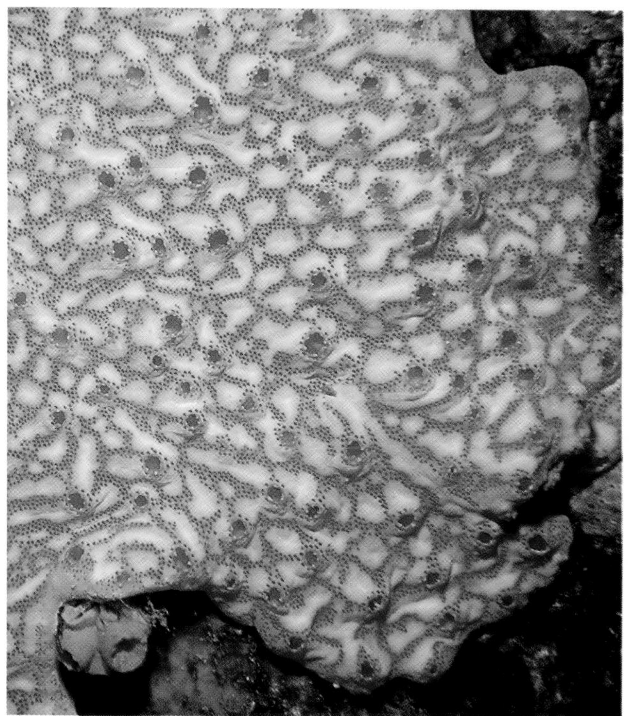

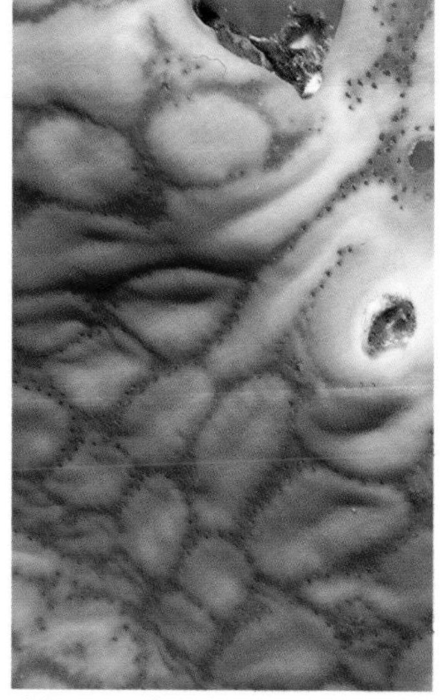

Close up of oral aperture pattern, Seychelles.

DIDEMNIDAE

Purple and white Didemnum

Didemnum sp.

Coral reefs, rocky reefs

10 to 20 metres (33 to 66 ft)

200 mm (8 in) colony

Seen at a number of Indian Ocean sites this investing ascidian does not seem to be as fixed as others to the reef and can be lifted as though it is growing across other organisms. Observations and photographs showed that this species is almost always variations of purple and white.

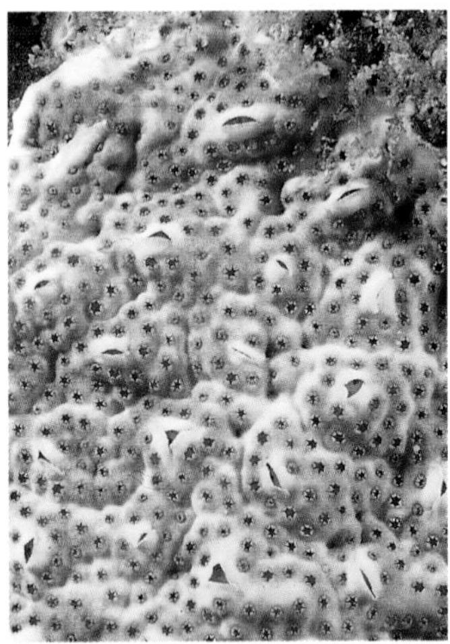

Close up showing cloacal apertures (large holes) closed as slits while the smaller six-lobed star-like oral apertures are open. Seychelles.

DIDEMNIDAE

Yellow Didemnum

Didemnum sp.

Coral reefs, rocky reefs

8 to 20 metres (26 to 66 ft)

250 mm (10 in) across

A brightly-coloured bulbous growing species, this ascidian did not appear common though it was easy to recognise whenever seen. It is firm to touch and quite spongy with high ridges and minimal attachment to the substrate.

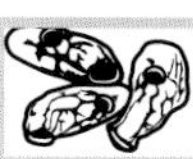

DIDEMNIDAE
Variable Diplosoma
Diplosoma varians
Coral reefs, rocky reefs
Lt to 30 metres (0 to 98 ft)
10 mm (0.4 in) colony

A common species found throughout the Indo-Pacific and at least from the Maldives to Lord Howe Island in the South Pacific this smaller species is often seen in large aggregations and is mostly bright green in colour.

PEROPHORIDAE
Red circle Ecteinascidia
Ecteinascidia sp.
Coral reefs, rocky reefs
10 to 25 metres (33 to 82 ft)
2 mm (0.08 in)

Established in small colonies along drop offs and walls this very distinctive little ascidian is not common in the Maldives. The animal has a barrel-shaped stalked zooid with patches of red dots on the sides. The larger inhalant siphon is transparent with around nine opaque white patches around the flared rim interspaced by red streaks. The exhalant siphon on top has less of each. A prominent red circle appears on the dorsal surface between the siphons.

STYELIDAE

Leach's Ascidian

Botrylloides leachi

Coral reefs, rocky reefs, rubble, seagrass meadows

1 to 25 metres (3 to 82 ft)

170 mm (6.8 in) across photo

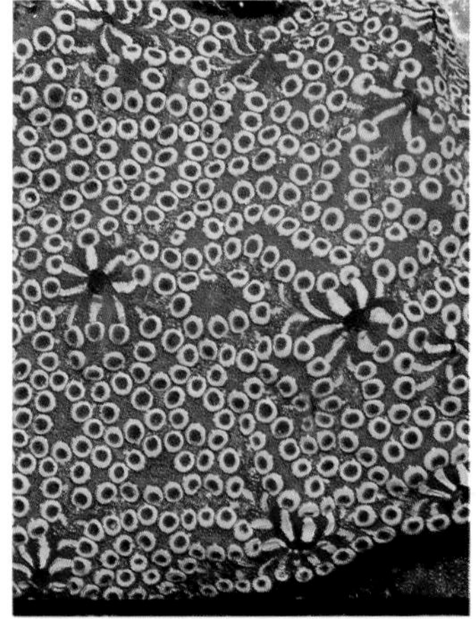

Colour is not a good criterion for species identification as it can vary from yellow to purple, white, brown, orange and various combinations. These variations fooled past scientists into describing it as 26 different species. Identification to genus level can be made in the field wherever sufficient growth of the colony is present. The surface is pocked with double rows of zooids leading to one or more exhalant siphons which are often surrounded by a rosette of zooids. The species and has been recorded from the Red Sea, to the Caribbean.

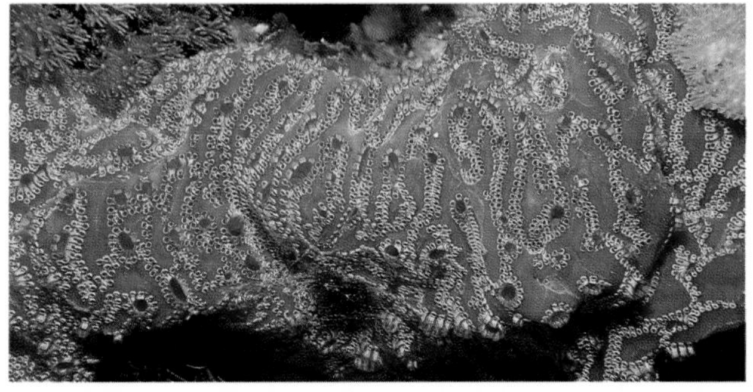

Colour pattern variation, Maldives (left).

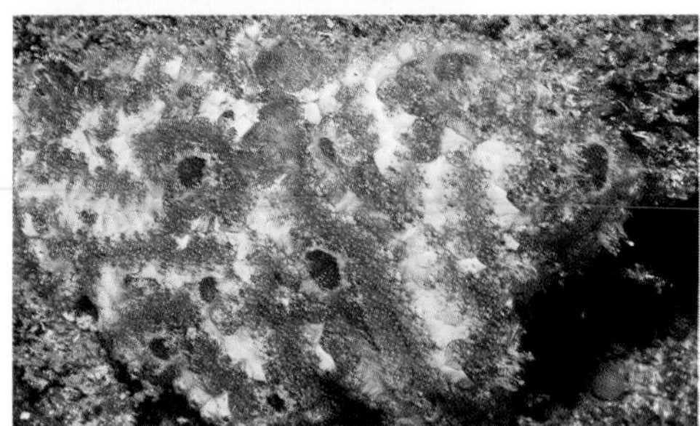

Colour pattern variation, Lord Howe Island, South Pacific.

Colour pattern variation, Maldives.

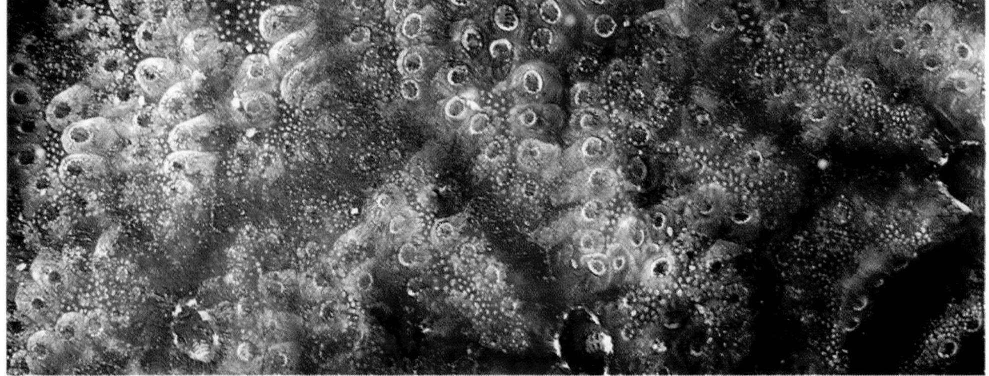

Colour pattern variation, Maldives.

STYELIDAE
Rock-wall Eusynstella
Eusynstella latericus

Coral reefs, rocky reefs

10 to 20 metres (33 to 66 ft)

35 mm (1.4 in) across

Frequently encountered beneath dead coral and under rocks this fairly distinctive little ascidian is generally red and yellow in colour. It is found from the Persian Gulf to the Maldives and across to Australia, the zooids are around 5 mm in size and grow very tightly together.

Colour variation, Maldives.

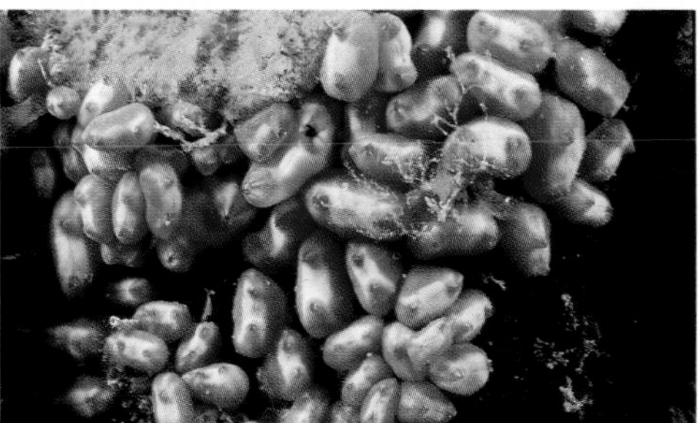

Variation, Port Moresby, Papua New Guinea.

STYELIDAE
Branching Semplegma
Semplegma sp.

Coral reefs, rocky reefs

1 to 5 metres (3.3 to 16 ft)

35 mm (1.4 in) across

This species has very characteristic side branching protuberances growing around the base of each zooid making it easy to recognise. It does not appear to be common in the Maldives and has not been published in any previous popular book. The zooids are around 5 mm across.

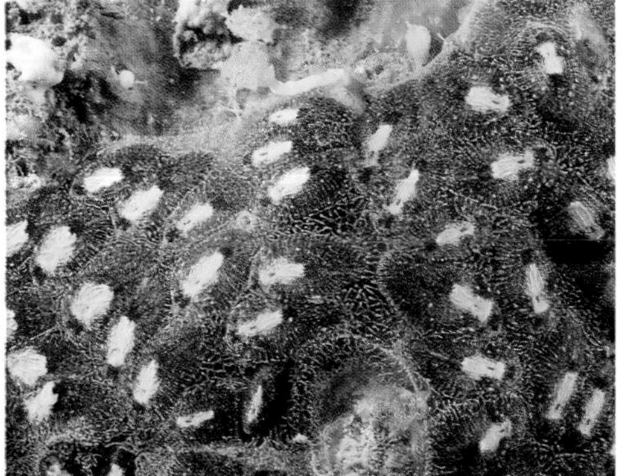

Colour variation appearance has occurred due to the colony being retracted, Maldives.

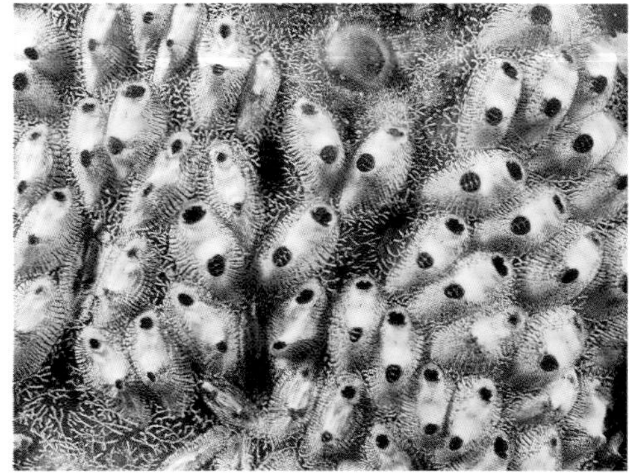

ASCIDIIDAE
Smooth Ascidia
Ascidia glabra
Coral reefs, rocky reefs
Lt to 10 metres (0 to 33 ft)
60 mm (2.4 in)

Reasonably common in the Maldives this species lives in shallow water where it resides beneath loose dead coral and rocks. Colour is a translucent white and yellow with a peppering of white or yellow opaque specks around and between the siphons.

PYURIDAE
Papillose Ascidian
Halocynthia papillosa
Coral reefs, rocky reefs
1 to 10 metres (3.3 to 33 ft)
50 mm (2 in)

A distinctive solitary species this ascidian is relatively well known from the Red Sea to Australia. It lives beneath dead coral and rocks and although colour may vary between individuals the test has many papillae and those around the siphons are very well developed.

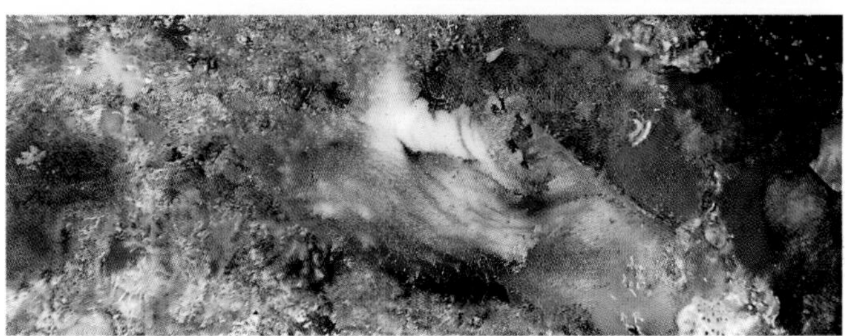

Colour variation, Maldives.

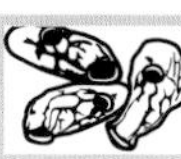

PYURIDAE
Four-lobed Pura
Pyura sp.
Coral reefs, rocky reefs, rubble
5 to 20 metres (16 to 66 ft)
120 mm (4.8 in)

Although this tunicate is usually very heavily encrusted with epizoic growths such as sponges, ascidians, hydroids and algae the yellow stripes and four yellow lobes on the inside of the siphons appear to be stable identifying features. It is common in the Maldives but has yet to be formally identified from a specimen.

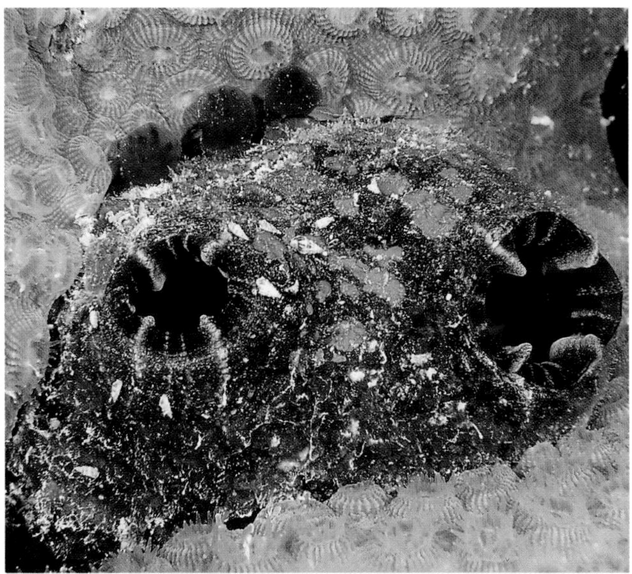

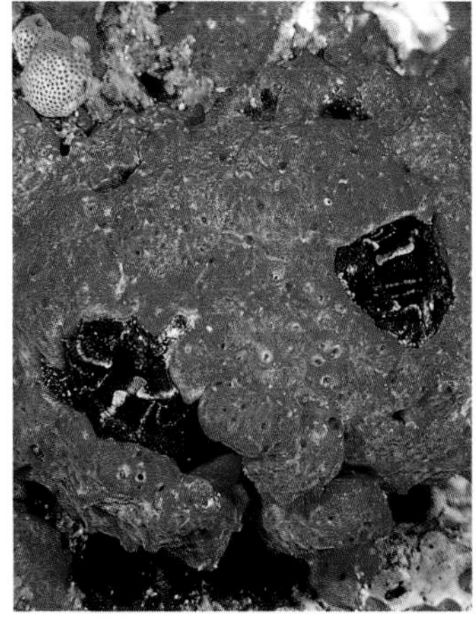

Heavily encrusted by a sponge, Maldives.

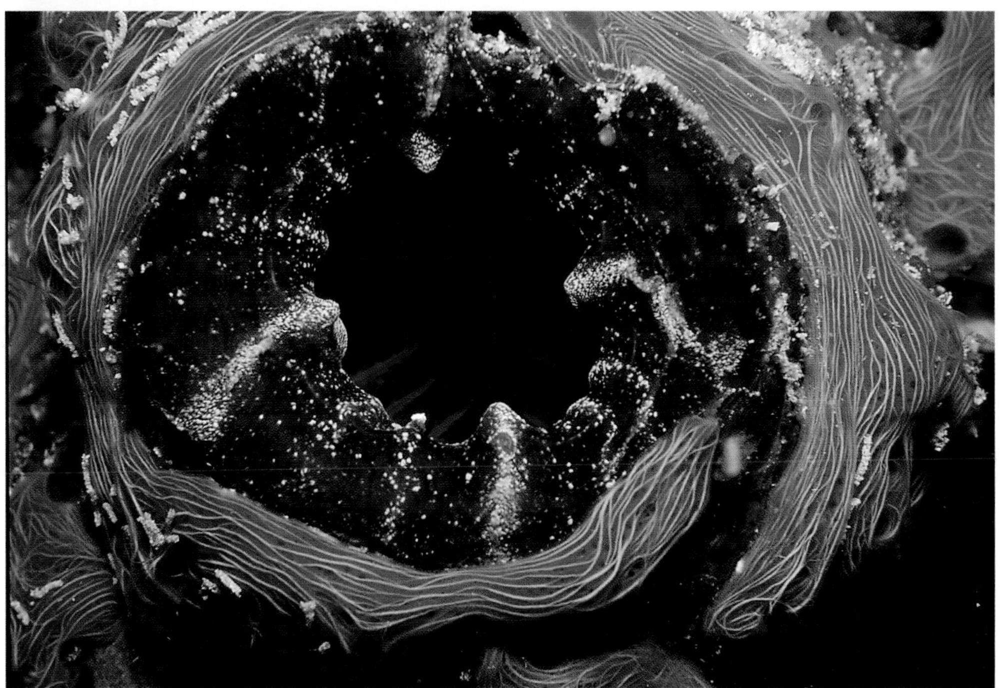

Close up of siphon, Maldives.

Reptiles

Chapter 10

Reptiles

PHYLUM: CHORDATA

CLASS: *Reptilia*

ORDER: *Chelonia* (Turtles)
Squamata (Sea snakes)

Features: In the reptiles the four-legged vertebrate plan (tetrapod) is well developed. The head carried eyes, nose, auditory canals and jaws and the brain is enclosed in a stout skull, or cranium. In the snakes, the limbs have been lost and in the turtles and tortoises, the body is housed in the shell, or carapace. While the terrestrial tortoises are cumbersome and slow walkers, their counterparts, the marine turtles, are swift and graceful swimmers.

Lifestyles: Present day reptiles are cold blooded, air breathing and for the most part land animals that have no internal mechanisms to control their body heat independently of their surroundings. Although land-based reptiles have scaly skins that allow little, or no loss of water from the body (sweating) and can conserve body fluids by reabsorption of moisture from urea and faeces, aquatic reptiles excrete fluid urine. Terrestrial reptiles control their body temperature by behaviour: movement towards, or away from heat and cold.

Of the 6,300 species of reptiles known throughout the world only 40 species have returned to the marine environment. Marine reptiles may be carnivores, herbivores, scavengers and some such as the crocodiles and alligators (not living in the Maldives) can be predators on humans.

Reproduction: Sexes are separate, males impregnate females internally. Most land reptiles lay shelled eggs, which are buried. This link with terrestrial ancestry is also followed in most marine reptiles, though the majority of sea snakes bear live young. Turtles are well known for their shore nesting.

Associations: Sea lice and barnacles infest the bodies of marine reptiles and quite often the larger species play host to suckerfish.

Identification: Most marine reptiles are readily identified due to their large size and well known content. Pictures are available in many books and magazines and the majority can be recognised visually. However, some sea snakes remain difficult due to lack of distinguishing features captured by most underwater photography. Unless close ups of heads and scales are available many may only be recognised to genus level.

Turtles

Features: Of the six species of turtle inhabiting the Indo-Pacific area only three are regularly seen in the Maldives.

Most turtles have strong bony shells covered by large overlapping plates (the carapace). The limbs are well developed, heavy and paddle-shaped with one or more claws on the anterior edge and this basic design has not changed for over 150 million years. Similar to all reptiles they breathe air yet they are able to slow down their heartbeats and sleep underwater for several hours.

Lifestyles: Marine turtles spend their lives in the sea, the only exception is that they are born on land and the females make short journeys up the beach to lay their eggs.

They feed on a variety of sea life including algae, barnacles, ascidians, sea jellies, fish, seagrass and crustaceans. Although they have survived throughout millions of years many species are now threatened, not only by increasing predation by humans but also from jettisoned waste in the form of plastic bags. The plastic bags (often bait bags thrown away by fishermen) may give off a marine smell (fish or prawns) and appear similar to a sea jelly. If eaten, the plastic blocks up the intestines and the turtle starves to death.

The mortality rate of turtles is high where there are large numbers of trawlers and fishermen with set nets with many becoming entangled and drowning.

Reproduction: Turtles migrate over long distances between feeding and breeding areas. Males and females mate during spring and summer after which the female crawls up the beach at night on the high tide to lay her eggs in a pit she digs above the high water line. Many turtles return to breed on the same islands or cays where they were born. Females may lay up to six clutches of eggs in one season and then remain barren for several years after. Once they are laid the 50 to 150 ping pong ball size eggs are covered with sand and left. The sex of the baby turtles is determined by the temperature inside the nest and incubation takes around six weeks. The baby turtles hatch at night and make their way down to the sea to face a myriad dangers in the forms of ghost crabs, land hermit crabs, night herons and once they reach the water, fish.

Associations: Marine turtles are often infested by boring barnacles which bury into their flesh, using them as substrate and a transport vehicle. Suckerfish often use them for transport and some turtles have a unique association with algae-eating surgeonfish, regularly visiting a cleaning station or sleeping area where their growths of filamentous algae are eaten off by the surgeons, result in less drag for them when swimming.

Identification: Most identification can be visually accomplished from a good colour photo. Taxonomically the plates on the head, the beak and shell shape are stable identifying features.

CHELONIIDAE

Loggerhead turtle

Caretta caretta

Coral reefs, rocky reefs, lagoons

Lt to 30 metres (0 to 98 ft)

1.5 metres (5 ft)

Found throughout most of the tropical waters of the world, the loggerhead turtle has a dark brown shell, With a yellow or cream underside and jaws with heavily expanded sheaths for crushing prey. The female lays eggs (50 at a time) on island beaches and coral cays during summer.

Male turtles have longer tails than females and as such are easy to distinguish, Great Barrier Reef.

CHELONIIDAE
Green turtle
Chelonia mydas
Coral reefs, rocky reefs, lagoons
Lt to 25 metres (0 to 82 ft)
1.5 metres (5 ft)

The most commonly observed in the Maldives it is imperative for their survival that any nesting sites are protected. The females come ashore at night on the high tides to lay their eggs in pits dug in the sand above the high-tide mark. Hatching takes place some six to eight weeks later, generally at night. The sex of a baby turtle is determined by the temperature of the nest. Males develop below 28.7°C. and at higher temperatures the baby turtles hatch as females.

Green turtle stranded on a reef flat at low tide, Dampier, Western Australia.

Close up of head showing the longer head scales between the eyes and shorter beak of the green turtle.

Mating green turtles, Great Barrier Reef.

Even after reaching the ocean unscathed there is still a long way to go and many dangers to elude.

Found across the Indian and Pacific oceans young hawksbill turtles have exceedingly beautiful shells known as "tortoiseshell" that almost led to the species demise from heavy exploitation by humans. Adult hawksbill turtles somewhat resemble older green turtles (*Chelonia mydas*), though at close range they can be separated by the scales behind the eyes, the hawksbill having three postocular scales and the green turtle having four or more.

CHELONIIDAE

Hawksbill turtle

Eretmochelys imbricata

Coral reefs, rocky reefs

Lt to 25 metres (0 to 82 ft)

1 metre (3 ft)

Female turtle with egg clutch.

Female hawksbill turtle laying eggs, Dampier, Western Australia.

Hawksbill turtle stranded in a pool at low tide, Dampier, Western Australia.

Sea snakes

Features: Most sea snakes belong to the family Hydrophiidae and as marine reptiles breathe air; many have valvular nostrils and a vertically compressed, paddle-like tail. The body is covered in scales and most species are highly venomous and kill their prey by biting and injecting venom.

Lifestyles: There are around 50 species of sea snakes known across the Indo-Pacific region and although most occur around the shores of continental islands and reefs, several species are known to drift and swim large distances across open ocean in the vicinity of sargassum rafts and driftwood.

Sea snakes feed on a variety of reef fishes and their eggs, and are able to hunt both day and night probing beneath rocks, in crevices, even under and around divers. They are especially keen on gobies and scorpion fish which are killed with venom and swallowed head first.

Although they are known to dive to depths in excess of 40 metres (131 ft) and sleep beneath coral slabs, or wrapped around coral for up to three hours they must return to the surface at various times to breathe. Sea snakes have poor eyesight and curious natures and for this reason have been feared by reefwalkers, snorkellers and scuba divers.

When sea snakes are mating they often appear to be aggressive and divers believe they are being chased to be bitten but this not the case. Although many Indo-Pacific fishermen have been bitten and killed by sea snakes when pulling nets, or when catching them underwater for their skins, no sport divers are known to have been killed in Southern Hemisphere waters. However, all sea snakes should be treated with caution as they have extremely strong venom – some of the deadliest known.

Reproduction: Sea snakes have separate sexes and although they mate in the sea, some give birth to live young and others, like the sea krait, go ashore at night and lay their eggs on land.

Associations: Periodically, sea snakes shed their skins so that many epiphytes are shed at the same time. However, one barnacle at least is known to become so firmly affixed that it remains attached to the snake's body after shedding takes place.

Identification: Although some of the more well-known and descriptively marked sea snakes can be relatively simple to identify others remain difficult and require close up pictures of heads and scales to determine specific identification.

Regularly observed throughout the Indian and Pacific oceans the olive sea snake is without doubt the most common of sea snakes encountered in the tropics. It is active day and night and moves along the bottom investigating crannies beneath coral and rocks searching for food. The olive sea snake generally surfaces to breathe at intervals of 10 to 20 minutes and ranges in colour from brown to yellow. The female produces up to five live young.

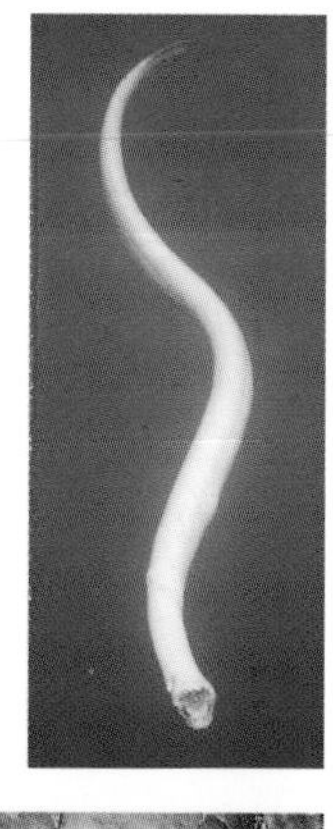

HYDROPHIIDAE

Olive sea snake

Aipysurus laevis

Coral reefs, rocky reefs

Lt to 25 metres (0 to 82 ft)

1.5 metres (5 ft)

Close up showing eye and head scales, Dampier, Western Australia.

Close up showing nostril flaps closed while underwater.

Sea snakes have a double penis, both armed with "stay-a-while" hooks.

Well known throughout the Indo-Pacific this sea snake is often seen washed ashore after rough seas or storms. The yellow-bellied sea snake is easily identified owing to its unique colour pattern, which is particularly noticeable on the flattened tail. This species is pelagic and feeds on ocean fishes found around sargassum rafts or floating debris.

HYDROPHIIDAE

Yellow-bellied sea snake

Pelamis platurus

Open ocean (washed ashore on beaches)

Surface

530 mm (21 in)

Sea birds

Chapter 11

Sea birds

PHYLUM: CHORDATA

CLASS: *Avres* (Birds)

Features: A sea bird is a warm-blooded vertebrate covered with feathers except for legs and feet which are scaly. The feet are generally webbed and the forelimbs are modified into powerful wings which enable them to fly and glide over wide expanses of the ocean. Most sea birds have well developed sharp beaks and many have the ability to dive from heights of 10 to 20 metres into the sea when hunting for prey species.

Lifestyle It is thought that the sea birds took to the water some 50 million years ago and their ancestors emerged as cormorants, frigate birds, pelicans and penguins which are living examples of today's ancient lineage.

Most sea birds spend the majority of their lives at sea feeding or searching for food. Many cover extraordinary distances from feeding grounds to breeding grounds making yearly migrations. Their hollow skeletons and large wingspans allowing them to soar or glide the wind current above the waves to keep them aloft for hours, days, week or in the case of albatrosses, months away from land. Some sea birds are so well adapted to a life in the air and on the sea surface that their legs and feet are relatively ineffective on land, making at best, clumsy progress.

Reproduction: Despite their open ocean nature sea birds are still dependant on land (mostly human uninhabited islands) to breed and reproduce, using whatever options are available for nesting sites; from nests built in trees to sand scrapes on the beach. Sea birds generally breed in colonies with many males and females having a life long bond, returning to the same nesting sites year after year.

Mating takes place on land and it is usual for one or two eggs to be laid in a season. However, in some species the earliest chick to hatch, (eventually the strongest) dominates the feeding and its sibling starves to death.

Associations: Sea birds are known to have lice and ticks which are transferable for a time to humans and, as such, injurious.

Identification: With a distribution spread across entire oceans it is natural that some forms prove a little different than the originally described species and many forms have been named as sub-species. However, this occurs in all species of animals with extended ranges and as most of the sea bird sub-species are unable to be distinguished in the field, only true species examples are shown. Sea birds have been studied for many years and the Maldivian species are easily separated by wing shape, colouration and head pattern.

PROCELLARIIDAE
Wedge-tailed shearwater
Bodu Hoagulhaa
Puffinus pacificus
(day time) open ocean
(night time) burrows in sand between tree roots
410 to 460 mm (16 to 18 in)
970 to 1040 mm (38 to 40 in)

Widespread across the Indo-Pacific this species is very common in the Maldives especially around fishing areas during early mornings where they congregate in flocks on the water (called rafts) and duck-dive for fish. They spend the entire day out at sea returning to their islands at sunset to find their burrows and mates.

Digging out last year's burrows, Great Barrier Reef.

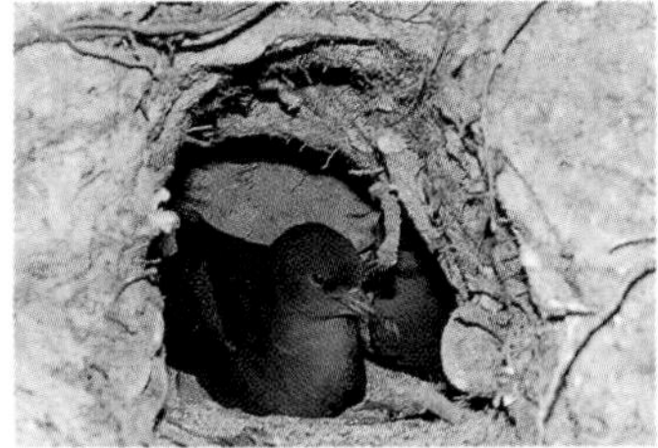
Birds in their burrow beneath tree roots, Great Barrier Reef.

Young Indian Ocean fledgling out of the burrow at night still wears a crown of "down", Houtman Abrolhos, Western Australia.

In good fishing seasons these birds are quite commonly seen in the Maldives and fishermen follow as the birds circle around an area where big fish are chasing little fish. They breed at Hithaadhoo in Gaafu Alifu Atoll and rest at Gallandhoo in Haa Alifu Atoll and Olhugiri in Baa Atoll. Their nests are built at the tops of tall trees and they feed on dead or injured fish floating on the surface (which they scoop up on the wing) or attack other birds and make them regurgitate their fish meals which the frigate bird catches in mid air.

FREGATIDAE

Lesser frigate bird

Hoara

Fregretta ariel

(day time) in the air at sea (night time) in the air at sea or roosting in trees on islands

1200 mm (47 in)

3400 mm (11 ft)

Female soaring on the wind currents, Great Barrier Reef.

Although this very striking sea bird is recorded from the Seychelles to the Pacific it is not considered common in the Maldives. Their black and white colours and long tail streamers make them easy to identify and they may be seen circling around islands such as Horubadhoo in Baa Atoll or at sea when they are fishing. They feed on squid and fish, often diving from heights of 20 metres (66 ft) and staying underwater for up to 30 seconds.

PHAEOTHONTIDAE

White-tailed tropic bird

Dhan'di Fulhu Dhooni

Phaeton lepturus

(day time) in the air at sea or around islands (night time) roosting in nest holes

400 mm (16 in) streamers 400 mm (16 in)

950 mm (3 ft)

Juvenile in nest, Seychelles.

LARIDAE
Bridled tern
Valli
Sterna anaethetus
(day time) in the air around reefs and islands (night time) roosting on islands
350 mm (15 in)
760 mm (30 in)

Although widespread across the Indian Ocean to Western Australia there are a number of subspecies which occur throughout most tropical oceans and these cannot be separated visually by a non-specialist. These birds are highly migratory and at times are quite common in the Maldives.

Landing on a perch rock, Lizard Island, Great Barrier Reef.

LARIDAE
Lesser crested tern
Gaa Dhooni
Sterna bengalensis
(day time) in the air around island and reefs (night time) roosting on the sand on islands
380 mm (15 in)
890 mm (35 in)

Generally seen in small fishing groups of three or four birds they dive into surface waters on shallow reefs and lagoons catching baitfish. Found throughout the Indo-Pacific this species is very common in the Maldives. They nest in a colony, laying a single egg in a sand scrape near bushes on uninhabited islands.

LARIDAE
Greater crested tern
Bodu Gaa Dhooni
Sterna bergii

(day time) in the air around islands and reefs (night time) roosting on islands

430 mm (17 in)

990 (39 in)

Common throughout the Maldives this species and its subspecies range throughout the Indo-Pacific. They are excellent divers and can be seen fishing in the shallows around islands. Nests are generally a sand scrape or grass hollow where a single egg is laid. Both parents care for the egg and chick.

Surface catch, full wing braking, New South Wales, Australia.

Skimming fish at the surface, New South Wales, Australia.

Close up of chick in nest, Tasmania, Australia.

LARIDAE
Roseate tern
Valla
Sterna dougallii

(day time) in the air around islands and reefs (night time) roosting on islands

360 mm (14 in)

630 mm (25 in)

Found from East Africa to New Caledonia, this species is not uncommon to the Maldives and generally forms large breeding colonies on uninhabited islands. Two eggs are usually laid in a sand scrape or amongst coral shingle and both parents look after eggs and young.

A mid-air scratch, Great Barrier Reef.

Landing approach glide to roosting site, Great Barrier Reef.

LARIDAE
Sooty tern
Beyn'du
Sterna fuscata
(day time) in the air at sea (night time) roosting on islands (nesting season) or at sea
430 mm (17 in)
860 mm (34 in)

A common Indo-Pacific tern this species is seasonally common in the Maldives. It generally breeds in large colonies and lays a single egg on the ground. Sooty terns do not dive, but skim flying fishes, crustaceans and squid from the surface waters and are able to hunt both day and night.

Dorsal aspect, Lord Howe Island, South Pacific.

LARIDAE
Black-naped tern
Kiru Dhooni
Sterna sumatrana
(day time) in the air around island and reefs (night time) roosting on uninhabited islands
320 mm (12 in)
640 mm (24 in)

Ranging throughout the atolls and across to New Caledonia this species lays its eggs once a year in a sand scrape amongst the coral clinker on uninhabited islands. The parents share in caring for the eggs and young catching small fish which are taken by diving or skimming surface waters around the reefs. Local "folklore" states that if eggs are taken the parent birds may follow and attack the person for up to a week after.

Eggs in a nest scrape, Great Barrier Reef.

Breaking into a dive, Great Barrier Reef.

LARIDAE
Brown noddy
Maaran'ga
Anous stolidus
(day time) in large flocks fishing at sea (night time) roosting on islands
400 mm (16 in)
790 mm (31 in)

This species is extremely common in the Maldives where it can be seen on island beaches in trees, or out fishing at sea. Due to their habit of flying around schools of tuna which are chopping into baitfish these birds act as guides to fishermen. Noddies do not dive for fish, but fly close to the sea surface (sometimes walking on it) and skimming or beaking up fish and crustaceans.

Bird on its nest, Great Barrier Reef.

Single egg laid in a grass nest, Lord Howe Island, South Pacific.

Close up at sea, Coral Sea.

LARIDAE
White tern
Dhon Dheeni
Gygis alba
(day time) at sea fishing (early morning) or perched in trees (night time) roosting in trees
280 mm (11 in)
700 mm (27 in)

Living only on Addu Atoll, where it is seen in trees on every island, the white tern is a very widespread from the Seychelles to the central Pacific. The birds are very tame and will tolerate close approach. In the Pacific a single egg is laid in the open in a small depression on a horizontal tree branch. When the chick hatches it has unusually large strong feet and claws to hang on to its precarious perch.

Adult on roosting branch, Lord Howe Island, South Pacific.

Fluffy chick in the open air "nest" site on a branch, Lord Howe Island, South Pacific.

Mammals

Chapter 12

Mammals

PHYLUM: CHORDATA

CLASS: *Mammalia* (Marine mammals)

ORDER: *Cetacea* (Whales, Dolphins)

Features: The word mammal refers to the female's mammary glands which provide milk for the young and are among the main distinguishing features of a mammal. Other features include hair, the birth of fully formed live young, ability to regulate body temperature and hold it constant, a brain of greater complexity than that of most other animals and breathing air. There are about 4070 species of mammals, many verging on extinction.

Ancestors of marine mammals are thought to have once lived on land. Returning to the sea, they have evolved to be the largest living creatures ever to exist on earth. Even so, by ignorance and over-exploitation humans have reduced many species almost to extinction in a mere 150 years. In some species only a few hundred individuals remain from original stocks often in the vicinity of 100,000. Small isolated populations were decimated by hunting and many specialised forms are now extinct.

Even though most marine mammals are now protected to varying degrees throughout the world seas, and reaction to their plight has been one of the greatest success stories in world cooperation, many are classed as endangered species and will continue to be so for decades. One significant fact remains: that for all the millions of individuals slaughtered over the past century the amount of natural history information obtained was remarkably small, so small that nations are still killing protected species in the name of science. So little is known about some that the entire specimen collection of a species may be represented only by a single skull.

Lifestyles: Although a number of Northern Hemisphere species have been studied quite extensively, knowledge of many of the Southern Hemisphere forms and such endangered species as river dolphins is almost non-existent. Few Southern Hemisphere species have been photographed underwater and those that have been, only in the last 10 years. Many cetaceans are open ocean dwellers. The immense size of the oceans and the inclement conditions there are factors that have maintained their secrecy.

There are about 76 recognised species of cetaceans including all the whales, dolphins and porpoises. Of these, 66 have teeth (feeding on an array of prey ranging from fish to squid and, in the case of killer whales, other mammals), and 10 (great whales) have a system of hair 'plates' called baleen that is used to strain planktonic organisms (krill) and fish from the sea. All cetaceans are excellent swimmers, using both body flex and powerful tail flukes for their main propulsion. Special physiological adaptations allow them to dive to great depths.

Most use echo location to detect prey and even those toothed whales and dolphins which are totally blind do not appear to be at a disadvantage in feeding. The ears may be of pinhole size or completely closed by a membrane. They breathe through one or two blowholes on top of the head and in some species the blowhole acts as a noise-producing mechanism. Some of the baleen whales (humpbacks etc) produce unique and complex songs. These are repeated according to identifiable patterns and some have been detected by hydrophones (185 kilometres (100 nautical miles) from their source. In a way similar to bird songs, the sounds consist of an ordered sequence of motifs and themes. Set songs follow set sequences with a beginning and end and each song may last from six to 35 minutes. Each animal may have its own version of a song, which the entire whale population in one region may sing over one season. Songs are thought to have a role in sexual attraction.

All cetaceans have very strong social ties and ocean-dwelling forms swim in family pods or combinations of social units forming schools. Although the strongest bonds are between cows and calves, each pod protects, assists and cooperates for the good of individuals within the pod. The strong assist the weak, calving mothers, etc. and there are even instances where deformed individuals incapable of feeding have been looked after and fed by the pod for over 16 years.

Mass strandings are now known to be due to entire herds going to the help of another cetacean in trouble. The pod picks up the distress calls

of sick, injured or confused individuals and responds to help, in turn stranding its members. While one live animal remains on a beach (even if all the others have been successfully returned to the sea), its distress signals will call them back to their deaths.

Reproduction: Like all mammals, cetaceans have mammary glands. The mammae (teats) and male sex organs do not protrude from the body, but are instead hidden within slits in the body wall. Very often there are long migrations from the winter feeding grounds to the summer breeding grounds. Set migratory patterns exist with old males, young males and females living in separate groups at certain times of the year. Cetaceans breed seasonally and bear one (rarely two) young at a time and have gestation periods of nine to 16 months. Newborn calves are often covered by a sparse stubble. In natural circumstances they may live at least 60 years.

Associations: Marine mammals are often accompanied by suckerfish and some whales are encrusted with giant barnacles which only live on a particular species of whale.

Identification: Most of the commoner species of marine mammals can be readily identified from a good colour photograph.

PHYSETERIDAE
Sperm whale
Physeter macrocephalus
Open ocean
Surface waters
20 metres (60 ft)

The largest of the toothed whales roaming world seas, sperm whales are known to dive to depths of 3200 metres (10,500 ft), though most records show averages around 1200 metres (4000 ft) are more common. They feed mostly on bottom-dwelling giant squid up to 12 metres (39 ft) in length and there is a very strong bond between individuals of specific pods or schools, with members combining to help sick or injured individuals. (Photo: Bill Rossiter)

DELPHINIDAE
Common dolphin
Delphinus delphis
Open ocean
Surface waters
2.2 metres (7 ft)

Found across the Indo-Pacific this species is often referred to as the saddleback dolphin owing to the markings on the dorsal surface being similar to a saddle. The species is distributed throughout world seas and can be common in coastal areas as well as open ocean. Occasionally groups come together and form huge aggregations numbering thousands. (Photo: Nigel Marsh).

DELPHINIDAE
Orca (killer whale)
Orcinus orca
Open ocean
Surface waters
10 metres (33 ft)

Orcas are the largest of the dolphin family and are easily recognised by their black and white markings and high dorsal fin. Pods range between 6 and 40 individuals and pod members remain together for life. Ties even exist from one generation to another and group co-ordination during hunting is highly advanced and implemented by close social cohesion. (Photo: Bill Rossiter).

Occurring in small pods in both temperate and tropical seas across the Indo-Pacific, the spinner dolphin is a much slimmer species than the bottlenose dolphin and its dorsal fin is smaller and more curved. It has well-defined markings and is easily distinguished from the bottlenose dolphin. Its name comes from the habit of spinning as it jumps out of the water.

DELPHINIDAE
Spinner dolphin
Stenella longirostris
Open ocean
Surface waters
2 to 3 metres (6 to 10 ft)

The bottlenose dolphin inhabits inshore waters and open ocean and can be various shades of grey on the back and white on the belly. The short, stout beak has 23 to 25 pairs of teeth in the jaws, and the lower jaw tends to jut out further than the upper jaw. Dolphins are social mammals and are generally seen in large herds or in pods. Their food is mainly schooling pelagic fishes, that are found by echo-location.

DELPHINIDAE
Bottlenose dolphin
Tursiops truncatus
Open ocean
Surface waters
4.5 metres (15 ft)

Bottlenose dolphin.

Maldivian sunset.

Index of common names

Index of scientific names

Index of family names

03-5431 ID-T

Further reading

For sea creatures:

Coleman, Neville
Nudibranchs of the South Pacific ISBN 094732502 6
Sea Australia Resource Centre, 1989
Rochedale, Qld

The Nature of Norfolk Island ISBN 094732506 9
Sea Australia Resource Centre, 1991
Rochedale, Qld

Australia's Great Barrier Reef ISBN 086777367 7
Child & Assoc 1990
Frenchs Forest, NSW

Encyclopedia of Marine Animals ISBN 0207 164 290
Collins, Angus & Robertson, 1991
Ryde NSW

Sea Stars of Australasia ISBN 0947 325 212
Sea Australia Resource Centre, 1993
Rochedale, Qld

Discover Underwater Australia ISBN 186436 007 0
National, 1994
Frenchs Forest NSW

Beautiful Great Barrier Reef ISBN 1 86436 0089
National, 1994
Frenchs Forest NSW

Dive Sites of the Great Barrier Reef and Coral Sea
(with Nigel Marsh) ISBN 1 864 36 095 X
New Holland, 1996
Frenchs Forest NSW

Sea Birds and others of the Great Barrier Reef, Australasia, South Pacific, Indian Ocean ISBN 0 947325123
Sea Australia Resource Centre, 1997
Brisbane, Qld

Diving Australia (with Nigel Marsh) ISBN 96 2593 104 X
Periplus, 1997
Singapore

Discover Loloata Island (Marine Life Guide
to Papua New Guinea) ISBN 0 646 31911 6
Sea Australia Resource Centre, 1997
Brisbane, Qld

1001 Nudibranchs, catalogue of Indo-Pacific sea slugs
(Identification – Biodiversity – Zoology) ISBN 0947325255
Neville Coleman's Underwater Geographic Pty Ltd, 2000
Brisbane, Qld

Dangerous Sea Creatures Aquatic Survival Guide ISBN 0947 325 247
Neville Coleman's Underwater Geographic Pty Ltd, 1999
Brisbane, Qld

For diving:

Godfrey, Tim (1998) *Dive Maldives, A guide to
the Maldives Archipelago* ISBN 1876 410 000
Atoll Editions

For fish:

Kuiter, Rudie H (1998) *Photo guide to
Fishes of the Maldives* ISBN 1876 410 183
Atoll Editions

For Maldives Maps:

Godfrey, Tim (1999) *Malways,
Maldives Island Directory* ISBN 1876 410 248
Atoll Editions